THE BIBLE IN MEDIEVAL TRADITION

GENERAL EDITORS

H. Lawrence Bond†
Ian Christopher Levy
Philip D. W. Krey
Thomas Ryan

The major intent of the series The Bible in Medieval Tradition is to reacquaint the Church with its rich history of biblical interpretation and with the contemporary applicability of this history, especially for academic study, spiritual formation, preaching, discussion groups, and individual reflection. Each volume focuses on a particular biblical book or set of books and provides documentary evidence of the most significant ways in which that work was treated in the course of medieval biblical interpretation.

The series takes its shape in dialogue both with the special traditions of medieval exegesis and with the interests of contemporary readers. Each volume in the series comprises fresh translations of several commentaries. The selections are lengthy and, in most cases, have never been available in English before.

Compared to patristic material, relatively little medieval exegesis has been translated. While medieval interpretations do resemble their patristic forebears, they do not simply replicate them. Indeed, they are produced at new times and in new situations. As a result, they lend insight into the changing culture and scholarship of the Middle Ages and comprise a storehouse of the era's theological and spiritual riches that can enhance contemporary reading of the Bible. They, therefore, merit their own consideration, to which this series is meant to contribute.

The Book of
REVELATION

Translated and edited by

David Burr

WILLIAM B. EERDMANS PUBLISHING COMPANY

GRAND RAPIDS, MICHIGAN

Wm. B. Eerdmans Publishing Co.
4035 Park East Court SE, Grand Rapids, Michigan 49546
www.eerdmans.com

25 24 23 22 21 20 19   1 2 3 4 5 6 7

ISBN 978-0-8028-2226-0

Library of Congress Cataloging-in-Publication Data
Names: Burr, David, 1934- translator, editor.
Title: The book of Revelation / translated and edited by David Burr.
Description: Grand Rapids : William B. Eerdmans Publishing Company, 2019. |
    Series: The Bible in medieval tradition | Includes bibliographical
    references and index. | Summary: "The author describes and provides
    freshly translated examples of medieval exegesis of the Book of
    Revelation from Richard of St. Victor through Nicholas of Lyra (from the
    twelfth through the fourteenth centuries)"— Provided by publisher.
Identifiers: LCCN 2019022634 | ISBN 9780802822260 (paperback)
Subjects: LCSH: Bible. Revelation—Commentaries. | Bible.
    Revelation—Commentaries—History and criticism.
Classification: LCC BS2825.53 .B77 2019 | DDC 228/.060902—dc23
LC record available at https://lccn.loc.gov/2019022634

Contents

CONTENTS

Editors' Preface

The medieval period witnessed an outpouring of biblical interpretation, which included commentaries written in Latin in a wide array of styles over the course of a millennium. These commentaries are significant as successors to patristic exegesis and predecessors to Reformation exegesis, but they are also important in their own right.

The major intent of this series, THE BIBLE IN MEDIEVAL TRADITION, is to place newly translated medieval scriptural commentary into the hands of contemporary readers. In doing so, the series reacquaints the church with its rich tradition of biblical interpretation. It fosters academic study, spiritual formation, preaching, discussion groups, and individual reflection. It also enables the contemporary application of this tradition. Each volume focuses on the era's interpretation of one biblical book, or set of related books, and comprises substantial selections from representative exegetes and hermeneutical approaches.

While interdisciplinary and cross-confessional interest in the Middle Ages has grown over the last century, it falls short if it does not at the same time recognize the centrality of the Bible to this period and its religious life. The Bible structured sermons, guided prayer, and inspired mystical visions. It was woven through liturgy, enacted in drama, and embodied in sculpture and other art forms. Less explicitly ecclesial works, such as Dante's *Divine Comedy*, were also steeped in its imagery and narrative. Because of the Bible's importance to the period, this series therefore opens a window not only to its religious practices but also to its culture more broadly.

Similarly, biblical interpretation played a vital role in the work of medieval theologians. Among the tasks of theological masters was to deliver ordinary lectures on the Bible. Their commentaries—often edited versions of their public lectures—were the means by which many worked out their most important theological insights. Thus the Bible was the primary text for theologians and the center of the curriculum for theology students. Some, such as the authors of *summae* and sentence commentaries, produced systematic treatises that, while not devoted to verse-by-verse explication, nevertheless often cited biblical evidence, addressed apparent contradictions in the scriptural witness, and responded under the guidance of nuanced theories of interpretation. They were biblical theologians.

Biblical commentaries provided the largest reservoir of medieval interpretation and hermeneutics, and they took a variety of forms. Monastic perspectives shaped some, scholastic perspectives still others. Some commentaries emphasized the spiritual senses, others the literal. Some relied more heavily on scholarly tools, such as dictionaries, histories, concordances, critical texts, knowledge of languages, and Jewish commentaries. Whatever the case, medieval commentaries were a privileged and substantial locus of interpretation, and they offer us fresh insight into the Bible and their own cultural contexts.

For readers and the church today, critical engagement with medieval exegesis counteracts the twin dangers of amnesia and nostalgia. One temptation is to study the Bible as if its interpretation had no past. This series brings the past to the present and thereby supplies the resources and memories that can enrich current reading. Medieval exegesis also bears studying because it can exemplify how not to interpret the Bible. Despite nascent critical sensibilities in some of its practitioners, it often offered fanciful etymologies and was anachronistic in its conflation of past and present. It could also demonize others. Yet, with its playful attention to words and acceptance of a multiplicity of meanings and methods, it anticipated critical theory's turn to language today and the indeterminacy characteristic of its literary theory.

What this series sets out to accomplish requires that selections in each volume are lengthy. In most cases, these selections have never been available in English before. Compared to the amount of patristic material, comparatively little medieval exegesis has been translated. Yet, the medieval was not simply a repetition of the patristic. It differed enough in genre, content, and application to merit its own special focus, and it applied earlier church exegesis to new situations and times as well as reflecting the changing culture and scholarship in the Middle Ages. The series, therefore, makes these resources more widely available, guides readers in entering into medieval exegetical texts, and enables a more informed and insightful study of the church's biblical heritage.

This volume addresses the book of Revelation with a focus on medieval Franciscan exegesis. It represents an oeuvre that would have important implications for this religious order, for the history of biblical interpretation, and for the life of faith more broadly. Because of the topic's difficulty, the volume's author, the scholar of the Spiritual Franciscans David Burr, does not confine his introductory remarks to a first chapter but includes substantial explanatory material throughout. Burr sets the stage by reviewing exegetes of the early church. He then turns to the influential Richard of Saint Victor before focusing on a procession of Franciscans that ends with the fourteenth-century Nicholas of Lyra. The volume revolves around John Olivi, a major apocalyptic commentator who changed the interpretive tradition dramatically so that later medieval commentators and even popes were forced to react to him.

Here we observe great biblical scholars contending with a notoriously difficult text. More than that, however, we also witness theologians struggling with what it means to live Jesus's message and negotiating the extent of compromise demanded by new times and new places, challenges that people of faith continue to face today.

Ian Christopher Levy
Philip D. W. Krey
Thomas Ryan

Preface

Few books of the Bible are greeted with more suspicion than Revelation. People who discover my interest in it often ask me why it's in the Bible at all. I try to satisfy them with a historical explanation, but they often want a good deal more. They want to know how I feel about religious discourse in the form of wall-to-wall visionary experience. They point out that the visions don't seem to furnish a coherent view of the future. They note that there seems to be a great deal of violence in Revelation, more than the gentle Jesus might have been expected to endorse. They vastly prefer the Jesus they find, or at least imagine finding, in the gospels to that strange, paradoxical Lamb they encounter in Revelation or, worse yet, to the figure with a sword coming out of his mouth. They wonder if John was entirely sane.

The uncertainty is hardly new. Even in the early church there were questions. Right down to the second half of the fourth century, there were many who would have been happy to eliminate Revelation from the New Testament canon. It was a bone of contention, and under slightly different circumstances Revelation might well have taken its place alongside works such as the Shepherd of Hermas as an also-ran.

I for one am glad Revelation made the cut, close call though it might have been. Over the years I have accumulated a great deal of respect for the author, John the Divine, who is not to be confused with either of the major gospel Johns; nor are his visions to be dismissed as some odd form of mental illness. I feel fortunate to have approached John from the vantage point of the Middle Ages, a period that was itself no stranger to mystical rapture, and thus was able to discuss the varieties of biblical visionary experience without any hint of superiority, any condescending smile or shake of the head.

Because so few people have bothered to look at Revelation seriously, I have decided to begin by explaining, not what it meant to the Middle Ages, but what it meant to John insofar as we can know that at all. Thus the first chapter, titled "Prolegomenon," means to provide a running start at the topic, providing a bridge of sorts over the early Middle Ages to what I see as my real starting point, the commentaries of Richard of Saint Victor and Joachim of Fiore. I have chosen to handle this transition by summarizing what I have always considered one of the best articles ever written, Robert Lerner's "Refreshment of the Saints." Here as elsewhere, Lerner manages to combine impeccable scholarship with a wry sense of humor. Using his article as the framework of that chapter allows me to offer a path through several centuries while reminding others how good a scholar Lerner is and, I hope, encouraging them to read his work.

From there we go on to our real twin starting points, Richard of Saint Victor and Joachim of Fiore. Years ago, in a book on Petrus Iohannis Olivi's Revelation commentary, I observed that Olivi had written that commentary with three books open before him on his desk: the Bible and the two commentaries on Revelation by Richard and Joachim. More recently, it has occurred to me that Olivi's choice of Richard and Joachim as traveling companions made perfect sense, even though they were not all traveling in the same direction. Richard blazed a popular trail leading into the thirteenth century, a path taken by most of the people we will encounter to at least some extent. Few stayed entirely on the path, but most felt it was necessary to acknowledge Richard as a guide.

Joachim's route was a road less traveled, but within the mendicant orders his influence was great. In fact, the next two chapters after Richard and Joachim turn seriously to the impact of Joachim during the first half of the thirteenth century, paying attention to the pseudo-Joachite materials and then to Alexander Minorita. Alexander is certainly the main attraction here, not only because of his connection with those pseudo-Joachite materials, but also because Alexander himself turns out to be oddly like one of those horses you encounter at the race track and find interesting, yet consider yourself too intelligent to actually bet on. Imagine your surprise when, at the end of the race, he finishes in the money.

The next chapter, "The Paris Mendicant Model," tries to describe an approach to the Apocalypse that dominated not only in Paris but elsewhere as well. It grew out of the approach already anticipated by Richard of Saint

Victor and even by Bede to some extent. Here again Lerner's work has been central, particularly his work on the Dominican Hugh of Saint Cher.

After paying serious attention to Hugh (or, more precisely, "Hugh," since I agree with Lerner and others in seeing the commentaries discussed at this point as the work of an *atelier*), I briefly examine a Franciscan installment of the Paris mendicant model that, if Alain Boureau is correct, is by Bonaventure, and then I follow with briefer attention to a later commentary perhaps by Vital du Four. If it is by Vital, as I assume here, it gives us some sense of where the Paris mendicant model was headed during Olivi's time. Here I face a problem: in 1993, when I sent *Olivi's Peaceable Kingdom* to the publisher, I was able to identify a substantial number of commentaries that fit within the Parisian mendicant model, but in a large number of cases I was uncertain who the authors were. It was a problem I was somehow sure graduate students everywhere would be eager to solve, but it seems they were not. Over two decades later I am still embarrassed at the number of commentaries I can see as related to one another without being able to explain how, let alone being able to assign them specific authors.

I then turn to Bonaventure's *Collationes in hexaemeron,* which is not technically a Revelation commentary at all but marks an important moment in Bonaventure's reading of Revelation (and, as a result, in Olivi's). The Bonaventuran and Olivian readings would have an impact on what followed. I have chosen to discuss the matter in the company of a man who, left free to do scholarship, would have proved himself one of the best scholars in the twentieth century. The chapter on Bonaventure's *Collationes* represents my own private tribute to Joseph Ratzinger.

The two chapters on Olivi may be excessive, but I have managed to convince at least myself that there is an important point involved. We tend to assume that Olivi and others must have worked out their apocalyptic views in the process of writing Apocalypse commentaries. In Olivi's case, at least, we have no reason to think so, and the same is probably true of many others as well. The first of these chapters argues that Olivi arrived at most of his key apocalyptic convictions early in his career while commenting on the Old Testament and the gospels. He would have seen nothing odd about that. His sense of how the various books of the Bible were interrelated made the process seem quite normal, even predictable to him. Certainly he was aware of the Apocalypse even then and cited it often; but there is no sign that from the beginning his vehicle for working out an apocalyptic scenario had to be a commentary on the Apocalypse. Joachim's biography may mislead us in that respect. If major Joachim scholars such as Gian Luca Potestà are correct (and I think they are), Joachim spent much of his time on consecutive revisions of his Revelation commentary. Olivi did not. He was always interested in the Apocalypse and cited it frequently, but he did so while working out an apocalyptic scenario that had a great deal to do with his reading of other scriptural sources. And we are extremely lucky that so many of his commentaries on those other sources survived.

Then I turn to Olivi's Revelation commentary, which has its own importance inasmuch as it represents a significant turning point in the development of Revelation commentaries. Olivi took interpretation of the Apocalypse in a recognizably Joachite direction at a moment when the church was notably unsure what it thought about Joachim and particularly uncertain about the value of reading Saint Francis in a Joachite context. This uncertainty became particularly dangerous when combined with the controversies going on both inside and outside the order concerning the value and even the legitimacy of the Franciscan life. The resultant condemnation of Olivi's Apocalypse commentary had wider implications, extending well beyond Olivi himself to the Franciscan order in general and, in a broader sense, to the church in general.

The two final chapters inspect this aftermath from a double perspective. They are conceived as a look at life after Olivi. Pierre Auriol and Nicholas of Lyra both reconceive the Apocalypse commentary, picking up the stray thread of thought developed in the early thirteenth century by Alexander Minorita and developing it in structurally similar yet emotionally different ways. Both, when seen in the light of Olivi's Apocalypse commentary and its condemnation in the early fourteenth century, are testimonies to the extent to which the Franciscan order and indeed the Franciscan ideal were moving on.

Given time and many more pages, a further point might be explored. One might ask whether what we actually see at this point is the entire church moving on. This latter question can hardly be ignored, but neither can it be explored seriously in this context. I have tried to stay on topic, stopping short of the point where I would venture into what someone once described as "wide-angle scholarship with no focus." Thus in a final chapter I offer some final thoughts and drop the matter.

During the last ten months of composing this work, I shared the couch where my writing takes place with a small black dog who was waging a brave but ultimately losing battle with kidney failure. Claire died on November 14, 2017. One month later I met yet another black dog named

Soledad, a Puerto Rican refugee who lost her family in the autumn hurricanes. Having survived the "beast from the sea," she washed up in Roanoke, Virginia, and now lies next to me as I write these words. There will probably be other, future projects, and Soledad will have a part in them, but this one belongs to Claire.

Prolegomenon

Every book must begin somewhere. This one begins with two major exegetes in the twelfth century, then settles into the thirteenth century. That leaves a huge gap in history. The book of Revelation has had its own story from its composition in the first century to the commentaries by Joachim of Fiore and Richard of Saint Victor in the twelfth; but all that falls within someone else's job description. My self-assigned task is to describe what happened from Joachim and Richard to Nicholas of Lyra.

Even granting that mission, something has to be said about the preceding period; yet it has to be recognized that any brief comments on it here must still be shaped by what this book is mainly about. The task in this chapter is not to present a very brief look at the earlier centuries in their own right, but rather to look at how they led up to and in fact contributed to the period this work actually covers. That means looking at them as they contributed to what Robert Lerner has described as the birth of medieval chiliasm, because the striking thing about all the works we will seriously consider here is their assumption that the book of Revelation is about historical development.

In what follows, I provide a bridge to my actual topic, and I do so in three stages. First, I offer a brief look at the book of Revelation itself, which is, after all, the book everyone else will be talking about throughout the rest of this story. Second, I offer a very rapid survey of where discussion of Revelation led between the first and twelfth centuries. Here I rest heavily on a single great article, as will be seen. Third, I say a few words about the legend of Antichrist.

Exhibit A: The Apocalypse as John Saw It

The subject of this book is what medieval exegetes thought the book of Revelation was about, not what modern scholars think it's about or, more implausibly, what it's actually about. Thus, one might ask how much any effort to address the latter topics would add to our project. Nevertheless, it seems worthwhile to say something about Revelation itself as scholars now view it, if only to provide a baseline against which medieval exegesis might be compared. The project will, of course, be too brief to do justice to the complexities of modern scholarship or to the complexities of the Apocalypse itself, and I freely admit to being well out of my field in pursuing it; but pursue it I must.

The book of Revelation—the Apocalypse, to use its alternate title (which is nothing more than a transliteration of the Greek word with which the book begins)—can be described as follows. It begins (1:1-3) with an announcement that it is a revelation given by God to Jesus Christ, who sent his angel to John. John in turn reported what he saw so that the world could share the message. Several things are worth noting here.

First, the passage establishes John as a prophet. That links him with the great prophets of the Old Testament. As a variety of scholars have established, John read the prophets well, probably in Hebrew or Aramaic rather than in the Greek Septuagint, and he read them in accordance with established Jewish hermeneutical procedures, although of course he saw Christ as their real subject.[1] The result, far from being a chaotic mélange of Old Testament references, is a carefully constructed argument for what John sees as the fulfillment of Old Testament prophecy.

Nor need we limit the matter to canonical Old Testament prophecy. Richard Bauckham's thorough familiarity with extrabiblical Jewish and pagan prophetic/apocalyptic writings enables him to place John in that context as well, and John emerges from the investigation as a man whose thought must be appreciated as part of an ongoing prophetic/apocalyptic conversation going on in his own century.

John's status as a prophet enables us to place him institutionally. Prophets played an important role in the early church, as we know from the apocalyptic passages in the Synoptic Gospels, from Paul and other New Testament

---

1. See especially Jan Fekkes, *Isaiah and the Prophetic Traditions in the Book of Revelation* (Sheffield: Sheffield Academic, 1994); and Richard Bauckham, *The Climax of Prophecy* (Edinburgh: T&T Clark, 1993).

epistles, and from later documents such as the Didache. Thus, the book of Revelation gives us an example of a prophet in action.

Where, though? Obviously in western Asia Minor, since his letters address seven churches there. The real question is whether he is characteristic of that area. The problem is an intriguing one because some scholars have tended to see John as an itinerant prophet who was more representative of a Palestinian-Syrian church rooted in primitive Christian apocalyptic expectation, one in which prophetic leadership was still central, than of the church in Asia Minor, which by the end of the first century had moved beyond all that and established a church polity guided by bishops and deacons, as Ignatius of Antioch attests in his letters.

Elisabeth Schüssler Fiorenza and Richard Bauckham produce a more complex and believable picture of the church in John's time, and in the process they read the evidence in a very different way. Schüssler Fiorenza manages to show that Ignatius can be seen as a witness, not of the strength of an institutionalized monepiscopate in Asia Minor at the end of the first century, but of its weakness; and she shows how Paul and John might have had more in common than previous scholarship suggested.[2] The common ground extends to sharing the same prophetic/apocalyptic traditions that also surface in the gospels.[3] John emerges as one voice, but hardly a lone voice, since he presides over a group of prophets active in the seven churches of Revelation 1–3. He is a community prophet, not a marginalized lone wolf, and his book tells us a great deal about Christian polity and aspirations in his time.

Second, John was a visionary. What he saw and heard was reported in his book, but necessarily filtered through language. What we have is not raw visionary experience but a literary composition that comes to terms, not only with the original vision or visions, but with John's reading of the Old Testament and extracanonical prophetic/apocalyptic literature. It includes elements of extracanonical literature that were available to him through what he read but also through what he heard from other prophets. The resultant work must be distinguished from the visionary experience to which John

---

2. Elisabeth Schüssler Fiorenza, *The Book of Revelation: Justice and Judgment* (Philadelphia: Fortress, 1985), especially ch. 5. This, to be sure, is painting with a rather large brush. Elaine Pagels, *Revelations: Visions, Prophecy, and Politics in the Book of Revelation* (New York: Penguin, 2012), tries to define more precisely the space between Paul's words and John's.

3. Schüssler Fiorenza, *The Book of Revelation*, 152: "Since Paul already had access to such apocalyptic-eschatological traditions handed down through early Christian prophets, we are justified in assuming a historical continuum running from pre-Pauline prophetic-apocalyptic circles to the Book of Revelation, Papias and the Montanist movement in Asia Minor."

testifies. We can come no closer to the latter than John allows us to come. When he tells us that he saw a figure whose eyes were like flames of fire and out of whose mouth protruded a two-edged sword, what did he *really* see? We will, of course, never know.

John's visionary experience was also an auditory experience, and we might be tempted to imagine that the words he reports having heard would have been less affected by that filtering process than what he saw; but even the words were experienced by him in a different way than we might recognize. In his first reference to hearing he reports, "I was in the spirit on the Lord's day, and I heard behind me a loud voice like a trumpet" (1:10). Immediately thereafter he describes the voice as "like the sound of many waters" (1:15). Clearly this is no ordinary voice John is hearing. Thus, even his original audience stood at one and probably two removes from the prophet's own experience. John saw and heard things, reflected on them, and turned them into an effective literary form. Greek was perhaps a second language for him, his first language being a Semitic one,[4] but his work shows concern for rhetorical effect, and some scholars suggest that even his rough style may be to some extent deliberate.

Third, his name was really John. Unlike any number of apocalyptic writings, this is not a pseudepigraphical work. Nor is it set in a time earlier than its actual composition in order to get a running start at the future by "predicting" things that have already occurred. By and large, John is predicting in real time. And—a fourth point—what he is predicting "must soon take place" (1:1). Two sentences later he announces that "the time is near" (1:3). The same point is made five times in rapid succession at the end of the book. Whereas in Daniel—which does get a running start on the future— the prophet is told to seal up his book until the end of time (Dan 12:4, 9), in Revelation John is explicitly ordered *not* to do so "because the time is near" (22:10).

The time for what? John answers that question almost immediately as he turns to his first vision, involving letters to seven churches in western Asia Minor. "Look! He is coming with the clouds; every eye will see him, even those who pierced him; and on his account all the tribes of the earth will wail" (1:7).

John tells us little about himself. He does say, "I, John, your brother who share with you in Jesus the persecution and the kingdom and the patient

4. Ben Witherington III, *Revelation* (Cambridge: Cambridge University Press, 2003), 11–12, and others follow Bauckham on this matter.

endurance, was on the island called Patmos because of the word of God and the testimony of Jesus" (1:9). Even that much tells us that it was a time when Christians in western Asia Minor were experiencing some degree of persecution, and we might conclude from the rest of the work that some Christians were being killed, although John himself was simply confined on Patmos, where he experienced some and perhaps all of the visions reported in this work. This must have occurred in the latter part of Domitian's reign, when we know there was persecution, though not a systematic, empire-wide persecution. If John was merely being confined on Patmos, then we can imagine that he was released after the close of Domitian's reign. That would eliminate the problem of how he managed to write the book on Patmos and then send it to the mainland.[5]

Are we dealing with the same author who wrote the Gospel of John and the Johannine letters? Probably not, on both stylistic and theological grounds.[6]

We now proceed to John's letters to seven churches or, as presented here, Christ's letters to them as delivered by John. Here we encounter the first of four sevenfold patterns—seven letters, seven seals, seven trumpets, and seven bowls—which will take us from 2:1 through 16:21, but with a few important interludes. Some scholars have gone further, seeing Revelation as composed of seven or even eight sevenfold patterns, but that may be pushing the matter too far. Even here we see important distinctions to be made. One is that the seals, trumpets, and bowls all involve punishments loosed upon the world, whereas the letters are just that, seven epistles addressed to specific churches. One could think of them as performance evaluations. We have no evidence that these letters existed anywhere except in the book of Revelation. They are, however, enormously valuable inasmuch as they contain information about these churches conveyed by a man who knew them well and who clearly addressed them on the assumption that they would recognize his prophetic authority.

If Schüssler Fiorenza is correct about John presiding over a group of prophets who in turn were associated with individual churches, that might explain why the letters are addressed, not to the churches themselves, but to the angels of those churches. He is writing to other prophets who are

---

5. For a discussion of these questions see Witherington, *Revelation*, 4–10. Witherington assumes, however, that he would have been unable to return to his old area.

6. See Witherington, *Revelation*, 1–3. In addition, and perhaps above all, see Schüssler Fiorenza, *Book of Revelation*, ch. 3, which lucidly presents the possibilities.

expected to present his message. His comments on Jezebel, the Nicolaitans, and Balaam tell us something about rival groups in the church. He is competing with one or more such circles, and in some cases the rivalry may involve challenging a libertine and/or enthusiastic theology that allows accommodation with Roman religious practices,[7] although one must proceed cautiously here, because John tends to use sexual imagery as a metaphor for such accommodation.[8] Again, his comment to the angel of the church at Ephesus concerning "slander on the part of those who say that they are Jews and are not, but are a synagogue of Satan," and his admonition immediately thereafter, "Do not fear what you are about to suffer" (2:9-10), might suggest that tension between the Jewish and Christian communities had led to Jewish denunciation of the Christians. In this chapter we will tend to concentrate (as John does) on the major rift between Christianity and the Roman Empire, but this contest was apparently accompanied by and closely related to intra-Christian and Jewish-Christian troubles.[9]

We move on to the other three sevenfold patterns. John is summoned to visit heaven by the same divine, trumpet-like voice he had heard before, again "in the spirit" (4:2), and sees God on his throne (he "looks like jasper and carnelian"). God is holding a scroll, and an angel asks ("in a loud voice"—heaven seems an oddly noisy place), "Who is worthy to open the scroll and break its seals?" (5:2). At first it seems no one can be found, but one of the attendant elders assures John that "the Lion of the tribe of Judah, the Root of David, has conquered, so that he can open the scroll and its seven seals" (5:5). Then John sees not a lion but a lamb. This is an important moment in the complex argument John is constructing, an argument constructed less of syllogisms than of symbols. The lion has conquered, but he has done so by dying on the cross. Those who "follow the Lamb wherever he goes" (14:4) must do the same. The message is both that they must be prepared for slaughter and that "they will reign on earth" (2:10).

When the first five seals are opened, we see four horses followed by an interlude in which the martyred souls under the altar cry out for vengeance and are told to wait until their number has been completed. With the open-

---

7. See Schüssler Fiorenza, *Book of Revelation*, especially ch. 4, which discusses the parallel with Paul's problems at Corinth.

8. Thus when he says of Jezebel, "Beware, I am throwing her on a bed, and those who commit adultery with her I am throwing into great distress, unless they repent of her doings," we can safely assume we're encountering a metaphor.

9. Pagels, *Revelations*, 46-47, offers a notably different interpretation of John's relation to Judaism, but we must keep moving.

ing of the sixth seal, the focus shifts back to worldly disasters, but this time they are cosmic in nature. "There came a great earthquake; the sun became black as sackcloth, the full moon became like blood, and the stars of the sky fell to the earth." In fact, "the sky vanished like a scroll rolling itself up, and every mountain and island was removed from its place" (6:12–14).

The people of the earth, understandably deciding that the day of the Lord is at hand, call for the mountains to fall on them and hide them from judgment, but what happens next seems more like another intermission. Four angels who have been given power to damage earth and sea actually hold back the winds, and another angel tells them, "Do not damage the earth or the sea or the trees until we have marked the servants of our God with a seal on their foreheads" (7:3). The number to be sealed is, John discovers, 144,000, allowing 12,000 from each of the twelve tribes. But this is the new Israel, not the old, so when John looks at those sealed what he sees is "a great multitude that no one could count, from every nation, from all tribes and peoples and languages" (7:9). They are the martyrs, who "have washed their robes and made them white in the blood of the Lamb. . . . They will hunger no more, and thirst no more; the sun will not strike them, nor any scorching heat; for the Lamb at the center of the throne will be their shepherd, and he will guide them to springs of the water of life, and God will wipe away every tear from their eyes" (7:14–17).

This is the first of two sealings. The other, the mark of the beast, will be seen in a moment. For the time being we await the opening of the seventh seal. When it happens, what we get is not judgment but "silence in heaven for about half an hour" (8:1). A great deal is about to occur, but that is the responsibility of seven angels with trumpets.

We have moved on to another set of sevens. Here again, the first four form a distinct unit, a series of natural disasters involving hail, fire, and blood hurled at the earth and destroying a third of its trees and grass; a mountain of fire hurled into the sea and destroying a third of the sea creatures; a star falling to earth and polluting a third of the waters; and selected other assaults on the environment. Then a break between the fourth and fifth trumpets is marked by an eagle that flies over, shouting, "Woe, woe, woe to the inhabitants of the earth" (8:13), and the fifth angel produces a whole other order of disaster by opening up a bottomless pit from which come creatures who attack and torture those who do not have the divine seal on their foreheads. Then the sixth angel improves on that result by releasing four angels hitherto bound at the Euphrates, who proceed to kill a third of humankind with the aid of two hundred million troops. The remaining two-thirds of humankind remain unrepentant.

We now expect to hear the seventh trumpet blow, but instead an angel holding a scroll descends from heaven, stands on the sea, gives a great shout, and seven thunders sound. John is about to write down what they said, but he is told to seal it up. The angel now swears that "there will be no more delay, but in the days when the seventh angel is to blow his trumpet, the mystery of God will be fulfilled, as he announced to his servants the prophets" (10:6–7).

So, we have another scroll and another sevenfold pattern, but nothing seems to come of the sevenfold pattern. On the other hand, quite a bit comes of the scroll. John is told to eat it. He is then told he "must prophesy again about many peoples and nations and languages and kings" (10:8–11). John is echoing Ezekiel 2:8–3:7, just as he echoed it in Revelation 5:1 when describing the scroll with seven seals. Richard Bauckham reasonably concludes that we're dealing with the same scroll in both cases. The seven seals were removed by the Lamb in heaven, and the scroll is now being taken to earth so that it can be presented to John, who eats it.

What, then, does the scroll say? We're not actually told, but we can guess. Certainly it cannot be identified with the events that are described as occurring when each of the seals was removed. Taking the seals off one by one would not allow the reader to read the scroll a little at a time. It could not be opened and read until all the seals were off. Only in Revelation 10 is it finally given to John, who in effect internalizes it and then is given a prophetic commission just as Ezekiel was. But—and we will come back to this in a moment—whereas Ezekiel was told to prophesy to Israel, John is told to prophesy about "many peoples and nations and languages and kings" (10:11). Bauckham suggests—again reasonably—that not only is the scroll John now receives and eats the one he saw in heaven in 5:1–9, but the angel who delivers it is the same one seen in 1:1 and 22:16. The scroll thus "contains the central and principal content of John's prophetic revelation." Since he receives the scroll in chapter 10, its content must follow chapter 10. "Everything which precedes John's consumption of the scroll is preparatory to the real message of his prophecy."[10]

In what follows, John is informed that "the nations" will be given authority to "trample over the holy city for forty-two months" (11:2). During this period they will be opposed by God's two witnesses, who will be given authority to prophesy for 1,260 days but will then be killed by the beast who arises from the bottomless pit. The precise locus of all this is veiled in metaphor. When they die, "their dead bodies will lie in the street of the great

10. Bauckham, *Climax of Prophecy*, 255.

city that is prophetically called Sodom and Egypt, where also their Lord was crucified" (11:8). John is tracing a prophetic itinerary that runs through all of these cities before reaching its fulfillment in Rome.

The two prophets will lie dead in the street for three and a half days before coming to life again and entering heaven. Again we are confronted with a variant on the 1,260 or three and a half already encountered. For three and a half days members of the peoples and tribes and languages and nations gaze at their dead bodies and refuse to let them be placed in a tomb. Inhabitants of the earth gloat over them, celebrating and exchanging presents, because these two prophets had tormented them. But after the three and a half days, the breath of life from God enters the prophets, they stand on their feet, and those who see them are terrified. Then the prophets rise up to heaven in a cloud while their enemies watch them. At that moment there is a great earthquake, and a tenth of the city falls; seven thousand people are killed in the earthquake, while the rest are terrified and give glory to the God of heaven (10:9–13). One might expect repentance, but apparently all we are seeing is fear.

Now at last we come to the seventh trumpet. When it sounds, there are loud voices in heaven saying, "The kingdom of the world has become the kingdom of our Lord and of his Messiah, and he will reign forever and ever" (11:15). In the worship that follows, the twenty-four elders around God's throne say to him, "You have taken your great power and begun to reign. The nations raged, but your wrath has come, and the time for judging the dead, for rewarding your servants, the prophets and saints and all who fear your name, both small and great, and for destroying those who destroy the earth" (11:17–18). At this point, God's heavenly temple is opened and the ark of the covenant is seen, accompanied by thunder, lightning, hail, and earthquake.

We arrive at Revelation 12, which actually seems to break the narrative, representing a leap backward in time. This is, perhaps, a good moment to push the "hold" button and make some general comments. Whether we choose to look at medieval or modern exegesis—or at least those medieval or modern exegetes who interpret Revelation as portraying a series of events— we find two general tendencies. One is to read the seven seals, trumpets, and bowls as a chronologically progressive development. They portray events that are successive in time. The other tendency is to see them as recapitulative. They cover the same events but, as some modern scholars like to say, they view the same events from three different perspectives.

If we consider only the seals and trumpets, which of these two patterns do we see? The answer, unfortunately, is "neither and both," which is why there are two different exegetical tendencies. Some of the ambiguities disappear once we give up reading the sevenfold patterns as linear temporal progression. Both patterns involve two groups, the elect and "humankind." The elect, those marked with and protected by God's seal, are identified predominately with the martyrs, but the rest of the book will clarify that there are some elect who are spared martyrdom. "Humankind" is ambiguous. It represents just that—all those who walk on the face of the earth—but the term is also used to describe those who (to anticipate a bit) receive that other seal, the mark of the beast. Thus, John can say that the locust-cavalrymen destroyed a third of humankind, but the other two-thirds "did not repent" (9:20–21). The difference between "humankind" in the more and less inclusive senses is, for John, statistically insignificant, because the true Christian community is, at least so far, an extremely small group. Everyone else is capable of seeing God's wrath and repenting, but in these two series they do not.

The leaders of this huge, stiff-necked group seek the destruction of the tiny Christian community, and they have the resources to kill a great many of them; yet at the same time they are engineering their own destruction. God is about to direct his heavy artillery at them in the form of invading armies—reference to the Euphrates suggests John has the Parthians in mind—who will soon be loosed upon the Roman Empire. The Parthians, of course, are equally a part of "humankind" in the bad sense and thus ripe for judgment, but in the meantime God can use one evil group to destroy another. He also has the ability to destroy them by his own nonhuman means, by bringing the natural world down on them. John seems less interested in telling us which of these things will happen first than he is in underlining God's immense striking power.

We have one more series of seven to work in, but first we must deal with some intervening material in the form of Revelation 12, the woman and the dragon. The woman bears a son and escapes a dragon with seven heads, seven crowns, and ten horns, who is eager to devour her child. She flees into the wilderness, where she remains hidden for 1,260 days. War breaks out in heaven. Michael and his angels defeat the dragon and his angels; then the dragon is cast down to earth, where he continues to prosecute his campaign against those who keep God's commandments. The point of this passage is that, although the dragon (i.e., Satan) is still able to attack God's people, in a larger sense he has already lost the war. He is raging precisely because "he knows his time is short" (12:12).

The dragon does have allies. He goes down to the seashore—John appreciates the long history of water as a symbol of chaos and rebellion in ancient Middle Eastern mythology[11]—and there John sees, rising from the sea, a beast with seven horns and seven heads, with ten crowns on its horns (13:1). One of those heads seems to have received a mortal wound, yet it has been healed. The beast resembles a leopard, but it has feet resembling those of a bear, and its mouth is like a lion's mouth. The dragon gives that beast power, which it exercises for forty-two months. The whole world follows it.

The beast from the sea is served by another rising from the land. It exercises power for the first beast and forces "humankind" to worship it. Aided in this task by wonders it is allowed to perform, it causes the world to worship an image of the beast. It insists that all be marked on the hand or forehead with the number of the beast's name (666), and none can buy or sell without that mark.

Compared with what we have been examining, this passage seems relatively straightforward. The beast from the sea is the Roman Empire. The sea may bear heavy mythological freight, suggesting the evil nature of the empire and its link with the dragon, but it also reflects the fact that, in the course of the century or so preceding John, the empire has washed up from the sea onto the shores of various lands. Once there, it functions through a partnership with the beast from the land, meaning those in the area willing to cooperate with the empire and further its aims. In Revelation 13, attention is focused on the imperial cult, and with good reason. Western Asia Minor, the locus of the seven churches addressed by John, was on the cutting edge when it came to the imperial cult.

Viewed from one perspective, residents of western Asia Minor had no reason to see themselves as occupied territory, having been incorporated into the Roman structure for over two centuries. From the time of Augustus, the elite of the area could hold dual citizenship. Under Rome, the area had become one of the most urbanized areas in the empire. Furthering the imperial cult could reap benefits for such cities, and some (in fact most) of the cities where John's seven churches were located seem to have pursued the practice vigorously.[12]

---

11. See Adela Yarbro Collins, *The Combat Myth in the Book of Revelation* (Missoula: Scholars, 1976). G. B. Caird, *The Revelation of St. John the Divine* (London: A & C Black, 1984), does an excellent job of tracing the mythological dimension. So do Bauckham and, more concisely, Schüssler Fiorenza, *Revelation* (Minneapolis: Fortress, 1991), 80–84.

12. See Witherington, *Revelation*, 22–25 and 192–95. Remember, though, that we are speaking of those socially prominent and economically comfortable enough to profit from the Roman connection. Those not in a position to profit from it might see the matter differently.

Thus, John's focus seems very particular. Nevertheless, his appropriation of imagery from Daniel 7 is suggestive. Daniel sees four beasts coming out of the sea. They represent a succession of kingdoms, and, since the author of Daniel leaves space for *ex eventu* prophecies by placing this vision in the past, it represents a tour of history capped by a look at the present and the near future.

John combines the four beasts into one, raising the question of whether his beast, while it represents Rome, is seen by him as applicable to other historical kingdoms as well, that is, whether the image represents a continuing uneasy relationship between God's people and great kingdoms throughout history.[13] But in the final analysis the question is not so much about what John intends as it is about what he actually produces. It is clear that not only his sensitivity to the mythological implications of water and his retrofitting of Daniel 7 but also his constant tendency to anchor his handling of the immediate future in allusions to Genesis, Exodus, and the entire Old Testament prophetic tradition; the complex Old Testament, intertestamental, and New Testament tradition of angelology; extracanonical prophetic/apocalyptic literature; and ancient Middle Eastern mythology give Revelation a depth and complexity that allow it to transcend his concern with what will happen next. Whatever happens next will be rooted in all of history and grow organically out of it. Intentionally or unintentionally, John has produced a work that deserves consideration alongside the other great mythology of the ancient Middle East, a work rooted in that mythology, and this fact is nowhere more apparent than in Revelation 13–16.

We can now proceed to the final seven-part series, the emptying of the bowls. The first angel pours his bowl on the earth, and a foul, painful sore appears on those who have the mark of the beast and who worship its image. The second angel pours his bowl into the sea, and it becomes like the blood of a corpse. The third angel pours his bowl into the rivers and the springs, and they too turn into blood. The fourth angel pours his bowl on the sun and burns people with fire; but they curse the name of God, who is responsible for these plagues, and they do not repent or give him glory. The fifth angel pours his bowl on the throne of the beast, and its kingdom is plunged into darkness. People gnaw their tongues in agony and curse God because of their pains and sores, but they do not repent. The sixth angel pours his bowl

13. Note that at 7:26–27 Daniel predicts that the fourth kingdom, usually interpreted by scholars as the Seleucid kingdom, will persecute the holy people for a time, two times, and half a time. Then it will be destroyed and be replaced by an everlasting holy kingdom.

on the great river Euphrates, and its water is dried up to prepare the way for the kings from the east.

Then demonic spirits go out to the kings of the world, to assemble them for battle at the place called Armageddon. The seventh angel pours his bowl into the air, and a loud voice comes out of the temple, saying, "It is done!" There are thunder and lightning and an earthquake that splits the great city into three parts. The cities of all the nations fall. God pours the wine-cup of the fury on Babylon, every island flees away, no mountain remains, and huge hailstones, each weighing about a hundred pounds, drop from heaven. The people again curse God (16:2–21).

By this point, much of the narrative has a familiar ring. Humankind is afflicted, nature is assaulted, and there is a great show of thunder, lightning, and earthquakes. To call this recapitulation makes some sense. The same elements keep appearing. The seven trumpets and bowls are directed at the same things in the same order: the earth, the sea, the rivers and fountains, and the sun; then darkness comes; then there is an attack from beyond the Euphrates; then there are voices in heaven followed by thunder, lightning, earthquake, and hail. The model is Exodus 7. In all three sevenfold sequences, God hurls his wrath down on humankind, but humankind refuses to repent. Those who bear the mark of the beast remain obdurate.

The idea that the three series can be arranged in any sort of progressive development makes substantially less sense if what we mean by that is arranging the twenty-one seals, trumpets, and bowls in such a way that we can match them with history. Here again, though, we might argue for a limited sense in which the three represent a progressive development. That possibility seems brightest as we arrive at the end of each series.

First, we have seen that the seven trumpets are folded into the opening of the seventh seal. It is at least possible to see the seven bowls as bearing an analogous relationship to the seventh trumpet, although that would be a harder case to make, particularly in view of the extensive detour the narrative takes before we arrive at the bowls. What seems more important is that the blowing of the seventh trumpet is greeted with the announcement that God has begun to reign and that the time has come to judge the dead, reward the righteous, and destroy those who destroy the earth. The pouring of the seventh bowl is followed by the words "It is done" and the splitting of the great city. One could argue that with each series we are inching our way closer to the end. That seems, however, an extremely slight foundation on which to build a theory of progressive development, or for that matter on which to build the notion that John even *wants* to present one.

When it comes to the seals, trumpets, and bowls, there is much to be said for Elisabeth Schüssler Fiorenza's suggestion that the text is more thematically than historically ordered.[14] Once we acknowledge John's debt to Old Testament precedents, we might be tempted to conclude that the images of divine wrath he is piling up make less sense as a plan of historical development, be it sevenfold or twenty-one-fold, than as a dramatic presentation of God's displeasure at human sin, God's repeated efforts to impress humanity with the depth of that displeasure, and humanity's oddly impressive refusal to repent. Nevertheless, the future anticipated by John does have discernible general contours. These will emerge in the course of examining the rest of the book.

What follows is relatively clear. One of the angels with the bowls says to John,

> "Come, I will show you the judgment of the great whore who is seated on many waters, with whom the kings of the earth have committed fornication, and with the wine of whose fornication the inhabitants of the earth have become drunk." So he carried me away in the spirit into a wilderness, and I saw a woman sitting on a scarlet beast that was full of blasphemous names, and it had seven heads and ten horns. The woman was clothed in purple and scarlet, and adorned with gold and jewels and pearls, holding in her hand a golden cup full of abominations and the impurities of her fornication; and on her forehead was written a name, a mystery: "Babylon the great, mother of whores and of earth's abominations." And I saw that the woman was drunk with the blood of the saints and the blood of the witnesses to Jesus. (17:1–6)

The whore is obviously Rome; and in case there was any doubt of that, the angel provides a succinct exegesis of the beast. It "was, and is not, and is about to ascend from the bottomless pit and go to destruction." The seven heads "are seven mountains on which the woman is seated; also, they are seven kings, of whom five have fallen, one is living, and the other has not yet come; and when he comes, he must remain only a little while." The beast "is an eighth but it belongs to the seven, and it goes to destruction. And the ten horns that you saw are ten kings who have not yet received a kingdom, but they are to receive authority as kings for one hour, together with the beast. These are united in yielding their power and authority to the beast; they will

---

14. Schüssler Fiorenza, *Book of Revelation*, 46.

make war on the Lamb, and the Lamb will conquer them." The beast and the ten horns "will hate the whore; they will make her desolate and naked" (17:1–18).

Here at last we find a sevenfold pattern that is obviously chronological. The passage assumes a succession of Roman emperors ending in Domitian— John says seven, but all such numbers in Revelation should be approached with caution—yet it also assumes the widespread legend that Nero actually did not die. According to some, he was hiding out among the Parthians and would return to power with their aid. That is essentially what we have in Revelation 17, except here we have Nero and ten royal allies attacking and destroying Rome.

We recall that the number of the beast is 666. We are dealing here with gematria, the ancient practice of transforming the letters of a name into the corresponding numbers of each letter, adding those numbers, then referring to the name by writing the total number. What makes the code particularly difficult to crack is that, whereas going from the name to the number is fairly straightforward, going in the opposite direction is complicated by the fact that a huge variety of names could add up to the same number. And, just to make it harder, the names were often transliterated into some other alphabet before the total of the letters was computed.

In effect, most numbers are translatable only if the reader is dealing with a limited number of possibilities and can test each of them. That is the situation if we decide we are looking for a Roman emperor, and especially if we begin with the assumption that Nero is a major candidate. Sure enough, if we take the Greek *Neron Kaisar* and transliterate the letters into Hebrew, the letters add up to 666. This solution appeared in the nineteenth century and has been adopted by a number of contemporary commentators.[15]

In the next chapter the expectation of Rome's destruction receives immediate gratification. Another angel arises and announces, "Fallen, fallen is Babylon the great!" (18:2). It is perhaps not quite that simple. John hears another voice saying, "Come out of her, my people, so that you do not take part in her sins, and so that you do not share in her plagues" (18:4). Thus, in rapid succession Rome is portrayed as about to fall, fallen, and in the process of falling.

In the rest of chapter 18, Babylon shifts between fallen and about to fall as John gathers testimonials from those who profited from her. What we read

---

15. Bauckham, *Climax of Prophecy*, 384–452, offers a thorough investigation of Nero as the beast.

here is in some ways remarkable. As much as John detests Rome, he seems to see what it signifies for many of its inhabitants. It represents a powerful stabilizing force that contributes not only to peace but also to prosperity.

> And the kings of the earth, who committed fornication and lived in luxury with her, will weep and wail over her when they see the smoke of her burning; they will stand far off, in fear of her torment, and say, "Alas, alas, the great city, Babylon, the mighty city! For in one hour your judgment has come." And the merchants of the earth weep and mourn for her, since no one buys their cargo anymore, cargo of gold, silver, jewels and pearls, fine linen, purple, silk and scarlet, all kinds of scented wood, all articles of ivory, all articles of costly wood, bronze, iron, and marble, cinnamon, spice, incense, myrrh, frankincense, wine, olive oil, choice flour and wheat, cattle and sheep, horses and chariots, slaves—and human lives. "The fruit for which your soul longed has gone from you, and all your dainties and your splendor are lost to you, never to be found again!" The merchants of these wares, who gained wealth from her, will stand far off in fear of her torment, weeping and mourning aloud, "Alas, alas, for the great city, clothed in fine linen, in purple and scarlet, adorned with gold, with jewels, and with pearls! For in one hour all this wealth has been laid waste!" And all shipmasters and seafarers, sailors and all whose trade is on the sea, stood far off and cried out as they saw the smoke of her burning, "What city was like the great city?" And they threw dust on their heads, as they wept and mourned, crying out, "Alas, alas, for the great city, where all who had ships at sea grew rich by her wealth! For in one hour she has been laid waste." (18:9–19)

Here for a moment John turns the microphone over to his adversaries. They are allowed to express what the great city meant to them, their grief at its collapse, and, beyond grief, their shock, "for in one hour she has been laid waste!" For a moment the mood is almost elegiac, but then it is shattered by a remarkable bit of divine theater as an angel takes up "a stone like a great millstone" and hurls it into the sea, announcing,

> With such violence Babylon the great city will be thrown down, and will be found no more; and the sound of harpists and minstrels and of flutists and trumpeters will be heard in you no more; and an artisan of any trade will be found in you no more; and the sound of the millstone will be heard in you no more; and the light of a lamp will shine in you no more; and

the voice of bridegroom and bride will be heard in you no more; for your merchants were the magnates of the earth, and all nations were deceived by your sorcery. And in you was found the blood of prophets and of saints, and of all who have been slaughtered on earth. (18:21–24)

John is now back on message. "After this I heard what seemed to be the loud voice of a great multitude in heaven, saying, 'Hallelujah! Salvation and glory and power to our God, for his judgments are true and just; he has judged the great whore who corrupted the earth with her fornication, and he has avenged on her the blood of his servants'" (19:1–2).

But just how does John think the great whore has accomplished that corruption? What sort of fornication are we dealing with here? It's easy enough to say that Rome has tried to substitute itself for the true God and to speak of the imperial cult as a form of idolatry, then to generalize from the Roman Empire to nineteenth-century colonialism and, more recently, global capitalism as forms of the same idolatrous substitution of some transient earthly institution for the eternal, transcendent God; but does John, too, see concrete political and economic crimes here? Most modern scholars would say that he does, and some of these scholars are willing to pursue the matter to remarkable lengths.[16]

From this point on, things happen fast. In Revelation 19, Christ, riding a white horse and wearing a garment soaked in blood, rides out accompanied by the armies of heaven to do battle with the unrighteous. What sort of battle it is seems less clear. The armies of heaven ride white horses and wear fine white linen. They could be the angelic host (cf. 2 Thess 1:7–10) or the martyrs (as Rev 17:14 suggests).[17] Their presence seems more ceremonial than warlike. No weapons or armor is mentioned, except for the sharp sword extending from Christ's mouth, with which he will strike down his adversaries.

No battle is described, though. John tells us instead that an angel appears and calls to the birds, "Come, gather for the great supper of God, to

---

16. Wes Howard-Brook and Anthony Gwyther, *Unveiling Empire: Reading Revelation Then and Now* (Maryknoll: Orbis, 2005), combine the idolatry theme with attention to the social injustice encountered once the beast and great whore are in charge; and Schüssler Fiorenza pursues the social injustice theme relentlessly, especially in *Revelation*. Bauckham, *Climax of Prophecy*, ch. 10, offers a detailed analysis of Revelation 18 as an economic critique of Rome.

17. Caird, *Revelation*, 242–44, suggests the latter and in the process presents an intriguing explanation of why Christ's garment is soaked in blood. It is the blood of the martyrs. Their garments have been washed white in the blood of the Lamb (7:14), while Christ's has been reddened by theirs.

eat the flesh of kings, the flesh of captains, the flesh of the mighty, the flesh of horses and their riders—flesh of all, both free and slave, both small and great" (19:17–18). Only the beast and false prophet are not killed by Christ's sword, and these two are thrown alive into the lake of fire. They will not reappear.

But what happens to everyone else? Revelation 19 is one of many passages that make exegetes uneasy. One is tempted to take advantage of the fact that the sword—first mentioned in 1:16—is located in Christ's mouth, not his hand, and to read it as an allusion to preaching the gospel.[18] We recall Revelation 5:5, where John is told, "See, the Lion of the tribe of Judah, the Root of David, has conquered, so that he can open the scroll," but what John actually sees is a lamb. When the Lamb takes the scroll, those in heaven "sing a new song, 'You are worthy to take the scroll and to open its seals, for you were slaughtered and by your blood you ransomed for God saints from every tribe and language and people and nation'" (5:9). One might be tempted to suggest that the "new song" is new precisely because it heralds a different sort of messiah, who reconciles the world to himself, not by violence, but by suffering love. Remember that Christ rides out to battle wearing a garment soaked in blood, and we might legitimately assume it to be his own.

Unfortunately, the book of Revelation will not fit comfortably into that mold. John says, "He will tread the wine press of the fury of the wrath of God Almighty" (cf. Isa 63:1–5), and he will rule the nations "with a rod of iron" (19:15; cf. Ps 2:9). Consider, too, that Revelation 19 closes with the announcement that "the beast and false prophet were thrown alive into the lake of fire that burns with sulfur; and the rest were killed by the sword of the rider on the horse, the sword that came from his mouth; and all the birds were gorged with their flesh." Or consider the earlier imagery in 14:19–20, describing the punishment of the ungodly: "The angel swung his sickle over the earth and gathered the vintage of the earth, and he threw it into the great wine press of the wrath of God. And the wine press was trodden outside the city, and blood flowed from the wine press, as high as a horse's bridle, for a distance of about two hundred miles." Or consider the reaction in heaven to the destruction of Babylon. However sad the merchants of this world might be, the celestial mood is marvelously improved.

> I heard what seemed to be the loud voice of a great multitude in heaven, saying, "Hallelujah! Salvation and glory and power to our God, for his

18. For references to that sword see 1:16; 2:12, 16; 19:15, 21.

judgments are true and just; he has judged the great whore who corrupted the earth with her fornication, and he has avenged on her the blood of his servants." Once more they said, "Hallelujah! The smoke goes up from her forever and ever." And the twenty-four elders and the four living creatures fell down and worshiped God who is seated on the throne, saying, "Amen. Hallelujah!" And from the throne came a voice saying, "Praise our God, all you his servants, and all who fear him, small and great." (19:1–5)

Once we take into account all that is said in heaven in the course of the work, and all the talk of vengeance, we might feel forced to conclude that the image of Christ as Lamb does not replace that of Christ as lion, but instead supplements it. Each describes an aspect of Christ's activity.

Nevertheless, a number of scholars have continued to protest that John's utilization of Old Testament imagery to describe Christ's victories has to be interpreted in a manner consistent with his realization that Christ has gained his victory on the cross and that the martyrs (or, as John calls them, "the conquerors") represent by their sacrifices an extension of Christ's saving activity. Thus, just as when we hear "lion" we should think "lamb," so when we hear other Old Testament references to divine vengeance we should transpose them into the key of New Testament sacrificial love.[19]

Richard Bauckham certainly does a good job of presenting the case for a nonviolent victory. In *Climax of Prophecy*, in a chapter entitled "The Apocalypse as a Christian War Scroll," he draws on his knowledge of extracanonical apocalyptic sources to demonstrate the variety of early Jewish and Christian opinion as to how or even if God's eschatological victory over evil involves human agency. The question would have been a live one in John's environment. Bauckham summarizes the problem as follows:

> No doubt in the Jewish circles with which John and his churches had contact—including Jewish refugees from Palestine who joined the great Jewish communities in the cities of Asia Minor after the fall of Jerusalem—ideas of eschatological holy war against Rome, such as the Qumran community had entertained and the Zealots espoused, were well known.

19. Howard-Brook and Gwyther, *Unveiling Empire*, 150, offer this view but then (155) seem to recant, settling merely on insistence that vengeance belongs exclusively to God. Caird, *Revelation*, is more resolute. He tries throughout the commentary to interpret John's use of Old Testament imagery in a way that either sees it as describing evil destroying itself (e.g., the destruction of Rome by Nero and the Parthians) or straightforwardly reinterprets it on the "hear lion, think lamb" principle.

Some Jews disillusioned with such expectations after the fall of Jerusalem may have joined the Christian churches to which John wrote. John's interaction with apocalyptic militancy will therefore have been a part of the churches' debate with "the synagogue of Satan who say they are Jews but are not" (3:9). He is not concerned *simply* to repudiate apocalyptic militancy, since he shares much of its general outlook: a strong critique of Roman power as antithetical to the rule of God, a perception of religio-political issues within an eschatological and dualistic framework in which God and his people are in conflict with the satanic power and destined in the end to triumph, and a conviction of the need for God's people to engage in the conflict with evil by active resistance to the religio-political claims of Rome and pagan society. Therefore, instead of simply repudiating apocalyptic militancy, he *reinterprets* it. . . . He aims to show that the decisive battle in God's eschatological holy war . . . has already been won by the faithful witness and sacrificial death of Jesus. Christians are called to participate in his war and his victory, but by the same means he employed, bearing the witness of Jesus to the point of martyrdom.[20]

Here we come to the cause of our hermeneutical confusion. Unlike apocalyptic writers of the period who utilized the full panoply of Old Testament holy war imagery and meant it quite literally, and unlike other apocalyptic writers of the period who eschewed that imagery as much as possible because they rejected the notion of the elect engaging in physical holy warfare, John retains the imagery but reinterprets it. He has no problem with the notion of God as judge and, more to the point, no problem believing in the notion that radical evil must be resolutely eliminated if we are to have a new heaven and earth. He knows that Christ has conquered by dying on the cross—that is what Revelation 12 is about—and he knows that the martyrs are now collaborating in Christ's work in that respect. Thus, they, like Christ, are to be considered victors.

The result is a notable disjuncture between how they are seen on earth and how they are seen in heaven. From an earthly perspective they are losing. From a heavenly perspective they are winning. "The heavenly viewpoint is destined to prevail on earth at the *parousia*."[21]

That, at any rate, is the way Bauckham states the matter; yet one wonders if a slight adjustment might be in order. In Revelation 19 we are actually

20. Bauckham, *Climax of Prophecy*, 233–34.
21. Bauckham, *Climax of Prophecy*, 235.

seeing the *parousia* and its victory, but even then Satan will be only temporarily defeated. The final victory of the heavenly perspective will come only with the descent of the new Jerusalem, when God comes to dwell among us. "See, the home of God is among mortals. He will dwell with them; they will be his people" (21:3). The solution to our dilemma lies, not in our moving on to a heavenly realm where our martyrdom receives full credit, but in a renewed heaven and earth. If we are to be saved, the earth must be saved and we in it.

At this point the narrative accelerates even more.

Then I saw an angel coming down from heaven, holding in his hand the key to the bottomless pit and a great chain. He seized the dragon, that ancient serpent, who is the Devil and Satan, and bound him for a thousand years, and threw him into the pit, and locked and sealed it over him, so that he would deceive the nations no more, until the thousand years were ended. After that he must be let out for a little while.

Then I saw thrones, and those seated on them were given authority to judge. I also saw the souls of those who had been beheaded for their testimony to Jesus and for the word of God. They had not worshiped the beast or its image and had not received its mark on their foreheads or their hands. They came to life and reigned with Christ a thousand years. (The rest of the dead did not come to life until the thousand years were ended.) This is the first resurrection. Blessed and holy are those who share in the first resurrection. Over these the second death has no power, but they will be priests of God and of Christ, and they will reign with him a thousand years.

When the thousand years are ended, Satan will be released from his prison and will come out to deceive the nations at the four corners of the earth, Gog and Magog, in order to gather them for battle; they are as numerous as the sands of the sea. They marched up over the breadth of the earth and surrounded the camp of the saints and the beloved city. And fire came down from heaven and consumed them. And the devil who had deceived them was thrown into the lake of fire and sulfur, where the beast and the false prophet were, and they will be tormented day and night forever and ever. (20:1–10)

So Satan is confined in the pit for a thousand years while Christ reigns on earth with the martyrs, who are resurrected at this point. At the end of that time Satan is released and gathers allies from all over. They march to battle against the saints and are consumed by heavenly fire. Again there is no description of the battle. Again, for all intents and purposes, there *is* no battle. The attackers are not so much defeated as summarily eliminated. Satan survives, but he is now cast into the lake of fire, where he will remain forever.

There are, of course, a few questions left to ponder. First, does John really mean to say that the elect is composed solely of the martyrs? Or are the martyrs simply the only elect invited to rule with Christ? Or are we reading the word "conquerors" too narrowly, and are those who remain true considered conquerors whether they die in the process or not? John doesn't address the issue, but it seems odd to imagine that no one could have avoided receiving the mark of the beast without being martyred in the process. When, just before the destruction of Rome, John hears a voice from heaven saying, "Come out of her, my people, so that you do not . . . share in her plagues" (18:4), that seems to suggest that there are still faithful Christians who have survived the persecution while living in Babylon, and now God wants them relocated to save them from the Parthians.

In the final analysis, these are the sorts of questions asked by those of us who look for an orderly, logically coherent philosophy of religion, and that is not what John gives us. He combines elements of the Old Testament and other ancient Middle Eastern mythology in such a way as to produce a complex, colorful tapestry that does have its own sort of coherence, but that coherence has more to do with T. S. Eliot's *Four Quartets* than with Paul Tillich's *Systematic Theology.*

For much the same reason, John remains unclear as to whether, during the millennial reign, those who have accepted the mark of the beast can still repent and be saved. John's tendency is to present a strongly dualist and absolutist distinction between those who bear the mark of the beast and those who bear the seal of Christ, but commentators tend to dwell on every word in Revelation that suggests a more complex situation. John's intent in this book is to warn his flock that serious persecution is about to befall them and to stress the absolute necessity of standing firm. Thus, it is understandable that he would present the faith as an existential choice to be made *right now.* In short, the rhetorical function of his work leaves him little incentive to discuss any opportunities sinners might later have to repent.

Here again, though, it is Bauckham who offers the most extended and convincing argument that John looks forward to the conversion of the nations.[22] This is not to say that everyone in every nation will be converted.

---

22. Bauckham, *Climax of Prophecy*, ch. 9, "The Conversion of the Nations."

Obviously some will remain obdurate. But neither is it to say that only a tiny group of elect will be saved. Bauckham documents a transition within Revelation from speaking of the church as drawn from the nations of the world to speaking of the church's witness to the nations of the world, and eventually a transition from rule over these nations by the beast to rule over them by God. Understandably, this transition begins at 10:9–11, when John discovers the true subject of his prophecy: "You must prophesy again about many peoples and nations and languages and kings." From that point on, John's tendency is to gravitate toward those passages in the Old Testament that present the hope for conversion of the nations in its most universalistic form.[23]

We must return to the subject of martyrdom. It is worth asking how much of it there actually was. Caird, who knows the sources as well as anyone, cites some evidence that Christians were executed during Domitian's reign, but he observes that in these few identifiable cases "it was their high rank that drew the emperor's attention to them and cost them life and liberty. There is no evidence that, at the time when John wrote, there had been any open and systematic persecution of Christians since the days of Nero."[24] Caird prefers to speak of John as predicting rather than reporting it. So does Bauckham. Perhaps, like the millennium, it was an expectation John would not live to see fulfilled.

John himself may be our best evidence on the matter. He names one person who was apparently martyred (2:13) and praises others for not denying their faith on that occasion. That suggests martyrdom did happen; yet the fact that he offers one solitary name encourages us to wonder how many more martyrs he could have added. John himself, of course, writes from confinement on Patmos, which itself suggests some degree of persecution; yet here again the evidence is ambiguous. John says he is living there because of his faith, but the fact remains that he is *living* there. We don't really know his situation there, but Tertullian tells us that John *in insulam relegatur*.[25] Tertullian is, to be sure, writing much later, but as a lawyer he probably understood the significance of his terminology. *Relegatio in insulam* was a milder form of banishment than *deportatio in insulam*. The latter could be issued only by the emperor, but the former lay in the power of the provincial

---

23. Bauckham, *Climax of Prophecy*, 311. As Bauckham notes, Daniel 7 is especially important to John, since it describes how, after the beast is slain, "one like the Son of man" is given everlasting dominion over all the nations (329).

24. Caird, *Revelation*, 20–21.

25. *De praescriptione haereticorum* 36, quoted in Caird, *Revelation*, 22.

governor, who had substantial latitude. It is perfectly possible that John could have been released from Patmos and could have returned to his province.

The Pliny-Trajan correspondence is often cited to show that there was in fact persecution in John's day. Certainly the correspondence offers us a window on the situation two decades after John wrote, during the reign of another emperor; and it suggests a situation in which, as Trajan himself says, it was impossible to offer any general rules dealing with Christians. Having said so much, Trajan does offer four rules: (1) Don't seek them out; (2) but if they are denounced to you, round them up; (3) then, if they worship our gods, pardon them; (4) or, if they refuse, punish them. Trajan doesn't say how they should be punished, but we know from Pliny's letter that Pliny himself gave them three chances to abandon their faith, then executed them. If they were adamant but were Roman citizens, he sent them on to Rome. Trajan assures Pliny that he is observing proper procedure.

In the course of describing his actions, Pliny notes that some of those apprehended said they had once been Christians but had since left the faith, "some three years before, some more than twenty years earlier." The three-year figure is interesting because one is tempted to connect it with a passage in which Pliny relays the suspects' description of a Christian worship service, then says they had given even this up "after my edict in which, according to your instructions, I banned organizations (*hetaerias*)." In other words, they were not reacting to explicitly anti-Christian legislation.

The twenty-year figure is interesting because it brings us back to John's time, and that has led some scholars to take Pliny's letter as evidence that there was persecution then; but Pliny doesn't really say that. He simply tells us that more than twenty years earlier some people left the church and never returned to it.

One is tempted to present something like an *a priori* argument for persecution in John's time. Western Asia Minor was, as we have seen, an area that had relatively less complaint with Roman rule than other areas (e.g., Palestine or Britain). It was an area in which cities actively contended for imperial honors by encouraging the imperial cult. In short, it was just the sort of province in which Christian intransigence of the sort John explicitly demanded might have led to frequent denunciations by fellow citizens. Thus, the sort of situation Pliny writes about is precisely what one might expect in John's time as well. We need not look for anything on the order of the later persecutions under Decius and Diocletian. We would expect something regional, the result of individual Christians being denounced by name to local officials. It would hardly be surprising if this sort of thing happened without producing the sort of evidence detectible by us. In fact, we know about Pliny's brush with Christians only because he tended to write the emperor asking his advice about a great many things that other Roman officials might well have settled on their own. It also seems likely that the Christian community in western Asia Minor—or, more precisely, John's Christian community as opposed to the less confrontational faction he denounces in the letters—was quite small. It would not have required many deaths to make the occasion register with them as a serious persecution. But this is all speculation.

Other questions are raised by Satan's millennial imprisonment. It is hard not to ask just what function it serves if he is released at the end of it and has to be defeated yet again. Here again, John doesn't say, nor would we expect him to do so.

While we are on the subject of that millennial imprisonment, how long is a thousand years? That is a question we can come close to answering. John's numbers tend to be more symbolic than literal. They are often symbolic in the sense that he chooses them because they mean something (e.g., seven suggests a totality, as in the seven days of the week); but some numbers have more to do with John's allegiance to his Old Testament sources (e.g., Dan 7:25 says "they shall be given into his power for a time, two times, and half a time," which can be converted into three and a half years or 1,260 days). In the final analysis, though, John's numbers seem to function as the equivalent of ballpark figures. A millennium presumably means a long time, just as "an hour" means a short time, and three and a half years or 1,260 days means that the period of tribulation will be long enough to be extremely unpleasant but short enough that the church can endure it.

But how soon does John expect that long time to begin? The first sentence of his prologue says that what he is predicting will happen soon. His epilogue says the same thing five more times. Obviously he doesn't mean *everything* will occur soon. He's telling us that Christ will come soon and the millennium will begin soon. In effect, he is telling us that the time between the composition of the book and the coming of Christ will be a bloody but limited period leading to a long one of relative peace.

That peace will be owed to the fact that Satan is restrained; but he is only temporarily restrained, and when he emerges he is still Satan. Only when he has again been defeated and this time put away forever can the world move on to its final state, a new heaven and a new earth.

At that point the earth becomes the abode of the holy city, the new Jerusalem. John receives a guided tour of the new Jerusalem, which is described with some care; yet it is unwise to be too concerned with its physical arrangement, which is, again, largely symbolic. The important thing is that God is there. "See, the home of God is among mortals. He will dwell with them; they will be his peoples, and God himself will be with them" (21:3–4). That is the central thing about the new Jerusalem: God abides there with his people, and by his presence all is made new. It is a world without evil. As John chooses to put it, "the sea was no more" (21:1). There is water, but the sea—that unpredictable, rebellious, chaotic element in the world as it existed—has been eliminated. And so has death, at least for those worthy to live in the new Jerusalem.

In short, John's eschatology takes seriously the fact that the earth, like humankind, was created by God and must attain fulfillment. The word "fulfillment" is perhaps more apropos than "restoration." Ben Witherington observes, "There is a sort of *Urzeit-Enzeit* pattern here. The end will be as the beginning. It is not accidental that John, like what we find in Isaiah 65–66, depicts the final state as like the first state in the garden of Eden."[26] Witherington is certainly correct in the sense that the eternal joy promised to humankind is a tangible, physical one in a tangible, material city and thus can be likened to the location of Adam and Eve in a physical garden (where God also dwells with them, just as he promises to do in Revelation 21); yet the absence of the sea reminds us that there is more involved in the heavenly city than mere restoration of an original state. It suggests that God has been struggling with unruly elements in the world he created since creation and has finally conquered them, a conclusion Teilhard de Chardin should have appreciated.

In short, Christ will come, pacify the world, confine Satan, and rule for a long time. Then the Satan will be released, organize a final rebellion, and be defeated yet again. This time he will be confined for good, and God will join his people, ruling forever over a new, perfected earth.

Who is the enemy that must be conquered in order to achieve this goal? In the letters to the seven churches we see evidence of internal dispute, just as we do elsewhere in the New Testament and in other early Christian documents. Christianity is in the process of defining itself. That certainly is important, but it receives nowhere near as much emphasis as the existential threat posed by paganism. This is a world in which the Christian element, engulfed by a pagan world, hardly registers as a power source. The punishment focused on that pagan world is described in terms of natural

---

26. Witherington, *Revelation*, 254.

forces such as falling stars and earthquakes, or scenarios in which one pagan kingdom, such as the Parthians, is deployed against another, such as the Romans. As time passes, this situation will change, but slowly. The Christian community will expand, but gradually.

That is, in a nutshell, this author's reading of Revelation. There are other readings—many others. It is, as Jerome said, a book with as many mysteries as words.

Athanasius, Augustine, Jerome, and the Open Window

We must now prepare for a great leap forward, all the way into the fourth century and the Constantinian rescue of Christianity. This is an equally important moment for the book of Revelation, a moment when it became something slightly different. Here Elaine Pagels shows us where to concentrate our attention by zeroing in on Athanasius, the iron-willed bishop who rode the Arian controversy into a whole new era of Christian history, one in which an establishment Christianity benefited from its imperial connections to impose a hitherto impossible ideal of orthodoxy on the church. That ideal of orthodoxy included not only the Nicene Creed but a canon of Scripture that included Revelation while excluding much else. Pagels makes it clear that Athanasius's Easter letter of 367 CE, which included Revelation as part of the canon, was hardly announcing the common opinion among scholars in his time, and she does well in emphasizing that Athanasius made his own battles easier to win by managing to shift the emphasis from John's attack on Rome to his concern about heresy. Key terms such as "the beast," "Babylon," and "the great whore" were at that point detached from the Roman Empire and reattached to heresy.[27]

How did that change affect the strongly historical emphasis of John's Apocalypse, particularly its sense of history as shaped by a specific set of periods in which Satan is bound, then released, then bound again? That particular pattern seems at odds with one in which order and, with it, sanctity can be enforced by an episcopacy enjoying a degree of imperial authority. One place to look for an answer is in the writings of contemporary scholars such as Augustine and Jerome. Historians often claim that Augustine spiritualized

27. Pagels, *Revelations*, is primarily concerned with Athanasius's impact on the "books of revelation" found at Nag Hammadi in 1945, but her book is equally important as an indication of his impact on John's Revelation.

the millennium, but he did not. In his *City of God* he notes that some people read the book of Revelation as promising that after six thousand years of world history there will be a bodily resurrection of the saints followed by a thousand-year rest period. This view, Augustine says, would be more tolerable if people who held it anticipated a millennium of spiritual delights, but in fact there are those who look forward to real banqueting. Thus, Augustine himself now thinks we can understand it in either of two ways. It might be taken as a synecdoche, the whole referring to one of its parts, and thus the word "millennium" should be taken as referring to whatever is left of the sixth and final part of world history; or it could be taken as simply a perfect number used to represent the entire Christian era. That definition leaves the historical period but seems to drain a great deal of the tension out of it.

Jerome is more interesting. As Robert Lerner wrote in one of the best articles ever written about medieval millenarianism,[28] Saint Jerome was as hard as anyone in the early church on the notion that Revelation 20 prophesied a thousand-year kingdom of earthly joy (something Jerome saw as crypto-Judaism); yet, even as he shut the door on a chiliastic reading of Revelation 20, Jerome opened a window to chiliasm with his exegesis of Daniel 12. It was, to be sure, a small window, only forty-five days wide; but a great deal came in through it.[29]

Daniel 12:11 announces that the impending abomination of desolation, which exegetes saw as the reign of Antichrist, will last 1,290 days; but then 12:12 adds, "Blessed is the one who waits for and reaches the end of the 1,335 days." Jerome decided that the latter interval was that between the death of Antichrist and the beginning of final judgment. Why should there be an interval of forty-five days after the death of Antichrist? God only knows, Jerome replied, "unless perhaps we can answer that it is to test the patience of the saints."[30]

By the time he commented on Matthew, Jerome could offer further thoughts on the matter. Pondering Matthew 24:37-39, he found what he saw as a reference to the behavior of sinners just before Christ's second coming in judgment. Matthew says, "As it was in the days of Noah, so it will be at the coming of the Son of Man. For in the days before the flood, people were

28. Robert Lerner, "Refreshment of the Saints: The Time after Antichrist as a Station for Earthly Progress in Medieval Thought," *Traditio* 32 (1976): 97-144 (hereafter "Refreshment").

29. My reference to a window amounts to artistic license. Lerner himself speaks of Jerome as opening a back door.

30. Hieronymus, *Commentariorum in Danielem* 3 (CCSL 75A:848).

eating and drinking, marrying and giving in marriage, up to the day Noah entered the ark; and they knew nothing about what would happen until the flood came and took them all away. That is how it will be at the coming of the Son of Man." So Jerome now had two reasons for the forty-five days. For the elect, it was a test of patience, which they, being the elect, were sure to pass. For the sinners, it was a final chance to repent, which they, being sinners, were sure to reject. Jerome summoned one more passage to bolster his argument, 1 Thessalonians 5:3: "When they say 'peace and safety,' then suddenly destruction will come upon them."[31]

Lerner does not deal at length with Augustine in the article, but it is worth observing that Augustine's discussion of Revelation 20:1–10 is in one respect quite unlike Jerome's discussion of Daniel 12:12–13. In suggesting that the millennium in Revelation might be taken as a synecdoche and thus could be seen as referring to whatever is currently left of the sixth and final part of world history, or that it could be taken as simply a perfect number used to represent the entire Christian era, Augustine effectively removes it from the list of periods that have to be accounted for in real time. He concedes that a more specific scenario appears right at the end of Christian history, a scenario involving Elijah, Antichrist, and Gog and Magog; but even here we should not try to discuss that scenario with undue precision, since we cannot predict the time, nature, and sequence of individual events.[32]

One other factor is important: for Augustine, these are not questions that need to be settled in his time. They are hardly just around the corner. For Augustine, Christ has come in the sixth and last period of world history. Thus, the world is in its final period, certainly; yet those who emphasize that fact can easily overdo it. Writing four centuries after the resurrection of Christ, Augustine feels he has some reason to take an exegetical interest in the identity of Gog, but not an existential interest in searching the horizon for his arrival.

Jerome's problem is a different one. There are those 1,335 days to be accounted for. There they are on the calendar, begging to be explained.

We return to Lerner, who then leaps from the fourth century to the eighth and examines Bede's commentary on Revelation.[33] He concentrates on Bede's historicization of the seven seals, pointing out that the first seal is seen as representing the primitive church; the next three allude to subse-

31. Hieronymus, *Commentarii in Mattheum* 4 (CCSL 77:233).
32. Augustine, *De civitate dei contra paganos*, section 20 (CCSL 48).
33. Bede, *Explanatio apocalypsis* (PL 93:129A).

quent unspecified warfare against it; and the fifth addresses the glory of those who will triumph in this battle. In the opening of the sixth seal we encounter those things to come in the time of Antichrist, and with the seventh we arrive at the beginning of eternal quiet.[34] He obviously thinks of this quiet (or rest, or peace) as beginning within history, because later he says, "After the death of Antichrist, some future rest is expected in the church, for Daniel predicts it. . . . Jerome exposits it in this way. . . . Note that he sees the greatest pressures on the church under the sixth seal, then rest under the seventh."[35]

How long will that rest last? Having followed Jerome this far, Bede balks at trailing him the rest of the way and taking the forty-five days literally. Here he simply doesn't commit himself, and in another work he explicitly states that, as the New Testament tells us, it is not for us to know that sort of thing.[36] As Lerner observes: "Ironically, however, Bede's theory of seven periods of Church history ending in one of this-worldly rest gave potentially greater cogency to expectations for the future than Jerome's isolated forty-five days, and his implication that the final period might last as long as God's pleasure made it possible to imagine that it could last considerably longer than Jerome's forty-five days. Both of these contributions were subsequently to prove very influential."[37]

Lerner looks only at that part of Bede's commentary mentioned so far; but it seems a shame to pass over the rest of it without indicating what Bede actually does with it. His treatment of the letters to the seven churches, the first vision, is historicized to the point that he recognizes he is dealing with seven churches in Asia Minor, but only to that extent. He shows little interest in placing them in their actual historical context, and he shows no interest whatsoever in reading them as a sevenfold historical pattern, as we will see some later exegetes doing.

The third vision, that of the seven trumpets, is another matter entirely. The trumpets suggest preaching, an association we will find to be common in subsequent commentaries. Bede sees the first trumpet as standing for "the destruction of the impious in fire and hail" and the second as the devil, having been ejected from the church, "more ardently setting afire the sea of this world." In an odd way, these two descriptions, vague as they seem,

---

34. Bede, *Explanatio apocalypsis* (PL 93:146D).

35. Bede, *Explanatio apocalypsis* (PL 93:154B–C).

36. Bede, *Chronica* (MGH Auctores antiquissimi 13:323–24). As Lerner observes, Alcuin represents Bede's opinion on the matter in *De fide sanctae et individuae Trinitatis* (PL 101:51D).

37. Lerner, "Refreshment," 105–6.

stretch in the general direction of what the first two trumpets will signify later in the Middle Ages.[38] The first will deal with preaching in the context of the battle between Judaism and the primitive church, while the second will address preaching in the face of persecution by that most prominent symbol of secularity, the Roman Empire. Thus, the image of the devil setting fire to the sea of this world meshes in an odd way with other imagery in Revelation pointing to the empire (e.g., the beast from the sea); yet a great deal of adjustment will be done in the future.[39]

Bede's approach to the third trumpet takes the words of Revelation 8:10 and retrofits them to match the image of heretics falling into and corrupting the rivers of holy Scripture. That works well enough for heresy to be associated regularly in future commentaries with the third trumpet. Likewise, Bede's description of the fourth trumpet (Rev 8:12) as obscuring the light by knocking out a third of the sun, moon, and stars and his identification of it with false brothers would stick, making the fourth trumpet about hypocrisy from then on.

In Bede's case, the preceding paragraph would apply to his initial listing of the seven trumpets, but less so once he returns for a second run-through. In the latter we find a smooth transition from heresy to *luxuria*, then suddenly the eagle in Revelation 8:13 is calling.[40] In other words, when he treats the trumpets for the second time, there is little sense of the third and fourth trumpets as standing for two separate things, let alone two different moments in a temporal progression.

In fact, there is little sense at this point that Bede is conscious of presenting a historical narrative at all as he examines these four trumpets. There is certainly a timeless story of confrontation between God and Satan, piety and sin, but no interest in how the history of the early church is the story of humankind moving through a series of periods in which one or another confrontation (with a particular sin or with a particular group) became particularly problematic. Yet there is a historical narrative of sorts here, as we are about to see.

The key to the trumpets lies in the voice of that eagle who, as Bede tells us, flies daily through the church, speaking through the mouth of the doctors,

---

38. Bede, *Explanatio apocalypsis* (PL 93:155C–156C).

39. In dealing at length with the first trumpet, Bede pays close attention to Tychonius and what he says about the third part. That introduces a degree of incoherence into Bede's interpretation and demonstrates that he is not really thinking in terms of the Judaism-Christianity split. Nor is he really thinking of martyrdom in the case of the second trumpet. The imagery might push him in that direction at times, but he is not interested in going there.

40. Bede, *Explanatio apocalypsis* (PL 93:157A).

telling us that in the latter days there will be dangerous times, and we will have to watch out for the son of perdition. When we hear the words "peace and security" we will really be in trouble. The eagle, in short, is delivering a message comprised of 2 Timothy 3, 1 Thessalonians 5, and 2 Thessalonians 2.[41]

That brings us to Bede's fifth trumpet, which anticipates one strain of future interpretation. He identifies it with what will turn into the precursors of Antichrist in later exegesis. Bede seems to confuse matters by returning a second time to heresy,[42] but oddly enough, this too belongs in the developing interpretation, as we will see later in this book. The imagery associated with the fifth trumpet suggests a wide variety of evils to Bede, but heresy is clearly his favorite, and he is not alone.

To summarize, we can say that Bede has little interest in laying out church history in a neat series of periods based on the seven trumpets; but his tenses are consistent with his sense of a serious temptation to come, an evil time announced by the eagle, a time already previewed in the earlier stages of church history yet still to come in force. Yet the eagle simply announces it. When can we expect it? Bede doesn't say.

That brings us to the sixth trumpet, which represents for Bede the preachers who detect the frauds of Antichrist during the open war of Antichrist and his people against the church, a war that will be followed by the destruction of these adversaries. Bede then moves smoothly to the seventh trumpet and the day of judgment in which the Lord will reward his people while he punishes those who corrupted the earth—too smoothly, perhaps. He seems to picture the scenario as moving directly from the death of Antichrist to resurrection, final judgment, and eternal rewards. If there is any delay for any purpose before the judgment, it does not register here. In fact, when the time arrives for the seventh angel to blow his trumpet, Bede says, "And the seventh angel sounded his trumpet, etc." The six prior trumpets correspond to the various battles of the church in different states of the present world. The seventh trumpet, however, is a message of the eternal sabbath, announcing only victory and the rule of the true king.[43] The difference between the seven seals and the seven angels with trumpets is that in the first case Bede feels required to do something with that silence in heaven. The second case places no such obligation on him, and he feels no responsibility to repeat the pattern seen in the seven seals, referring a sec-

41. Bede, *Explanatio apocalypsis* (PL 93:157A). All three passages are cited by Bede.
42. Bede, *Explanatio apocalypsis* (PL 93:157B and 157C) explicitly makes the connection.
43. Bede, *Explanatio apocalypsis* (PL 93:165A).

ond time to the space for Jerome's forty-five days. One might expect later Apocalypse commentaries to repair that omission, but what we find instead is more thought-provoking.

The next stop on Lerner's itinerary is the ninth-century scholar Haimo of Auxerre. In commenting on 1 Thessalonians, Haimo decides that the forty-five days represent extra time for those elect who had faltered a bit during the time of Antichrist, time for them to do penance and be saved. Antichrist's followers, or at least those followers who remain, will miss the point of that hiatus and spend their time getting married, banqueting, and generally enjoying themselves, saying, "Our leader may be dead, but we have peace and security." And once they have said that, destruction will suddenly fall upon them.[44]

But Haimo isn't through with the matter at that point. In another work he returns to the forty-five days, saying, "Note that the Lord will not come immediately to pronounce judgment once Antichrist has been killed, but rather forty-five days will be granted to the elect for penance, as we learn from the book of Daniel." Then he adds one more sentence that changes everything: "But as for how much time it will be until the Lord comes, that is entirely unknown."[45] Thus, the forty-five days become, in effect, a minimum figure that might be followed by an indeterminate number of days before judgment; yet Haimo actually says *quantulumcumque vero spatium temporis*, "whatever little space of time," not *quantumcumque*, "whatever space of time." The uncertainty and the brevity implied by that *quantulumcumque* invite low expectations. In any case, Matthew 24:36 becomes the ultimate word on the matter, but only once the forty-five days have expired.[46]

We now arrive at Adso of Montier-en-Der and his tenth-century treatise on Antichrist.[47] Adso is one of several authors from this time on to speak of forty days rather than forty-five. On the other hand, the amount of extra time after the forty days is left wide open, with no implication that the delay will be a brief one. (The forty-day minimum had its own biblical rationale, of course, as we will see.)

---

44. *In Epistolam I ad Thessalonicenses* (PL 117:773D–774A), under the name of Haimo of Halberstadt.

45. Haimo, *In Epistolam II ad Thessalonicenses* (PL 117:781D).

46. Lerner notes in passing that the Old Saxon Genesis, probably datable to the first half of the ninth century, speaks of humanity returning to the kingdom of God after Antichrist "for a long time" before the end.

47. Ernst Sackur, *Sibyllinische Texte und Forschungen* (Halle, 1898; reprint, Turin, 1963), 113; Robert Konrad, ed., *De ortu et tempore Antichristi* (Kalmünz, 1964), 28–34.

As we move from Adso into the next two centuries, there is much to notice, but one thing in particular catches our eye. The *Glossa ordinaria* took shape and began its remarkable career as a major exegetical aid.[48] It was the *Glossa ordinaria* on Daniel that provided what would become a popular way of describing the forty-five or forty days, possibly because it emphasized, not simply the further testing or penitential striving of the elect or the self-destructive behavior of the hardened sinners, but a positive reward for faithful service. The period was seen as a time for "the refreshment of the saints" (*refrigerium sanctorum*).[49] Thus, while those elect who had blotted their copybooks during the days of tribulation could use their final time to make amends, and while the damned were using theirs to eat, drink, and make merry, thus assuring their damnation, the saints could spend their last days "chilling."

Lerner is particularly interested in the way expanding the time from the death of Antichrist to the final judgment—turning it, in effect, into a period—allowed twelfth-century theologians to envisage a broader conversion program. Conversion of the Jews had been built into the eschatological scenario from the beginning, but the gentiles were another matter. Tracing twelfth-century thought on conversion from Honorius Augustodunensis through Otto of Freising and Hildegard of Bingen, Lerner shows how the period after Antichrist came to be seen as a time when both the Jews and the gentiles turned to Christianity. Thus we see the development of an idea that became an established apocalyptic commonplace: the Jews would be seduced by Antichrist, then after his death they would realize that they had been misled and would turn to Christianity. That left a great many gentiles to be converted.

Lerner also notes that neither Otto of Freising nor Hildegard of Bingen was interested in mentioning a forty- or forty-five-day period. Lerner suggests that, once the likes of Adso and Haimo had rendered these figures almost meaningless by making room for another period after them, they might just as well abandon them. That may well be the case, but it is worth noting that the forty- or forty-five-day period didn't simply go away after that point. We will encounter it again in the thirteenth century.

One more theologian is important for Lerner before he arrives at Joachim of Fiore, and with good reason. Around 1160, Gerhoch of

---

48. On the *Glossa ordinaria* and other aids to scholarship, see chapter 11, "Nicholas of Lyra," below.

49. In the *Glossa ordinaria* (Nürnberg, 1481), vol. 3, regarding Daniel 12:12: "dies quietis et pacis post mortem Antichristi xlv superioribus adduntur ad refrigerium sanctorum et ad penitentiam subversorum."

Reichersberg wrote in his *Investigation of Antichrist* that before the last judgment the church would be reformed by "spiritual men" and returned to the apostolic state. Lerner acknowledges that Gerhoch never explicitly places these events in the time between Antichrist's death and the final judgment, but in the context of the *Investigation* it is hard to place it anywhere else. In any case, *On the Fourth Nightwatch*, written circa 1165, portrays Gerhoch's own age as the last storm brought by Antichrist, which will be followed by purification of the church. Only then will the church be ready for Christ to come in judgment. In both works Gerhoch employs the same image. The relationship between the purification before judgment and the consequent peace in heaven is that between the glow of sunrise and the full light of day.

Note, though, that Gerhoch never foresees anything resembling a long period in which a new age will unfold. He simply assumes it will be short. His concentration is more on what will happen than on its duration.

The Legend of Antichrist

The preceding represents a brief word on the way, by the year 1200, scholars had begun to find ways of imagining the possibility of an interval at the end of time that would last, if not a thousand years, at least long enough to merit consideration as a period in its own right. Before we conclude this chapter, we should also mention something else that was happening simultaneously: not the birth of Antichrist, which even in the thirteenth century most scholars would still prefer to project into the future, but the birth of the *idea* of Antichrist, the *legend* of Antichrist and its relation to western history. It sprang from several roots.[50]

The sources are varied. We can start with the five times in John's letters that we actually find the term "Antichrist." It is questionable whether any of the five can be taken as referring to a single person. Here, in four passages, are the five references:

> Children, it is the last hour! As you have heard that antichrist is coming, so now many antichrists have come. From this we know that it is the last hour. (1 John 2:18)

50. On the Antichrist legend see especially Bernard McGinn, *Antichrist: Two Thousand Years of the Human Fascination with Evil* (New York: Columbia University Press, 2000).

Many deceivers have gone out into the world, those who do not confess that Jesus Christ has come in the flesh; any such person is the deceiver and the antichrist! (2 John 7)

Who is the liar but the one who denies that Jesus is the Christ? This is the antichrist, the one who denies the Father and the Son. (1 John 2:22)

By this you know the Spirit of God: every spirit that confesses that Jesus Christ has come in the flesh is from God, and every spirit that does not confess Jesus is not from God. And this is the spirit of the antichrist, of which you have heard that it is coming; and now it is already in the world. (1 John 4:2–3)

Thus if we seek evidence of a single individual, we must look elsewhere, namely, at a passage in 2 Thessalonians 2:1–10 that does not even use the word "Antichrist":

As to the coming of our Lord Jesus Christ and our being gathered together to him, we beg you, brothers and sisters, not to be quickly shaken in mind or alarmed, either by spirit or by word or by letter, as though from us, to the effect that the day of the Lord is already here. Let no one deceive you in any way; for that day will not come unless the rebellion comes first and the lawless one is revealed, the one destined for destruction. He opposes and exalts himself above every so-called god or object of worship, so that he takes his seat in the temple of God, declaring himself to be God. . . . For the mystery of lawlessness is already at work, but only until the one who now restrains it is removed. And then the lawless one will be revealed, whom the Lord Jesus will destroy with the breath of his mouth, annihilating him by the manifestation of his coming. The coming of the lawless one is apparent in the working of Satan, who uses all power, signs, lying wonders, and every kind of wicked deception for those who are perishing, because they refused to love the truth and so be saved.

Although the word "antichrist" (Greek *antikhristos*) is used only in the epistles of John, the word "pseudochrist" (Greek *pseudokhristos*, meaning "false messiah") is used by Jesus in Matthew 24:24 and Mark 13:22: "For false messiahs and false prophets will appear and produce great signs and omens, to lead astray, if possible, even the elect."

Finally, we have the book of Revelation, where the major contribution to the legend of Antichrist (again without actually using the term "Antichrist") is the beast from the sea in Revelation 13:1–10, supplemented by the beast from the land in 13:11–18 and by the various other references to the beast in Revelation 11, 14, 15, 16, 17, and 20; which is to say that, if we consider the various references to the beast from the sea, the beast from the land, and the beast unspecified as to land or sea, and then we assume that some or all of these references can be taken as contributions to our notion of the Antichrist, then the Apocalypse becomes a major source concerning the matter.

It is hardly surprising that the church fathers should have followed up on all these New Testament passages, amplifying them when they saw the possibility. Writers as early as Irenaeus tried their hand at teasing a name from the number 666; recognized that any decent reading of Revelation might profit from consideration of Daniel 7; and read the ten horns of the beast as a prediction that the Roman Empire would dissolve into ten kingdoms. The notion that the Roman Empire would collapse led naturally to the idea that it was the restraining force mentioned in 2 Thessalonians 2:7–8, and that in turn might allow connection of the developing Antichrist legend with the Nero legend.

All this ties the Antichrist legend to Rome but not to Jerusalem; yet the latter was happening too. As early as Irenaeus, writers were willing to suggest that Antichrist would be from the tribe of Dan, and Hippolytus suggested that in the process of setting himself up as the true messiah Antichrist would rebuild the temple at Jerusalem. Thus the Antichrist legend took on anti-Jewish features in addition to its anti-pagan features.

One other important ingredient should be added. We saw earlier that, during the christological struggles of the fourth century, Athanasius himself was willing to label his opponents as heretical. He was also willing to label them as precursors of Antichrist.[51] Thus Antichrist by that point was tied not only to paganism and Judaism but to Christian heresy; and in fact, here again as early as Irenaeus, one can see a connection being made between Antichrist and heresy, a connection that began through an identification with Gnosticism but in the fourth century managed to expand to Athanasius's enemies in general. We will see all of this working itself out in the thirteenth century. The aim here is not to offer a detailed picture of what the fathers said about Antichrist but merely to suggest that they already had said a great

51. Pagels, *Revelations*, chs. 4–5, does a thorough job of revealing Athanasius's role in the polemical use of Antichrist language.

deal by the end of the fourth century; that by the tenth century Adso had access to an Antichrist legend that attempted not only to make sense of the biblical sources but also to improve on them through later additions; and that the result encouraged scholars in the period we are actually covering to look especially closely at the way the legend related to political structures, Jewish-Christian relations, and heterodoxy.

We can now turn to Richard of Saint Victor and Joachim of Fiore.

RICHARD OF SAINT VICTOR

With Richard of Saint Victor we enter a new era in biblical scholarship, in fact a new era in scholarship generally. The Victorine school at Paris was a part of the twelfth-century intellectual leap forward that also included Peter Lombard and Peter Abelard. In biblical studies it included the literal exegesis of Andrew of Saint Victor, who consulted not only Hebrew texts but also Jewish scholars.[1] Richard of Saint Victor represented something quite different, an attempt at an alliance between biblical scholarship and mystical theology. His Revelation commentary is important as an anticipation of much to come in the next century. When, at the end of the thirteenth century, Petrus Iohannis Olivi produced his own Apocalypse commentary, he wrote with two previous commentaries open before him: those by Richard and Joachim of Fiore. Most scholars would have seen Joachim as more problematic than Olivi did, although a surprising number did cite Joachim as an authority. The question was *how* they cited him, whether they did so in ways that came to terms with what was characteristic of his exegesis. Richard was a different matter. His importance was indisputable.

Tradition has it that Richard was a native of Scotland, was received at the Abbey of Saint Victor by Abbot Giduin (1114–1155), and was a disciple of the great theologian Hugh of Saint Victor.[2] Recent scholarship is less sure

---

1. On Andrew, chapters 3 and 4 of Beryl Smalley, *The Study of the Bible in the Middle Ages* (Notre Dame: University of Notre Dame Press, 1964), are still insightful and instructive.

2. See John of Toulouse's seventeenth-century biography of Richard reprinted in PL 196:9–14.

that Richard arrived at Saint Victor in time to study with Hugh,[3] but his Scottish provenance is still accepted,[4] and it is generally agreed that he was a master during the 1150s, was promoted to subprior in 1159, then served as prior from 1162 until his death in 1173. Thus his Revelation commentary must have been written sometime in the 1150s.[5]

Richard begins his exegesis of Revelation with two short prefaces. In the first, he announces that his work will be divided into seven books corresponding to John's seven visions. In the second, he deals with John's biography. He informs us that, after John's exile on Patmos, finding the faith threatened by heresies, he wrote his gospel to strengthen his followers in the faith. Thus Richard follows the general assumption of the time that the John who wrote Revelation was also the one who wrote the Fourth Gospel.

Book I begins with yet another prologue, this one extremely important. In it, Richard addresses the question of what he means by "vision." The question is a very old one, and for medieval scholars Augustine's views on the matter loomed large, at least in theory. In fact, Augustine's thought had been bent into various shapes by succeeding writers. A. B. Kraebel's introduction to his own translation of selections from Richard's commentary on Revelation does a good job of tracing the way Ambrosius Autpertus (d. 784) and the Revelation commentary attributed to Anselm of Laon altered medieval thought on visions, then showing how Richard altered it still more.[6] He also shows how Richard profited from the work of Pseudo-Dionysius. We find all this spelled out by Richard himself in his exegesis of John's first vision, which comprises our first excerpt.

The Victorine school of exegesis is known for basing its interpretation on the literal sense of Scripture, and Richard fits neatly into that generalization, although those dealing with literal interpretation among the Victorines have not normally been all that interested in Richard. His interpretation of Revelation contains allegorical, anagogical, and tropological interpretation, but the literal interpretation is central.

---

3. Boyd Taylor Coolman and Dale M. Coulter, eds., *Trinity and Creation* (Turnhout: Brepols, 2010), 198.

4. Franklin T. Harkins and Frans van Liere, eds., *Interpretation of Scripture: Theory; A Selection of Works of Hugh, Andrew, Richard and Godfrey of St Victor, and of Robert of Melun* (Turnhout: Brepols, 2012), 289.

5. The translation here is taken from the Latin text of *In Apocalypsim Joannis Libri Septem* published in PL 196:683–888.

6. In *Interpretation of Scripture: Theory.* Kraebel's introduction and translation are on 327–70.

That might seem odd considering the content of Revelation, but the literal sense was never considered by the Victorines to be devoid of metaphor. In fact, the prologue that begins Book I goes a long way toward explaining why metaphor is not only accepted but necessary. Richard informs us that, as we as individuals travel through life, and as the church as a whole travels through history, the prophetic word functions as a lamp that illuminates our way and keeps us from straying off the path through human ignorance. The book of Revelation is particularly instructive, describing "many tribulations, pressures, and persecutions the church suffers in the world, as well as the supernal rewards that follow in heaven after the passage of time."

Helpful though that may sound, Richard is equally aware that the guidance offered us is itself difficult to decode. He cites the patristic warning that Revelation "has as many mysteries [*sacramenta*] in it as it has words, . . . for a host of meanings lie hidden in each word." Here Richard presents us with the basic dilemma inherent in prophetic discourse, particularly in apocalyptic discourse. It intends to tell us what we need to know, but its very subject matter forces it to address us in language we may not understand. Yet Richard soldiers on, knowing that while the narrative he is about to consider may not be completely comprehensible, some meaning can be teased from it, and we are better off having even that much light than walking in complete darkness.

Richard proceeds to a discussion of visionary experience. There are, he tells us, "four types of vision, of which two are inner and two outer. Two are corporeal and two spiritual." The first kind of corporeal vision is, in effect, our normal eyesight, which is useful as far as it goes, but it is too weak to take in either the greatest things or the smallest things. "Because it is weak, it cannot reach out to distant things. Because it is not keen, it cannot penetrate to [tiny] hidden things." In our modern world of deep space and subatomic particles, Richard's words seem oddly evocative; yet he means a great deal more by them than we might imagine. Since our normal vision discovers only that which is available to the corporeal senses, it contains little of mystical signification in itself.

Thus we proceed to a second type of corporeal vision, in which things are seen by us and register with us as having mystical meaning, as was the case with the vision in which Moses saw the burning bush. Here the important thing is not what Moses physically saw but what it meant, its "typical significance," as Richard says.

> For what do we take the flame to mean except the grace of the Holy Spirit? What do we understand by the bush . . . except the blessed virgin Mary? . . .

> The Lord appeared in flame in the bush, yet the bush was not consumed. In like manner, the Son of God took on flesh within the virgin through the overshadowing grace of the Holy Spirit, yet her virginal modesty remained unaffected. . . . Moses said of the vision, "I will go and see this great vision" (Exod 3:3). And indeed it was a great vision, for it showed the miraculous incarnation of the Word and perpetual integrity of his virgin mother.

The difference between the first and second type of vision is that the first simply sees what is there and what the limits of physical sight allow us to see, while the second is a window to something more. It radiates mystical meaning.

The third type of vision is not physical. In it, "the mind is illuminated by the Holy Spirit with forms that are similitudes of visible things," and through them we are led to invisible things. Richard says little more about this type of vision, preferring to move on to the fourth type, in which, "through internal aspiration, the human mind is subtly and sweetly raised to celestial contemplation without the mediation of any figures or qualities or visible things." Here again Richard says little, but refers us to Dionysius. So here we have two types of vision that are not physical at all, in which the mind is directly illuminated, the difference between the two being that in one case "the truth of hidden things is concealed in forms, signs, and similitudes. In the other it is shown nakedly and purely, uncovered as it were."

How, then, did John see these visions? Not in either of the first two ways. He says he saw them "in the spirit." But he did not see them in the fourth way either, and on this matter Richard cites Dionysius on the impossibility of ascending to celestial things except through material means. This leads him to a relatively extended meditation on the need for and nature of symbolism in theology, a passage included at length in the readings at the end of this chapter. It is in the context of this meditation that we are introduced to John, the author of Revelation, as a contemplative whose exile on Patmos, whatever its inconveniences, is portrayed as an excellent setting for mystical experience.

> Thus the blessed John, sent into exile, removed from the hustle and bustle of the world and given over to peace and quiet, received this revelation (*apocalypsim*) from the Lord in the third way of seeing . . . and recorded it in writing for the utility of holy church. The fact that, when put in a place of quiet, he received this revelation signifies to us that those who love

internal quiet know the joy of invisible blessings, and the more they can distance themselves from temporal things, the closer they are to eternal things.

John thus becomes a model for all of us.

> For whoever involves himself in worldly affairs alienates himself in that measure from internal and eternal things, and he who cannot pull his mind away from visible things finds it impossible to devote any great attention to invisible things. Thus, if we wish to approach God, we must turn our minds from external to internal things, so that, placed thus in quiet, we can contemplate heavenly things. "Be still and see that I am God" (Ps 45:11). It is as if he said, "Unless you separate yourself from the perturbations of the world, you will not succeed in contemplating me. Thus separate yourself from externals and internally, through quiet, see who I am." For the more the human mind comes close to spiritual things, the farther behind it leaves temporal or corporeal things; and the more clearly and perspicaciously it reaches out to grasp the highest things, the more it averts its eyes from the rays of its own light shining up from below. And although the sea of secular perturbations flows out through the world in a great circle, if we can confine it within ourselves through internal desire (as if we were placed within the stability of a certain island) we can inhere in divine things through contemplation.

Richard seems in no great hurry to embark on a line-by-line exegesis of the text. When he arrives at the first line, **The apocalypse of Jesus Christ**, he notes that Jesus cleansed his people from their sins, and that sets him off on a lengthy meditation concerning the two principal vices, malice and luxury. When he finally gets around to examining the next words of the text, **Which God gave to him to make known to his servants**, that leads him into another digression on the way God's gifts descend hierarchically to us.

> **Which God gave to him to make known to his servants.** Note the order of giving. God gave it to Christ, Christ to an angel, the angel to John, John to the seven churches of Asia, and the churches of Asia to the universal mother church. The universal mother church, through the voices of its doctors, dispenses and distributes it daily into the minds of the individual faithful. Thus every perfect gift descends from the Father above to the predestined to give them life, and proceeds variously, beautifully, and

multiformly in them, and gathers them to the breast of the mother who calls them and unites them together into her unity.

Thus the phrase becomes a model of God's work in the world, reminding us of, among other things, the difference between ourselves and the angels, who receive the splendor of the divine light directly; yet when we mortals put on immortality and the corruptible achieves incorruption, then we, transferred to the same fate as the angels, will participate in the same contemplation, and we too will receive in greater measure the divine goods that we now sometimes receive through the ministration of angels. In the meantime, all proceeds according to grade and merit.

Richard still has not quite finished with the first sentence. He now focuses on the words **to make known**. God gave John this revelation in order that he should make it known. "For there is no use in hidden wisdom and in undiscovered treasure. Thus, just as it is a sin for him who knows how to do good not to do it, so it is a sin for him who knows how to say good things not to say them."

Yet that in itself invites another set of considerations centered on the words **to his servants**. To whom should the revelation be distributed?

> Not to proud philosophers, not to unbelieving Jews, not to impure Christians. For holy things should not be given to the dogs, nor should pearls be cast before swine. The dogs are infidel persecutors of the sacred faith, barking dogs who snap at it. The pigs are false Christians who have faith in the sense of belief but soil themselves with vices like pigs. From each of these groups the sacred mysteries are hidden, from one because of their blindness and from the other because of their polluted lives. But these things are to be revealed to those who studiously serve the Lord.

Richard is now ready to take on another line, **Which must come to pass soon**. This too calls for serious consideration.

> Whatever happens in the present passes quickly, for all things subject to time pass quickly. This life is brief, the way is slippery, and the moment of death is uncertain. "What will come to pass soon" refers to what will happen to the church in this world, whether good or bad, or what retribution will be handed out at the end of this world. And all these things come to pass soon because the present passes soon, being soon suc-

ceeded by the future. And the sooner the things contained in this book must necessarily be completed, the sooner and the more studiously they should be announced, lest, death coming upon them unexpectedly, he who should be justified through hearing these things should die without hearing them and the Lord should hold the preacher who has failed in his duty responsible for that sinner's damnation. There is no more listening to sacred doctrine after you are dead, but as long as you are alive it can still be heard.

Richard can now move on to another line.

> **And he made it known by sending his angel to his servant John.** Here he shows the mode of sacred revelation by saying "made it known." He "made it known" in the sense that he revealed sacred mysteries through certain signs, figures, and seals similar to sensible things. For he wished his mysteries to be demonstrated through figures so that they could not be understood without effort, because that which is acquired through labor is retained more deeply and firmly. Moreover, he wished the figures to be exposited elsewhere, in order that through this means he could indicate an exposition to be sought in other senses, and thus the faithful who seek it could find it while the infidels who seek to pervert and attack the sacred mysteries would not understand it.

Richard has already addressed this point earlier, but from a different perspective, emphasizing a slightly different reason for resorting to metaphor. What follows has also been covered earlier.

> **Through his angel to his servant John.** For the vision was shown to Saint John through an angel in the form of the Son of Man, as he declares in the following, where he says, **And having turned I saw seven golden candlesticks, and in the middle of the seven golden candlesticks one similar to the Son of Man.** And thus Christ according to his humanity accepts the sacrament from the Father, and, through an angel in the appearance of Christ, he transmits it to Saint John, who in turn transmits it to the seven churches, or rather to the entire universal church.

So far, Richard could be described as teasing a general, timeless sort of theology out of the text without much attention to either the precise historical context of the work or the future events projected by it. The same could be said for his exegesis throughout chapter 2 of the commentary.[7] Chapter 3 offers a change at least insofar as he addresses the sevenfold nature of the visionary pattern in Revelation.

> Holy mother church, which is regenerated through the sevenfold grace of the Holy Spirit, justified in time that unfolds in the number of seven days, and represented through the seven churches of Asia, is enlightened through the seven prophetic visions presented in this book, which assure us that the present adversities will soon pass and encourage us to long for the good things that will come in the future, remaining forever. For although this prophecy is particularly directed to the seven churches, it more generally addresses the present and future states of the holy catholic church. And its structure is rightly sevenfold, for that number points to the perfection of the doctrine contained in the prophecy. Seven represents the fourfold nature of that which is visible and the threefold nature of that which is invisible. Thus the sevenfold nature of the prophecy represents all things.
>
> As we enter the profound obscurity of these heavenly mysteries [*sacramentorum*], we will look briefly at each of the seven visions, just as one about to enter a dense, dark woods might first consider with care the path he should follow in order to make his way through the woods in the best possible way. Thus, as we pass through the obscure places in this book, we can hope to come away with a few twigs of meaning lest we seem to have read the whole thing to no purpose.

The first paragraph quoted above does little except set the scene for an initial tour through the seven visions. The second paragraph is included, not because it advances the argument in any important way, but because it demonstrates what a remarkably skillful writer Richard can be.

Most of what we find in the next chapter of Richard's commentary is less striking. He again calls our attention to the advantages of John's situation.

> An authentic and noted person, honest and friendly, a place remote, quiet, secret and private. In these two things, the person and the place, we are shown how anyone who wishes to contemplate heavenly things should comport himself. He should separate himself from worldly affairs and seek quiet. But because I already have written about this above, let us go on.

---

7. "Chapter 2 of his commentary" refers to just that, the chapters of the commentary, not the chapters of Revelation itself. The two are not concurrent.

Even the time works in John's favor. Richard emphasizes that it was the Lord's day, a good time for a revelation. "The holier the day, the more fitting for divine revelation, the more tranquil because of the cessation of external labor, and the better for internal contemplation."

The Letters to Seven Churches

Richard briefly lists the seven churches to which John wrote, then asks whether the letters should be envisaged as having been seen by him successively or all at once. Richard suggests that "it seems more fitting and truer" to say the former; yet almost immediately afterward he offers a slightly different answer.

> Distanced from subordinates and sent into exile, removed from the hustle and bustle of the world and given over to quiet, he left all pastoral care, all visible things, and everything similar to visible things far behind him, and, extending himself through pure intelligence, he stretched out to contemplate supernal and invisible things removed from any imagination; and when the experience was recast for the instruction of his subordinates and written down in similitudes of sensible things, it was narrated as if in a series of events running from earlier to later. And while the Holy Spirit was concerned with that which led him to celestial things through simple contemplation, John was told to respect the formal qualities of things in his narration, as if his hearing the voice occurred within a succession of events.

So far we have spoken as if the vision was just that: a matter of sight. In fact, Richard is aware that it involves not only sight but also hearing. Thus what John experiences is not only spiritual vision but spiritual hearing.

At Revelation 1:12–20, the vision of the seven lampstands and one like a Son of Man, Richard is for the first time sufficiently engaged with an image to grant it extended commentary. (The commentary on this passage will be found in the sources at the end of this chapter.) It is interesting partly because John's description is nothing one can easily make sense of within the context of the message John is delivering to the seven churches. Thus it functions oddly like a Rorschach test for Richard. He strives to turn it into Christian doctrine, and the result is impressive if not convincing. Richard goes on to interpret the letters to the seven churches in Revelation 1–3. However uninterested he might be in exploring the historical context of these letters, and however committed he might be to seeing the text as timeless spiritual instruction, there are moments when he has to face the fact that these chapters address a particular time and place. For example, reference to the Nicolaitans in Revelation 2:4 demands that we know who the Nicolaitans were. On the whole, though, Richard stays as far away from history as possible. The letters offer him a sevenfold pattern, but he does not attempt to read it as seven periods of church history.[8] The following passage is typical. Richard is considering Revelation 2:10.

> Fear none of those things which you will suffer. Beware, the devil is about to throw some of you into prison so that you may be tested, and for ten days you will have affliction. It is as if, concentrating on higher things, he openly said, "Since as you have heard you are already rich with the good things I have given you (Rev 2:9), you should not only bear patiently your present adversity but also endure any future persecution patiently and securely for the sake of my name. Thus I tell you, marshal your strength, be faithful until death, and I will give you the crown of life."

The Seven Seals

Although Richard does not correlate the seven churches with periods of church history, he comes closer to doing so when he deals with the seven seals of Revelation 6–8. He begins by seeming to acknowledge the essentially ahistorical nature of his exegesis so far; then he announces a change, not so much in his exegetical style as in the text itself. He has a point.

> **And I saw that the lamb opened one of the seven seals, and I heard one of the four animals saying with a voice like thunder, "Come and see." And I looked, and behold, a white horse, and he who sat upon it had a bow, and a crown was given to him, and he came forth conquering, that he should conquer.** Everything contained in the three preceding chapters of this vision[9] seems to pertain especially to the sacrament of

---

8. A number of thirteenth-century commentaries will follow his lead here. The seven letters are hard to envisage as a sevenfold historical progression.

9. Again, remember that he is referring to the chapters in his commentary, not those of Revelation itself.

human redemption. What follows in the seven following chapters, that is, what we find in the opening of the seven seals, refers to the redemption and sequence of events during the time following. There we find described the virtues of the elect and the persecutions of the elect by the reprobate, that is, the tribulations of those who have suffered from the birth of the church to the end of the world. These persecutions are described not all together in a single statement but in order. Gradually, over time, according to the opening of the seals, the persecutions are completed and the hidden things made manifest, as the opening of the seals shows us in multifold fashion. The mystery of human redemption having been described, the book informs us concerning the merits of the just, the persecutions of the reprobate, and the rewards to be given, in order to provide for all the elect, diligently instructing them concerning future events.

Taking what is about to come in Revelation 6–8 as a whole, we can see the logic of this description. The aim is, as Richard says, to "forearm the elect against adversity" and "to comfort them by informing them of the reward promised them" if they manage to bear up under it.

Richard then turns to the first seal, which he correlates with "the first period of the church in which it is reborn from old age to new life through baptism in Christ by the reception of spiritual gifts and set on the way to heavenly rewards. **And I saw that the lamb had opened one of the seven seals.** Christ opened the first seal of sacred Scripture by redeeming the world and filling the primitive church with the gift of the Spirit." We are introduced to the first of the four animals, the lion, Mark, who represents the apostles preaching the resurrection; and the white horse is the number of those washed clean of their sins through baptism. The bow represents either preaching or damnation of the evil. The basic theme here is not so much persecution of the early church by the Jews as it is celebration of those elect who come out of Judaism and are rewarded.

Richard does explicitly identify the second seal with the persecution of the church. The second animal stands for Luke, who in turn stands for preachers speaking of Christ's passion. The instrument of this persecution is the Roman Empire, but the whole thing is inspired by the devil, who is set on destroying the church. The result of the persecution, however, is that, inspired by the martyrs, many become Christians. The devil, recognizing that open persecution has proved ineffective, tries another tack, heresy, and so we arrive at the third seal, in which heresy is combated by preachers of orthodoxy. This time the horse is black, symbolizing hiddenness. Heresy is an inside job, the devil operating under cover within the church. This animal has a human face, representing Matthew and also representing the preachers of this third period who emphasize Christ's humanity.

Once the devil realizes that both persecution and heresy have failed, he introduces hypocrites sabotaging the church from within, as do the heretics. This is represented in the opening of the fourth seal, featuring those who falsely pretend to be pious, thus necessitating another order of preachers to oppose them. Now we meet the pallid horse, which stands for those whited sepulchers, the hypocrites themselves, who afflict themselves with fasts and the like in order to hide their malice. We also meet the fourth animal, similar to an eagle, representing the Gospel of John and the preachers of Christ's divinity.

Thus the first four temptations are presented as arriving successively, but after Richard's mention of the Roman Empire he proceeds without much specificity as to when the two succeeding temptations take place. Then comes the opening of the fifth seal, which marks a break with the tight structure of what has gone before, a structure ordered by the four horses and four animals. In fact, the fifth seal interrupts the whole story of diabolical anti-Christian machinations and saintly reaction. This seal shows the martyrs seeking retribution and being assured that the time left will be short.

The sixth seal describes the tribulation to come in the days of Antichrist. Richard stays close to the text, saying little more than that a great number of those who seemed upright will fall. The angel who ascends from the place of the sun is Christ, who shows us the way to heaven. He descends through the assumption of flesh and ascends through glorification of that same flesh. The seventh seal brings us to the end of the world, judgment, and to heavenly bliss.

We have completed our first trip through church history and will now do it again with the seven trumpets.

The Seven Angels with Trumpets

In approaching this vision, Richard begins by noting that "God in his ineffable goodness has predicted the future clearly, showing us what is to be done, what avoided, what endured, what hoped for." In this vision, due to the great extent of time involved, God has followed an order of narration. The seven angels with trumpets represent all the preachers throughout time, described here as proceeding through seven days.

Besides the seven angels, the vision refers to

another angel, that is, Christ, who is an angel of great council, rightly
described as "other" because he is far removed from the other angels
(that is, all the preachers) in grace of sanctity, excellence of dignity, and
power of virtue. He came when he assumed the fragility of our nature.
And he stood before the altar. And of this altar it is typologically written, "Make for me an altar of earth" (Ex 20:24). The altar of earth is his
assumed humanity. But just as to come pertains to his assumption of
flesh, to stand pertains to the immutability of divinity. Therefore he who
comes through flesh stands before the altar through divinity, because
through the divinity in which he remains immutable he was prior to and
more sublime than the humanity that is to us an altar. **Having a golden
thurible in his hand.** The thurible is the holy apostles who in the holy
church are principally ordained to offer up the prayers of the elect to the
highest divinity. They are fittingly called gold because they shine like
gold, because they have within them wisdom through which they illuminate everything in the world. This angel had the thurible in his hand,
for Christ chose the twelve apostles.

And so it goes. The incense we next hear about represents the prayers offered
to God by the apostles. The altar before which the prayers are offered is gold
"because in it are all the treasures of wisdom and knowledge." The thunder
represents the threat of damnation.

When we finally arrive at the first trumpet-blowing angel and hear that
the result of his blast is hail and fire mixed with blood, Richard explains that the
hail signifies persecution, the fire envy, and the blood killing, because the first
order of preachers, when they were preaching in Judea, were cruelly persecuted
by the Jews, who were excited to do so by the devil.

The second angel represents the order of preachers who preached the
gospel among the gentiles. Here again the devil stirred up hostility leading
to persecution. Richard never mentions the Roman Empire, but that is obviously what he has in mind.

When he arrives at the third angel, Richard notes the strong parallel
between the second and third visions. The second trumpet, like the second
seal, deals with persecution, and the third trumpet, like the third seal, addresses heresy. The fourth seal and trumpet both tell us of hypocrites, while
the sixth seal and trumpet both announce the persecution of Antichrist. The
seventh seal and trumpet both signify the end of the world.

What, then, of the fifth trumpet? For the moment Richard ignores it, although he does acknowledge its existence in summing up: "First with first, second with second, third with third, fourth with fourth, fifth with fifth, sixth with sixth, seventh with seventh, seal matches angel."

Of course, all of this is preparatory to a fuller treatment of the third angel, which is followed by a fuller treatment of the fourth. Then Richard arrives at the fifth, and we see that he actually does have something in mind. He explains that since neither persecution, nor heresy, nor hypocrisy taken separately was successful in preventing the preachers from proclaiming the gospel, the devil decided to try them all at once.

This combination inspires Richard to provide a long, full treatment of the fifth angel. Presented with the task of describing all three evils in a single temptation, Richard consciously favors heresy,[10] but that makes little difference to his presentation, because he tends to look beyond particularities and focus on evil in general. What comes out of the abyss is, in Richard's phrase, the *malorum universitas*, evil people of all kinds introducing all kinds of evils. That description includes some who immediately seek to assume power, which functions as a leitmotif of sorts throughout Richard's commentary, although it is inspired here by the locusts who are given authority (Rev 8:3).

The varieties of evil may be many, but their end is the same, a point Richard makes rather neatly by employing the reference to chariots and war horses (8:7–9). The voices of the reprobate "are like the sound of different chariots and horses dashing into battle because, however the chariots and horses may differ in various ways, they are all headed into the same battle. Thus evil people with their various heresies and tumultuous contention are all led into the same battle; that is, they all aim to destroy the church."

Richard is following the logic of the seven angels with trumpets and not explicitly relating them to specific periods of church history, but his sequential presentation certainly invites the reader to think of the various trumpet blasts as introducing specific periods. Moreover, his description of the fifth trumpet as ushering in a combination of all three major evils introduced by previous trumpets makes it easy to see the fifth angel as setting the stage for the sixth, who will announce the advent of Antichrist. Richard recognizes as much in introducing the sixth angel. He speaks of the angel as a sixth order of doctors who preach in the time of Antichrist.

The other angel who descends is Christ. He places his right foot on the sea and his left foot on the land, signifying that he subdues the gentiles and

---

10. A number of thirteenth-century commentators will also emphasize heresy.

Jews to his power. He places his right foot on the sea, then his left on the land, because first he calls the gentiles to salvation, and then, when all the gentiles have been admitted, all Israel will be saved. The angel also announces that the time left will be short. The elect can look forward to their heavenly reward. "The time of the reprobate will be in this world," meaning presumably that their happiness will be here, before the end of time. The impression projected by Richard is that he sees a world dominated by the powers of evil giving way soon to final judgment and the end of the world, followed by heavenly bliss in which "all things are made new." In considering the "liberty of the sons of God," he explains that the creation is currently subjected to "vanity, that is, mutability," but awaits the liberation of the sons of God, when, in the end, they will be glorified, liberated "from vanity, that is, from mutability." For the creation will be changed into "a permanent state of newness." There are, he says, three kinds of vanity or mutability:

> Those in man, those caused by man, and those that happen because of man. In man there is the vanity of mortality, in those things caused by man there is the vanity of curiosity, and in those things that happen because of man there is the vanity of mutability. And because man is the cause of all vanity, it is aptly written, "All vanity, every living man" (Ps 38:6), and "vanity of vanities, all is vanity" (Eccl 1:2). If man were removed from the world there would be no vanity. Thus when it says here, "There will be no more time," it means "There will be no more vanity of mutability." We can believe that the planets will be moved no more, nor will clouds gather, rivers flow, the wind blow, the earth germinate vegetation, or animals bear their young. It can be concluded that all elements, that is, all bodies composed of elements, will be dissolved in the fires of justice and reduced to elements, nor will other bodies be composed from them, but instead the elements will remain forever in their purity. We can opine that in that ultimate conflagration the air, which now through continuous agitation is cloudy and dense, will be purged, made fine, and the sun, because of its fine texture, will produce no heat, but it will have a marvelous brightness, fulfilling that which is written: "And the light of the moon will be like the light of the sun, and the light of the sun will be seven times greater than the light of seven days" (Isa 30:26). The creation is now subjected to the vanity of mutability; it groans and gives birth, for all elements now complete their work with labor. But this is because of us. When we are removed, the creation will be quiescent; it will be liberated in the freedom of the sons of God. The sons of God will be liberated from the vanity of

mortality, and the creature will be liberated from the vanity of mutability.
The sons of God will be liberated through immortality and the creation
will be liberated through immutability. And lest the sons of God in the
time of Antichrist, afflicted long and late by the persecutions of Antichrist,
be disheartened in their expectation of this liberation, it is intimated that
its appearance will be speedy and soon when it is said, "In the days of the
seventh angel, when he begins to sound his trumpet," that is, in the days of
the final preachers, after the time of Antichrist, when they begin to preach,
that is, in the beginning of their preaching, the mystery of God will be
consummated, that is, the secret promise that the eye does not see nor the
ear hear, nor does it ascend into the heart of man. That which is begun
here on earth is consummated in heaven. Thus the prophets evangelized
to Christ's servants, because through them he prophesied it from the beginning to his elect. Great, therefore, in the days of Antichrist, despite the
doubt produced by enemies, will be that consolation which is promised
to the elect and which is to come immediately, the stability of eternity.

This is arguably one of the most intriguing passages in the commentary. Richard has begun with a reflection on the negative influence of mutability and proceeded to a prediction concerning its abolition, not only
in human nature, but also in nature as a whole, and this change seems to
be portrayed as beginning in time, then extending into eternity. Richard is
reading Revelation 10, but he is importing a great deal into it.

From here on, he follows the text rather closely, proceeding through
Revelation 11 and commenting at one point that "because we discern that
much of what is said here is to be interpreted according to the literal sense,
we go through it more lightly in its exposition." There is in fact little added
concerning Antichrist except that he will reign for three and a half years and
that he is very evil.

At length Richard arrives at the seventh trumpeter and the words "the
kingdom of this world has become the kingdom of our Lord and his Christ,
and they shall reign forever" (Rev 11:15). Richard says, "At the end of the
vision he deals with the end of time and the reward of just retribution." He
paraphrases the words "kingdom of this world" as

all the faithful who are still in the world and exercised by tribulations and
prepared for the reward of heavenly mansions. They are not yet perfectly
of God as long as they are subjected to the mutability of time and the
corruptibility of mortality proving and persecuting them, which afflicts

them through the cunning of Antichrist the enemy. Thereafter they will be perfectly of God and Christ, that is, of divinity and humanity coreigning, when, removed from the present world, they will give themselves over to nothing but divine praises in heaven, and the perfidious enemy no longer will exert power over them. The tranquility of Christ's reign will then begin in the world, when Christ kills Antichrist with the spirit of his mouth, and the holy church, in the silence of half an hour, rests peacefully to the end. Thus when the seventh angel sounds his trumpet, and the just are saved and the wicked are sentenced to their foreknown damnation, it can now be said not "it will be" but "it is done," for the fraudulence and ferocity of the devil will be utterly eliminated, and God in all his faithful will rule in peace and tranquility, *in secula seculorum*, that is, forever. Amen, truly and faithfully. For God, as has been said, will truly reign forever, and his people will not, as some heretics imagine, remain holy for a defined time in the life of the world and then return to their old ways.

There are three senses in which we speak of "the world." There is the sense in which it is meant when the doctors speak of God as creator of the world; and the sense meant when they speak of the savior of the world; and that meant when the devil is said to be prince of the world. There is, then, the world of which God is creator, the world of which God is savior, and the world of which the devil is the prince. The world of which God is creator is the total fabric of the world, as when John says, "He was in the world, and the world was made by him" (John 1:10), etc. The world of which God is savior is the total church of God, of which it is written, "God so loved the world that he gave his only begotten son" (John 3:16). The world of which the devil is prince is the total concupiscence of the world, of which it is said, "Do not love the world or those things that are within it" (1 John 2:15). The world in the first sense, the total fabric of the world, is always of God, never of the devil. The world in the third sense, that is, the total concupiscence of the world, is always of the devil according to depraved action but always of God according to the disposition of the depraved action. For God, although he is not the author of evil, is nevertheless its disposer, for although it does not originate from him, he nonetheless does not leave it unordered. In a marvelous way, that which does not originate in him is ordered by him.

The world in the second sense, the universal church of God, even those predestined to eternal life, will sometimes, with the permission of divine providence, stray from the path for a while, and persecutors, incited by the devil, will vent their rage atrociously on those who wish to live piously. Although they are heatedly accused, bitterly attacked, and cruelly savaged, they retain their firm foundation. For God knows who his own are, and for those who are called his saints according to the plan, that is, according to predestination, "all things work together for good" (Rom 8:28). The kingdom of this world will perfectly and manifestly be of God when the holy and universal church in all its sons is completely liberated from the temptation and persecution of the devil, and in time (or rather in eternity) under the trumpet of the seventh angel the church gives itself over to divine praise and contemplation. The kingdom as it is then provided to us will in no way be temporal but rather eternal, just as the sacred page (*sacra pagina*) tells us when it says *in saecula saeculorum.*

When he arrives at Revelation 13, the beast from the sea, we find Richard returning to the Antichrist, but in a somewhat confusing way. He begins by placing the passage in the context of persecution by pagan gentiles, particularly princes of the gentiles who attack the saints "through various assertions of the philosophers." All this, plus the fact that he begins in the past tense, might give the impression that he has returned to the time of the early church; yet he soon announces that "Antichrist will be the head and prince of the general persecution." He cites Revelation 13:3, "one of the heads who seemed to have been slain but the wound was healed," explaining that Antichrist will pretend to be mortally wounded and then come to life, imitating Christ. Thus what Richard essentially gives us is a narrative concerning the ongoing persecution of the elect by the forces of evil, of which Antichrist will be the greatest prince.

Turning to the beast from the land (Rev 13:11–18), Richard remarks that the devil, seeing the holy church armed with virtues and divine help, attempts to attack it, not with one way of expunging it but with several combined, and thus he calls upon the beasts from the sea and land. Thus he calls not only on cruel princes of the gentiles but also on false masters and princes of the false Christians.

The number of the beast presents an irresistible temptation to most exegetes, and Richard is no exception. He decides, as most do, that it must be solved by converting the number to letters of the alphabet, and he chooses Greek. That gives him the name "Antemos," which he interprets as "contrary." He notes that the number could be parsed differently, giving him different names, but for the sake of brevity he will end the matter at this point. Then he continues with a different approach. The number six stands for perfection. The number six by itself indicates minimum perfection, sixty middling perfection, and six hundred consummate perfection. Thus in the number 666 we have a fitting description of one who is perfectly evil in every type of evil and contrary to every type of good.

When Richard arrives at the seven plagues (Rev 15), he explains that they are called "final" (*novissimae*) because there will be no more in the world after them. They represent the wrath of God visited on the evil. God's wrath is said to be consummated in them because after them, all the evil having been removed from the world, God will pass judgment on the world no more. Here Richard says much about the punishment of the evil and little about rewarding the good, for his intent is to show that, since the good are freed from the depravity of the evil, they are not involved in the punishments described here.

> And I saw, through spiritual understanding, something like a glassy sea, that is, baptism, which is the beginning and the doorway of salvation through remission of sins, glassy through the pure and lucid clarity of faith, mixed with fire through the inflammation of the Holy Spirit. Baptism is aptly compared with a glassy sea mixed with fire because in it remission of sin, cognition of God, and grace of the Holy Spirit are conferred. And when it adds **I saw those who defeated the beast**, that is, Antichrist, it means they did so by patiently sustaining his persecution, not believing his miracles, and condemning his riches and blandishments. When it speaks of victory over his image that means they did not imitate the impious who conformed themselves to him, and they rejected his mark, standing for firm faith and right intention upon the sea, that is, through a higher perfection, having cithars of God through good action, singing a song of Moses the servant of God and a song of the Lamb through profession and preaching of both Testaments, the Old and the New.

Richard then repeats the next few lines of the text, **Great and marvelous are your works, eternal king**, and expands on them, turning them into an extended hymn of praise.

Here, as at the end of every section, Richard offers a brief summary in which he tersely repeats the major images and what they mean. This one is significant in its first four items: "Seven angels, all preachers. Seven final plagues, tribulations of the evil in the present time. Glassy sea, baptism. Beast, Antichrist." The summary is interesting because of its complete lack of interest in preserving any sense of historical sequence; yet notice the ambiguous characterization of "final plagues" as tribulations "in the present time."

The Seven Angels with Vials

We go on, however, to the seven angels with vials. In this section, Richard establishes early in the game that he will be moving chronologically, beginning in first-century Judea and ending at the eschaton. The angel with the first vial is preaching the destruction of Judea and the dispersion of the Jewish people, "who have the mark of the beast." Not only is Judaism given a terrible, savage wound of reprobation for its infidelity; it is physically cast into exile. The Jews, configured to Antichrist, have the mark of the beast and adore his image.

The second angel pours his vial into the sea, which Richard advances as evidence that we are dealing here with the gentile world, persecutors of the early church. The third vial is thus predictably aimed at heretics.

We might now logically assume that Richard will talk about hypocrites in dealing with the next vial. He does not. The fourth vial alludes to Antichrist, the head of all evildoers; the fifth to the impious who "are minimally baptized"; and the sixth to those who are baptized but apostatize from the faith and are considered to be fighting for Antichrist. Given the fact that the last section ended with an apparent coupling of Antichrist and "the present time," and the fact that the first three vials have apparently moved sequentially through phases of the early church, we might be eager to see which tense Richard will now be using. It is in fact the future tense. He again has jumped over the present, as he did in interpreting the seven seals.

We now encounter the fifth vial (Rev 16:19) and learn that Richard's earlier reference to those "minimally baptized" actually refers to infidels who have not been baptized at all. The beast will sit securely on such people, whereas he will not always sit on those who have been baptized, for as long as they preserve their grace he will not achieve dominion over them.

The sixth vial, as advertised, is aimed at apostate Christians. The seventh introduces us to the final order of preachers after the death of Antichrist. The words *factum est* are spoken as if the voice were to say, "All things have been consummated, the end of the world is at hand." But history will not proceed directly from the death of Antichrist to the end, for some are to be converted through preaching while others remain obdurate.

Babylon is predictably divided into unconverted Jews and gentiles along with apostate Christians. Their sins are predictable, too.

We now come to one of the most striking visionary experiences in the entire book: **Then one of the seven angels who had the seven bowls came and said to me, "Come, I will show you the judgment of the great harlot** who is seated upon many waters, with whom the kings of the earth have committed fornication, and with the wine of whose fornication the dwellers on earth have become drunk." And he carried me away in the spirit into a wilderness, and I saw a woman sitting on a scarlet beast which was full of blasphemous names, and it had seven heads and ten horns (Rev 17:1–3). Richard begins his interpretation as follows: "Come through spiritual knowledge and I shall show you, through typical vision, the damnation of the great harlot." (Later Richard describes John as seeing "through spiritual contemplation.") The waters, he says, are its people, for just as waters flow away, so people pass on through mortality. Babylon sits on them because it exercises rule over them. It has fornicated with the kings of the earth by adoring demons or loving the world. The kings of the earth are those who are accustomed to ruling by worldly cupidity; or, taken literally, they refer to the kings of the earth who are more malicious the more powerful they are. The more they fornicate with Babylon, the more involved they become with demons or the impurity of the present age. Later, encountering the information that the woman is "drunk with the blood of the saints and the blood of the martyrs," Richard identifies this with "persecution of the elect" but takes "the saints" to mean "the lesser people" and the martyrs to mean "the greater people." He identifies the beast on which the woman rides as the devil. The beast "was" before Christ's advent because he ruled powerfully in the world then, but he "is not," because Christ sent him away; yet in the days of Antichrist he will return to exercise authority, then perish at the day of judgment.

Why does the beast have seven heads and ten horns? The first two times Richard encounters the question he waves it away, promising to explain it later. When he finally does face it, he begins by saying that the number seven signifies universality. Time flows along a repeating path of seven days, as well as along larger paths. The seven heads, mountains, or kings signify the universal principality of evil seen in seven ages of the world: first, Adam to Noah; second, Noah to Abraham; third, Abraham to Moses; fourth, Moses to David; fifth, David to Christ; sixth, Christ to Antichrist; seventh, under Antichrist. Of these five heads, mountains, or kings, five have died because they occurred before Christ's advent and before this vision. One now exists who, because of Christ's grace, is the weakest of the lot, although he exercises his power against the good insofar as possible. Another has not yet come, for Antichrist has not appeared yet, and when he comes he will remain for only a brief time, three and a half years. "Therefore he should not be overly feared, because, although he will be fiercer than all his predecessors, he will soon disappear." In view of the importance given to Antichrist and the attention normally lavished upon him, this seems a remarkably cavalier attitude. There are other commentaries that note the brevity of Antichrist's reign but manage to turn that fact into an advertisement for the horrific nature of that brief period. In reality Richard himself normally takes Antichrist more seriously.

And the beast who was and is not, he is the eighth and one of the seven, and he will go to his destruction. And the ten horns which you saw are ten kings who have not yet received royal power, but they are to receive authority as kings for one hour, together with the beast. These are of one mind and give over their power and authority to the beast (Rev 17:12-13). The beast is the devil, as Richard has already said, and he has also explained why he was and yet is not. He is the eighth because he transcends all others in his evil but also in his punishment, for he will go to eternal destruction. The ten horns are ten kings who, according to Daniel, will reign in the time of Antichrist, then go to war with Christ and lose. As Richard's exegesis proceeds, he turns from the business of projecting an apocalyptic future to pondering the implications for theodicy of John's statement that **God has allowed them to do as he wishes, so that they give their kingdom over to the beast until the word of God is fulfilled.**

It might strike the reader that Richard has never really explained what he takes Babylon to be. As he finishes his exegesis of this vision, he finally offers that explanation. "**And the woman you see is a great city which rules over the kings of the earth.** The woman is clearly the sum total of evil. That is what is meant by the woman, the great city, the harlot, and Babylon. It is the woman because it softens; the city because it gathers many; great because of its pride; a harlot because it subjects itself to the devil, the corrupter; Babylon because it is disordered and causes disorder. It reigns over the kings of the earth because all serve it and expand its control insofar as they are able." Note that he has said all this without mentioning the name "Rome." His interpretation is too general to call for specificity.

Like most commentators, Richard is predictably—in fact, totally—negative in his description of Babylon, portraying it as something the world is well rid of. One of the most fascinating elements in John's description of the destruction of Babylon has always been the chorus of mourners who tell us how much they are going to miss it (Rev 18:9-19): kings, merchants, shipmasters, and sailors, and we know that John could easily expand the list if he wanted to do so, throwing in the prostitutes, tavern-keepers, and all the rest. What may surprise us is the genuine grief John depicts; yet anyone who has lived in (and loved living in) a big city can understand the mourners' grief. Of course, it has to do with losing a source of profit, but it involves much more than that. We can appreciate how those merchants and shipmasters might have felt. What is fascinating is John's ability and willingness to portray it.

Richard, like most medieval commentators, has little sympathy for these mourners. He sees that they are lamenting the loss of their worldly status, wealth, and pleasures. He tersely and perhaps a bit smugly informs us that they will still be mourning in hell. Beyond that he cannot go. For Richard the moral is that these people, blinded by their pride, greed, and love of earthly pleasures, fail to recognize how short life is and how all that we possess can be taken away in an hour (Rev 18:19). They invested in earthly pleasures when they should have been concentrating on heavenly rewards.

And then he surprises us. "In Babylon is found the blood of the prophets (that is, the greater), and the saints (that is, the lesser), **and all who are killed in the land**, not only, that is, the good but the bad, and the killing of each is a sin. For even if the bad kill the bad, the evil nature of the one killed does not excuse the killer. We are going through this rapidly because we are hurrying on to other things, and we are not discussing the spiritual sense of material we judge to be understood mostly according to the letter." What about the good killing the bad, though? Or is this simply irrelevant when we're speaking of Babylon? Richard offers no further comment. He is, as he promised, hurrying on and has already dropped the matter.

The following section, in which the faithful give thanks for their delivery, places Richard in familiar and friendly territory. It is the sort of thing he enjoys discussing. Commenting on the line **I heard, as it were, the great voice of many trumpets in heaven** (the Vulgate actually says *turbarum*, not *tubarum*, "a great multitude" rather than "many trumpets," but that does not affect Richard's point), he settles on *quasi*, "as it were," to highlight the way what is heard from heaven transcends the earthly categories in which we must describe it. He also accentuates the other association tied to the trumpet image, namely, preaching, noting that those who are like trumpets in the word, preaching the faith and precepts of God, will later rejoice in heaven. Shortly after, when the heavenly voices announce the marriage of the Lamb (Rev 19:7), Richard has a chance to expand on the theme of preparing for heavenly joy by faithful service on earth, in the process reminding us what lack of preparation did to the foolish virgins.

Revelation 19–20 is likely to present problems for any exegete. There is, first of all, the warrior Christ in chapter 19 to be dealt with, not to mention the sword sticking out of his mouth and, after the battle, the heavenly invitation to the birds to come and eat the slain. Then there is the fact that in Revelation 20, with only two more chapters left to go, the devil is cast into the abyss for a thousand years. Richard seems to find neither text particularly surprising or troubling. He doubles down to some extent by identifying Antichrist as the leader of the opposing soldiers. He also spiritualizes the text to some extent by seeing the sword as Christ's judgment, exercising inflexible justice, and by staying far away from the question of whether the text refers to a real physical battle. The heavenly invitation is also spiritualized to the extent of interpreting the birds as actually demons, which turns the meal into a way of describing the eternal punishment of the damned. Richard is still left with the problem of explaining how Antichrist, whom he sees as coming at the end of history, could be slain *and then* the devil could be cast into the abyss for a thousand years, at the end of which he is set loose for a short time. He solves the problem in a single sentence in which he accepts Augustine's identification of the millennium with the period from Christ's incarnation to the time of Antichrist. How long this period will actually last and when it will end are unknown to us. Viewed through the lens of spiritual understanding (*intelligentia spiritualis*), the millennium will end only when holy mother church attains perfect justice. Seen from this perspective, the millennium signifies not a literal thousand years but perfection.

The seventh and final vision might be expected to pose another challenge to Richard because Revelation 21 seems to describe a change on earth, not our ascent to heavenly realms but rather a descent of those heavenly realms to us. First we hear of a new heaven and a new earth; then we are told that the heavenly city Jerusalem will descend from heaven; then we are told that henceforth God will live with his people. Richard nods briefly to the idea of voices from the throne (announcing God's habitation among his people) as a reference to "holy fathers, rulers of our souls, in whom God resides and through whom he reigns, piously and justly governing their inferiors," but on the whole he takes chapter 21 as describing Christ's preparation of his elect for celestial joys "in the heavenly homeland." Richard devotes some time to explaining what is involved when the voice from the throne announces that **they will be his peoples, and God himself will be with them**. Certainly God is already with his people in the world, but "as long as they live in this mortality" he is not seen by them plainly. But then, glorified, they will be his people, never offending him, and he will truly be with them, never deserting them, and thus he will show his face to them. This can occur only in heaven, when the elect are washed clean of all evil.

From verse 11 on, chapter 21 gives Richard everything he could ever dream of asking in a text. The description of the holy city provides him a treasure trove of symbolism he can apply to Christ, the church, holy Scripture, the Trinity, the apostles, and much else. And chapter 22 is equally generous, providing him with images such as the stream of living water and the tree of life. **Then he showed me the river of the water of life, bright as crystal, flowing from the throne of God and of the Lamb through the middle of the street of the city; also, on either side of the river, the tree of life with its twelve kinds of fruit, yielding its fruit each month; and the leaves of the tree were for the healing of the nations.**

> The tree of life is in the middle of the street in the city, offering twelve kinds of fruit, because Christ offers himself as refreshment to all his elect, greater and lesser alike, on earth and in heaven. He refreshes them on earth through their partaking of his body and blood, and in heaven through perpetual contemplation of his divinity and humanity. On each side of the river, therefore, the tree of life offers us fruit, justice on this side and glory on the other. On this side eating makes us just, on the other it makes us blessed. He who is not refreshed by the fruit of justice on this side will not be sated by the fruit of glory on the other. The tree of life yields fruit every month because Christ feeds his elect continuously and without any break, on earth and in heaven. The leaves of the tree for the healing of the gentiles are his precepts, which are for the healing of the gentiles because, if they are fulfilled, then with the help of grace the souls of the gentiles will be made just. For he who is justified will be healed.

Richard's approach is not structurally complex. He recognizes that there are seven visions and divides the text accordingly. He also recognizes that there is a historical dimension to be addressed, although the text itself as Richard sees it might point in this direction less obviously than many exegetes throughout history have assumed. Certainly, given Richard's identification of the beast from the sea as Antichrist, he finds it easy to see the text as anticipating a future "age of Antichrist," an age of tribulation involving increased persecution and temptation. Richard's predecessors have furnished him with at least a vague scenario for these events. He remarks at one point that Antichrist will be from the tribe of Dan, which would make sense to Richard since, like most medieval exegetes, he has a tendency to play the Jews off against the Christians. Nevertheless, the scenario remains undeveloped. The time of Antichrist tends to appear as an intensification of the temptations and tribulations already experienced throughout Christian history, a final, desperate satanic counterattack leading into an equally final judgment. The road to that counterattack leads through several temptations thrown in the path of an advancing Christianity, and these could be arranged sequentially, allowing us to recognize a series of stages in the journey; yet the stages do not coalesce into watertight periods. Richard has other interests.

Nor is Richard's view of the time after Antichrist particularly complex or surprising. Richard is willing to acknowledge the validity of John's hint that the elements will be reconstituted, but his emphasis in Revelation 21–22 is on eternal bliss after the end of history.

In fact, Richard is less interested in assigning a shape to earthly history than are those we will be investigating from here on. He makes little effort to discuss history in terms of seven periods of church history, as others will do. This might seem odd in view of the fact that he does spend considerable time talking about what later exegetes will consider the first four periods: persecution by the Jews; persecution by the Roman Empire; the rise of heresy; and the rise of hypocrisy. If, as in the vision of the seven trumpets, we throw in what Richard describes as the time when the devil tries using all of the original elements at once, and then we add the period of Antichrist, that gives us six of what will eventually be accepted by some commentators as the seven periods. Richard has given succeeding exegetes that much to work with. He simply doesn't concentrate on seeing it in those terms, although most historians familiar with what is to come might be tempted to read that into him.

That seems to leave us with a historical pattern characterized by a notable gap between the "was" and the "will be." Perhaps what Richard sees as the present is identical with that period when the devil is using all the elements he previously used singly, but Richard doesn't say that clearly. It doesn't qualify as the sort of thing he feels an urgent need to clarify.

What really interests Richard is not what particular period he is in but the human condition in general, a condition that, even as it has varied and will vary to some extent, remains essentially constant. As Richard sees it, most of those many preachers depicted in Revelation have essentially the same message: our salvation depends on Christ, who died for us. Those who accept that message are the elect, and those who do not are the damned.

Richard's comment on mutability, brief as it is, should also be taken seriously. Our true joy awaits us in heaven, beyond this temporary, disruptive process we call history.

*   *   *

Richard is the first medieval scholar we have examined in any depth, and before we leave him it behooves us to pause and point to the obvious. For Richard, twelve centuries have passed since John wrote his Apocalypse. Many things have happened in the meantime, and one would hardly expect Richard to read Revelation in precisely the same spirit John wrote it; yet he is still expected to read it as a part of holy Scripture and make sense of it. He can do so only by ignoring a great deal that was important to John and by reading in a great deal John would never have taken as central to the book's meaning.

Both John and Richard are mystics, but in different senses. In essence, John is a visionary while Richard is a contemplative more or less in the spirit of Pseudo-Dionysius. He says more than once that John was on Patmos, and he seems to understand why, what Patmos was *for*; yet he cannot resist talking about it as if it were a contemporary meditation center. There are, of course, historical cases of prisons that functioned in that way for their inmates, but John gives us no reason to assume that his did, or even that the visions he describes occurred on Patmos.

Nor does John's description of the divine decision to come down and live with his people fit without notable adjustment into Richard's notion of heavenly bliss. John was hardly the last visionary to think in those terms, but by the end of the fourth century the course of theological speculation favored travel in the opposite direction, with the saved joining God in heaven rather than God joining them on earth.

Nor by the end of the fourth century had the Christian world found it any easier to verify John's identification of the beast. In fact, it would arguably get harder in Richard's time, and once the papacy consolidated a very earthly brand of power during the century following Richard, the task would become even more complicated. Richard does in fact have some interesting things to say about the distinction between the two beasts from land and sea, taking it at one point as a distinction between "cruel princes of the gentiles" and "false masters and princes of the false Christians," an intriguing effort to repurpose a metaphor that no longer meant precisely what it meant for John.

To say this much is not to say that Richard got it wrong, much less that he was unique in getting it wrong. Everyone we will cover in this book has to explain away at least part of the Johannine text in order to make sense of it. Some will find the task less difficult than others, but none will be able to inhabit John's world without either distorting or simply ignoring parts of his message. The shoe will pinch in different places, but it will inevitably pinch.

READINGS

The First Vision

Prologue[11]

The immense and eternal God, who is neither limited to a single place nor changed by time and who, by his great and eternal deity, has powerfully created all things, has in his goodness mercifully redeemed his spouse, the holy church, from all guilt and punishment and, enriching it with spiritual goods, has brought it out of exile and pointed it toward the heavenly beatitude prepared for it in the course of time. The Father of Lights, author of our spiritual gifts, from whom all the good things given to us descend daily, has established and now rules through fitting ministers of the New Testament and leads us to heavenly bliss along the strict and arduous way that leads to life. Along this way, as we follow in the footprints of holy church from the valley of tears to supernal joy, the prophetic word is a lamp that illuminates the places and keeps us from straying from the path through human ignorance. The prophecy of the blessed John, contained in this book, revealed to him by God's mediator and man among men Jesus Christ so that the holy church might be illumined, advances all the more gloriously and brilliantly in the measure that the oracles it describes are more brilliant and more sublime. In this way it is more excellent than the other prophecies, and, just as the gospel excels over the observances of the law, so this prophecy excels over those of the Old Testament in which the great mysteries concerning Christ and the church are only partly revealed. Indeed, this prophecy has as many mysteries [*sacramenta*] in it as it has words, and all praise comes short of describing its value. For a host of meanings lie hidden in each word.

Exhorting the holy church to patience, this Apocalypse (that is, revelation) describes many tribulations, pressures, and persecutions the church suffers in the world, as well as the supernal rewards that follow in heaven

---

11. *In Apocalypsim Joannis Libri Septem* (PL 196:685).

after the passage of time. First it describes the work in terms of its title. Then it adds a salutation to the seven churches of Asia to which the book is sent. Then it turns to a narration of the seven visions that form of the content of this book.

Chapter I

Concerning the title and the four types of vision[12]

The Apocalypse of Jesus Christ. There are four types of vision, of which two are inner and two outer. Two are corporeal and two spiritual. The first kind of corporeal vision is when we open our eyes to exterior and visible things and see the heavens and the earth, figures and colors of visible things. But this sort of vision is inferior and weak. Because it is narrow, it does not take in the greatest things. Because it is dull, it does not discern the smallest things. Because it is weak, it cannot reach out to distant things. Because it is not keen, it cannot penetrate to hidden things. Hence it contains nothing of mystical signification, but discovers only that which is available to the corporeal senses.

In the other type of corporeal vision, something external to us is seen and registers within us as having great mystical signification, as was the case with the vision in which a bush externally appeared to Moses. It did so visibly, but it was full of typical signification. For what do we take the flame to mean except the grace of the Holy Spirit? What do we understand by the bush—young, harsh, full of vitality, blooming—except the blessed virgin Mary, humble in her self-contempt, harsh against softness through exercise of the virtues, vital through faith, blooming through chastity? The Lord appeared in flame in the bush, yet the bush was not consumed. In like manner, the Son of God took on flesh in the virgin through the overshadowing grace of the Holy Spirit, yet her virginal modesty remained unaffected. This second type of vision is thus much more sublime and excellent than the first, because the first is empty of mystery, while the second redounds with the power of a celestial sacrament. Thus Moses said of the vision, "I will go and see this great vision" (Ex 3:3). And indeed it was a great vision, for it showed the miraculous incarnation of the Word and perpetual integrity of his virgin mother.

---

12. *In Apocalypsim Joannis Libri Septem* (PL 196:686–90).

The third type of vision is seen, not with the eye of flesh, but with the eye of the heart. That is, the mind is illuminated by the Holy Spirit with forms that are similitudes of visible things, and, through these images presented to it more or less as figures and signs, it is led to cognition of invisible things.

The fourth type of vision occurs when, through internal aspiration, the human mind is subtly and sweetly raised to celestial contemplation without the mediation of any figures or qualities or visible things. Concerning these two types of vision, which occur not corporeally but spiritually, the blessed Dionysius the Areopagite speaks in his book, *The Hierarchy*,[13] when he says, "Let us pay attention, when possible, to the illuminations symbolically and anagogically radiated down to us in most sacred oracles, that is, let us consider, as far as is attainable, the hierarchies of heavenly minds."

A symbol is a collection of visible forms to demonstrate invisible things. "Anagoge" refers to an ascension or reservation of the mind to the contemplation of heavenly things. He notes here the double mode of divine revelation infused in the minds of theologians and prophets. The Greeks call these "theophanies," that is, divine apparitions, by which invisible things are sometimes shown through signs resembling sensible things. At other times it occurs through anagogy alone, that is, ascension of the mind to pure contemplation of heavenly things. From these two types of vision are formed two types of description in sacred discourse. In one, the truth of hidden things is concealed in forms, signs, and similitudes. In the other it is shown nakedly and purely, uncovered as it were. And thus when what is hidden is made manifest by forms, signs, and similitudes, or what is manifest is so described, that is symbolic demonstration. When it is shown by pure and naked revelation or taught by plain, transparent reason, it is anagogical.

Since, according to what has been said, there are four types of vision, two external and two internal, two corporeal and two spiritual, we must ask in what way Saint John saw this Apocalypse, that is, this revelation. But it is clear that he did not see it in either of the first two ways, since he says he saw it in the spirit. He says, **I, John, your brother and fellow participant in tribulation, and in the kingdom, and in suffering in Jesus, was on the island called Patmos on account of God's word, and testimony to Jesus Christ. I was in the spirit on the Lord's day.** He who sees in the spirit does not see with eyes of the flesh, but rather with eyes of the heart. But neither did he see it with the fourth type of vision, since the fourth type of vision is believed to occur without the forms of any corporeal substances mediating,

13. *Celestial Hierarchy*, ch. 1, section 1.

which is to say, there are no words through which what was seen is hidden from evil persons. Nor could we understand the things John saw without his using and our understanding words that refer to the forms of visible things. It is clear, therefore, that this case involves the third form of seeing, particularly because this book is filled with the likenesses of temporal things such as the heavens, the sun, the moon, clouds, rain, hail, lightning, thunder, winds, birds, fish, beasts, serpents, reptiles, trees, mountains, hills, air, sea, land, and other things, though not as we normally experience them. For it was necessary, given our infirmity, that higher things should be grasped only by lower things, and spiritual things only by corporeal, so that we can come to know the unknown, not through what is even less known, but through what we know. Thus the blessed Dionysius says in the aforementioned book, "Nor is it possible for our minds to ascend to imitation and contemplation of the immaterial celestial hierarchy unless it is led there by material means." The material means he has in mind are images of corporeal things used in sacred Scripture to represent incorporeal and invisible things. Saint Dionysius explains these things with marvelous subtlety, showing us how we should understand formative images of angelic powers, how we should interpret fingers, eyes, noses, ears, mouths, eyelids, eyebrows, teeth, shoulders, arms, hands, hearts, chests, backs, feet, bright cloaks, priestly garments, purses, rods, arms, axes, winds, clouds, various metals, the colors of diverse stones, lions, eagles, horses and the various colors of horses, rivers, chariots, wheels, the joy of the angels.[14] Our mind, because it knows visible things, does not know invisible things unless it is led to them through material things; that is, unless it is led through similitudes of corporeal things, which it knows, it cannot rise to the contemplation of the immaterial. Thus visible images of many kinds are used in sacred revelations, so that, through those things to which our mind is accustomed, it learns to habituate itself to seeing the good things that are hidden. Nor are they represented only through similitudes of the most excellent things, but also by similitudes of middling and inferior things. For because nothing that exists is deprived of participation in the good—as the Scripture says, "God saw all that he had made, and it was very good" (Gen 1:31)—even the least things that, in comparison with others, seem deformed, can fittingly represent invisible things, and on this score the aforementioned theologian says, "Sometimes those theologians (that is, those who speak of divine Scriptures) praise the invisible Wisdom through reference to precious lights like the sun of justice, as the morning star arising

14. Taken from *Celestial Hierarchy*, ch. 15. I have abridged the list slightly.

divinely in the mind, as light revolving and invisibly resplendent. Sometimes they use middling things, such as fire burning without damage, or water, giver of a fullness of life, and, symbolically speaking (that is, figuratively speaking) flowing into the stomach and returning in immeasurable volume to refill rivers. Sometimes they use the newest (that is, the lowest) things, like sweet ointment or a cornerstone. But they also employ the forms of beasts, such as the lion or the panther, and describe it as like a leopard or a savage bear. But what seems more vile than all the rest, yet more significant, those wise in knowledge of divine things (that is, the theologians) have presented them in the form of a worm.

Note that he says what is more vile than all the rest is more significant: that is, it is the worm that signifies Christ. According to the prophet, Christ born according to the flesh says of himself, "I am a worm" (Ps 22:6). For a worm is born from the earth without coitus, just as Christ was born of Mary without virile seed. A worm, therefore, is said to be more vile than all else, yet it seems to signify Christ more fittingly. That is because figures demonstrate the truth more evidently in the measure that they represent themselves to be dissimilar similitudes and do not prove the truth; and dissimilar similitudes lead our minds to the truth inasmuch as they do not permit them to remain in similitude alone. Thus holy Scripture, by a marvelous providence, descends to the deformed qualities of deformed things in representing immaterial, invisible things. Such deformed things do not permit our minds to rest in themselves but force us by their deformity to push on to immaterial things far beyond any similarity to material things, because by their deformity and temporality they show (though not in a demonstrative way) that the divine and spiritual is something quite beyond them. For if, in sacred speech, similitudes were always taken from bright, lucid, and precious things, the human mind would easily be seduced, especially the minds of those who understand nothing else except visible goods, and, according to the aforesaid theologian Dionysius, we would perhaps imagine that in the heavens there were certain golden essences, and certain bright men dressed in lovely clothing, and other such things, taking for reality the images used by sacred theology to veil mysteries in presenting them to our minds. Sometimes Scripture praises the blessedness of superessential divinity in lauding its rationality and wisdom and calling it the existing subsistence and the true cause of the subsistence of all those things which proclaim its existence, and in describing light as its form and life. And although these material images can be shown to be superior in some way and certainly seem to be a more chaste way of referring to ineffable, incomprehensible, and interminable divinity, they too are incapable of expressing the truth of it as it is in itself. It is above any essence, nor can it be characterized through reference to any light, and it is in fact incomparably beyond any similitude our reason and intellect might use to describe it. Although a rational creature is made in the image and similitude of the Creator, we cannot really compare the former to the latter.

Thus the blessed John, sent into exile, removed from the hustle and bustle of the world and given over to peace and quiet, received this apocalypse from the Lord in the third way of seeing (as has been shown) and recorded it in writing for the utility of holy church. The fact that, when put in a place of quiet, he received this revelation signifies to us that those who love internal quiet know the joy of invisible blessings, and the more they can distance themselves from temporal things, the closer they are to eternal things. For whoever involves himself in worldly affairs alienates himself in that measure from internal and eternal things, and he who cannot pull his mind away from visible things finds it impossible to devote any great attention to invisible things. Thus, if we wish to approach God, we must turn our minds from external to internal things, so that, placed thus in quiet, we can contemplate heavenly things. "Be still and see that I am God" (Ps 45:11). It is as if he said, "Unless you separate yourself from the perturbations of the world, you will not succeed in contemplating me. Thus separate yourself from externals and internally, through quiet, see who I am." For the more the human mind comes close to spiritual things, the farther behind it leaves temporal or corporeal things; and the more clearly and perspicaciously it reaches out to grasp the highest things, the more it averts its eyes from the rays of its own light shining up from below. And although the sea of secular perturbations flows out through the world in a great circle, if we can confine it within ourselves through internal desire (as if we were placed within the stability of a certain island) we can inhere in divine things through contemplation.

At this point the introductory part ends and the line-by-line exegesis begins.

Chapter One[15]

The apocalypse of Jesus Christ. "Jesus" and "Christ," the two principal names of the savior, are often recited in the divine page. But "Jesus," although

---

15. *In Apocalypsim Joannis Libri Septem* (PL 196:690–98).

it has great significance in itself, is acknowledged to be a proper name, while "Christ" signifies a mystery. "Jesus" is interpreted as "savior." Many were called by this name, "Jesus," before this man, but none of them saved anyone from his sin. This man truly cleansed his people from their sin.

Some sin is original, some actual. Original sin is what we contract by being born from our parents. Actual is what we ourselves later do. Jesus, our savior, saves us from both, because through the grace of baptism he frees us from both. There seem to be two principal vices, malice and luxury, from which two other evils flow like rivers. For, although gluttony is a vice of the flesh, luxury seems to be greater than gluttony, because, although we can contain gluttony, luxury never ceases to flow.

After two columns of commentary on the two major vices, Richard finally arrives at John's next sentence.

Which God gave to him to make known to his servants. Note the order of giving. God gave it to Christ, Christ to an angel, the angel to John, John to the seven churches of Asia, and the churches of Asia to the universal mother church. The universal mother church, through the voices of its doctors, dispenses and distributes it daily into the minds of individual faithful. Thus every perfect gift descends from the Father above to the predestined in order to give them life, and proceeds variously, beautifully, and multiformly in them, gathering them to the breast of the mother who calls them and unites them together into her unity. But the heavenly good that we see in a mirror dimly, the angelic minds contemplate face-to-face. What we know in part, they know as they are known. Just as a healthy eye gazes purely at the solar brilliance, so an ailing eye can discern it only with some obstacle interposed. Thus the invisible minds of celestial essences, which no malice of the reprobate fallen angels could corrupt, receive directly the splendor of the divine light, while the minds of humans are darkened by sin, and they cannot see it except through figures. But when the mortal puts on immortality and the corruptible incorruption, then human beings, transferred to the same fate as the angels, will participate in the same contemplation, and the divine goods that they now sometimes receive through the ministration of angels and through figures they will then possess in eternity, without requiring either the angels or the figures. In the meantime, however, until we join together in the unity of the faith, all proceeds according to grade and merit, and goods are dispensed by superiors to inferiors.

This last sentence represents a summary of what Richard says at some length.

The cause of the divine revelation is declared in the title of the book when it is said, **made known**. For God gave him this Apocalypse for that purpose, that he should make it known. For God wants the talent to be increased and a profit returned to him (Matt 25:14–30). He told us to make known the good that we know, and to teach to others what we have learned. He wishes that we should preach from the roofs what we have heard in chambers, and, the light of divine knowledge having been illumined in our souls, we should not hide it under a bushel basket (Matt 5:15) of taciturnity but rather broadcast by lighting the candelabra of preaching. As it is said at the end of the Apocalypse, **Let he who hears say, "Come"** (Rev 22:17). For there is no use in hidden wisdom and in undiscovered treasure. Thus, just as it is a sin for him who knows how to do good not to do it, so it is a sin for him who knows how to say good things not to say them. Those to whom sacred revelation should be revealed are clearly identified when it is added, **to his servants**. Not to proud philosophers, not to unbelieving Jews, not to impure Christians. For holy things should not be given to the dogs, nor should pearls be cast before swine. The dogs are infidel persecutors of the sacred faith, the barking dogs who snap at it. The pigs are false Christians who have faith in the sense of belief but soil themselves with vices like pigs. To each of these groups the sacred mysteries are hidden, to one because of their blindness and to the other because of their polluted lives. But these things are to be revealed to those who studiously serve the Lord, because they patiently hear what is said and devoutly do what they hear. And just as the divine good should not be made manifest to the evil, so it should not in the least be hidden from the good. And just as it is a grave sin to reveal the sacred mysteries to the reprobate, so it is a grave sin to hide them from the elect. Thus the unprofitable servant who is slothful in the office of teaching should not feel secure, because on the day of judgment he will have to account for the talent given to him.

Which must come to pass soon. Whatever happens in the present passes quickly, for all things subject to time pass quickly. This life is brief, the way is slippery, and death is uncertain. "What will come to pass soon" refers to what will happen to the church in this world, whether good or bad, or what retribution will be handed out at the end of this world. And all these things come to pass soon because the present passes soon, being soon succeeded by the future. And the sooner the things contained in this book must necessarily be completed, the sooner and the more studiously they should be announced, lest, death coming upon them unexpectedly, he who should be justified through hearing these things should die without hearing them and the Lord should hold the preacher who has failed in his duty responsible for that sinner's damnation. There is no more listening to sacred doctrine after you are dead, but as long as you are alive it can still be heard.

And he made it known by sending his angel to his servant John. Here he shows the mode of sacred revelation by saying **made it known**. **He made it known** in the sense that he revealed sacred mysteries through certain signs, figures, and seals similar to sensible things. For he wished his mysteries to be demonstrated through figures so that they could not be understood without effort, because that which is acquired through labor is retained more deeply and firmly. Moreover, he wished the figures to be exposited elsewhere, so that the faithful who seek it could find it, while the infidels who seek to pervert and attack the sacred mysteries would not understand it. **Through his angel to his servant John.** For the vision was shown to Saint John through an angel in the form of the Son of Man, as he declares in the following, where he says, **And having turned I saw seven golden candlesticks, and in the middle of the seven golden candlesticks one similar to the Son of Man**. And thus Christ according to his humanity accepts the sacrament from the Father and, through an angel in the appearance of Christ, transmits it to Saint John, who in turn transmits it to the seven churches, or rather to the entire universal church. And in this John's authority is made clear, for it is added, **Who has given testimony to the word of God, and testimony of Jesus Christ, concerning all he saw**. In fact, great was the man who gave testimony of Christ according to both his divine and human natures. That he did so is announced here inasmuch as it speaks of his having **given testimony to the word of God and testimony of Jesus Christ**. He gave testimony to his divinity where, as one who has contemplated heavenly secrets, he says, **In the beginning was the Word, and the Word was with God, and God was the Word** (Jn 1:1). He gave testimony to the Christ's humanity when he described how Christ preached to the crowds, performed miracles, died, was resurrected, and appeared to his disciples. In this passage, indeed, when he says "word of God" he speaks of the divinity, and where he says "Jesus Christ" he refers to the humanity. And John **has given testimony to the word of God, and testimony of Jesus Christ, concerning all he saw**. For what he saw through spiritual eyes concerning the hidden things of the sempiternal God he understood, or what he saw (insofar as he could) with eyes of flesh of the works of Christ's humanity he preached in word and passed along in writing.

He then says, **Blessed is he who reads and hears the words of this prophecy, and observes those things that are written in them**. At the end of his opening passage, to encourage good will and diligence on the reader's part, he offers a reward: beatitude, that is, eternal joy. And when he says **he who reads** he is speaking of the educated or doctors. But when he says **he who hears** he is speaking of the laity or hearers. For nothing read or heard contributes to our salvation unless it is diligently observed in our acts. Thus if we wish to attain beatitude we should studiously attempt, not only to understand what we read or hear, but to fulfill what we understand by living well. For the servant who knows the will of his lord but does not perform it will be beaten severely. For understanding is good (that is, it is useful) to those who act on it. But he who observes what is written keeps inviolate the faith of Christ and the church. He who fears the mandates seeks that which is promised.

He then says, **For the time is near**. The time, that is, when our labors will be ended and we will receive our rewards. Because the time is near when the evils will be over and the good things will follow. So in this short remaining time, rather than being broken by adversity or softened by prosperity, let us be strong and strive to attain eternal life. He stands at the beginning of the book as one who opens the door so that he can discern clearly who is within the house (Rev 3:20).

> *The Vulgate says that once the door is opened Christ will enter the house and eat* (cenare) *with those within. Richard says he enters so that he can discern clearly* (patenter cernare) *who are within. This seems to be a creative misreading of the Vulgate text.*

We have hurried through this introductory section so that we could inspect in greater detail the arcane material contained in the rest of the book.

The Salutation[16]

John to the seven churches in Asia, grace and peace to you from him who is, and was, and is to come, and from the seven spirits who are before his

16. *In Apocalypsim Joannis Libri Septem* (PL 196:698–700).

throne. In order to declare clearly what is to follow, he adds this salutation to the aforementioned title, so that he can describe more fully to whom this prophecy is especially addressed.

> From this point until the end of chapter II Richard is teasing a general, timeless sort of theology out of the text without any attention to the precise historical context.

The General Meaning [Sententia] of the Seven Sacred Visions[17]

Holy mother church, which is regenerated through the sevenfold grace of the Holy Spirit and justified in time that unfolds in the number of seven days and is represented through the seven churches of Asia, is enlightened through the seven prophetic visions presented in this book, which assure us that the present adversities will soon pass and encourage us to long for the good things that will come in the future and remain forever. For although this prophecy is particularly directed to the seven churches, it more generally addresses the present and future states of the holy catholic church. And its structure is rightly sevenfold, for that number points to the perfection of the doctrine contained in the prophecy. Seven represents the fourfold nature of that which is visible and the threefold nature of that which is invisible. Thus the sevenfold nature of the prophecy represents all things.

As we enter the profound obscurity of these heavenly mysteries [*sacramentorum*], we will look briefly at each of the seven visions, just as one about to enter a dense, dark woods might first consider with care the path he should follow in order to make his way through the woods in the best possible way. Thus we, as we pass through the obscure places in this book, can hope to come away with a few twigs of meaning lest we seem to have read the whole thing to no purpose.

The first vision deals with the similitude of the Son of Man, which appeared through the angel to Saint John, showed him heavenly mysteries, and ordered him to write. It deals, too, with the seven churches and their seven bishops, and the rebukes directed at those seven bishops as well as the praise and commendation given them, and the rewards that will be given to the victors.

---

17. *In Apocalypsim Joannis Libri Septem* (PL 196:700-702).

The rest of the chapter proceeds on that level, simply describing in the most general way the images presented in each vision. From there Richard proceeds carefully through the rest of Revelation. The exposition in the earlier part of this chapter, preceding the readings, offers an extended treatment of Richard's commentary with substantial citations, and giving it here again in full seems unnecessary.

JOACHIM OF FIORE

Our knowledge of Joachim's life is dependent on two biographies written by people who knew him, but it is also dependent on what we can gather from his own writings. The biographies tell us a great deal if we can trust them, while Joachim himself tells us little. We can gather from the biographies that he was born around 1135 in Calabria and that he was a chancery official until he went on pilgrimage to the Holy Land around 1167. He may have had visionary experiences at that point, but he himself does not tell us so. Upon his return to Italy, Joachim lived for a while as a hermit on Mount Etna and then in Calabria before becoming a monk at Corazzo around 1171.

By 1177 he was their abbot and sought to bring them into line with Cistercian practices. He was successful, but he found it harder to incorporate the house fully into the Cistercian order. The Corazzo monastery was poor, and established Cistercian monasteries in the area were hesitant to assume the responsibility of acting as its mother house. Much of Joachim's activity over the next few years was dedicated to this project, but it need not concern us here. The important thing for our purposes is that in late 1182 or early 1183 he went to the monastery at Casamari in pursuit of the same goal and ended up staying there for a year and a half. While there, he had the opportunity to think and write. During his stay he began not only his Apocalypse commentary but also his *Liber concordiae* and *Liber psalterii decem chordarum*.[1]

---

1. As Joachim studies became a growth industry in the twentieth century, textual scholars had a hard time keeping up with intellectual historians. Scholars examined his thought in a number of excellent studies, but they had to work with unreliable sixteenth-century editions

Joachim tells us in the introduction to the last work that it was inspired by a Pentecost vision in 1183 or 1184, presenting the mystery of the Holy Trinity in terms of a ten-stringed psaltery.[2] More interesting from our perspective, in his Apocalypse commentary he reports a vision in connection with that work.[3] The entire passage in which Joachim describes it is included in the selections at the end of this chapter. For the moment it will suffice to say that his problems began when he reached the words of Revelation 1:10, "I was in the spirit on the Lord's day." According to Joachim, he was disturbed by the passage. Why he felt that way is less clear. He says he felt "as if [he] was being shut out by the stone blocking the entrance to the tomb." The Easter symbolism is clear enough, but what tomb was Joachim excluded from entering? It seems hard to believe that it was the meaning of the words, "I was in the spirit on the Lord's day." They seem straightforward enough, and what Joachim himself says suggests as much.[4]

Perhaps what bothered Joachim was not so much the meaning of the words as their implication. He tells us, "I left the passage unexplained and went on to what follows, reserving that particular difficulty for the Universal Master, in order that he who opened the book and loosened its seven seals might, if he pleased, open it to me or to others." The point seems to be that he understood the precise words of Revelation 1:10 all too well. They reminded him that the contents of this book had been revealed to John through a vision, and the discovery of its meaning would depend on God providing another

---

of his three major works, the *Liber concordiae novi ac veteris testamenti* (Venice, 1519; repr., Frankfurt am Main: Minerva, 1964); *Expositio in Apocalypsim* (Venice, 1527; repr., Frankfurt am Main: Minerva, 1964; the text used for translation here, hereafter *Expos.*); and *Psalterium decem chordarum* (Venice, 1527; repr., Frankfurt am Main: Minerva, 1965). Until recently, the main exception to that situation has been E. R. Daniel's 1973 edition of the *Liber concordiae*, books 1–4 (Philadelphia: American Philosophical Society, 1973). Even here, though, the important fifth book remains available only in the 1519 edition.

An editorial commission is currently presiding over the preparation of Joachim's works. Several of the minor works have already received modern critical editions, and recently Kurt-Victor Selge has presented us with an excellent edition of the *Psalterium decem cordarum*, Monumenta Germaniae Historica, Quellen zur Geistesgeschichte des Mittelalters, vol. 20 (Hanover: Hahnsche Buchhandlung, 2009).

2. *Psalterium decem chordarum*, 227va.

3. *Expos.*, 39rb–vb.

4. Nevertheless, after reporting his insight, he says, "When, therefore, after some time, I had the opportunity to go again through the little bit that I had done earlier, and I came to the passage where it is said, 'I was in the spirit on the Lord's day,' I understood for the first time what John's words, 'I was in the spirit on the Lord's day,' meant to say as far as mysteries are concerned." This helps somewhat, though not much.

mystical enlightenment. So Joachim was quietly waiting for God to present him with the key, not simply to Revelation 1:10, but to the entire book.

He tells us it took close to a year, during which occupation with other matters kept him from dwelling on the problem. Then, the following Easter, around the hour of matins, he awakened and began to think about the Apocalypse. Joachim says explicitly that he was not thinking about Revelation 1:10 at that moment. Then, "around the middle of the night's silence, I think, at the hour when our lion of the tribe of Judah is thought to have risen from the dead, as I was meditating, suddenly something of the fullness of this book and of the concord of the Old and New Testament was revealed to me with a certain clarity of understanding in my mind's eye."

According to Robert Lerner, the revelation can be dated, because in yet another work, the life of Saint Benedict that he wrote in 1187, Joachim says he was endowed with "divine gifts" at Easter three years earlier. Thus, the Easter vision occurred in 1184.[5] Even so, it seems to have taken him a long time to finish the commentary, although we cannot know how long. We can only say that it was completed by his death in 1202.

What did Joachim learn from his Easter vision? Obviously, he discovered "the fullness of this book and of the concord of the Old and New Testaments," but what does that mean? The second part concerning "the concord of the Old and New Testaments" seems clear in the light of Joachim's total thought. It seems to mean that he was granted insight into the parallel between Old Testament history and the history of the church. In Joachim's developed view of history, this parallel meant that the course of Old Testament history reflected in a general way the historical development from Christ to the eschaton. The parallel did not add up to an absolute identity, but it was close enough so that each series clarified the other. Joachim felt we could see the significance of Old Testament events if we read them in the light of the corresponding New Testament events, and the reverse was also true. That assumption was given extra importance by the fact that church history was still in process.

Unfortunately, according to Robert Lerner, this notion of Joachim as discovering the concordance of Old Testament and church history in an

---

5. "*De vita sancti Benedicti ed de officio divino secundum eius doctrinam*," in *Analecta sacra Tarraconensia* 24 (1951): 65. This passage is noted by Stephen Wessley, "Bonum est Benedicto mutare locum," *Revue Bénédictine* 90 (1980): 322. Robert Lerner, "Joachim of Fiore's Breakthrough to Chiliasm," *Cristianesimo nella storia* 6 (1985): 495, demonstrates that the same date can be arrived at by other means. Bernard McGinn, however, in *The Calabrian Abbot* (New York: Macmillan, 1985), 22, seems to suggest that both the Easter and Pentecost revelations took place in 1183.

1184 revelation is compromised by the fact that elsewhere he himself tells us he began writing the *Liber concordiae* before he began his Apocalypse commentary, and the concordance of Old Testament and church history is what the *Liber concordiae* is essentially about.[6] There is perhaps no good way of explaining this disparity.

What, though, are we to make of the earlier part of the statement, his reference to "the fullness of this book"? Robert Lerner suggests that it refers to Joachim's decision that the book of Revelation had to be read "progressively as one unit." In other words, he believed that it should be read "as a continuous story which revealed the entire history of the Church—past, present and future."[7] This conclusion had profound implications, according to Lerner, for "as soon as one read Revelation developmentally, with the last chapters standing in sequential order for earthly history's final events, one perforce became a chiliast."

Whether Joachim's reference to "the fullness of this book" can be explained as a reference to reading the book of Revelation "progressively as one unit" might be debatable, but Joachim's interest in such a reading is not. Lerner is hardly alone in saying that Joachim interpreted the Apocalypse in this way. Bernard McGinn comments that Joachim "saw the Apocalypse primarily as a *continuous prophecy* of the Church's history through the sixth and seventh *aetates* of history, as well as the eighth period (if we can call it that) of eternity."[8] It would be hard to deny that Lerner and McGinn are correct, since Joachim himself says the same thing explicitly and more than once.[9] Nevertheless, all those sevenfold patterns in the Apocalypse are hard to ignore, and Joachim treats them as miniature tours of church history, at least up to the destruction of Antichrist.[10] Thus, whereas in a consistently continuous reading of the Apocalypse the letters to the seven churches in Revelation 1–3 would be taken as applying to the first period of church history, Joachim actually reads them as the first of these tours stretching from Christ to Antichrist.[11]

As for the seven seals of Revelation 5–8, the first is referred to the primitive church, the second to the persecution of the church by the Roman

---

6. *Psalterium decem chordarum*, 227va.

7. Lerner, "Joachim of Fiore's Breakthrough to Chiliasm," 501–92.

8. McGinn, *The Calabrian Abbot*, 147.

9. See, for example, the excerpt from *Expos.*, 16ra, entitled "On the Eight Parts of the Book of the Apocalypse" included in the readings below.

10. He also explicitly says that they are to be read in this way. See the excerpt from *Expos.*, 15vb–16ra, entitled "On Recapitulation in the Apocalypse."

11. *Expos.*, 48ra–92va.

Empire, the third to the Arian heresy, the fourth to the rise of Islam, the fifth to contemporary attacks on Christians in Muslim Spain, and the sixth to contemporary troubles within the church.[12] We also see here a progression through Joachim's five orders tied to the first five periods: the apostles in the first, martyrs in the second, doctors in the third, virgins in the fourth, and the general order in the fifth.

The seven trumpets of Revelation 8–11 follow the same trajectory.[13] The first of the seven angels blowing those trumpets designates Paul and his colleagues, sent not to baptize but to evangelize. The second designates the doctors who combated early heresy within the church in the period of the martyrs. Joachim especially mentions the Nicolaitian heresy. The third represents the doctors in the time of Constantine who opposed the Arians. The fourth represents the monks and virgins who were decimated in the process of withstanding both the early Muslims and hypocrisy within the church. The fifth symbolizes those battling, not only heretics like the Cathars in Joachim's own day, but also corrupt clergy. The sixth describes the battle just beginning in Joachim's own time.

Much the same could be said for the seven vials of God's wrath.[14] The first angel is placed in the primitive church, and Joachim speaks of the battle with those who insisted on circumcision. The passage concerning the second angel speaks of the Nicolaitian heresy. The third angel attacks those infected with the Arian heresy, the fourth angel preaches chastity against the self-indulgent in the post-Constantinian Christian empire, and the fifth speaks to Christian decay in the fifth period, while both the sixth and seventh angels train their fire on the sixth period.

Thus, of the first five visions, only the fourth does not essentially deal with some sevenfold pattern. Even here, though, the same temptations beckon in the seven heads of the dragon and of the beast from the sea (Rev 12:3; 13:1). In dealing with the woman clothed in the sun, Joachim stays focused on the fourth period for a while,[15] but he warns us in the process that "what is said in this fourth part applies generally to the time of the entire church and in a special way to the fourth period."[16] Soon he encounters the dragon and recognizes in the seven heads seven rulers who have persecuted

---

12. *Expos.*, 113vb–120vb.

13. *Expos.*, 127va–137ra. Note, however, that the pages of the 1527 edition repeat themselves in this section.

14. *Expos.*, 177ra–191va.

15. See *Expos.*, 153ra.

16. *Expos.*, 153vb.

the church in successive periods.[17] In fact, his exegesis of the entire fourth vision ranges widely over history.

Just how it ranges over history will become apparent when we arrive at the selection concerning Revelation 13. For the moment, speaking generally, we can say that the idea of Joachim's reading of the Apocalypse as a continuous history is not a misunderstanding on our part, but neither is it the thing most likely to strike a reader who turns to the book unfortified by scholarly commentary concerning its author. What may strike that reader instead is the sheer complexity of Joachim's enterprise. So far, we have seen that he is conscious of each vision as applying especially to its corresponding period but generally to all of church history. We have seen, too, that he approaches the book believing in a concordance between Old Testament history and church history.

And there is more, much more. Joachim also divides history into three *status*, a word translated in what follows here as "ages." They were ascribed to the Father, Son, and Holy Spirit, respectively. In the first age, the spotlight was on married laity; in the second, it is on clerics; and in the third, it will be on monks. Here we see another way of integrating the Old and New Testaments. Thus, Joachim thought in terms of two different systems described as the *diffinitio alpha* and the *diffinitio omega*. In the first, history is seen as tripartite, reflecting the Trinity. In the second it is seen as two concordant series of sevens.

Probably no element in Joachim's thought is more misunderstood than his threefold division of history, and the misunderstanding is hardly limited to modern historians. It began almost immediately after Joachim finished writing. One serious misreading arises from identifying the age of the Son with that of the church and thus projecting a third age of the Holy Spirit, which, in effect, supersedes the Christian dispensation. Joachim never meant to suggest that Christ would become irrelevant when the third age began, any more than he intended to imply that God the Father lost his function after the resurrection. All three members of the Trinity remain active throughout history, and the contemplative *ecclesia spiritualis* Joachim anticipates in the third age is definitely a new, improved Christian church. His use of the Father/Son/Holy Spirit distinction to divide history into three ages is meant simply to differentiate dominant functions within the life of the faithful in

---

17. *Expos.*, 156vb. He does not go into the matter at this point, however, merely noting that he has discussed it earlier in the preface and will do so again while dealing with the sixth vision.

each of these ages and to suggest that the history of humankind is really a progressive history.

Joachim's other pattern, the *diffinitio omega*, based on two concordant, parallel, sevenfold patterns of Old Testament and New Testament history, underscores the permanence of the Christian dispensation through the age of the Holy Spirit.

Another common misreading of Joachim sees the three ages as succeeding one another. To some extent they do, but they also overlap. The age of the Father, particularly identified with the *ordo conjugatorum*, the order of married people, is contiguous with what we would consider Old Testament history, but the other two ages both began within Old Testament times. The age of the Son, particularly identified with the *ordo clericorum*, began in the age of King Uzziah (2 Kgs 15; 2 Chr 26), that is, in the early eighth century BC. The age of the Holy Spirit, particularly identified with the *ordo monachorum*, had a double beginning (due to the double procession of the Holy Spirit), first in Elijah, Elisha, and the sons of the prophets (1 Kgs 17–22; 2 Kgs 1–10; and elsewhere), then later in Saint Benedict and his disciples. Thus—puzzling though it may seem—in its first beginning, the third age is actually close to a century earlier than the second. Joachim projects concordances among these three ages as well. This gives him a complex series of historical relationships to develop in his exegesis.[18]

But are these ages at all? Is that word a decent translation for Joachim's *status*? Some historians would say that it is not, that the word should be rendered as "state" or something similar, something that does not reduce it to a period.[19] Certainly we should not reduce it to a period and nothing else, but it remains true that Joachim does see a development in human history in which the sort of spirituality practiced on a limited scale in earlier times will become more characteristic in later times. And, in striking contrast with Augustine, who saw the millennium of Revelation 20 as the period of church history running from Christ's resurrection and Satan's confinement to the period (in what for Augustine must have seemed a very distant future) when Satan would be unleashed for a while, Joachim sees the thousand years of Revelation 20 as designating, among other things, a future period of uncertain duration in which the church will be free from assault by the devil and

---

18. See the selection entitled "On the Three Ages of the World," pp. 97–98 below.

19. Marjorie Reeves, one of the truly great Joachim scholars, was eager to remind readers that *status* was at best an ambiguous word. More recently, E. R. Daniel has made the same point with considerable effect.

will enjoy contemplative experience beyond what could have been attained in earlier times. He identifies that period with the period immediately following the tribulations of the sixth seal, which he thinks he is currently entering;[20] and he sees it as symbolized by "the silence in heaven for the space of about half an hour" after the opening of the seventh seal (Rev 8:1).

The twofold and threefold divisions of history are just the beginning for Joachim. He also accepts the traditional sevenfold division of world history in which the entire Christian era makes up the sixth period, and he can discover concordances between it and his smaller sevenfold patterns. The life, death, resurrection, and ascension of Christ provide another fertile area for comparison with his historical schema, and we find several other numerical patterns being exploited in the commentary, particularly fivefold patterns. The effect is—to use a word employed by two of the most eminent Joachim scholars—kaleidoscopic.[21]

In achieving that end, Joachim distinguishes among a remarkable number of senses in Scripture. If by the end of the twelfth century most scholars had come to agree that there were four senses in Scripture, it was a consensus Joachim did not share. He counts them differently in different works, and in one work he is able to find fifteen.[22] He shifts his ground on this matter so often that it is tempting not to take his enumerations entirely seriously, but Joachim scholars certainly do. How badly one needs to understand the nature of these senses in order to comprehend Joachim depends on how thoroughly one wishes to comprehend him. For our purposes we can (indeed we must) largely ignore the problem.

So far this introduction to Joachim has relied largely on American and British scholars. Until recently it has been possible to do so without feeling that one was missing what was new and important in Joachim scholarship. This situation began to change in a major way when, in 2004, Gian Luca Potestà published *Il tempo dell'Apocalisse*.[23] Potestà proceeds from the premise that Joachim's later writings were often composed by combining and

---

20. Joachim located himself in the fifth period but felt the sixth period had begun. Thus he was in a time of transition between periods.

21. Marjorie Reeves, *Joachim of Fiore and the Prophetic Future* (New York: Harper Torchbooks, 1977), 8; McGinn, *The Calabrian Abbot*, 124.

22. *Psalterium decem chordarum* (Venice, 1527), 262v–271v. McGinn explores this problem in *The Calabrian Abbot*, ch. 4, and provides an informative chart on p. 129. He notes that Joachim offers us, at various moments, enumerations of three, four, five, seven, twelve, and fifteen senses.

23. *Il tempo dell'Apocalisse: Vita di Gioacchino da Fiore* (Rome and Bari: Laterza, 2004).

expanding on his earlier works, and thus not only the extant writings but also their component parts must sometimes be dated and examined more or less as independent works. Thus, understandably, Potestà pays particular attention to dating.

Potestà is aware that this situation presents problems especially for Joachim's three major works. The *Psalterium*, the *Liber concordiae*, and the Apocalypse commentary all evolved gradually, and they lack internal consistency. For example, the fact that the Apocalypse commentary was begun in the early 1180s and completed just before Joachim's death in 1202 means that it covers every chapter of the Apocalypse, but that should not encourage us to believe that the apocalyptic role assigned to the Holy Roman Empire in part 6 of the work is identical with the one assigned to it in part 5.

What Potestà gives us is an intellectual biography of Joachim in the form of a guided tour in which, thanks to a great deal of careful historical reconstruction, he traces Joachim's intellectual pilgrimage from the 1170s to 1202. He offers us a Joachim who arrived at some of his most important ideas early, developed others along the way, and was never afraid to change his mind. He became fascinated with the Trinity early and progressively discovered its implications for a theology of history. Potestà argues that he first linked the three persons with the three orders of laity, clerics, and monks, then proceeded from there to a further link with the three ages of Father, Son, and Holy Spirit. The result of this change in focus was a much more pronounced sense of historical development. The three orders—like the Trinity itself—continue to exist through time, but the three ages do not. The church evolves in history, and a remarkably complex evolution it is. Potestà has little patience with the notion that the three *status* should be understood in any way other than historically. He emphasizes that Joachim himself refers to them as *tempora*.

Thus, for Potestà, Joachim's Apocalypse commentary is very much about history. Joachim was keenly sensitive to his total milieu, observed contemporary events with great interest, and altered his reading of the Apocalypse accordingly. A particular contemporary pope, Holy Roman emperor, or Muslim leader could have a profound impact on his reading of the passage on which he was working at the moment. Yet it remains true that he was deeply rooted in the monastic world of his time and saw the world essentially from that perspective. His works are also very much about monasticism and its role in history.

The revolutionary aspect of Potestà's book can be overstated. Obviously, scholars such as Robert Lerner have been sensitive to the changes that took place in Joachim's thought over time. Nevertheless, it is hard to read Potestà's book carefully without recognizing a qualitative difference in the way he handles Joachim's works. That same difference can be seen in the way another Italian scholar, Marco Rainini, treats the *figurae* Joachim employed to present his thought in visual form.[24] Most of us know these *figurae* as Marjorie Reeves and Beatrice Hirsch-Reich described them close to a half century ago,[25] and as a result we are inclined to think many of them were combined into a single work produced late in Joachim's life, the *Liber figurarum*. The fact that Rainini places the words *liber figurarum* in quotation marks goes a long way toward suggesting what he thinks of that view. He agrees that Joachim produced individual *figurae* but thinks it likely that they were collected together only after Joachim's death, and he sees the collection as more like a portfolio of designs or an envelope of photographs than like a book with its own internal consistency.

Following in Potestà's wake, Rainini uses the minor works to date individual *figurae*, and in the process he shows how both the works and the *figurae* within them illustrate various moments throughout the long, slow evolution of Joachim's thought. The *figurae* may strike us as less important than the works, but one of Rainini's accomplishments is to place Joachim's *figurae* in the context of what he and others call "visual exegesis," the use of *figurae* to present complex interpretations of Scripture and, more generally, of Christian doctrine. Thus, he manages to place Joachim's *figurae* within a historical context we might otherwise have neglected. In the course of the work he at least makes a start on explaining how such *figurae* were used: for didactic purposes, but also for individual meditation. He also has some thoughts on the question of which authors Joachim was consulting—in fact, he makes interesting comparisons with the Victorines, especially Hugh of Saint Victor—and he does a good job of explaining how Joachim would have had access to good libraries and thus would have been aware of "visual exegesis" as developed by others in his time. The Joachim who emerges from this book is a man who, although he was an autodidact in the sense that he was a mature adult when he entered monastic life and thus was not shaped by the standard monastic education, nonetheless had the resources to do a great deal of catching up on his own. Yet in the final analysis Rainini sees

24. *Disegni dei tempi: Il "Liber Figurarum" e la teologia figurativa di Gioacchino da Fiore*, Centro Internationale di Studi Gioachimiti, Opere di Gioacchino da Fiore, testi e strumenti, 18 (Rome: Viella, 2006).

25. *The Figurae of Joachim of Fiore* (Oxford: Clarendon, 1972).

Joachim as belonging only partly to the Victorine age. He also points forward to scholasticism.

The absolutely central thing to remember when reading Joachim is, however, that not only his exegesis of Revelation but the entire body of his work is tightly focused on Scripture. It is about the interpretation of Scripture, and the meaning of Scripture is, for Joachim, very much a historical meaning. Bernard McGinn comments that "with Joachim . . . the brunt of the biblical message shifts away from a concern with cosmic truths, that is, the revelation of the nature of the universe and man's place in it, to truths about what the abbot called the *plenitudo historiae*. . . . No exegete before him made the world-historical message of the Bible so central or carried it through with such consistency and power."[26] Our understanding of this message, according to Joachim, is enhanced with the progressive development of God's people through the three ages. The *intellectus spiritualis* of the third age will entail a fuller understanding—a spiritual understanding—of both the Old and New Testaments. Joachim says, "Just as the letter of the New Testament proceeds from the letter of the Old, so from the wisdom of the Father is born the wisdom of the Son. And just as, from the letter of each proceeds one spiritual understanding, so one Holy Spirit proceeds from both the Father and the Son." This spiritual understanding began with Christ, but its fullness is yet to be revealed. Nor will it be completely revealed even in the third age. That will occur only beyond history in heaven.

Reading Joachim is not easy. The passages translated here will illustrate that much. In dealing with all the various dragon heads and kings, Joachim often gives the impression of a man thinking out loud. His sense of what the Apocalypse says might be summarized in the words "It's complicated." That should hardly be surprising. The task of blending Daniel and Revelation into a consistent pattern that does justice to every chapter of each work is hardly a minor one for any exegete, medieval or modern. Moreover, if Potestà's approach tells us anything, it warns us to be prepared for genuine changes of opinion on Joachim's part and to be prepared for the discovery that he does not always manage to keep his work abreast of those changes. His work is like a palimpsest in which old ideas, never quite erased, keep bleeding through.

Nevertheless, we should recognize that what we find in the passages translated here does reveal a general sense of how historical events have

26. McGinn, *The Calabrian Abbot*, 124.

heretofore fit into a discernible pattern and how that pattern will unfold in the future. Perhaps Joachim often envisages the general pattern much more clearly than he sees how individual passages in the Apocalypse can be made to fit into it, although he finds it easy to show how some of those passages are compatible with it. Thus, we are left with the question of whether he derives the pattern from his reading of history and then does his best to impose it on the Bible, or whether the pattern emerges from his reading of certain scriptural passages and then he does his best to turn it into a consistent reading of Scripture as a whole.

In any case, the historical pattern is clear enough. Joachim sees a church composed of both sheep and goats, in traditional Augustinian fashion. To switch the metaphor, Babylon and Jerusalem coexist within it. At the moment Babylon is doing quite well, and God is faced with the task of wreaking retribution on Babylon while furthering the cause of Jerusalem. This results in a two-stage process involving two battles. In one, a non-Christian power attacks Christianity intending to destroy it but actually destroys corrupt elements in the Christian church. In the other battle, Christ and his elect destroy the non-Christian power.

Joachim is reticent when it comes to identifying the non-Christian power, but what he does say suggests that he is thinking of Islam. Note that he sees it as having apparently been defeated earlier, but then having rallied. He is thinking of the first crusade and then, more recently, Saladin's reconquest of Jerusalem. Joachim sees the latter as introducing a religious crisis within Christianity in which the faithful despair, concluding that God has given up on Christianity and is now channeling his support to Islam. Yet at other times he sees the despair as generated, not so much by a perception that God has turned his affections to the Muslims, as by the decision that belief in heavenly rewards is illusory and God has placed his stamp of approval on the search for worldly rewards. In either case, though, it is impelled by a despair that leads to questioning Christian values. And in either case, whatever the earthly manifestation, it should be recognized as the work of the Old Deceiver, described here as the Dragon, who moves behind the scenes and, when allowed, derails sacred history until God gets it back on the tracks again. But history is the stage on which we see this sacred drama played out and on which we perform in it as actors. Thus history, meaning the concrete events of both church history and secular history, is the subject of Joachim's intense interest. Thus his concern with popes, kings, and emperors. Joachim's God is very much a God who presides over the vast panorama of historical development, shaping it to his favored ends.

Nor is the drama over. Joachim foresees great battles yet to come before the final one described toward the end of Revelation. They all bear watching. This is Joachim's major contribution: he implores us to look carefully at current events, to read them in the context of a pattern that encompasses all of history. Thus, we have two missions: to discern the pattern in history and to apply it to our own time. This is his major contribution to thirteenth-century study of the Apocalypse and perhaps to ours as well.

At the end of the chapter on Richard of Saint Victor, I noted that, whereas John was a visionary, Richard was more a contemplative. One might be tempted to ask which of the two Joachim was. Here we encounter the difficulty with the question itself. Joachim's experience with Revelation 1:10 (which is included in the readings) would seem to mark him as a visionary; yet the very fact that the issue is Revelation 1:10 serves as a reminder that, if Joachim is to be considered a visionary at all, he must be a different kind than John. His vision in this case involves the interpretation of John's vision, which has taken its place within the canon of Scripture. Thus, along with the rest of Scripture, it both defines and limits what can be said in the future. Seen from this perspective, John is simply in a different league than Joachim.

But is this also too simplistic? In following chapters we will look at thirteenth-century Joachism from pseudo-Joachite writings through Olivi. Do we see a definable tradition carried through here? Or do we see several recognizably different sorts of Joachism developing?

At this point we must ask if we have robbed ourselves of an important aid in answering the question: Joachim's *figurae*. He is the only commentator studied here about whom this question can even be asked, the only one whose verbal exegesis comes accompanied by visual aids. His *figurae* were ignored here more for reasons of convenience than because they were considered unimportant. Rainini is the most recent scholar, though not the only one, to treat them as an important part of his theology. And it is worth remembering that he sees the *figurae* as suggesting at least a partial connection with Hugh of Saint Victor. This is not to say that Joachim brings us back to the Victorines. It is simply to say that our comparison between Joachim and one prominent Victorine in this chapter may be in itself too simplistic.

Preface

On the Seven Seals[27]

> *The notion of seven seals is important to Joachim, but he does not apply it only to the book of Revelation or even only to Christian history. In fact, he pays close attention to its value in interpreting Old Testament history. He begins by establishing that the Old Testament has one general history and four special ones. The general history is found from Genesis to Chronicles, while the special ones are Job, Tobias, Judith and Esther. Thus we have Ezekiel's wheel (Ezek 1).*
>
> *The New Testament too has four special histories (the Gospels) and one general history (Revelation). Thus we again have Ezekiel's wheel.*

The Old Testament from Abraham to Christ was bound with seven seals, because we read that seven spiritual battles, distinguished by time and figures, occurred. These signify ecclesiastical wars as well as spiritual battles and labors of the saints.

But it is pointless for us to seek to undo the seven seals unless we first explain what these seven seals sealing the book actually are. This book was sealed with seven seals; but there is something important here which should be pointed out. Five of them are uniform, but the sixth and seventh are dissimilar. Five are simple, while the sixth is double. The seventh is sabbatical (*sabbatizat*, sabbatizes). Thus in six seals some labor is designated. In six seals, therefore, there are six general wars from the time of Moses to the death of Esdras, which Malachi the prophet says occurred in six periods. These were written about by the prophets in the sacred books. The first of these battles was with the Egyptians, the second with the Canaanites, the third with the Syrians, the fourth with the Assyrians, and the fifth with the Chaldeans. The sixth, which we already have said to be double, was with the Assyrians and Macedonians. The sixth is contained in the book of Judith. The seventh pertains to the history of Esther. Holofernes was Assyrian, though, while Hamon the Agagite was from the Macedonian

---

27. *Expos.*, 2vb–4rb.

nation. Nevertheless, some people tentatively say that the history of Esdras was written before that of Esther. According to the opinion (not the assertion) of some there were two Artaxerses ruling one after the other, and this story took place in the time of the second, rather than the first, which was the time of Esdras. For Scripture clearly says Mordecai was among those captives transferred by Nebuchadnezzar, king of the Babylonians, with Jeconiah, the king of Judah. And according to the calculation of years from the migration into Babylon to the second Artaxerses, more than two hundred years would have passed, and it seems absurd that a man of two hundred would have been considered fit to serve in the king's palace and would have a young niece, his brother's daughter. Even if Mordecai had been a septuagenarian when his brother was born, and his brother was a septuagenarian when Esther was born, how could one describe her as a young girl when she was betrothed to the king? She would have to have been at least a sexagenarian. This is based on the historian Esdras, who was the last of those who wrote the true histories, by which I mean, not just any histories, but the authentic ones. For the books of the Maccabees are extracanonical.

Odd as such an opening might seem to a modern reader, Joachim continues in this vein for some time. He has to establish the importance of Old Testament history as early as possible, because his exegesis is predicated on a concordance between Old and New Testament history. They are like two trains moving on parallel tracks, but in different time frames. One train already has completed its journey and the other is just going through the sixth part of its trip. If the book of Revelation outlines the entire itinerary of that second train, it also clarifies the itinerary of the first. We know the significance of Old Testament history because we can read it in the context of New Testament history. But the reverse is true, too. Precisely because Old Testament history is complete, the fact that it moved in concordance with church history gives it a degree of predictive value. It supplements the knowledge we derive from reading the book of Revelation.

On the Concordance of the Two Testaments[28]

> *Here Joachim is mainly concerned with the* diffinitio omega, *but at times he comes close to echoing the* diffinitio alpha.

The first course of time began with Jacob the patriarch and was terminated with Christ. The second runs from Christ to the end of the world, when Christ will come in glory to pass judgment. The first was initiated in Abraham, though, and the second in Zechariah, John's father. But the New Testament is twinned, double as it were. Not only did the Son appear in flesh, but the Holy Spirit, designated by a dove and fire, was revealed to humankind. Not only was the Son sent that he might redeem the world, but also the Holy Spirit who proceeds from him, in order to complete what he had begun. This time, which is called the time of grace, is divided into two parts, and that is entirely necessary, for we see in the three ages the great works of the Lord distinguished by their properties. To all of this a threefold concordance should be assigned. First, we have the concordance of the two testaments. For the Son and Holy Spirit are not something more than the Father alone, nor is the Son alone something less. And thus there is a simple relation of the New Testament to the Old, and an equal relation of the second age to the first and the third to the second. Thus it is also that in the two testaments commemorated by Scripture, and in the works of the three ages, which are equally great in each, a simple likeness is recognized. In the first distinction the concordance is to be assigned in this way: the time of the first seal runs from the patriarch Jacob to Moses and Joshua; the time of the second from Moses and Joshua to Samuel and David; the time of the third from Samuel and David to Elijah and Elisha; the time of the fourth from Elijah and Elisha to Isaiah and Ezekiel; the time of the fifth from Isaiah and Ezekiel to the Babylonian exile; the time of the sixth from the Babylonian exile to the death of Esther or the prophet Malachi; and the time of the seventh from the death of Malachi to Zechariah the father of John the Baptist. So much for the Old Testament. In the New Testament it is as follows: the opening of the first seal goes from John's father Zechariah—but more from the Lord's resurrection—to the death of Saint John the evangelist. The opening of the second is from that time to the emperor Constantine. The opening of the third is from then to Justinian. The opening of the fourth is from then to Charles. The opening of the fifth is from then to the present days in which, the opening

---

28. *Expos.*, 6rb–7vb.

of the sixth seal having begun, the new Babylon is to be struck, as is shown in the prophets and as this book of the Apocalypse clearly demonstrates, although not until the fifth is consummated. When the opening of the sixth seal is completed, there will be a holy Sabbath of the Lord. The apostle says of this, "A Sabbath remains for God's people" (Heb 4:9), until the Lord comes in final judgment, with Elijah preceding him as John the Baptist once did. For laborers come before the Sabbath and struggle before they rest. Thus the wars of the Israelites should be mentioned in connection with the first series, and the wars of the church in connection with the second. The former were fought for the faith of the one God who is creator of all things, while the faithful are read to have waged the latter for the name of Christ, who is true and one with God the Father, through whom all things are made.

In order to weigh accurately the similarities between the wars waged in the two testaments, we should know that the Savior speaks truly when he says, "My father works up to now, and I work" (John 5:17). In the time of the first seal Israel had a conflict with Egypt, who inflicted many griefs upon them and kept them fettered with the chains of servitude, so that they were not allowed to fulfill the Lord's commands in the desert, nor were they allowed to cease from the brick-making duties imposed on them. And in the time of the opening of the first seal under which, the Old Testament having been ended in the fathers, the new one began, a new and spiritual Israel arose for the fathers, and it entered into a spiritual struggle with the new Egyptians, the Jews. And there came a new Moses, a faithful bearer of the law and prophets, the Lord of all. Just as, in a certain way, the sons of Israel remained silent in that first conflict while Moses, the servant of the Lord, struggled and was victorious, so, in this one, the elect remained quiet (who, oppressed by the burden of the law and the letter, were engaged in unnecessary labor), while Christ Jesus alone fought and conquered, extending his strong hand and snatching them away from superstition concerning the letter and servitude to the law.

> There follows an elaboration of concordances within the first seal, including one between the twelve sons of Jacob and Christ's twelve disciples, as well as one between Moses and Aaron on the one hand and Paul and Barnabas on the other. Eventually Joachim returns to his enumeration of the seals.

While the battle with the Egyptians pertains to the first seal, that with the Canaanites pertains to the second; yet the latter was not held off until the beginning of its period. Instead, the second battle was begun while the first period still remained. This is something one can observe in other seals as well. And thus in the time of the second seal the battle with the Canaanites took place, and in the same way, in the church of Christ, in the period of the second seal the struggle with the pagans took place, but it was begun during the opening of the first seal and consummated in the days when the second seal was opened.

In the period of the third seal, there was a split between Judah and Israel, and various errors sprang up in each kingdom (though more in the tribes of Israel), causing them to fight longer among themselves. And there were wars with other peoples.

In the period of the fourth seal, the battles involving the Syrians were followed by those involving the Assyrians; and, just so, in the period of the fourth opening in the church of Christ, the wars involving the Persians were followed by those involving the Muslims, the cruel savagery of whom endures into the present period.

In the period of the fifth seal, some battles with the Egyptians still went on, and some storms from the Assyrians still affected the tribe of Judah, but these were followed by the attack of the Chaldeans, through which the kingdom of Judah was scattered.

> *Joachim goes on to mention the previous defeat and exile of Israel at the hands of the Assyrians, then draw a concordance between the ten uprooted tribes of Israel and the Byzantines, both of which have, on the whole, wandered away from the faith (although Joachim is willing to say of the eastern church, as Elijah—speaking for God— says of Israel, "I shall leave for myself seven thousand who have not bowed the knee to Baal" (1 Kgs 19:18). The other half of the simile involves Judah and the western church.*

It was not thus with Judah. Although it suffered exile for its sins, even in Babylon it was not deprived of the comfort of its prophets. When seventy years were over and Babylon and its king were struck, then with the aid of Cyrus, king of the Persians, Judah was restored to the land from which it had been exiled. Soon it restored the altar and began to rebuild the temple. Due to the troubled times, it restored the walls of the city since other powers in the area were threatening and its enemies were attacking.

> *At this point, Joachim is concerned that the reader might remember the role played in all this by the Hellenistic successor states that came*

into being with the collapse of the Macedonian Empire and might thus be tempted to draw a false concordance.

Nor should we be led astray by the fact that a Greek empire remains to this day. Just as the Roman Empire is assimilated to that of the Chaldeans, so that of Constantinople is to that of the later Egyptians, because Samaria and Egypt are contained in spirit in the kingdom of the Greeks, while Jerusalem and Babylon are contained in the kingdom of the Latins. So in the fifth time the kings of Egypt and Babylon, who sometimes seemed to be friendly with the kings of Judah, afflicted them more sorely than did any of the other gentiles. In the same way, in the fifth time of the church, and especially in the days of Henry the first German emperor, the worldly princes, who were said to be Christian and who at first seemed to venerate the clergy, turned out to be worse than the gentiles who did not know God. They sought to deprive the church of its freedom and are known to have done so insofar as they were able.

Joachim assures us, however, that God will exercise justice upon those who oppress his people.

In the period of the sixth seal, the Medes were let out of their prisons to strike the Chaldeans, and through them the pride of Babylon, which had risen to the heavens, was brought low and the humility of Jerusalem raised on high. For as we read in the book of Ezra and at the end of the book of Kings, in the first year of Cyrus's reign his contemporary Darius the Mede struck at Belshazzar and his kingdom, and we read that he was the first of the Medes to rule in Babylon. He ordered that an edict be written to his entire kingdom stating that anyone in it who was of the seed of the Jews and wanted to return to the land of Judah to restore God's house should be allowed to go there freely and securely.

Joachim continues to outline what and who is involved in the period of the sixth Old Testament seal, carrying the story through the time of the Hellenistic rulers. When he turns to the ecclesiastical side of the equation, however, he is largely unspecific, preferring to speak in the terms given him by the Apocalypse (especially Rev 17) and Daniel 7, although he does tell us that "the beast ascending from the abyss" designates some particular kingdom of pagans allied with that other beast ascending from the earth, which John names as the pseudo-prophets, and that "the many kings who will be seduced by

*them will join together and persecute the church, as will be described
more clearly in the sixth chapter of the fifth part of this work." Moreover, he suggests that, just as in the period of the sixth seal in the Old
Testament we see Babylon being attacked once and the sons of Israel
being persecuted twice, so in the sixth period of the church the new
Babylon will be destroyed by foreign armies, but God's people will
be afflicted by two forces, one of which will strike soon and the other
not long after. Then he offers a terse finale:*

After King Antiochus, the Old Testament was at an end. So after the
arrival of Gog, the world will come to an end. So much for the concordance
involving the two testaments.

On the Three Ages of the World[29]

*Joachim needs to supply one more basic piece of information before
he can begin to interpret the Apocalypse. He must also prepare us
for the threefold division of history, the* diffinitio alpha. *We are rear-
ranging his text slightly at this point, since he actually begins on the
three ages before he arrives at the two-part concordance.*

The first of the three ages concerning which we speak was during the time of
the law, when the Lord's people were still little servants, unable to attain the
freedom of the Spirit until he should come who says, "If the Son shall have
freed you, you will be truly free" (John 8:36). The second age was under the
gospel and remains, up to now, in freedom as compared with the past but
not compared with the future. For the apostle says, "Now we know in part
and prophesy in part, but when that which is perfect comes that which is in
part will pass away" (1 Cor 13:9–10). And in another place he says, "The Lord
is spirit, and where the spirit of the Lord is, there is freedom" (2 Cor 3:17).

The third age will come, therefore, around the end of the world, not
under the veil of the letter but in full freedom of the Spirit, when the pseudo-
gospel of the Son of Perdition and his prophets is destroyed and those who
teach justice to the many will be like the splendor of the firmament, like
stars in perpetual eternities. The first age, which flourished under the law
and circumcision, began with Adam. The second, which flourished under

29. *Expos.,* 5rb–va.

the gospel, began with Osia. The third, insofar as it can be estimated by the number of generations, is said to have begun in the time of Saint Benedict, but its preeminent excellence should be expected from the time Elijah is revealed and the unbelieving Jewish people is converted to the Lord, so that in it the Holy Spirit should seem to cry with its voice in Scripture, "Until now the Father and Son have worked, and now I work" (cf. John 5:17). For as the letter of the prior testament, with a certain quality of similitude, seems to pertain to the Father, and the letter of the New Testament to the Son, so the spiritual understanding proceeding from each pertains to the Holy Spirit. Furthermore, just as the order of married people, which flourished in the first age, seems to pertain to the Father by the property of similitude, and the order of preachers, which flourished in the second, seems to pertain to the Son, so the order of monks, to whom the final times are assigned, seems to pertain to the Holy Spirit. And according to all this the first age is ascribed to the Father, the second to the Son, and the third to the Holy Spirit, although in another way it should be said that there is one age of the world as well as one elect people, and the Father, Son, and Holy Spirit are all simultaneous. Nor should all this be considered contrary to the authority of the fathers when they speak of a time before the law, a time under the law, and a time under grace, for that in its own way was considered necessary, and so is this. For if we accept both, a three-age assignment of times is to be added: the time under the letter of the gospel, the time under the spiritual understanding, and the time of manifest vision of the Lord. That gives us five times in all, although it is abusing the word "time" rather than using it in its proper sense when we apply it to what goes on in heaven. Nevertheless, if we do speak of eternity as a time, we have, first, the time before the law, second that under the law, third that under the gospel, fourth that under spiritual understanding, and fifth that involving manifest vision of God. For it belongs to God's elect to go from virtue to virtue, from clarity to clarity, until the God of Gods is seen in Zion: from natural law to the law of Moses; from the law of Moses to the gospel; from the gospel of Christ to spiritual understanding; from spiritual understanding to true and eternal contemplation of God. In a marvelous way we find the sacred mystery of the Trinity bound up in and signified by these five distinctions, so that it remains in its integrity without compromising the mystery of unity.

Joachim proceeds to demonstrate how this is so, first using the relationship of the patriarchs Abraham, Isaac, Jacob, Joseph, and Ephraim as a scale model, then applying it to the larger picture.

The twofold and threefold divisions of history, along with the con-cordances they engender, might seem tangential to Joachim's exegesis of the Apocalypse, but by laying them out in the preface he is reveal-ing the superstructure on which the entire commentary is erected. This complex series of relationships is, indeed, what the commentary is about, and in calling it to his readers' attention Joachim is telling them precisely what they need to know if they are to make sense of what follows. No prologue to a work of medieval exegesis is more important than this one.

One might imagine that Joachim has now cleared the way for a chapter-by-chapter exegesis, but he is still embroiled in introductory matters. He turns to the question of Antichrist and his minions. We will see that he covers much of the same territory in expositing Rev-elation 13, but he says some things here that he will not say again at that point, and some of what he says here was echoed so regularly by thirteenth-century exegetes that it is worthwhile for us to pay some attention to it.

On Antichrist and the Heads and Members of the Dragon[30]

Since it is clear to all that there are now many antichrists, we must ask who that one is of whom the apostle says, "Until the rebellion occurs and the son of perdition is revealed. He will oppose and will exalt himself over every-thing that is called God or is worshiped, so that he sets himself up in God's temple, displaying himself as if he were God" (2 Thess 2:3). And when will this be revealed? But we can show this better (insofar as we can do such) if we interject that passage from the Apocalypse, "A great sign appeared in heaven, a red dragon with seven heads and ten horns, and his tail swept a third of the stars from the sky, casting them to earth" (Rev 12:3–4).

This dragon is the devil. His body is made up of all the reprobate. His heads are those who rule among the reprobate and who are the leading, most accomplished evildoers among them. The first head through which the dragon discharged his venom was Herod, who, when Christ was born, sought to devour him and, when he was unable to do so, slaughtered the innocents. Along with him are to be grouped all the kings of the land of the Jews, who succeeded him both in rule and in the persecution of Christ.

30. *Expos.*, 10ra–11ra.

The second head was Nero, killer of the principal apostles. And along with him should be included all his successors who, up to the reign of Julian the Apostate, persecuted the church of God. The third head of the dragon was Constantius the Arian, who, along with his successors (in perfidy, I mean, not in reign), afflicted the church down to the time of the Saracens.

The fourth head of the dragon was Cosdroes, king of the Persians, whose kingdom was, after a few years, given over into the hands of the Saracens and the sect of Mohammed established in it. (The latter was begun in the time of Cosdroes himself in Arabia.) The fifth head of the dragon was one of the recent kings of Babylon who, wishing to sit on the mountain of testament and appear like the Most High, launched many persecutions against the church. The sixth head of that dragon is that one of whom Daniel says, "Another king will rise up after them, and he will be stronger than the earlier ones" (Dan 7:24), although the sixth head should, I think, be taken as beginning from that king of the Turks named Saladin, who, as a result of our sins, not long ago began to trample on the holy city and on the necks of Christians. What John says in the sixth part—"And there are seven kings; five died, one is, and one has not yet come" (Rev 17:10)—should be taken as if it were spoken in reference to us in the sixth period, because undoubtedly this was meant to be revealed to those in the sixth period. And only in the sixth period, and in the sixth part of his book, did the angel speak to Daniel, teaching him about the mystery of that beast with ten horns. And only in the sixth period and in the sixth part of the book did the angel speak to the blessed John, teaching him in a similar way about the mystery of the beast with ten horns, in order that they should consider the matter, understand it, and reconsider it in similar manner. It is given to those represented by Daniel and John, men dedicated to God and preeminent in chastity, to know in this sixth period the mysteries of the kingdom of God and to know the sacrament that existed from ancient days but was hidden from generations of humankind until the present.

Whether this Saladin is the person written about in the book of the prophet Daniel or Daniel was writing about another to come after him, in either case all of this is to be applied to the sixth king of which John says, "one is," for it is possible that all of this will be completed under this one, but it is also possible that under the name of the sixth king another will come along after the present one, and in him will be fulfilled what is written concerning the eleventh king, who, "when he has humbled three kings, will speak against the Most High, thinking he can change times and laws, and they will be given over into his hand for time, times and half a time" (Dan

7:24–25). Nevertheless, the seventh king, of which it is said, "He has not yet come," is the one concerning whom it is said in Daniel's sixth vision, "There will arise a king with an impudent face and deep knowledge, and he shall be strengthened, but not through his own powers" (Dan 8:23–24), and he will, we can believe, destroy all. This is the seventh head of the dragon and seems to be the one of whom the apostle says, "He will oppose and will exalt himself over everything that is called God or is worshiped, so that he sets himself up in God's temple, displaying himself as if he were God" (2 Thess 2:3). This is that great tyrant who will do much evil in the world, although there will be another designated by the tail. Thus in a marvelous way another is to come in the spirit of another, just as John was to come in the spirit of Elijah. It is, indeed, as if one prophet had been promised by the Lord through the prophet, saying, "Behold, I will send you Elijah the prophet" (Mal 4:5), and nevertheless we knew two Elijahs would be sent to us by the Lord, one of whom now comes and the other of whom is to come. And it is as if the holy men had spoken of one great tyrant, and nevertheless two were to come toward the end, one of which is the man of iniquity and greatest enemy of the Christian faith, he of whom John says, "One has not yet come, and when he comes, it is necessary that he remain only a brief time" (Rev 17:10), and the other of whom is the one called "Gog" (Rev 20:8).

Nor should it be surprising that the devil will attempt to fool human-kind with two wicked men, for there is nothing under heaven he likes more than to do the opposite of God. Thus whereas the Lord placed Adam in Paradise, the devil (with the permission of the just God) took King Herod as his own. In place of Noah, the just man, he placed that most impure man Nero in the city of Rome. For the faithful Abraham he produced Constantinus the Arian. For Moses, the legislator, Muhammad the inventor of an iniquitous and spurious law. For David, the king of Jerusalem, he offered the king of Babylon. For John the Baptist, that eleventh king of whom Daniel the prophet writes. And in place of Elijah, who is to come, he will send that seventh king of which it is said in this book, "And one has not yet come, and when he comes, he must remain only a short time."

Whether the devil will speak more especially through one of these or through someone else is, however, uncertain. Whoever that great Antichrist will be, however, he will come secretly with false signs and prodigies, just as Christ did with true ones, and he will deceive an infinite multitude of Jews and gentiles, so that there will be few who escape his evil trickery. But just as Christ Jesus is called king, pontiff, and prophet, so he will pretend to be now prophet, now pontiff, now Christ the king. So great will be the signs he performs that, although they are actually all false and full of lies, the signs performed by Christ will be deemed nothing in comparison with his. And the devil will do all this, either through that seventh king who is to come after the sixth, or through someone else whom he takes as his own.

Because the Lord is still to come in the glory of his Father, and all his saints with him, the devil will also depart for the peoples at the four corners of the earth, and he will suddenly appear with them as if he is to judge the world, so that he can pretend to be he who is to come to judge the living and dead and the world by fire. Thus many believe he will be that last tyrant called "Gog," but one might perhaps also say this Antichrist will not be Gog but rather a certain prince in the army of that king, whom the devil will inhabit.[31] After doing many evil things through pseudo-Christs and pseudo-prophets, he will openly come forth (totally possessed by the Man of Sin) and seduce Gog and his army into persecuting the church. That is what John seems to expect when he says, "And he will seduce the peoples at the four corners of the earth, Gog and Magog" (Rev 20:8).

It is not against the faith to believe that perhaps the devil himself, having assumed the body of a man, will first work in hidden fashion through sons of unbelief, sending kings of the earth and pseudo-prophets to deceive even the elect if he can manage to do so, but these will be defeated and he will not succeed because the power of Christ will be too great for him. He will then retreat to barbarian nations, remaining imprisoned among them for some days or years while the church of God enjoys a rest and Sabbath. After that peace, he will lead with him Gog and his army, whom he has seduced, and do all the evil written in the book of Ezekiel the prophet. However this occurs, this tribulation will come at the end, like the tail of the dragon, for the heads will by that point be destroyed in their own times.

On Recapitulation in the Apocalypse[32]

In six of its parts, this book extends to the third age so that, beginning with the Lord's resurrection, it proceeds to its end, then returns again and again to its beginning. In each of five parts there is recapitulation, and to the end of the second age it is directed into individual treatments of that age. These recapitulations are to be taken, not according to the whole, but according

---

31. Literally *induet*. The devil will put him on like a suit of clothes.
32. *Expos.*, 15vb–16ra.

to part. Thus each of the single parts refers generally to all the times of the second age, but each of the single parts is also especially and more properly related to a specific part or order. That is, the first is related especially to the first, the second to the second, etc. Hence, although in the final parts there are some elements that involve recapitulation, we attribute recapitulation more particularly to the first five parts, for it is there that it is more manifest. Six parts relate in common to laborious struggle, while the seventh part is distinct and separate from the other six, although the number of years of Satan's incarceration seems to pertain partly to the second age. For he is not incarcerated all at once, but rather the heads of the dragon are weakened one by one in each of the five periods of the second age, and in the sixth period two are weakened, in order that, having none left by which to exercise his powers, he is forced to remain incarcerated without any hope of working his evil until the end of history, which will be the time of the tail. And in this sense the thousand years seems to designate the entire time from the Lord's resurrection to the time of Gog, not because it will be precisely a thousand years but because that figure represents a great many years.

On the Eight Parts of the Book of the Apocalypse[33]

We said above that there are seven parts of the book and the same number of periods from the coming of our savior to final judgment. In the first part the topic is those prelates who took on the first war in that time. In the second it is the martyrs, in the third the doctors, in the fourth the virgins. The fifth part deals with the general church and the conflict between four orders and the four special beasts which the prophet Daniel says he saw in a vision, that church which is the new Jerusalem versus the most impious Babylon. That new Babylon, as it is shown in the sixth part of the book, is to be judged in the sixth period, and afterward the beast and pseudo-prophet—who, as we have said, will rise up more audaciously than usual against Christ in that same sixth period—will also be judged.

After that, the devil will be incarcerated, and the people of God will enjoy a Sabbath, but around the end of that Sabbath the devil will be released from his prison and will seduce the peoples at the four corners of the earth, Gog and Magog. At the end the devil will placed in a lake of fire. The universal judgment of the living and dead will take place.

33. *Expos.*, 16ra–rb.

Once that is completed, there will be no more worldly time, but only one eternal day. Nor will earthly kings reign anymore, but only the one king, the Lord of Armies. Nor will there be any longer cities of various nations, but only the city of God, our mother Jerusalem, the glory of which is pursued in the eighth part, as is shown where John is invited to contemplate its glory. The invitation comes from one of the seven angels with seven vials of God's wrath. John says, "One of the seven angels with seven vials filled with the seven new plagues came and spoke with me, saying, 'Come and I will show you the bride, the wife of the Lamb.' And he transported me in the spirit onto a great, high mountain and showed me the holy city Jerusalem descending out of heaven from God, having the splendor of God" (Rev 21:9–11), and all the rest that follows there.

Revelation 1:10 and a Personal Revelation[34]

In the process of interpreting Revelation 1:10, "I was in the spirit on the Lord's day," Joachim offers an autobiographical note that bases his exegesis of the entire book on a purported personal revelation.

When I had gone through the preceding verses of this book and arrived at this place, I experienced so much difficulty and felt my understanding was constrained so much more than usual that, feeling as if I was being shut out by the stone blocking the entrance to the tomb, my mind remained darkened and, giving honor to God who closes and opens as he wishes, I left the passage unexplained, went on to what follows, and reserved that particular difficulty for the universal master, in order that he who opened the book and loosened its seven seals might, if he pleased, open it to me or to others. Occupation with other matters kept me from thinking about this passage. Then, a year later, Easter having come around, at the hour of matins, having awakened from sleep and begun to meditate on this book, by God's gift I was made confident and found myself bolder when it came to writing. Indeed, I found myself more timid about remaining silent and not writing, lest if I remained silent the judge should say to me, "You bad and lazy servant, you knew I reap where I did not sow and gather where I did not scatter. Therefore there was all the more reason to deposit my money with bankers so that on returning I might receive back what is mine with interest" (Matt

34. *Expos.*, 39rb–vb.

25:26–27). And since at that point I understood some things but still did not know other, greater mysteries, it was as if a battle were going on in my mind, with those things that were clear enjoining me to be bold while the others threatened difficulty.

And, on that night, something like this happened. Around the middle of the night's silence, I think, at the hour when our lion of the tribe of Judah is thought to have risen from the dead, as I was meditating, suddenly something of the fullness of this book and of the concord of the Old and New Testaments was revealed to me with a certain clarity of understanding in my mind's eye. Nor was I remembering the above-mentioned verse at the time, why, that is, John should have said, "I was in the spirit on the Lord's day," and whether it might be pertinent to this matter that the revelation of this book is said to have been made on the Lord's day. This, I say, did not occur to me; nor did it occur to me that Christ leaving the tomb signified the spirit which is to proceed from the letter; or that the seven days of Easter week, along with the eighth day following, are concordant with the parts of this book in mysteries; or that on the same day he opened the meaning to his disciples so that they would understand the Scriptures.

When, therefore, after some time, I had the opportunity to go again through the little bit that I had done earlier, and I came to the passage where it is said, "I was in the spirit on the Lord's day," I understood for the first time what John's words, "I was in the spirit on the Lord's day," meant to say as far as mysteries are concerned. Upon thinking through what occurred and what I had written about that day, it became clear that henceforth the spirit began to be raised up from the letter, and much else, too much else to be contained in this passage.

"This is the day the Lord has made, let us rejoice and be glad in it" (Ps 117:24). This is the day in which Christ rose from the dead, that great stone having been removed from the door of the tomb. This is the day in which he opened the meaning to his disciples so that they might understand the Scriptures. The eight days in which the Easter festivities are so solemnly celebrated by the whole church conform in meaning to the eight parts of this book.

Joachim has just presented us with an excellent example of one type of concordia, *this one between the resurrection story in John and Revelation 1:10 as Joachim interprets it, or, better, all of Revelation, its eight parts correlated with the eight days of Easter. The stone sealing Christ's grave is the hermeneutical blockage that has kept Joachim from understanding the passage. Its removal symbolizes*

the transition from literal to spiritual understanding. That Joachim
sees John as author of both the eponymous gospel and Revelation is
significant, though not crucial.

On Revelation 1:20, concerning the Seven Churches[35]

What is said here concerning the meaning of the stars is not meant to be an allegorical interpretation, but rather an introduction of mystical eloquence and, as it were, the explanation of a vision having the integrity of an allegorical explanation of truth concerning hidden things. For example, Joseph, interpreting the pharaoh's dream, said the seven meager ears of grain devouring the seven fat ones, as well as the seven meager cows eating the seven fat ones, meant that seven years of sterility would consume seven of fertility. Here the interpretation of this passage is not to be considered allegorical, but rather the dream itself was allegorical, and that is how Joseph explained it. For the first seven years designate seven ages of the Hebrews in this book in which seven seals of the book are consummated and the grains of sacred words are collected in heaps. The seven sterile years are seven periods of church history to which specific parts of this book are dedicated, except that the sixth part contains two within this one part. Because the seventh part is excluded from this law, it covers only the first six parts. It is similar to the way Rachel corresponds to Leah.

Revelation 7[36]

And I saw another angel ascending from the rising of the sun, having the sign of the living God. And he cried with a loud voice to the four angels to whom it was given to hurt the earth and the sea, saying: Hurt not the earth nor the sea nor the trees, till we sign the servants of our God in their foreheads (Rev 7:2–3). Is this angel Christ, who ascended from the rising of the sun when he rose from the dead, and who is so worthy to bear the name of the living God, he who alone in his deity is life and the author of life, the great clamor of whom is clear and open preaching and whose prohibition demonstrates the authority of his power? Or should this angel be interpreted

---

35. *Expos.*, 48ra.
36. *Expos.*, 120va–vb.

as a Roman pontiff since his ascent in the spirit seems to refer to Zerubbabel of Babylon under whom the Lord's temple was rebuilt? If the latter, then it is nonetheless Christ who conquered and triumphed in these actions.

Revelation 13[37]

And he stood upon the shore of the sea. And I saw a beast coming up out the sea, having seven heads and ten horns: and upon his horns, ten diadems (Rev 12:18–13:1). The shore of the sea is sterile. It is sometimes flooded by the sea, and sometimes burned by the heat of the sun. It signifies those people who are halfway between. They do not seem to be entirely infidel, but neither do they adhere piously to the entire purity of the Christian faith. The devil stands on this group as he watches the beast ascending from the sea, for false Christians who withdraw from the breast of mother church, concurring with the devil and his displays, offer infidels an example of their depravity with which they infect the church, and thus the infidels are all the more strongly incited to persecute the Christian church. The devil, in his depraved shrewdness, sees this. To take only a few of the many possible examples, the Jews would hardly have found an opportunity to capture Christ had one of the disciples, into whom the devil had entered, not betrayed him. Again, the emperor Nero would hardly have bothered the apostles had that treacherous Simon not forced him into action against them. Again, Constantinus the Arian would hardly have taken up arms against the pious Christians had impious bishops not provoked him to such presumption. Thus the devil stands on the shore and sees the beast arising from the sea. For when he is seen to reign in these reprobate Christians, there can be no doubt in his mind that he can count on the aid of many infidels to aid him in his battle against Christ.

Note that the prophet Daniel represents the thing signified by this beast with his four beasts; and, although we already have mentioned these matters in this work, we must nevertheless say something about them here as well. "Four winds," he says, "the four winds of the heavens, strove upon the great sea, and behold, four great beasts, different one from another, came up out of the sea" (Dan 7:2). In this book, the heavens often signify the church or holy Scripture. There is no doubt that the sea signifies the world. The four winds are the four special meanings of the four gospels. The first of these special

37. *Expos.*, 162rb–168vb.

meanings is the typical, the second the historical, the third the moral, and the fourth the contemplative. The first is especially suited to pastors, the second to deacons, the third to doctors, and the fourth to virgins and hermits. Why? Because the first teaches ecclesiastical events recorded through the writings and actions of the fathers, and through these things pastors prove that the church's confession of faith is true. The second is what the faithful, babes in Christ, receive through example as if nursing. The third demands that one be a perfect disciple progressing toward higher things. For this one instructs in morality, forms actions, and reveals the deceptions of vices that sometimes mask themselves as virtues. It shows, too, how the virtues can be defeated by vices. It illustrates all these things through fitting examples taken from the past, in order that we may understand what happens to us daily in the spirit by hearing what has been done in the flesh, and so that we can try all the harder to trample down the vices and vigilantly work at the virtues. Thus we understand it was not in vain that the Spirit of the omnipotent God decided to ordain this sense just for the salvation of humankind.

The fourth meaning, called the contemplative, takes flight like an eagle (to use an image from earthly matters) and deals with celestial things. It is this meaning which most teaches us to despise worldly things and love heavenly things, to have contempt for the temporal and seek the eternal. These are the four spiritual meanings which, like the four rivers of Paradise, water the hearts of those who have faith in God. Because, however, contrary powers hide in this world and stir it up like the winds of heaven stirring up the roiling waters, thus the four winds of the heavens do battle in the great sea. For the world battles the four special meanings through which men learn to despise earthly things. Ezekiel the prophet writes about the four meanings and the four animals: Where the spirit moved them, there they went, nor did they turn back when they moved (Ezek 1:9).

But in what way did these four winds of heaven do battle in the great sea? In what way did they *not* do battle, they who stirred up the entire world? The sea is stirred up when the heavens produce winds. The world is also stirred up when the saints preach God's word, because such preaching is contrary to the world's works and aspirations. And there are four evangelists who wrote the gospels, as well as four orders of preachers (as I have said) who depend on these four meanings: the apostles, martyrs, confessors, and virgins.

But perhaps virgins and hermits do not preach God's word, because (as some say) they are dead to the world. Yet I say they do preach, and they preach well because what they proclaim with their voices they demonstrate with their behavior. But in order to move on to other matters, let us simply say that they do preach at least to themselves and their disciples, sacred legions of which, waxing healthy in their monasteries, have filled the world.

Therefore, four orders are designated by four animals, from the mouths of which, out of the secret places of the heavens, come forth spirits of wind, as it were, which battle to collect together the schools of fish in the sea of this world. But it occurs to those so engaged that not only do they catch and remove many fish, but also great beasts emerge and devour many of the fish they have taken. The first beast is the synagogue of the Jews, the second that of the pagans, the third that of the Arians, and the fourth that of the Muslims. When the apostles, the order identified with the lion, was breathed forth, the lion of the Jewish people went forth first to counter them. When the evangelists, also called deacons, were breathed forth, especially those holy deacons the martyrs, who were obedient unto death, the bear of the pagan people came forth against them. When the doctors, also called confessors, were breathed forth, the leopard of the Arian sect came forth against them. When the hermits were breathed forth, there came forth against them a beast different from the others, from the savage Saracen people. Daniel says, "The first beast was similar to a lion" (Dan 7:4). John tells us what he saw when he says of that beast, "Its mouth was like that of a lion" (13:2). And what Daniel says, "The second beast looked like a bear" (7:5), John echoes in what he says, "And its feet were like a bear's feet." And what Daniel offers, "The third beast was similar to a leopard" (7:6), is also suggested by what John says, "And the beast that I saw was similar to a leopard." And what Daniel says, "And behold, a fourth beast, terrifying, horrible, and of extraordinary strength," to which he later adds, "It had ten horns" (7:7–8), etc., John reflects in speaking of the ten horns and of the head that seemed mortally wounded but was revived from death. One beast seen by John is described by him as having seven heads, and one of the beasts Daniel saw he describes as having four heads, while the four beasts seen by Daniel had a total of seven heads, because the third beast is said to have four heads.

But we will understand these matters better if we touch summarily on them, exposing whatever does not seem too tedious to repeat. The sea or abyss represents the present world and, along with the earth, the infidel people. From this world or infidel people have emerged at various times diverse sects who have persecuted the church with bestial ferocity. The first of these, similar to a lion, was the Jewish synagogue. The two wings bearing it aloft, swollen with pride, were doubtless two sects of the Jewish people who labored for its advancement, the Sadducees and the Pharisees. These two wings were, however, quickly clipped from the lion, and the beast was given over to the Roman army. Soon these two sects, and whatever others there might have been, perished. Thus it makes sense that the text adds, "And it stood on the ground like a man" (Dan 7:4). For earlier, as if it were not part of the sinful human mass, it scorned the gentiles. Once given over to the power of the Romans, though, it was shown to be of the same nature and to share the same misery as other human beings. It was chastised horribly and still has not been recalled to the faith of God. Thus the passage goes on to say, "And a human heart was given to it" (Dan 7:4). It has not been consummated down to the present day because up to now it still has not been granted to it to know him who suffered for its salvation and for that of the entire world. Unless perhaps this is said ironically: its heart is hard because it was always hard-hearted and stiff-necked, with an unconquerable heart.

The second beast similar to a bear was the vast multitude of pagans, then stretched out over the world. Nor is it unfitting that what is said to it is, "Up, devour much flesh" (Dan 7:5), for an infinite number of the saints were killed by the pagans, as the psalmist predicted long before, saying, "O God, the nations have come into your inheritance, they have defiled your holy temple, they have laid Jerusalem in ruins, they have given the bodies of your servants as food for the birds of heaven and the flesh of your faithful ones to the beasts of the earth; they have poured out their blood like water round about Jerusalem, and there is no one to bury them" (Ps 79:1-3). And shortly thereafter, "Pour out your wrath on the nations that acknowledge you not, on the kingdoms that call not upon your name. For they have devoured Jacob and laid waste his dwelling" (Ps 79:6-7). Thus it is said to this beast, "Up, devour much flesh," just as the psalmist says, "For they have devoured Jacob and laid waste his dwelling." I believe that the three rows of teeth it had in its mouth stand for the tyrants, priests of the temples, and worshipers of idols, who proceeded against the saints with greater zeal than others.

The third beast similar to a leopard refers to the multitude of Arians. This beast is described as having four heads because four peoples joined together in this heresy: the Greeks (from whom it began), Goths, Vandals, and Lombards. The third beast is described as having four heads because the four above-mentioned peoples joined together in persecuting the church during the third course of time. They were joined together not in body but in malediction. And this beast is rightly likened to a leopard, which is a mixture of white and black, because some Arians were pagans and converted to Arianism from paganism, while others were unfaithful Christians, but all were unified in persecuting catholics. They had four wings like birds, because ecclesiastical history tells us that the Arians, Macedonians, and Eunomians all were of different opinion on Christ and the Holy Spirit, and the Eutychians, who were contemporary with the Arians, blasphemed in a still different way about Christ, adding yet more pain to the wounds of the church. Thus, by order of the emperor Constantine, Pope Martin died in exile.

They erred in four ways concerning the Son and Holy Spirit, but they are all called by the name of Arius, because he was first of the four who dared raise his mouth to heaven and tell whatever lies he wished about Christ's ineffable nature, so that he and his followers began to stray from the way of truth that is Christ, and as a result several heresies espousing various errors were ushered in. Thus this third beast, divided by four heads and wings, lacerated the catholic church.

These three beasts were succeeded by the fourth one, who exceeded the others in bestial savagery. This beast was, Daniel says, "terrifying, horrible, and of extraordinary strength. It had great iron teeth with which it devoured and crushed, and what was left it trampled with its feet" (7:7). It was dissimilar to the other beasts seen earlier, and it had ten horns. Later Daniel says, "I approached one of those present and asked him what all this meant in truth. He said to me, 'These four great beasts stand for four kingdoms which shall arise on the earth. But the holy ones of the Most High shall receive the kingship'" (7:16–17). If we study the ecclesiastical histories diligently we will note that the Arian persecution was moderated and in some places abolished with the reign of Cosdroes, king of the Persians, who preceded Muhammad and his followers in his persecution in the east. The persecution of this sect is so monstrous as to be considered not one of men but of some terrible beast, especially since its error does not seem to be fortified by any human argument, but to be defended only by the madness of detestable untruth and the tyrannical power of arms. The way it quickly gained strength and advanced in its malice, undoubtedly due to sin, is witnessed by the desolation of the churches in Syria, Phoenicia, Palestine, and Egypt, as well as Africa and the isles of the sea, in which Christ's name has been abolished and the detestable teachings of Muhammad are preached as if they were those of a great prophet of the Lord and herald of the Most High. Alas if Antichrist performs such evils as this one through his falsehoods! Just as Moses, giver of the law long before Christ, led the way for Christ, so this giver of lies has prepared the way for Antichrist.

But lest the savagery of this beast should seem similar to that of the other beasts, the Jews fought against the faith of Christ; yet despite their opposition the churches of Jerusalem were built, and after not all that many days the Jews were swallowed up by the Romans. From that time on they persecuted the churches no more. The pagans too battled against Christ but were daily defeated by his warriors, so that in the days of Pope Sylvester they practically gave up their arms and turned the imperial scepter over to the vicar of Christ. The Goths, Vandals, Lombards, and other Arian heretics were partly wiped out by the Roman army and partly converted to the catholic faith. But this fourth beast was so indomitable that it is easier to fear than to explain how, although it appeared at times humiliated and almost dead, it again became great and ready to devour others. This, then, is that beast that Daniel called extremely terrifying. John included it and the other three when he spoke of one beast with seven heads, on one of which were ten crowns.

But more of this in what follows. For now, we will look at the battle. We said above that the fourth period pertains to the virgins and hermits, that is, to those holy men who were, John says, of the seed of woman. And the red dragon, overcome in three battles, went off enraged to do battle against those holy men who were from the seed of the woman and who guard God's commandments, John says, and give witness to Jesus (Rev 12). Thus one beast John saw, the dragon ascending from the sea, is equivalent to the four beasts seen earlier by the prophet Daniel. And four battles were fought and are being fought by these four beasts (i.e., the dragon). The fourth is the one designated by the aforementioned words of John, when he says the dragon, angry at the woman, went off to make war against those who were left of the woman's seed, who guard God's commandments and give witness to Jesus. It is as if John had said that the red dragon knew and was jealous that not only were those saints to be crowned who, for God's honor and glory, exposed themselves to tortures or at least, once captured by infidels, persisted in the faith, but also those who led the solitary life, winning the victory of chastity, were to be raised up. He was unable to bear the sight of this new genus of martyrs, the hermits, destined for the kingdom. Thus he who had sent the Jews into battle against the apostles, the pagans against the martyrs, and the Arians against the catholics, now arrayed against the hermits the Muslims, a sect more monstrous than the others, the fourth beast spoken of by Daniel, because in the fourth period of the church, going forth ahead of the others, they rose up to battle the fourth order.

"After this," he says, "I saw in a night vision a fourth beast, terrifying, horrible, and of extraordinary strength. It had great iron teeth with which it devoured and crushed, and what was left it trampled with its feet." And when the angel says to him, "These four beasts are four great kingdoms that will arise from the earth," he goes on to say, "After this, I strongly desired to learn more of the fourth beast, who was very different from the others, terrifying, and had iron teeth with which it devoured and crushed, trampling what was left with its feet" (Dan 7:19). From this it can be gathered that the ferocity of the three preceding beasts was nothing compared that of this fourth one.

Joachim continues in this vein, adding little to his thought so far, until he turns to the head that seemed dead but then recovered, which he identifies with Islam. He notes that this head has indeed been impossible to kill, but then he has to face the question of why John describes it as having seemed to die. Perhaps, he suggests, this refers to the future, when the Christians will prevail (more by preaching than by battle), but then Islam will again become strong. Then he turns to another possibility.

But there are, perhaps, some who think this already has occurred through material arms. For, as they say, in the year 1015 of our Lord's incarnation there appeared in the sky a marvelous sign, countless stars traveling every which way in the sky, wandering around the sky like birds. After that sign had occurred, at the exhortation of Pope Urban, the Christians were inspired to go beyond the sea and liberate Christ's sepulcher. After this, the Christians gained so much courage that you would have thought practically the whole multitude of pagans destroyed or reduced to nothing through Christ's victory. To sum it up in one example, the Saracens in Egypt rendered tribute to the Christians who had invaded the Holy Land.

Joachim goes on to survey the general progress of Christian armies against the Muslims in the eleventh and twelfth centuries, then comments:

Who, then, seeing so many victories by that indomitable people, would not conclude that the Christians had undoubtedly conquered and that head of the beast was dead? But any sane person need only look around today to see that there is little peace and the nations are rising up around us like the tide of the sea. The head that seemed dead has been restored to health and is ready to go back to killing and devouring, just as the Lord predicted. But if indeed, as we said above, the prophecy has not yet been fulfilled, it may possibly be fulfilled without delay by another order. The spiritual sense seems to favor this opinion more, namely, that it is not yet fulfilled but will be fulfilled without delay by another, higher order.

As for what follows, "And all the earth admired and followed after the beast" (Rev 13:3), although that still has to be fulfilled, there are nonetheless many even now who admire and even begin to stammer, as it were, saying, "What sort of judgment is this, that such a multitude of people oppose the faith and are allowed to triumph against the Christian people? Do you think a thousand people are to be damned as if they were one person? Do you think God is permitting these things to occur without cause?" The unhappy people saying this fall from the faith, in ignorance of what is written: "How great are your works, Lord, how deep are your thoughts! A senseless man knows not, nor does a fool understand this" (Ps 92:6–7). For sinners have sprung up like hay and all those who do evil have appeared, that they might die for all time. Yet you, Lord, are supreme throughout eternity. This, in truth, is unknown to the foolish who esteem the beast and desert the faith of Christ, inclining themselves to the bestial power, going over to its uncleanness, and making themselves heirs of its perfidy. This is already true in part, and in the near future it will be completely fulfilled. That is, the whole world will esteem the beast, and those who gape at him, filled with earthly desires, will adore the dragon, who gave power to the beast. And they will adore the beast himself, saying, "Who is like the beast, and who can battle with him?" (Rev 13:4).

In what immediately follows, Joachim blends Daniel and Revelation in a mix that more or less repeats what he already has said. He speaks generally, not mentioning the Muslims. Eventually he arrives at Revelation 13:11 and the second beast rising from the earth with two horns like those of a lamb.

Just as in Daniel the he-goat (Dan 8:5–26) signifies not a person but a kingdom, so in this place the beast ascending from the land should be taken, not as some person, but as a sect or kingdom. The author of this book manifestly demonstrates that this beast ascending from the land should be taken as a sect of pseudo-prophets. If this is clear, then whom should the two horns like those of a lamb be taken to be? For it is clear from many places in Scripture that the horns of some beasts should be interpreted as persons. But there is a difference between the horns of a sheep and those of many other beasts. The horns of many beasts are sharp and rigid, designed to wound, but those of a sheep are curved and excite little in the way of terror. Our lamb who took away the sins of the world, however, is said to have had seven horns, for seven men were sent in various times. We mentioned them in the first part of the book. Two were sent especially to prepare the way, namely, John and Elijah. But two were also seen with Christ on the mountain, that is, Moses and Elijah. Now two are expected to come, Enoch and Elijah. Let him who fears to be deceived or seduced pay careful attention to all this, and examine the matter carefully, for the father of deception is a very good mimic and can do some funny things to deceive the careless or resemble the creator. For the Lord having found David to reign in Jerusalem, his chosen city, the father of deception found Nebuchadnezzar to rule in Babylon, and the latter persecuted Jerusalem all the days of his life. Because the Lord redeemed all of humankind through his Christ, the father of deception worked falsehood through Antichrist. For just as the omnipotent God is the father of truth, so the Antichrist is, as the Lord says, the father of falsehood. Beyond that, we can believe that he will destroy all. All of the faithful, therefore, should be ever watchful and careful, lest perhaps he, knowing that the faithful are prepared to receive Enoch and Elijah, whose coming is predicted by the doctors, will first find and dispatch a false Enoch and a false Elijah. These latter are the two horns similar to those of a lamb, the horns of the master of the bestial crowd concerning which the Lord thought it worthwhile to warn his disciples, saying, "Beware of the false prophets who come to you clothed like sheep but are ravenous wolves on the inside" (Matt 7:15). I say this, though, not because I am sure, but so that we might be careful in all things and suffer no shipwrecks. What we say seems likely, though, even if we cannot back it or disprove it with authority. Everything that is likely but lacks certain authority must remain suspect and subject to caution until its actual occurrence shows the truth of the matter.

> *Joachim continues in this vein for some time, underlining at great length the dangers of deception and the limitations of our knowledge. We rejoin his commentary at the moment when he begins to deal with 13:12.*

And he made the earth and those inhabiting it adore the first beast, whose death wounds had been healed. And he performed great signs, making fire come down from heaven in the presence of onlookers (Rev 13:12–13). These words and those that follow are partly obscure (because they deal with future things) and partly clear. For the time being, let us put aside what is obscure and concentrate on what is clear until the course of events makes clear that which was obscure. For what do we gain by chasing after curiosities when war is imminent and events expected in the present can quickly be interrupted? The following, therefore, represents what can be examined. We will leave the rest to its own time.

The emperor Nero was a pagan. Simon Magus, however, was a Christian and was made, as it were, not one of the pagans but one of the great demons. The faith he left he held in great hatred, and he especially hated Peter, who pronounced sentence against him. Having become an apostate, he detested Christians; but, because by himself he could not hinder them, he stirred up the ruler against them. He took his conflict with the apostles before the emperor, deferring to him in all things, not because he truly loved him but so that he could arm his malice with imperial power. Pseudo-prophets are made in this way. It happens frequently, and there are clear examples in both the Old and New Testaments. In the time of the Maccabees, the evil Alcimus, wishing to usurp the priesthood illicitly, appealed to a gentile power (2 Macc 14). The Jews often went before Roman judges for aid against the apostles. The Arians stirred up worldly princes against the church. The Patarene heretics looked to worldly powers for protection. Even so, once the evils are multiplied, the new Babylon will be given over into the hand of the beast and his kingdom so that it can be struck by them, and gentile power will be strengthened due to sin. This will occur at the time when that eleventh and last king of the Saracens will reign. The pseudo-prophets (whom the devil will unceasingly join to himself in order to increase the misery), seeing an opportunity to exercise their treachery, will go to gentiles and, receiving from them a peace treaty, will preach that their power and rule is from God, as if they were speaking of the faithful. And they will say that the religion of those who worship the crucified man is false. Not only that, but they will prefer the bestial law given to them by the father of lies, as if the Trinity were nothing. And they will gather the entire Christian people to [their bestial law], because of the signs they are able to produce through their false religion. But who knows what sort of law will be given by that prince of the beast of whom Daniel writes? He will think himself able to change the times and laws, and it shall be handed over to him for times, time, and half a time (Dan 7:25). Of whatever sort that blindness might be, the pseudo-prophets will teach that it should be accepted by all, and they will reinforce it with signs and prodigies. Comparing these two beasts, it seems that the first one coming out of the sea is in concordance with Daniel's sixth vision, in which he speaks of the four beasts coming out of the great sea, while the second beast ascending from the land is in concordance with Daniel's seventh vision dealing with the he-goat, except that in connection with the first beast we see that the eleventh king who considers himself able to change times and laws will rule. In connection with the second we find other things already mentioned, especially that he will destroy all. Neither in the first nor in the second is there mention of any particular king, except that in this fourth part solemn mention is made of the dragon with seven horns (Rev 12:3 [which actually speaks of a dragon having seven heads and ten horns]), which signifies seven kings, and in the sixth part it is said of the last two kings, "One is and one has not yet come, and when he does come he will remain only a short time" (Rev 17:10). This is said in order to make clear that these are two kings written about in the prophet Daniel's two visions.

But why two kings, since the dragon himself is singular, unless according to the type of the one Christ who came to redeem humankind and will come again in judgment? And two persons are anointed in the church of God, that is, kings and popes. Because undoubtedly the pope is more truly king. And Lord Christ can be called both, because he is God and man. Thus it seems likely that, just as that beast who ascends from the sea will have a great king of his sect similar to Nero and, as it were, emperor of the whole world, this beast who ascends from the earth will have a certain great prelate, similar to Simon Magus, who will be, as it were, universal pope of the whole world. He will be Antichrist, concerning whom Paul says that he will be exalted over and opposed to everything that is called God or is worshiped, so that he sits in God's temple, displaying himself as if he were God (2 Thess 2:4). This can be related to what Daniel says: "There will arise a king with an impudent face and deep knowledge, and he shall be strengthened" (Dan 8:23–24), but not (it is added) through his own powers, because, just as it was not through his own power that Simon Magus persecuted the apostles but rather through Nero's power, so in the case of this one it will be through the power of that eleventh king who, it can be believed, will destroy all. And perhaps he himself will not go to the king at first but will send two of his leading prophets to him. They will perform signs and say they have a prince by whom they are sent. Some doctors, however, call that eleventh king Antichrist, like the one who is called Gog, which seems true to me, for the dragon is one, but it has many heads, and the malice it does not fulfill in one Antichrist it will fulfill in another, and whoever is the worst, that one should be called the greatest Antichrist.[38]

---

38. Robert Lerner explores Joachim's shifting thought on Gog and Antichrist in "Antichrists and Antichrist in Joachim of Fiore," *Speculum* 60 (1985): 553–70.

At the end of chapter 13, Joachim encounters the passage about the number of the beast, another key passage in determining what the work is about: "Here is wisdom. Whoever considers the matter will compute the number of the beast. For it is the number of a man, and his number is 666" (Rev 13:18). After driving home the obvious message of this passage, namely, that the number must be comprehensible by us through human intellect even now if we think carefully about it, Joachim turns to the harder question of just what it does mean.

And its number, a number expressed in its name, he says, is 666. Why this number? Because this number signifies the totality of all worldly time from Adam to the end of this beast, which will be in the time of Antichrist. For six hundred signifies the six ages of the world in which this beast reigned in his members from the beginning of history, while sixty signifies the six periods of this sixth age, in which, by a special power accepted from the dragon, the church of God has been more atrociously persecuted. The six signifies the period of that eleventh horn, that is, forty-two months, in other words six times seven months, a time during which his anger will burn especially and inexpressibly strong, inflamed no doubt by that ancient dragon, who knows he has little time left. Thus in the six hundred is comprehended all that pertains to the six ages of the world, in the sixty that part pertaining to the sixth age, and in the six that sixth time of the sixth age in which that eleventh horn is to reign, that is, for time, times, and half a time. As for no one having the power to sell or buy unless they have the mark of the beast, the beast's name or the number of the beast's name, on their right hand or forehead, what does that mean except that those will not be judged worthy and faithful who approve only of temporal things, deriding and mocking those who promise eternal life? For those who themselves so despair that they cannot see the light of heaven, whom can they love except desperate men? For on their right hand or on their forehead they bear the mark of the beast, his name or the number of his name. Those who are of his party are seen to bear it because it is not sufficient that they do it unhappily or from necessity. They do it happily and openly, speaking out clearly in their synagogues, saying, "If this kingdom were not of God, it wouldn't be able to accomplish anything. Thus whoever resists it is resisting what God ordains." For to bear on their right hand or on their forehead the mark of the beast, his name or the number of his name, is to show oneself happy in the accomplishment of bestial deeds as will be contained in his letters, or to publicly preach these things in their convents, or certainly to praise the beast's power, or to show no shame in the commission of whatever crime or in the enjoyment of whatever sin. For this is what the dragon demands of his soldiers. Of course, these things are said according to the spirit, and insofar as one can conjecture concerning future things. For that one who will believe he can change times and laws is not yet revealed. These things will be given over into his hands in time, times, and half a time. When this actually begins to occur, then the bare facts of the matter will make its meaning clear.

On Revelation 17, the Beast and Babylon[39]

The beast you saw was and is not. It will come up from the abyss once more before going to final ruin. All the men of the earth whose names have not been written in the book of life from the creation of the world shall be amazed when they see the beast, for it existed once and now exists no longer, and yet it will exist again. Here is the clue for one who possesses wisdom! The seven heads are seven hills on which the woman sits enthroned. They are also seven kings. Five have already fallen, one lives now, and the last has not yet come; but when he does come he will remain only a short while (Rev 17:8–10).

It has been said already that this terrible, hateful beast signifies all the infidel peoples who were at some point subjected to the Roman Empire and persecuted Christ and his church, beginning with Herod and running through various times in seven heads, the seventh of which, as we said, has held forth from the time of Muhammad to the present. What the angel says, "he was and is not," is to be ascribed to the sixth period of the church, during which, Babylon first being struck, the beast will be defeated by Christ, as will be shown later in its proper place when the relevant words are exposited. The angel says, "he is not," because it is necessary that his ferocity should cease because Christ and his army prevail.

Yet the beast, though thought to have been slain, will arise again after a while from the abyss of an infidel people through the instigation of the dragon, and worldly, carnal people, those whose names are not written in the book of life from the creation of the world, will be scandalized, saying together in their hearts, "If this Jesus whom we worship were the true son of God, then this persecution by infidel nations, which has only recently calmed down, would not have begun again with such power to scatter the

---

39. *Expos.*, 196ra–197va.

remainder of the Christian people. But when the confessors of his name are driven from the land, it is clear that he can do nothing." For they do not believe that this could occur by the Son of God's permission, or that he permits the beast to be raised up to the clouds just as Simon Magus was, so that he may fall into the depths and be ruined at the end, but they believe rather that it occurs by the judgment of God's wrath, for he wishes to wipe from the earth the Christian people who have been seduced by the crucified man. They are especially prone to believe this because of the pseudo-Christs and pseudo-prophets, who come forth to seduce even the elect, if that were possible. This is the hour of that temptation of which the Lord speaks to the angel of Philadelphia: "I will serve you in that hour of temptation which is to come throughout the whole world to tempt its inhabitants" (Rev 3:10).

Hear what the angel says next: **Here is the clue for one who possesses wisdom! The seven heads are seven hills on which the woman sits enthroned. They are also seven kings. Five have already fallen, one lives now, and the last has not yet come; but when he does come he will remain only a short while** (Rev 17:9–10). This clearly indicates that his meaning is hidden and in need of exposition, or certainly that there should be wise people by whom these words might be explained so that what is said can be understood. As the apostle says, "We speak wisdom among the perfect" (1 Cor 2:6).

First, however, the angel said, "The beast you saw was and is not." Yet then he says, "The seven heads are seven hills on which the woman sits." If the beast was but now is not, how can the angel say the heads are hills unless it is the custom of holy Scripture to speak in the present sometimes when referring to the past or future? Thus he says "are" meaning "were," just as we ourselves often do. Who these hills were, however, is touched upon in the preface of this book and, unless I am mistaken, repeated more carefully in the fourth part. The first head was King Herod and his successors, while the second was the Roman Empire through Diocletian. The third, fourth, fifth, and sixth heads were four Arian kingdoms, remembered for their deeds. The seventh head is the Saracen kingdom.

He does not say, "And the seven heads are seven kings," suggesting that each head represented one of seven kings (particularly since he says that the ten horns designate ten kings). Instead he says, "And there are seven kings," without implying that each of the seven is identified with a particular head. They are, instead, understood as arising in another way, that is, in each of seven periods, those of which we have spoken frequently and at greater length elsewhere in this work. For each of the seven heads of the beast did not arise in one of the seven periods, but rather, as it is shown better in Daniel, the first head arose in the first period, the second in the second, the next four in the third, and the seventh in the fourth. The seventh has persevered to the sixth period, in which it will be weakened, or at least appear to be weakened, only to rise again after a short time, then disappear for all eternity.

Thus the seven kings are not equivalent to the seven heads, but are assigned to seven periods, and thus he says, "And there are seven kings." The first of these (as we have just written) is Herod with his successors; the second Nero with his successors; the third Constantius the Arian with his successors; the fourth Muhammad, or rather Cosroes, king of the Persians, and his successors; the fifth he who first began to tire the church in the west with investiture of churches, a practice from which there arose in God's church, from that time on, many schisms and tribulations. The sixth king, of whom it is said, "one is," is the eleventh king in Daniel, in the time of which this revelation is to be opened in clear fashion. The new Babylon will be struck down by this same king and his accomplices; then, after this occurs, the seventh head of the beast will itself be struck down as if dead and the church of Christ will be granted peace. Between that sixth persecution and the other that will occur under that king of which it is said, "one has not yet come," there will be a brief space of time for the faithful to catch their breath, because both the empire of Babylon within and the empire of the beast without, having died, will cease to persecute them. The beast will again arise like a demon, rising from the abyss to conduct one more persecution as if in the eighth place, but then he will go to destruction, and he will rise no more.

The beast who was and is not, he is the eighth, and he is one of the seven, and he will go to destruction (Rev 17:11). If the beast had eight heads, he would not have said, "he is eighth, and he is one of the seven," but only "he is eighth." For he would be the eighth, in the eighth head, the last one left. But because the seventh head of the beast will die and rise again, and also all the rest of the errors of the other heads will appear together, there will be that terrible congregation which is eighth according to time and succession, yet it will be one of the seven, because it will have in it a collection of all the errors already displayed in the seven heads. The seventh king, who will be a fountain of evil and vessel of errors, and in whom will abide a plenitude of iniquity and a wellhead of badness, will reign. All these iniquities will spring forth so that all that has been written might be fulfilled. In the meantime, under the sixth king, Babylon will be struck down by the beast and his kings. Nonetheless, these kings will fight with Christ, and he will defeat them by the sword of his mouth, not a material sword but a sword of the spirit, the word of God. For there will not be lacking a remnant through which he will fight and win, because whatever he wants to do he can accomplish, in heaven and on earth.

And the ten horns you saw are ten kings who have not yet assumed their kingdoms, but they will have power for an hour after the beast. They will fight with the lamb, and the lamb will defeat them, for he is lord of lords and king of kings, and they will also conquer who are with him, those called his elect and faithful (Rev 17:12–14).

In Daniel it is said that one king will arise after the ten. Here, however, it is said of the sixth king, "one is," and of the ten horns, "they are ten kings who have not yet assumed their kingdoms." I do not see what this could mean unless under the sixth king one is expected to arise after another. Thus John says, "one is," which, historically speaking, I understand to refer to Saladin, that most renowned king of the Turks, by whom the city in which Christ suffered was recently captured. Another will rise up as his successor, and he will be that one of whom it is said by Daniel, "And another will arise after them" (Dan 7:24). And he will be more powerful than the earlier ones. If that is the case, he should not rightly be called one of the ten kings. He will assume his kingdom for an hour, after the sixth king, but after the beast, because one king will perhaps reign over the beast when those ten kings will reign, and another when that which is said, "and one is," begins to be fulfilled. For according to Daniel, while the ten kings are reigning, each in his place, a certain small king will arise from the midst of them and, laying low three of them, he will make war on the saints (Dan 7:24–25).

This raises some questions. One of them is whether earlier the ten kings, joining together with some single great king who will rule over that kingdom called the beast, will together strike down Babylon, then later he who will lay low three of them will reign and make war on the saints, or will both things occur under one and the same ruler? Whichever will be the case, the basic battle will be between these kings and the lamb, because their whole intention, their whole battle, will be against Christ and those who confess his name. But Christ and his soldiers will triumph, because those who are with him are called his elect and faithful. It may be, however, that both are simultaneous, the striking down of Babylon and the persecution of the elect by those who do not understand the cause of the judgment inflicted on Christians, not knowing, I mean, that they are destined to win over that part which pertains to Babylon but be defeated in battle by Christ in that part which pertains to Jerusalem. They will win there because God is angry at false Christians, but lose here because he is pleased with his faithful elect. Thus both things are said to happen simultaneously because both occur in the same sixth period. The beast will be vanquished by Christ the victor, however, and he who was will cease to be. As it is said, "he was and is not." But along with this it can be held that one king, who is called the eleventh by Daniel, will unexpectedly rise (as we believe) against the ten and, having brought low three of them, will be greatly exalted and will do all those evils which were sufficiently discussed by us in the fourth part. This will be fulfilled after the fall of Babylon and the war these kings will have with the martyrs of Christ.

Next we hear something about Christ's victory and the fall of Babylon. For the text continues: **The waters on which you saw the harlot enthroned are large numbers of peoples and nations and tongues. The ten horns you saw on the beast hate the harlot and will turn on her. They will strip her nude and leave her naked. They will devour her flesh and set her on fire** (Rev 17:15–16). As long as these waters remain in their present condition, the kings of the nations cannot prevail over Babylon, because these waters represent the forces fighting against the nations in Babylon's defense. But because the vial cast by the sixth angel dries them up, it is clear that there is no faith involved in their power, for it is the Lord himself fighting against the harlot through impious forces.

> *In what immediately follows, Joachim does not elaborate on the nature of that "drying up" except to say that, when the attack occurs, the Roman Empire will then be divided under many kings. He does stress, however, that they will be attacking because "all with one soul hate Christians and especially the Roman Empire." That is, they are attacking not corruption but what they see as Christianity. When he reaches Revelation 17:18, he underlines a point already made earlier.*

The woman you saw is the great city which has sovereignty over the kings of the earth (17:18). Not only do we have it on the authority of this book that Rome is in the place of Babylon, but also from the words of Peter who, writing to some people from the city of Rome, says, "The church that is in Babylon sends you greetings" (1 Pet 5:13). But with these words a great deal of consolation is given to the people who are called "Roman," for the city of Jerusalem lives as a pilgrim in the very city that is called "Babylon." One can judge who in it are sons of Jerusalem and who sons of Rome only by their end. One should not be confident in sterile fashion because of the good things promised to Peter by Christ when he says, "You are Peter, and upon this rock I shall build my church, and the gates of Hell shall not prevail against it" (Matt 16:18), nor should one lose faith because of all the bad things written in this book. Even if the sons of Jerusalem reside like pilgrims in Babylon according to their bodies, that does not make them sons of Babylon. They are still sons of Jerusalem. Both emerge together from one womb like Esau and Jacob, for God is powerful, as Peter says, when it comes to rescuing pious people from temptation. Nor should it be imagined that the city is confined to those within its walls. It includes all who are a part of its imperial rule. Although it is divided and torn into parts, thus portending that its desolation is near, it is nonetheless one in the Christian people, especially in its Latin part, which is accustomed to be subject to the Roman pontiff in all things.

On Revelation 20–22, the Seventh Period, and Satan's Last Stand[40]

With chapter 20, Joachim arrives at what he sees as the seventh part of the book and the seventh period of church history. He begins with an introductory look at the new territory he is entering.

We have gone through six parts of the Apocalypse in which six laborious periods have been dealt with. Now we come to the seventh part dealing with that great Sabbath at the future end of the world, which can be called the third age, or also the seventh age of the world designated by that seventh day concerning which Scripture says, "And on the seventh day God rested from all his works that he had accomplished. And he blessed the seventh day and sanctified it" (Gen 2:2–3). As we have said in this work, Saint Augustine, in his book *The City of God*, wrote of this final period designated in the Sabbath that the entire church of God confesses, "We believe Christ will come from heaven to judge the living and dead." This final day of divine judgment we consider to be the final period, for it is uncertain how many days this judgment will last. Now no one, no matter how negligently he has read this work, can doubt that it is the habit of holy Scripture to use the word "day" to designate a period of time. The blessed Remigius also taught that it is uncertain how much time will elapse after the fall of Antichrist, thus demolishing the opinion of those who believe that with Antichrist's fall world history will immediately end and so will the world. Such people do not realize that reference to the last day or the end of the world does not

---

40. *Expos.*, 209vb–212ra.

always mean the very last moment of the world's end, but can mean instead the time of the end, that is, the final age of the world, especially in view of the fact that over a thousand years have elapsed since the blessed John said, "Children, it is the final hour" (1 John 2:18).

Thus there will be a time after the fall of Antichrist. But as to whether the Lord will come in judgment at the end of that period or at the beginning, some feel this question should be left open rather than decided, even though the Lord says, "Immediately after the tribulation of those days," that is, the tribulation the beast and pseudo-prophet will cause,

> the sun will be obscured and the moon will not give its light, and the stars will fall from the sky, and the powers of the heavens will be moved, and then the sign of the Son of Man will appear in the sky. And then all the tribes of the earth will lament, and they will see the Son of Man coming on the clouds of heaven in power and majesty, and he will dispatch his angels with trumpet and loud voice to gather his elect from the four winds from one end of the heavens to the other. (Matt 24:29–31)

And the apostle makes the same point when he says concerning Antichrist, "And the wicked one will be revealed, he whom the Lord Jesus shall slay with the breath of his mouth and destroy by the manifestation of his coming" (2 Thess 2:8).

We have said in this book, though, when discussing the dragon, that with the defeat of the six heads in which the dragon has fought through six consecutive periods, in the seventh head there will be a battle even more desperate than normal, and all the dragon's poison will be poured out through its mouth, for it knows that the time of its damnation is at hand. For that which the Lord says must be completed: "And the prince of this world will be cast out" (John 21:31). Thus even if in the sixth part, in what we already have said, the result of this battle was not spelled out, it is nonetheless known. In that battle of the beast and pseudo-prophet against Christ, the Antichrist deployed by the dragon will be the worst prince in that evil alliance of kings of the earth who rise up to battle against the King of Kings. This is seen in the sixth of the angels who pour out vials of God's wrath on the earth, where it is said, "I saw go forth from the mouths of the dragon, the mouth of the beast, and the mouth of the pseudo-prophet three unclean spirits in the manner of frogs. They are the spirits of demons producing signs. They went forth to the kings of the earth in order to assemble them for battle on the day of the great God Almighty" (Rev 16:13–14).

Thus whatever the beast and pseudo-prophet do they will do by the decision and order of the dragon speaking through the mouth of that seventh king written about in this book. And because the blessed John has taught us in what was said above that the beast and pseudo-prophet will be sent live into the fiery lake of burning sulfur, but the others will be killed by the sword that comes out of the mouth of the one sitting astride a horse (Rev 19:20–21), it must still be decided what is to be done with the dragon. He is the author of the evils through the seduction and trickery of which the kings and princes of the earth will oppose the Lord and his Christ, leading the Lord to address them in his wrath and pronounce punishment on them.

Thus he says, **Then I saw an angel coming down from heaven, holding the key to the abyss, and a huge chain in his hand. He seized the dragon, the ancient serpent, who is the devil and Satan, and bound him for a thousand years, and sent him into the abyss, and closed and sealed it over him, so that he would not seduce the nations anymore until a thousand years had been completed, and after that he must be released for a little while** (Rev 20:1–3). What has been said so far seemed clear enough. We have a story that proceeds smoothly from beginning to end through six periods and also six parts of the book. Now, however, when we hear that Satan is to be bound, then released again, the senses of many are dulled by it, because this news is a long way from what many think. It would seem more likely if the number 1000 were not to be applied to the entire duration of church history through recapitulation. As for that common opinion, that is, the view of those who think the thousand years should be seen as signifying the Sabbath and not the entire duration of church history, I say that, even if we can have no certainty in this matter, I think their view can be seen as a rational opinion that does not contradict the faith. For note that the dragon and beast are said to have seven heads, and these heads were to be destroyed in seven periods. Once the seven have been destroyed, it seems part of the logic and mystery that a Sabbath of a seventh period should follow. But who knows how short it will be? If the time of this Sabbath should be brief, and Antichrist will actually be present when the beast and pseudo-prophet are defeated, what prevents us from thinking that he too will be banished from the sight of the elect, and, because he has been unable to conquer in either the first or second battle of the sixth period, he will transfer himself for a while to the Scythian nations and, when Gog and his army are called forth, numerous as the sands of the sea (Rev 20:7), he will do all the damage God's patience allows?

This seems implied by the passage in which the beast and pseudo-prophet fight and then are thrown into the lake of fire. It does not say the dragon will be thrown into that lake of fire. Instead, it says he will be incarcerated for a while and then, for a short time, released. And on this basis we can accept as true the opinion of those who say there will be some time remaining after the fall of Antichrist. That is, God will slay the beast and pseudo-prophet in battle. And they speak truly who say the dragon will truly be slain by a breath from the mouth of Christ, destroyed by the manifestation of Christ's coming. For perhaps the first of these battles will be the penultimate victory, when those who are in the beast's army will be slain by the sword proceeding from Christ's mouth. But in the final battle the Lord will appear manifestly.

The text of this book seems to say that at the beginning of the sixth period the devil will bring forth the Saracens against the Christian empire, and after many evils have occurred he will be defeated by the armies of Christ. Thus it is said, "they will fight with the Lamb, and the lamb will defeat them, for he is lord of lords and king of kings, and those who are with him are the called, the elect, the faithful" (Rev 17:14). And Babylon will be given over into their hands to be judged by them, as was said earlier. When this battle is over, there will be peace and rejoicing in the church of Christ. Once this time is past he will rouse the dead beast (that is, the pagans), and for extra help he will add to them the pseudo-prophet. The more strongly the beast fights, the more strongly he will be defeated by the army of Christ. The beast and pseudo-prophet will be thrown into the fiery lake of burning sulfur, and the others will be converted to God. After that battle is over, there will be a great peace, the likes of which has not been seen since the beginning of the world. When it ends is up to God. When that peace is completed, the devil will emerge with Gog's army and the third battle, worse than the first two, will take place. After that one is over and all who came with him have been punished, he himself, after all the others, will be cast into the lake of fire. These three battles will perhaps take place close together, so that the man of sin can be involved in all of them, but especially the second and third.

Having touched upon these matters as efficiently as necessary in the introduction to this seventh part with which we have begun to deal, we now turn to its orderly exposition. As Augustine says in *The City of God*, some people gather from this passage that there will be a thousand-year seventh period in which the Christ will reign with his saints after the resurrection, six thousand years already having passed since the beginning of the world. And they add certain other things that are entirely contrary to the Christian faith.

He seems to agree with this opinion in part and reject it in part, since part of it is true and part vacuous and worthless. For their opinion was true insofar as a seventh period and Sabbath will come after the aforementioned battle. In fact, such is not so much an opinion as a most serene understanding. Insofar as they say that that seventh period will be a seventh thousand-year period, however, they are wrong both according to the Greeks and according to the Latins. For they assert themselves to have more and we a great deal less, and we think they stray far from the path of truth. Insofar as they said the Lord and his saints would give themselves over to carnal banquets for a thousand years after the resurrection, that idea is entirely against the faith and certainly took shape, not in spiritual souls, but in carnal ones. For food is for the belly and the belly for foods, but God will destroy both one and the other.

Because, however, different people say different things about this, per-haps, moved by the urgency of the time rather than by an idle desire to write something, we should state our own opinion. Earlier, in the fourth part, in connection with the seven heads of the dragon, we said that its individual heads are conquered at different times, but two are to be conquered in the sixth period. It follows that some part of him has been incarcerated ever since Christ defeated him on the day of Christ's death. As far as all the heads are concerned, however, the imprisonment occurs from the day or hour that the beast and pseudo-prophet are cast into the lake of fire. And, seen from this perspective, the thousand years refers to the entire time from the Lord's resurrection to the end of the world, but especially to that great mystery of the Sabbath by which we have said the seventh period is begun concurrently with the sixth, yet is not consummated concurrently with it, just as John was called by Christ at the same time as Peter but nevertheless did not pay the debt of death at the same time as he, but remained alive a long time after Peter's demise. For we said this pertains to the mystery of the Trinity and is intended to demonstrate that the Holy Spirit, through which freedom was given to men (and is still given to them), proceeds from the Father and the Son, one of whom manifestly imposed labor on people of the Old Testament and the other of whom imposed it on men of the New Testament, although neither acted without the other, for the Father, when the labor involved in servitude to the law was completed, gave to people that spirit of adoption which is Sabbath and freedom, and the Son, when this laborious time is completed, will give it even more abundantly. This is not to imply that the Father gave it without the Son, or the Son will give it without the Father, for they are one in essence. On the contrary, it is understood by evident signs specific to each time that it proceeds from both.

Because, therefore, at the end of the first age freedom from servitude to the law was granted to the faithful, and at the end of the second freedom is to be given more fully and perfectly, this time in relation to bondage by the passions—since it is clear that the freedom that the apostle says is found where the spirit of the Lord is (2 Cor 3:17) pertains to the Sabbath, it is clear that the seventh period, in which that great Sabbath is located, partly began with that Sabbath in which the Lord rested in the sepulcher, and it will be present in its fullness with the ruin of the beast and pseudo-prophet. For that reason, although that which is written concerning the incarceration of Satan will be perfectly fulfilled only at that time, nevertheless the thousand years begins from the Lord's resurrection. Not that one should expect one thousand years precisely. Rather, because one thousand is a perfect number, it signifies a great fullness of years.

> *Before completing his exegesis of Revelation 20:3, Joachim offers one final clarification concerning the period when Satan is to be bound and the church will enter a time of peace.*

But lest someone imagine that this is said of that eternal peace which will be enjoyed in the eighth period, he adds, "And after this he must be loosed for a short time." Thus after the destruction of the seventh head there will be peace, and after that peace a persecution designated by the dragon's tail. In the meantime, however, that which the apostle says of Christ will be fulfilled: "He must reign until he puts all his enemies under his feet," that is, the Jews and gentiles.

EARLY JOACHISM

Joachim had received the moral support of three popes: Lucius III, Urban III, and Clement III. They had protected him and encouraged his writing as well as his order. His good fortune ran out with the election of Innocent III. The issue was a treatise in which Joachim attacked Peter Lombard's theology of the Trinity.[1] Joachim was hardly the only theologian to disagree publicly with the Lombard. Richard of Saint Victor, among others, had done so; yet it was Joachim's treatise that was condemned in 1215 at the fourth Lateran council. The decree is understandable, since Innocent III was himself a product of the Parisian education system and thus more in harmony with the newer scholastic method represented by the Lombard. In fact, the wording of the decree produced by the council is relatively mild, since it is careful to avoid labeling Joachim as a heretic, noting that Joachim submitted all his works to the pope for correction.[2]

More important from our perspective, the decree deals with a single treatise concerning the Trinity and not with Joachim's apocalyptic theology. Some have tried to see Joachim's argument on the former as intimately connected with his views on the latter, but it is not an easy argument to pursue if in making it one is aiming at demonstration that Joachim's idea of the

1. The treatise was long thought to have disappeared, but Selge, in his recent edition of the *Psalterium decem chordarum*, argues that it was absorbed into the early part of the *Psalterium*. See *Psalterium decem chordarum*, modern edition edited by Kurt-Victor Selge, Monumenta Germaniae Historica, Quellen zur Geistesgeschichte des Mittelalters, 20 (Hanover: Hahnsche, 2009).
2. Mansi, *Sacrorum conciliorum* 22.986.

three *status* and his association of them with the Father, Son, and Holy Spirit somehow precluded a satisfactory doctrine of the Trinity. One might ask the more relevant question, namely, whether Joachim's criticism of the Lombard's formulation made all that much sense or whether he even understood the Lombard's formulation; but that is another matter entirely and might entail a much deeper dive into the question of how radical a change was represented by the move from Joachite (and indeed Victorine) scholarship to the newer, shinier model represented by the Lombard and those who followed him.[3]

In any case, while the 1215 decree cast a shadow over Joachim's reputation, it hardly prevented his works from being widely disseminated after his death. Just how that occurred is open to question. On the one hand, there is some question as to how and when Joachim's authentic writings were disseminated. Traditionally the argument has centered around Calabria, Naples, and Pisa, and it has depended heavily on piecing together various comments in Salimbene's chronicle. The result was a dramatic story of a Florensian abbot fleeing the threat of attack by Frederick II around 1243,[4] taking the collected works of Joachim with him and arriving at the Franciscan house in Pisa. There Salimbene was launched on his path toward Joachism. If E. R. Daniel is correct, however, the Franciscans at Naples were already familiar with Joachim by the early 1240s.[5]

The introduction of Joachim north of the Alps is another problem for which various solutions have been offered. Salimbene tells us that when he visited Hyères in 1248 he found all of Joachim's works there. One common theory as to how they got there is that Hugh of Digne was introduced to Joachim's writings when he went to Italy in 1240 for the Siena general chapter, but more recently Fabio Troncarelli has suggested that Joachim's works arrived in southern France during the legation of Raniero da Ponza between 1198 and 1202.[6] This theory is supported to some extent by the fact

---

3. On this subject see Marco Rainini, *Disegni dei tempi*, mentioned in the previous chapter, and, more recently, Luca Parisoli, *Gioacchino da Fiore e il carattere meridionale del movimento francescano in Calabria*, Collana Pensatori Italiani (Davoli Marina: Associazione Radici del Tempo, 2016).

4. Damien Ruiz, "Hugue de Digne Provençal, Franciscain et Joachite," in *Il ricordo del futuro*, ed. Fabio Troncarelli (Bari: Mario Addia Editore, 2006), 83, says 1243 or a little later, which makes sense since Salimbene claims to have been there.

5. Daniel, "A Re-examination of the Origins of Franciscan Joachism," *Speculum* 43 (1968): 671–76.

6. Troncarelli, "Fiorenzo d'Acri e la condanna di Gioacchino," *Frate Francesco* 68 (2002): 111–36; Troncarelli, "La chiave di David," *Frate Francesco* 69 (2003): 5–56.

that Salimbene tells us there was a complete set of Joachim's works at Hyères, including his commentary on the Gospels, the latter being a final, unfinished work that exists today in very few manuscripts and, according to Salimbene, was not available to John of Parma, an ardent Joachite, until Salimbene copied it for John while in Hyères.

The important thing here is that Joachim's *oeuvre*, legitimate and illegitimate, was large, complex, and fascinating enough to keep a subset of Franciscans very busy exploring it. These were the people Salimbene called variously *Ioachite, magni Ioachite*, and even *maximi Ioachite*. Nor were they all Franciscans. They could also be Florensians, Cistercians, Dominicans, or secular clergy. At Hyères, if we can trust Salimbene, they could include judges, notaries, physicians, and other learned laity who came to hear Hugh of Digne expound on Joachim.

There were elements within Joachim's thought that could easily be claimed as joint property of the Franciscans and Dominicans. Joachim spoke of two new orders who would lead the church into the third age. As Marjorie Reeves observes,

> They were not "religious" in the traditional sense of withdrawing from the world, but rather intermediaries between the life of contemplation and the active life of secular clergy and laity. [Joachim] distinguishes two degrees of involvement in the world: one order will preach among the people, living an active life; the other will live the hermit life on the mountain top, interceding for the salvation of the world but finally descending in fiery denunciation of sin. Joachim describes the intermediate position of the first order under various figures, and notably under that of the Son of Man seated upon a white cloud in Revelation 14:14. This figure signifies "a certain order of just men to whom it is given to imitate perfectly the life of the Son of Man" (*quendam ordinem iustorum cui datum sit perfecte imitari vitam filii hominis*). These men will be learned enough to evangelize, yet their conversation will be light and spiritual as a cloud. The cloud itself symbolizes their position midway between heaven and earth, for their life will be contemplative in comparison with those involved in earthly affairs, but not as high as that of the hermits figured in the angel who issues from the temple in heaven (Revelation 14:17).[7]

---

7. Marjorie Reeves, *Joachim of Fiore and the Prophetic Future* (London: SPCK, 1976), 29–30. Reeves pursues the problem of the two new orders at greater length in *The Influence of Prophecy in the Later Middle Ages* (Oxford: Clarendon, 1969), especially 142–44.

For a while both the Franciscans and the Dominicans on the highest of official levels were apparently open to applying this notion of the two new orders to themselves. In 1255 the leaders of the two orders, John of Parma and Humbert of Romans, issued a joint encyclical suggesting as much;[8] but events would soon encourage the Dominicans to create a safe distance between themselves and Joachim, although a few individual Dominicans retained an interest in him. As we will see in a moment, some *magni Ioachite* in the Franciscan order were less cautious and would suffer for it.

So far, we have been speaking largely of Joachim's authentic works. In addition, there were various inauthentic ones. If we can believe Salimbene, Hugh of Digne had access to some of them, too, and deployed them skillfully in an argument with a Dominican who said that he valued Joachim as much as he valued the fifth wheel on a cart.[9] The opening words of that sentence, "If we can believe Salimbene," raise an important question to which we will return in a moment. First we should say something about the inauthentic works, or at least the most important of them for our purposes, the commentary on Jeremiah.

Labeling the commentary *Super Ieremiam* as inauthentic may distort the facts to some extent. In reality, the commentary might straddle the "authentic" and "inauthentic" categories in an interesting way. Damien Ruiz sums the matter up neatly:

> It has been demonstrated convincingly that we are dealing with a composite work within which we can identify a primitive stage probably due to Joachim of Fiore (ca. 1197). This first stage of the text was then glossed a first time within the Florensian order, giving birth to a brief revised text of the *Super Ieremiam* (ca. 1223) which was in turn the subject of a commentary within the Franciscan Order in Italy around 1243. As for the longest revision of the text, it would have been composed within the Franciscan milieu between 1248 and 1249.[10]

---

8. Luke Wadding, *Annales minorum* (Rome: Typis Rochi Bernabò, 1731), 3:380.

9. *The Chronicle of Salimbene de Adam*, trans. Joseph L. Baird and John Robert Kane (Binghamton, NY: University Center at Binghamton, 1986), 231–48. The debate would have taken place in 1248.

10. Ruiz, "Es tu infatuatus sicut alii qui istam doctrinam secuntur?," in *Experiences religieuses et chemins de perfection dans l'occident médiéval* (Paris: AIBL, 2012), 277–92; Robert Moynihan, "The Development of the 'Pseudo-Joachim' Commentary 'Super Ieremiam,'" *Mélanges de l'Ecole française de Rome, Moyen Age* 98 (1986): 109–42. But see Stephen Wessley, *Joachim of Fiore and Monastic Reform* (New York: Peter Lang, 1990), 101–13, and Daniel, "A Re-examination of the Origins of Franciscan Joachism," 671.

Whether everyone would agree with every part of Ruiz's summary is less important to us than the fact that by the late 1240s the *Super Ieremiam* was being read by Franciscans on the assumption that it was by Joachim. Salimbene describes how, when he was at Provins with Gerard of Borgo San Donnino and Bartholomew Guiscolo, they received news that King Louis IX was preparing to go on crusade. Gerard and Bartholomew predicted that it would turn out badly for Louis and proved as much by showing Salimbene a prophecy from the *Super Ieremiam*.

That brings us to another matter, the relevance of a work like the *Super Ieremiam* to the subject of Revelation commentaries. Despite the fact that, as Ruiz's brief history of the various redactions suggests, what we have in the printed editions is a palimpsest informed by different concerns at different levels, and despite the fact that it is, after all, purportedly a commentary on Jeremiah rather than Revelation, it nevertheless reflects a series of concerns that, by the middle of the thirteenth century, could be voiced in a number of contexts including Revelation commentaries. In fact, they were especially suitable for inclusion in Revelation commentaries once those commentaries began to reflect the sorts of prophetic concerns found in Joachim's authentic works.

Certain elements in the *Super Ieremiam* presumably can be traced back to specific concerns in the life of the Florensian order;[11] but Franciscan Joachites such as Gerard, Salimbene, or, for that matter, John of Parma, minister general of the Franciscan order and *magna Ioachita*, were not interested in what it had meant a half century earlier. They expected it to make sense for their own time. Nor were they interested in tracing the history of its various redactions. It was, for them, all of a piece and all the work of Joachim. That is the way they read it, and that is how we will read it here.[12]

The commentary was in some ways a trendsetter. Among other things, it projected an apocalyptic role for the empire (especially Frederick II, although it claims to have been written in 1197 and to be addressed to Henry VI) and for the church hierarchy, which it charges with greedily pursuing wealth and neglecting the faithful. What impresses the reader is not the idea that the church has faults but the sheer magnitude of those faults. The whole church from top to bottom is corrupt, with the exception of a few *spirituales* who are, of course, persecuted by the hierarchy.

Change will soon arrive in the form of a hostile power that intends

11. Reeves, *Prophecy in the Later Middle Ages*, 34–36, points to a passage she sees as reflecting anger at the condemnation of 1215.

12. What follows is taken from the Venice 1525 edition.

to destroy the church but will actually exercise God's vengeance on it, re-forming it. The hostile power will then in turn be destroyed. The document speaks of a threefold attack by the empire, the Cathars, and the Muslims. The imagery tends to shift, but Revelation 13 is used effectively, with the dragon and two beasts representing the empire, heretics, and Muslims (although elsewhere the two beasts are made to stand for the empire and Muslims).

One must avoid stating the matter too clearly. More is shifting here than the imagery. Sometimes the commentary seems to depict the emperor as protector of the Christian borderlands whose weakness allows the eastern power to attack Christendom, a scenario based to some extent on Revelation 9 and 16. At other times the widespread image of Frederick II as a friend of Muslims and heretics manages to produce a very different scenario in which the empire is allied with the Muslims and heretics in despoiling the church. We have here a treasure trove of possible scenarios that could be (and was) exploited by thirteenth-century Revelation commentaries.

In any case, the long-range result for the church will be positive. The effect of these attacks will be to purify the church, robbing it of the wealth it shouldn't have anyway. A group of *spirituales* will survive, functioning for a while without an official hierarchy, and from this righteous remnant a new order (or orders) will grow. The church—symbolized by the figure of the woman in Revelation 12—will survive the threat and emerge from it uncor-rupted by wealth yet rich in its new *intellectus spiritualis* and contemplative experience. The result will be conversion of the Greeks, Jews, and infidels. This optimistic prophecy did not fall on deaf ears. We will hear it echoed later.

But for the moment we must take stock of how much we know con-cerning what the *magni Ioachite* were saying in the mid-thirteenth century. Salimbene tells us that by 1247 he was already being warned about his fas-cination with Joachim, but he is remarkably lax when it comes to telling us what Joachite ideas he was being warned against. If we were to accept what he says about Hugh's use of the Jeremiah commentary and other pseudo-Joachite works, that might give us at least some insight, and we desperately want to trust Salimbene's stories because they are so engagingly presented and we have so little else to fall back on; yet a great many historians, from Oswald Holder-Egger[13] to Damien Ruiz,[14] have expressed skepticism on just that point, although for different reasons.

---

13. Editor of the chronicle as published in the Monumenta Germaniae Historica, Scrip-tores, 32 (Hanover and Leipzig, 1905–1913).

14. Ruiz, "Es tu infatuatus sicut alii qui istam doctrinam secuntur?"

In order to understand Holder-Egger's distrust, we must return to that debate mentioned earlier between Hugh and the Dominican (whose name was Peter). Here as elsewhere Holder-Egger is almost instinctively suspicious of Salimbene's narration of extensive conversations, which sometimes read as if Salimbene was working from a transcript. Holder-Egger's instinct seems a sane one to follow if what we seek is a verbatim report of what was said. Even today, with all our recorders and television cameras, we find ourselves trying to decide what was said a great deal of the time. Even if our security services were to succeed in preserving everything that was said by all of us all the time, we would simply be presented with new problems. How would we access it in a meaningful way? How would we present it in a useful manner?

Salimbene and other historians solved their own problems, and to some extent ours, by seeing history as a literary discipline. The historian's task was not to preserve every word spoken but to present an entertaining narrative that could be considered accurate insofar as it encapsulated the essence of the problem being discussed. Thus Salimbene, looking back on an event that took place over thirty years earlier, might have considered his narrative of the Hugh-Peter debate a success if he managed to hold the reader's attention while presenting what he saw as the basic issue at hand. That was the most one could expect of someone who moved around a great deal without a laptop or a smartphone with access to the cloud. And that is what would have been entailed if we were to expect a factually accurate general report, let alone a verbatim report.

Holder-Egger, however, thinks he has found a smoking gun that will convict Salimbene of historical malfeasance. The debate as recorded by Salimbene centers around four numbers from inauthentic sources,[15] all of which are seen as important in predicting the date of Emperor Frederick II's death. In the course of this conversation Hugh seems to leap from 1248 to a time after Frederick's death, noting that "he lived thirty years and eleven days, so that the prophecy of the [Erithean] Sibyl should be fulfilled." Holder-Egger is struck not only by the chronological leap but also by the reference to prophecies (the *Dicta Merlini* and the Erithean Sibyl) that he feels were written after Frederick's death. Thus he concludes that Salimbene made up the entire conversation.

In his doctoral dissertation, Robert Moynihan has several important things to say concerning this passage, but one thing in particular seems to

---

15. Particularly the *Dicta Merlini*, although other sources, including the *Super Ieremiam*, are involved.

solve the problem. Mohynihan suggests that the passage in which Hugh seems to stray into post-1250 territory is actually "a kind of *post factum* gloss" inserted by Salimbene.[16] This, like much of Moynihan's work, seems based more on instinct than on polished historical argument, but Moynihan's instincts are themselves impressive and strike one as worth taking seriously.

One could also raise a question about Salimbene's narrative based on the dissonance between his description of Hugh's ardent Joachimism and the fact that Hugh's writings as we have them seem innocent of any Joachite influence. That dissonance is an important factor in Ruiz's uncertainty as to whether Salimbene is reporting Hugh's thoughts on the death of Frederick or his own thoughts on that event. It remains an important but largely unanswerable question. Here again we have a scholar with excellent instincts pursuing a topic that seems to defy any demonstrable solution.

John of Parma, who became minister general in 1248 and who, a decade later, became inextricably enmeshed in a scandal over Joachism that forced his resignation, is described by Salimbene as fanatically devoted to Joachism, but Salimbene's portrayal never really goes on to tell us what John fanatically believed. Angelo Clareno does, but he is writing substantially later than Salimbene, seems remarkably uninformed about the causes of John's resignation, and has a huge axe to grind.

Ubertino da Casale is a more promising source. He tells us that he visited John at his hermitage in Greccio four years before John's death (i.e., probably in 1285). During that visit John told him that the sixth seal took its beginning from Francis and his state. John went on to bewail the damage done to the Franciscan life and rule caused by Francis's transgressing sons and to condemn the carnal church, which should be called Babylon rather than Jerusalem. He predicted that the carnal church would receive the just punishment described in the sixth vision of the Apocalypse.[17] Ubertino thus seems to suggest that in 1285 Hugh recognized Francis as the angel of the sixth seal, saw Francis as ushering in the sixth period of church history, distinguished between a spiritual and carnal church, and thought the latter would be punished; but the word "seems" should warn us that we are reading a great deal into very little and that the opinions we see described here, however well or poorly they describe John's beliefs, certainly resemble Ubertino's own. Moreover, at best what we see here could tell us what John

16. Robert Moynihan, "Joachim of Fiore and the Early Franciscans: A Study of the Commentary 'Super Hieremiam,' Volume 1" (dissertation, Yale University, 1988), 118.

17. Ubertino da Casale, *Arbor vitae* (Turin: Bottega d'Erasmo, 1961), 422.

believed in 1285, not what John had believed three decades earlier. We will return to John in a moment.

While we are inspecting notable Joachites, we would do well to look more closely at Salimbene himself. Robert Moynihan reminds us that, "of the 652 pages of text in Holder-Egger's MGH edition of the chronicle, two-thirds are devoted to a twenty-year period from the late 1230s through the mid-1250s."[18] Whatever else Salimbene chose to include in his description of this period, he gave ample space to the flowering of a Franciscan Joachism in Italy and France. His narrative can be read as the bittersweet recollection of a love gone sour. As one might expect from a man who threw himself into the affair so enthusiastically, Salimbene provides us with a lively sense of his initial interest, growing obsession, eventual disillusionment, and yet continuing attraction.

Part of this process is encapsulated in his exchange with Brother Bartholomew. The original topic of their conversation is John of Parma's Joachism, not Salimbene's. There is agreement between them that John could have done great things as minister general had he not clung stubbornly to "the prophecies of fantastic men." But John was not the only one attracted by those prophecies. "Brother Bartholomew said to me, 'And you likewise were a Joachimite.' I said, 'What you say is true. But after the death of the Emperor Frederick and the passing of the year 1260, I laid that doctrine completely aside, and now I plan to believe in nothing save what I can see.'"[19]

We sense here the theme of countless mid-twentieth-century songs: "I'm through with love, I'll never fall in love again"; yet, like other songs from that period, the narrative Salimbene spins out for us in that critical section of his chronicle leads him back on a trail of remembrance that allows him to revisit the old places and recall the past, reliving some its happier moments. That, too, is the stuff of mid-twentieth-century love songs. "I'll be seeing you in all the old familiar places."

There is a point to all this recollection, though. Reading Salimbene's trip down memory lane reminds us of those songs commemorating a love that ended but probably shouldn't and wouldn't have if the participants had only behaved more sensibly. At times Salimbene seems intent on defending Joachim against the later Joachites. For example, at one point he announces that, "although Abbot Joachim was a holy man, his doctrine has three main defects."[20] The first defect turns out to be Joachim's criticism of Peter Lombard on the Trinity; yet

---

18. Moynihan, "Joachim of Fiore and the Early Franciscans," 114.
19. *The Chronicle of Salimbene de Adam*, 302.
20. *The Chronicle of Salimbene de Adam*, 230–31.

Salimbene goes on to mention the problems he himself has in agreeing with the Lombard. The second "defect" is that Joachim predicted future tribulations, which is "the very reason, in fact, why the Jews killed the prophets. . . . For carnal men do not hear about future tribulations gladly; they prefer consolation." Thus this "defect" places Joachim alongside prophets like Jeremiah.

The third "defect" involves not Joachim but those of his followers who laid out a precise timetable, something Joachim refused to do, offering at most a series of possibilities. We will hear Salimbene launch a similar charge (or the same charge aimed more specifically) later when he talks about Gerard of Borgo San Donnino. We will turn to Gerard shortly. For the moment we need only note the way Salimbene describes Gerard's book. He says it "contained many lies against the teaching of the Abbot Joachim, which the Abbot had never written."[21] The point here is that when Salimbene enumerates the three defects of Joachim's doctrine, they tend to resolve into the defects of people other than Joachim.

Salimbene's criticism of the Apostles, the rival group led by Gerardo Segarelli, is interesting in this regard. Salimbene points out that Joachim predicted the Franciscans and Dominicans but made no mention of the Apostles; nor can they be identified with any of the seven orders delineated in Joachim's *Liber figurarum*.[22] In short, the Apostles cannot be legitimate because Joachim did not predict them.

In these passages we again get the sense of a layered Joachite tradition. One might think that Salimbene was familiar enough with Joachim's genuine writings—remember, he was at Hyères and participated in the copying of Joachim's commentary on the Gospels—to recognize that the Joachite Gerard of Borgo San Donnino, as Salimbene describes him, was delivering a message Joachim himself would have rejected; yet Salimbene had no reason to see a work like the commentary on Jeremiah as inauthentic. Here we see the significance of his conversation with Brother Bartholomew. Salimbene accepted both the authentic Joachim and the inauthentic works that had been developing throughout the early thirteenth century. Thus he, like several others, defended a "Joachism" containing much that was truly in line with Joachim's own thought, but also much that was not, including much involving prophecy concerning Frederick, the empire, and the apocalyptic change that would be discernible around the year 1260. When Frederick died in 1250, well before his death was expected, and when the year 1260 came and went

21. *The Chronicle of Salimbene de Adam*, 463.
22. *The Chronicle of Salimbene de Adam*, 293.

with some evidence of apocalyptic turmoil but not enough to really satisfy expectations, the result was a crisis of confidence on the part of people like Salimbene, although less of a crisis for some others who stuck to their beliefs. It is roughly the same in modern apocalyptic movements, where the same degree of negative evidence encourages some to create psychological distance between themselves and the group while others decide to double down.

But then—and here we return to the layered tradition—Joachism was visited with a major shock in the form of Gerard of Borgo San Donnino's heresy of the eternal gospel. Here Salimbene is a remarkably helpful source. He met Gerard at Provins in 1247, when Louis IX was preparing for his disastrous crusade in Egypt. He and another Joachite, Bartholomew Guiscolo, had what struck Salimbene as an impressive library of Joachim's works, and they did their best to turn Salimbene into a serious Joachim afficionado. He tells of their showing him the passage in the *Super Ieremiam* that prophesied the crusade would turn out badly for Louis. That news understandably irritated the French Franciscans, who tried to counter it by insisting that the prophecy had already been fulfilled in the preceding crusade. Salimbene describes Gerard as "a well mannered young man, honorable and good, but with the single exception that he was too obstinate in the teaching of Joachim and could never be swayed from his own fixed opinion."[23]

From there Salimbene went to the Franciscan house at Auxerre, Bartholomew to the one at Sens, and Gerard to Paris where he studied four years, preparing himself to teach in the province of Sicily. But then, Salimbene says,

> [Gerard] thought out the foolish plan of writing a little book, and he showed his foolishness by publishing that book among the brothers. (I shall speak again of this book when I come to Pope Alexander IV, who condemned it.) And because of this book, the order was brought into shame, both in Paris and elsewhere. Therefore, Brother Gerard was, as a result, deprived of his office as lector, and relieved of his duties of preaching, hearing confession, and every other legitimate act of the order. And because he refused to mend his ways and admit his guilt humbly, but, rather, obstinately and shamelessly, persevered in his pertinacity and contumacy, the friars placed him in chains in prison and fed him "with the bread of affliction and water of distress." . . . Indeed, he allowed himself to die in prison and was buried in a corner of the garden, deprived of Christian burial. May all men know, therefore, that the rigor of justice is preserved in the order of the friars minor against

23. *The Chronicle of Salimbene de Adam*, 228–29.

transgressors of the order. There is not a single act of foolishness that can be imputed to the entire order.

Later in the *Chronicle*, Salimbene returns to the matter, furnishing new information. He says Gerard's book "contained many lies against the abbot Joachim, which the abbot had never written. For it maintained that the gospel of Christ and the teaching of the New Testament had never led anybody to perfection and that they were to be superseded in the year 1260." Salimbene says Gerard "wrote this little book in Paris and made its contents known to certain ignorant brothers." As a result, "he was sent back to his own province, and, because he would not recant his foolish errors, Brother Bonaventure, who was in France, sent for him."

Salimbene follows this rather harsh assessment with an anecdote that casts his relationship with Gerard in a somewhat different light.

> And when Brother Gerard came through Modena, I was living there and I told him that I had been with him in Provins. . . . Therefore I said to him since he was an acquaintance of mine, "Shall we debate about Joachim?" Then he said to me, "Let us not debate, but let us simply compare notes in some secluded place." Therefore I led him behind the dormitory and we seated ourselves under a vine. And I said, "I wish to know when and where the Antichrist will be born." Then he answered, "He has already been born and is a grown man, and soon the mystery of iniquity will work itself out."

Gerard went on to support his view by citing Isaiah 18, which he interpreted as referring to the present king of Castile. At that point a group of friars and others passed in the meadow behind the dormitory, and Gerard sent Salimbene to discover what they were upset about. Salimbene returned with the news that the archbishop of Ravenna had been captured by Ezzelino. Gerard's response was, "See, the mysteries now begin!"

Gerard then asked Salimbene about a certain man in Parma who had the prophetic spirit, and Salimbene replied that he knew the man well. Gerard asked if Salimbene could get the man's writings for him, and Salimbene told him that the man now lived at the Cistercian monastery at Fontevivo. Salimbene suggested that Gerard could visit the man, who would gladly give him the writings. He noted that the man lived scarcely two miles off Gerard's route. "But he said to me, 'My companions do not wish to turn aside from the way. Therefore, I beseech you as a favor to me to go and get them for me.' Then he went his way, and I never saw him again."

Salimbene did try to fulfill Gerard's request, but when he went to the monastery where the man had been living, he found that the man was dead and his writings had been destroyed, partly to prevent any scandal from falling on the monastery because of them. The anecdote apparently reminds Salimbene of an occasion many years later at Imola when someone brought him a copy of Gerard's book and asked him what should be done with it. Salimbene told him to burn it, for it contained "many frivolous words worthy only of scorn" and had been condemned.

Salimbene goes on to say more or less what he has said earlier about Gerard. He was "a friendly, courteous, generous, religious, honorable, modest, well-mannered man, temperate in word, in dress, in food, and in drink," but "the perversity of his opinions destroyed all of these good qualities."[24]

Those opinions must have been very perverse indeed to counterbalance such virtue. In fact, by the standards of the time they actually were perverse, and here we return to what Salimbene describes as Gerard's "little book." In 1254 Gerard produced his *Evangelium aeternum*, or at least part of it. He intended it to consist of an introduction by himself followed by Joachim's *Liber de concordia*, *Expositio in apocalypsim*, and *Psalterium decem chordarum* with glosses by Gerard. We know that the "little book" offered by Parisian booksellers in 1254 contained at least Gerard's introduction and the *Liber de concordia*. It came at a bad moment, a time when the battle between the mendicants and Parisian secular masters was in full swing. The secular masters excerpted some of Gerard's most inflammatory ideas and made sure the pope was alerted. The pope formed the so-called Anagni commission, which produced its own list of passages. The result was that the pope condemned Gerard's introduction in 1255, although it should be added that at that point it was not all that obvious who had written it. John of Parma was accused of doing so, and the Dominicans were suspected as well.

Among the propositions considered by the papal commission, the following are significant:

1. Around the year 1200 the spirit of life departed from the two testaments so that there might be an eternal gospel.
2. Joachim's *Liber de concordia* should be considered the first book of the eternal gospel, the commentary on Revelation the second, and the *Psalterium decem chordarum* the third.

24. *The Chronicle of Salimbene de Adam*, 463–69. The word translated as "perversity" here is *protervitas*, which in this case might rather be translated as "boldness" or "impudence" or "recklessness."

3. At the beginning of the first *status*, three men appeared: Abraham, Isaac, and Jacob, the third of whom had twelve sons. At the beginning of the second *status*, three more appeared: Zechariah, John the Baptist, and Christ, the third of whom had twelve disciples. At the beginning of the third *status*, three more appeared: the man in linen (cf. Dan 12:7), the angel with a sharp sickle (Rev 14:14), and the angel bearing the sign of the living God (Rev 7:2), who originally was one of twelve. Joachim is the man in linen, and the people of the third *status* are committed to following his writings. The angel bearing the sign of the living God is Francis.

4. The eternal gospel was especially committed to that order which proceeds equally from the orders of laity and clerics, a barefoot order.

5. While we do not know how long the generations of the third status will be, we know from Scripture that they will be brief.

We should remember that the main target here was Gerard and his "little book," but neither the papal commission nor the Paris masters preceding them were all that skillful at separating Gerard's version of Joachim from the real one. There is one important difference, though. The Paris masters were out to smear not only Gerard but the mendicants in general, and in the process they were willing to offer an unflattering interpretation of Joachim. The Anagni commission, however, was composed of mendicants and their supporters, so their targets were primarily Gerard and secondarily Joachim.

Enter Florentius, bishop of Acre and future bishop of Arles, who appeared before the Anagni commission with a list of passages from Joachim he considered suspect. Here was a man primarily concerned, not about the mendicants or even about Gerard, but about Joachim. His presence undoubtedly nudged the commission toward greater concern about Joachim's orthodoxy.

What, then, was it primarily concerned *about*? Following Florentius, the commission decided that "the foundation of Joachim's teaching" is his theory of three *status*. The commission reads Joachim's prediction of a third *status* as implying that the second one will pass away, taking with it the church as they know it. The *ordo clericalis* will be replaced by a new order of monks. The sacraments will disappear. And according to Joachim's timetable the change will begin to occur in the very near future. Nor is the focus only on positive change. A great spiritual and physical tribulation will begin around 1260, and then, after a short respite, a great, mostly spiritual tribulation will follow and the Antichrist will be revealed.

All this may have been more or less in line with Joachim as Gerard interpreted him, yet it also reflected Joachim as Florentius wished the commission to see him. Nevertheless, when Pope Alexander finally spoke in October 1255, he condemned Gerard's introduction and not Joachim's writings. The result was profoundly unsatisfying for Florentius, and in 1263, as bishop of Arles, he tried to correct the oversight at a provincial synod. The acts of the synod forbid the use of Joachim's writings, attacking those who accept the idea of three *status* and who postulate a necessary concordance among them; venerate the Holy Spirit and expect the Son's role to end after a specific time; assume the Holy Spirit will be infused in that period, as if it had not been given at Pentecost; see the three *status* as involving three orders as well as a threefold pattern of Old Testament, New Testament, and eternal gospel of the Holy Spirit; and describe the spiritual gospel of the Son as literal. All this, according to the synod, implies that the redemption performed through Christ will be superseded and the sacraments of the second *status* will end.

Thus the result of the scandal was immediate and disastrous for Gerard and, to a lesser but nonetheless significant extent, for John of Parma, who had to resign his position as minister general. What happened to him next is unclear. Angelo Clareno offers the fullest narrative but also the most questionable one. According to Angelo, John was subjected to a hearing presided over by Bonaventure, whom John had recommended as his successor. It included everything but waterboarding. Bonaventure was seized with something resembling pathological rage. He himself would have preferred to see John spend the rest of his life in prison, but a cardinal friendly to John intervened, and John was allowed to slip away into obscurity in the form of a hermitage at Greccio.

It is tempting to dismiss Angelo's version of events out of hand. Angelo was not even in the order at the time, gets key aspects of the story wrong, and homogenizes Franciscan history, presenting John and Gerard as martyrs to the same cause Angelo himself was serving, as if throughout all of thirteenth-century history the order was fighting the same battle. He depicts not only John but also Gerard as defiantly defending, not Joachim's three *status*, but his doctrine of the Trinity; and he underlines Bonaventure's hypocrisy, claiming that Bonaventure told John in private that he shared his opinions yet informed someone else that, if he had not been concerned about the honor of the order, he would have had John openly punished as a heretic.[25]

---

25. On Angelo see Burr, *Olivi's Peaceable Kingdom* (Philadelphia: University of Pennsylvania Press, 1993), 9–14.

Nevertheless, once we have finished trashing Angelo's story we must acknowledge some odd resonances. Granting that Angelo is probably wrong in emphasizing Joachim's thought on the Trinity as he does, we might still wonder if, given the outrage expressed in the *Super Ieremiam* concerning the condemnation of Joachim's thoughts on the Trinity, either Gerard or John or both might have conducted some sort of rearguard defense of Joachim on that subject; and, given Salimbene's emphasis on John's almost fanatical Joachism, a harried Bonavenure, thrust into leadership at a moment of extreme crisis, might have looked to John for some flexibility on that score, found none, and said some things he later regretted.

The long-term effects for Bonaventure are worth pondering. The political aspects of his position—for example, his lack of leverage in negotiations concerning the order and its function within the church as a whole—are less relevant to the subject at hand, but his loss of leverage in the shadowy area of apocalyptic thought might be worth considering. If he really told John he agreed with him on Joachim, one might assume that he soon found he could afford to do so no longer; yet, curiously enough, he did go on to engage in some adventurous apocalyptic speculation himself. That story must be reserved for a future chapter, however.

As for Joachim, he managed to emerge from the crisis without papal condemnation, but the Anagni commission was clearly doubtful about his three *status*, and, thanks to Florentius, a provincial synod had produced the condemnation that could serve as a precedent.

One other result of the crisis should be noted. Franciscans were forbidden to publish any new writings outside the order without first receiving approval from the provincial ministers and diffinitors.[26] As we will see, that certainly did not mean the end of Joachite influence, but one might have expected it to limit the sort of influence scholars considered acceptable. That too must be reserved for a future chapter.[27]

---

26. *The Chronicle of Salimbene de Adam.*

27. Moynihan, "Joachim of Fiore and the Early Franciscans," 158–61, conducts an interesting survey of the evidence, which leads him to conclude that "Joachim's thought would have been within easy reach of virtually any mid-century Franciscan who wished to have contact with it." This is a useful reminder that, although few friars were willing to pay the heavy price of adhering to Gerard's extreme position and perhaps few were even tempted to do so, a substantial number of friars were at least in a position to know something about Joachim.

ALEXANDER MINORITA

Saint John, apostle and evangelist, was sent into exile on the island of Patmos by the Caesar Domitian because he preached the word of God. There he saw, heard, and wrote down this apocalypse. Great as is the concord between law and gospel, equally great is the concord between this book and the volumes of the ancient prophets. Thus the Lord says, I have not come to destroy the law but to fulfill it. Ezekiel saw four animals and so did John. Zechariah saw four horses that were red, black, white, and of mixed color, and so did John. And the prophets are concordant in various things so as to show that there is one God of the New and Old Testament.[1]

Thus at the beginning Alexander states his mission. He fits within the early thirteenth-century Joachite tradition. Exegesis is all about *concordia*; but the *concordia* to which he calls attention is not so much between Old Testament and New as it is between the Apocalypse and an apocalyptically oriented Old Testament prophet like Ezekiel.

Alexander goes on to note that "John saw these things not with corporeal eyes but through images he perceived in his mind, and he understood the truth contained in them." That brings him to the seals, which in turn brings him to Jerome, like others before him.

---

1. Alexander, *Expositio in apocalypsim* (hereafter Alexander, *Expos.*), Monumenta Historiae Germanica, Quellen, I (Weimar: Hermann Böhlaus Nachfolger, 1955).

The Blessed Jerome says, "In the Apocalypse the book is seen to be sealed with seven seals, and if you were to give it to someone who was literate and asked that person to read it, that person would reply to you, 'I cannot, it is sealed.' No matter how literate people today might consider themselves to be, they would judge that the book was sealed and could be opened only by one who had the key of David, the power to open and no one can shut, or to shut and no one can open." And again Jerome says, "The Apocalypse of John has as many mysteries [*sacramenta*] as words. I have said little here, for anything that could be said in the way of praise would be insufficient. Multiple meanings are concealed in every word of this work."

Like Joachim before him, Alexander has a story to tell us about how the scales fell from his eyes. At that point in his life he was searching for yet another form of *concordia*, that between the Apocalypse and church history.

Since our interest was turned toward the history of the church, and was focused on the relationship between prophecies and events, we searched for some concord between events and the words of this book. We found none; but then on a certain Lord's Day, as we were preparing as best we could for communion, certain things about this book appeared to us, albeit obscurely. But then, as our mind fluctuated on this matter, on the third day, having taken in communion the body of our Lord, the lamb without whom the book cannot be opened in heaven, on earth, nor under the earth, on that same day we were able to understand the greater part of the book according to the order of history, and later we were taught how other parts should be understood. What does this book teach us that we would consider useful? Among other things (and this would be a long story to tell) an angel identified himself as our fellow servant of the Lamb and called us blessed for being such. Those who believe that the Lamb would graciously deign to reveal such things to an unworthy layman will render thanks to God and the Lamb. Others, not wishing to believe that what we say has now been fulfilled since it does not appear to have been according to the surface of the letter of this sealed book, are like the Jews refusing to believe that the messiah (that is, our Lord Jesus Christ) has come since, according to surface meaning of the prophet, the lion still does not live with the lamb nor the leopard with the kid.

After a few more pages of general introduction, Alexander launches into the exegesis of chapter 1, and we begin to see what sort of structure the

Lamb recommended to him. It is, indeed, a very historical reading, but in a different sense than either Richard of Saint Victor or Joachim offers. Joachim views the Apocalypse as a sequentially arranged trip through church history, but in fact both Richard and Joachim offer an obvious recapitulative element. Here in Alexander's commentary the book of Revelation is presented as a progressive trip through church history, beginning at its beginning and ending at its end. We begin with chapter 1 and the first vision, that of the letters to seven churches in Asia Minor, which is in one sense the easiest vision to fit into Alexander's pattern since it deals specifically with the early church.

Alexander is comfortable with a word-by-word exegesis that reveals his desire to place the text in historical context. He describes the heresies and persecutions experienced during the author's time, always assuming that the seven churches in question are primarily the seven churches of Asia Minor and that Ephesus is its metropolitan seat presided over by John, but also that reference to seven churches is a way of referring to all existing churches.

The latter focus allows Alexander to refer once more to his own status in the process of expositing the words "blessed is he who reads and he who hears" (Rev 1:3). He says, "Blessed is he who reads, as do those who are literate or clerics, and he who hears, as do laity, because many can hear when someone is reading to them. This person speaks to learners. What is said earlier of laity refers to someone in no religious order and instructed in no liberal art." Then he again drops the matter. If he himself is the layman he has in mind, he is using the term in a special sense. He knows a great deal of early church history and much previous exegesis of Revelation. Nor was it read to him. His reading is narrower when we compare him to some other, later exegetes (particularly Nicholas of Lyra, who offers a wider reading list and uses it to greater effect); but Alexander supplies a great deal of data. Perhaps he is *laicus* in the sense that he is not a priest or has not received the sort of formal education young Franciscans had begun to receive, but he is by no means uneducated.

When Alexander arrives at chapter 4 and John's second major vision, that of the book with seven seals, the scene shifts to heaven, but Alexander's reading of the seals will continue the sequential historical exposition.

> Some people interpret the seals in this way: the first seal is the Lord's incarnation; the second his nativity; the third his passion; the fourth his resurrection; the fifth his opening the disciples' sense so that they can understand Scripture; the sixth the Lord's ascension; and the seventh

the final judgment.[2] But this exposition is not very intelligible, because later they do not interpret the first seal as the Lord's incarnation; and they interpret the red horse not as Christ's nativity but as persecutors of the martyrs and say the rider of the horse is the devil. And we find the black horse identified by them not with the Lord's passion but with heretics, and again the rider is identified as the devil. Moreover, they interpret the fourth seal not as Christ's resurrection but as false brothers, and the rider of the pallid horse is, again, the devil. And in the case of the other seals we do not find this order observed, so that the white horse stands for the incarnation, the red one for the nativity, the black one for the passion, the pallid for the resurrection, the souls under the altar for the opening of their senses, the earthquake for the ascension, and the opening of the seventh seal as future judgment. We, however, according to the revelation of the Lamb, exposit the seals according to an order of many kings, for the angel tells John, "You must prophesy concerning many peoples and kings."

Alexander takes the kings absolutely seriously as an ordering principle. The opening of the first six seals tells the story of Christian martyrdom under ten Roman rulers from Gaius through Domitian. Of course, he sees the Jews, too, as persecutors, and he sees history as the story, not only of Christian martyrdom, but of divine affliction visited on the Jews and Romans for their part in that martyrdom.

He is obviously aware that some exegetes prefer a recapitulative approach when dealing with the seven seals. In fact, the passage just quoted openly acknowledges as much. He is also aware that in treating the seals as a history of Christian persecution under the pagan emperors, he is breaking with those exegetes who see the seals as containing a prophecy of Antichrist. Having brought his narrative into the fourth century, Alexander pauses to recognize that, too, noting that he has fitted into a consistent historical narrative of the past what other commentators interpret as pertaining to Antichrist in the future. He offers no complicated rationale for his decision, simply observing that their behavior seems irrational. As for passages that might seem to demand discussion of Antichrist, he prefers to see them as referring to lesser antichrists in the spirit of 1 John 2:18.

Alexander is still thinking about the problem as he begins to exposit Revelation 7.

2. Those so arguing include Bruno de Segni, Rupert of Deutz, and Haimo.

After this I saw (7:9). He doesn't say "before." Because it would be absurd if we treated **the wrath of the lamb** (6:16) as referring to the day of judgment and then immediately returned to the devil and the four kings, because immediately after in the narrative come those four kings, of which John says, **After this I saw four angels** (7:1), that is, four kings through which four evil angels were working.

Why are they called angels? Because by "angels" John means messengers, and these four are messengers of Satan. Alexander names them, then goes on to Revelation 7:2 where the angel rising from the place of the sun turns out to be Constantine, the messenger of God. He defeats his political rivals, the persecution ends, and by 7:3 the bishops are at Nicaea. Alexander's success in steering the narrative toward this goal says a great deal about his *modus operandi*. He proceeds by what we have been referring to as a line-by-line exegesis in which he identifies John's rich symbolism with very specific persons and events. The exegetical rules he applies in effecting this translation allow him substantial freedom. For example, at Revelation 7:2, "I saw another angel ascending from the place of the sun," he reminds us that "in the person of angels this prophecy speaks of men, as was clear with the bishops of Asia." That was, we realize, a major assumption in dealing with the angels of the seven churches. The angel of 7:2 is also a man, but this time a political leader, because, for Alexander, the vision of the seven seals is largely about political leaders. This one is said in the book of Revelation to have the sign of the living God, because he is said in the early Christian sources to have looked up and seen the cross of Christ in the sky. He calls out in a loud voice to the four angels who have been given power to harm the land and the sea, **"Do not harm the land or the sea or the trees until we put a seal on the foreheads of the servants of our God"** (7:3). Alexander identifies the four angels (for the third time) with the emperors Maxentius, Licinius, Maximus, and Severus, whom Constantine prevents from harming the Christians by defeating them. He put a seal on the foreheads of Christians by bringing peace to the church and acknowledging its authority, most specifically at Nicaea. Alexander describes the council in terms of Constantine and his supporters placing a seal on the foreheads of Pope Sylvester and the 318 bishops who attended.

All this is, in a sense, impressive. Like a magician reaching into his hat and pulling out a rabbit, Alexander has reached into Revelation 7:2-3 and extracted a basic historical structure that he can embellish with whatever else he feels he knows about the Constantinian era, including the story of how Constantine was cured of leprosy.

The vision of the seven seals gives us an opportunity to mention in passing another aspect of Alexander's exegesis, his tendency to personalize imagery. That is, things are interpreted as people. That is hardly something only Alexander indulges in. Alexander simply does a great deal more of it, and it becomes an important element in his translation of the Apocalypse into ecclesiastical history. For example, in dealing with Revelation 6 he sees himself as, in effect, demythologizing the apocalyptic language and finding beneath it a story of human beings struggling to survive in the midst of persecution. When he comes to Revelation 6:13, **and the stars fell upon the earth**, he says,

> that is, when those in the church who seemed to shine with right faith and just works were struck with these terrible persecutions, they left the faith and fell into the enjoyment of earthly delights, as we read in the *Ecclesiastical History.* For if men could not be seen as stars who fell from heaven, then Jeremiah would never have said, "The Lord has hurled the splendor of Israel down from heaven to earth" (Lam 2:1), when he ejected them from the synagogue. For to that point the people of Israel never had ascended to heaven. **And the stars in the sky fell to earth, as figs drop from a fig tree when shaken by a strong wind.** The figs he refers to here are the early fruits that, before they come to maturity, are blown off and fall to the ground. In the same way those who had not yet matured in good works were struck by persecution and fell into error. It could not happen, however, that the elect could be led into error. **And heaven,** that is the church, receded like a scroll being rolled up. In Isaiah it says, "My sword will be drunk in heaven," that is, in the church. On a rolled-up scroll, what is inside cannot be seen. Thus the saints of that time manifested themselves to some and hid themselves from others, for, as it is written, the faithful celebrated the divine office in crypts underground. If the elect and the church could not be designated through the sun, moon, stars, and heaven, the prophet Joel would never have said, "A large and mighty army comes, such as never was from the beginning. Before them the earth shakes, the heavens tremble, the sun and moon are darkened, and the stars no longer shine" (Joel 2:2, 10). For it seems impossible that the sun and moon should have been concealed from the view of anyone and the heavens moved. But as was said above, through this the faithful and the church are designated. **And all the mountains and islands were moved from their places** (6:14). He calls the more eminent and notable people "mountains," as the Lord says to the people of Israel when he says,

"Mountains of Israel, hear the word of the Lord" (Ezek 6:3), because a literal mountain cannot hear. Thus by this the more excellent men are designated. The islands denote the more humble who patiently sustain the inundations of the impious, who, "like the tossing sea, cannot rest" (Isa 57:20). These are moved from their places by permission of the Lord, who says, "If you are persecuted in this city, flee to another" (Matt 10:23). Here the sense is: **Then the kings of the earth, the princes, the generals, the rich, the mighty, and everyone else, both slave and free** (6:14). Here, as is said, the faithful fled the kings of the earth as persecutors, but the kings of the earth of whom we spoke, once they became Christians, sought aid from the saints. For then two emperors, Marcus and Philippus, who reigned in the year 247, were the first to become Christians, well before Constantine, just as Abimelech reigned before Saul and David. And then along with **the princes, the generals, the rich, the mighty, and everyone else, both slave and free hid themselves in caves and among the rocks of the mountains,** because whatever the emperors did, good or bad, they had many helpers. They hid in caves. The caves represent the aid of the saints. The rocks represent the aid of the elect. **And they said to the mountains** (6:16), just as the prophets said to the mountains, "Mountains of Israel, hear the word of the Lord" (Ezek 6:3; 36:1). These mountains, as we have said, are unable to hear, but by them men are meant. Thus these, under the name of mountains, cry out to the saints, contemplating celestial things. That is what Pope Fabian and others did.

The passage is worth examining because it goes a long way toward explaining Alexander's approach to exegesis, and Alexander's approach is hardly unique. One might start by reading all of Revelation 6–7 and then asking whether anyone reading it without Alexander's guidance would deduce that it intended to present a sequential narrative tracing a history of the church around the time of Constantine. Certainly not. Alexander has chosen the sequential narrative approach and then done his best to read the text in that way. To say that much is hardly to dismiss Alexander as a fool. We all have to do *something* with the Apocalypse. Laying the seven visions end to end and treating them as historical narrative may overlook a great deal about the structure of Revelation, but it is not entirely inaccurate to see a temporal progression in the work. Alexander's fault lies in not knowing when to stop, not knowing that the Holy Spirit did not expect us to look specifically for the emperors Marcus and Philippus, let alone Muhammad (as we will see shortly).

Another way of approaching the same problem would be to examine Alexander's understanding of symbolism. He is, as we have seen, fond of suggesting a one-to-one correspondence in which things stand for people. Perhaps the most interesting part of his approach is his appeal to Old Testament prophets such as Joel and Ezekiel in justifying his reading. Ezekiel, for example, must have been addressing people instead of literal mountains because, as Alexander has informed us, mountains cannot hear. The problem here is that anyone reading Ezekiel 6:3 in context would recognize that he actually *is* addressing literal mountains because Ezekiel, like Joel and like Saint John the Divine, is a poet and speaks the language of poets. Alexander, like Moliere's bourgeois gentleman, speaks prose, which places him at a disadvantage when it comes to reading things like Ezekiel and the Apocalypse. Yet even Alexander will have his poetic moments before he finishes his commentary.

It is worth noting that Alexander imports Revelation 20:4 into the narrative at this point.[3] He observes, "The priests will reign one thousand years." He seems to offer a more or less firm date for the beginning of the millennium when he says, "From the days of Jesus Christ the son of God, around 325 years passed before priests began to rule as judges. They first began to rule, the persecution having ceased for the most part, after the seventh year of Constantine's reign, when the cross of Christ appeared to him."[4] Thus, if he is serious about the thousand years (and he is), Satan is due to be released around 1325 CE.

Revelation 7 yields to Revelation 8, the opening of the seventh seal, the death of Constantine, and all the troubles that followed. Alexander's attitude toward the period is neatly encapsulated in his presentation of Revelation 8:2: "**And I saw seven angels**, all of whom were heretics except one." His interpretation of the vision of seven trumpets features Arians and Germanic tribes. The next ray of hope shines forth at Revelation 10:1 when an angel descends from heaven wrapped in a cloud, with a rainbow above his head and his face like the sun, which Alexander manages to reduce to Justinian

---

3. Alexander, *Expos.*, 114.

4. The reference to priests ruling as judges refers back to a *concordia* of sorts that Alexander has delineated between the Old and New Testaments. He notes that "from the time of Jesu Nave, who was also called Josue, 325 years passed until the end of the book of Judges, and during twenty-five of them Jesu ruled the people." Then he makes the comment about 325 years passing from the days of Jesus Christ until the priests ruled. In fact, he regularly draws, if not Joachite *concordiae*, at least parallels based on numbers between the Old Testament and the Christian history he sees unfolding. This is another aspect of Alexander's exegesis that merits more attention than it will receive here.

coming from the church supported by the testimony of those in religious orders and bringing peace.[5] Later Alexander returns to 10:1 once again to present the credentials of Benedict of Nursia.[6]

Benedict died in 547 and Justinian in 565. The next genuinely dramatic figure to appear on the scene in Revelation is the beast from the sea (Rev 13), which Alexander squanders on a description of the Byzantine-Sasanid conflict in the early seventh century. He redeems himself, however, by identifying the beast from the land with Muhammad, whose historical role he fully appreciates.[7]

By the time Alexander arrives at Revelation 15 and the angels with seven vials, he is up to the eighth century and ready to describe how these angels avenged the blood of the martyrs by reversing the work of the seven angels with trumpets. Whereas the earlier seven persecuted the just, these persecuted the reprobate. The seven are identified as King Charles, Pope Leo, Emperor Charles, Crescentius the Patrician, Emperor Otto, Pope Gregory VII, and Emperor Alexius of Constantinople. One might assume that the first Charles represents Charles Martel, but Alexander explains that it is the same Charles who later became emperor and was then like another man, as 1 Kings 10:6 says of Saul. He begins the narrative with Charles's struggle against the Saxon king Widikind, who by virtue of Revelation 15:2 is temporarily identified with the beast. Alexander observes that 15:2 simply refers to the number of the beast without mentioning the number 666. He takes that to mean that John is referring to the number of the word "beast." He takes the numerical meaning of "beast" in Greek to yield a word that, translated into Latin, means "liberty." He moves from there to the idea of the Saxons surrendering their own liberty and subjecting themselves to Christ, voluntarily agreeing to be baptized in the year 780.[8]

Alexander goes on to describe Charles pouring out the vial of his wrath in various other directions, creating an empire and a papal-imperial alliance in the process. Alexander's beast/liberty formula allows him to indulge in reflections that are somewhere between Augustinian and Orwellian. Charlemagne's divinely dictated task is to make sure various sinful peoples renounce the wrong sort of freedom and find true godly freedom by putting on the yoke of Christ.

5. Alexander, *Expos.*, 153–54.
6. Alexander, *Expos.*, 162–82.
7. Alexander, *Expos.*, 282–92.
8. Alexander, *Expos.*, 320–21, 327.

Alexander doesn't stop there, however. His interest in the vision of the vials extends not only to the continuing relationship but also to the tension between empire and papacy. Thus he goes on to report on the investiture crisis, in which the pope poured out the vessels of divine wrath on the emperor. Then, still expounding on Revelation 16, he discusses the foundation of the Cistercian order and its flowering at Clairvaux.[9]

This good time was also a bad time. Alexander explains that, at the very moment the Cistercians came into being, ecclesiastical and secular leaders were living dissolutely. He describes the situation by recalling the ingratitude of the Israelites in the desert, quoting Numbers 11 and 20. In the latter case even Moses and Aaron are accused of failing to trust God sufficiently. The point is not lost on Alexander, who is using it to show how the people can be scandalized by the bad example set by their leaders.[10] He sees his own time as one in which bad example is encouraging contrarian behavior, and that leads him to cite Joachim of Fiore: "From the year 1200 and beyond all times are suspect to me."[11]

Then he goes on to quote Hildegard of Bingen: "I looked to the north, and behold, there stood five beasts. One was like a fiery dog, but he was not burning. Another was a lion of yellow appearance (*fulvi decoris*). The third was a pallid horse, the fourth a black pig, and the fifth a grey wolf."[12] Alexander explains that, according to Hildegard, these five animals signify five ferocious styles of temporal rule. The dog symbolizes men who fiercely defend their power but are not ardent in seeking justice. The lion stands for men who war without rectitude and in time begin to weaken through exhaustion. The horse signifies men who leap over the exercise of their virtues as they race headlong in pursuit of lascivious behavior and eventually lose their strength. The pig symbolizes leaders rolling around in the mud of fornication and other forms of uncleanness. The wolves work through cunning to overthrow the leaders of kingdoms by dividing them. These five will lead to the entanglement of many souls. The five began serious operation around the year 1100 and will end with the death of Antichrist. Hildegard describes what follows as "blooming" because of the restoration and strengthening of virtue.

At this point Alexander shifts back to the Bible, quoting Jeremiah 6:4, "the shadows of evening are longer," by which he means that as the world

---

9. Alexander, *Expos.*, 347.
10. Alexander, *Expos.*, 350–51.
11. *Concordia novi ac veteris testamenti* 3.2.6 (Venice, 1519), f. 41d. Alexander, *Expos.*, 351.
12. *Scivias* 3.11 (PL 197:709–11).

enters evening, heading toward the end, the shadows of sin grow longer. "Thus," Alexander says, "Jeremiah confirms the things said above about the beasts. And the malice of these beasts—that is, the unjust biting of the dog, the bellicose ferocity of the lion, the lascivious desire of the horse, the filthiness of the pig, and the cunning of the wolf—is concisely expressed by John through the dragon, beast, and pseudo-prophet." He is referring to Revelation 16:13, **Then I saw three impure spirits that looked like frogs; they came out of the mouth of the dragon, out of the mouth of the beast, and out of the mouth of the false prophet**. These are, he says, the same vices that afflict the church today.[13]

Note that Alexander has gone from Revelation to Joachim to Hildegard to Jeremiah and back to Revelation, always assuming that his sources are saying the same thing. The allusion to Jeremiah is hardly surprising. He is, of course, a prophet, and Alexander regularly cites Old Testament prophets as if they were speaking about the church. The inclusion of Joachim gives us pause, although there is nothing said about him to prevent us from assuming that Alexander is citing Joachim as an exegete rather than as a divinely inspired prophet (although either might seem justified). The same cannot be said about Hildegard. She is clearly included as the recipient of an extrabiblical prophetic vision that Alexander sees as reinforcing a passage in Revelation. We will see this mixing of biblical and contemporary visionary experience occur in even bolder form when we get to Petrus Iohannis Olivi.

Chapter 16 is still in progress. The final vial of divine wrath is to be poured out in the holy land, and the story carries over into the following chapter because of the angel who takes John to see the damnation of the harlot. The woman is the kingdom of Persia, and the beast on which she sits is "the king of Babylon, which is in Egypt."[14] The king of Egypt ruled Jerusalem but was expelled by the king of Persia, who will in turn be expelled by the king of Egypt. The latter will reign for only a brief time, for he will be defeated the same year by the Christians, as will the other rulers in the area symbolized by the ten kings, who are symbolized in turn by the ten horns of the beast. (The symbolism in the chapter extends to John himself, who actually represents the church.)

Thus Alexander is still talking about the capture of Jerusalem when he arrives at Revelation 18. The context encourages us to read the chapter with new eyes. Our normal tendency is to concentrate on the words **Then**

13. Alexander, *Expos.*, 52.
14. Alexander, *Expos.*, 367.

I heard another voice from heaven say: "Come out of her, my people, so that you will not share in her sins, so that you will not receive any of her plagues" (Rev 18:4). That gives us the opportunity to see the destruction of Babylon as something God does. We are merely warned to get out of the way before it happens. If we ask how all of this relates to Jesus and the Gospels, we do have something to compare it with: the little apocalypse, in which Jesus describes the destruction of Jerusalem by the Romans and warns his listeners to take to the hills.

In Alexander's scenario, we are deprived of even that much comfort. As he describes the crusader army about to wreak God's vengeance on a defeated city, the emphasis falls, not on 18:4, but on 18:6–7: **Give back to her as she has given; pay her back double for what she has done. Pour her a double portion from her own cup. Give her as much torment and grief as the glory and luxury she gave herself.** The reader is invited to become a participant in the slaughter. For those lacking either the will or the imagination for such an activity, Alexander provides a passage from Fulcher of Chartres's description of the event. The resulting scenario seems oddly at variance with anything the reader might expect to find in any passage of the New Testament before this one, so much so in fact that several modern New Testament scholars have attempted to argue that we are misreading the passage if we claim to find such an admonition there.

Throughout the next chapter the focus remains on the Holy Land, as we witness the birth of new crusading orders and the capture of the beast and pseudo-prophets, who are obviously Muslim. With chapter 20 we finally arrive at something other than the first crusade, although we are merely returning to the investiture controversy, with the emperor now playing the role of dragon and serpent. When Alexander arrives at 1122 and the concordat of Worms, he takes up the language of Revelation 20, because that is where he is: **And I saw an angel coming down out of heaven, having the key to the Abyss and holding in his hand a great chain. He seized the dragon, that ancient serpent, who is the devil, or Satan, and bound him for a thousand years. He threw him into the Abyss, and locked and sealed it over him, to keep him from deceiving the nations anymore until the thousand years were ended** (20:1–3). It seems an odd thing to say about Henry V, but Alexander does what he can with it. The Concordat is presented as a great victory for the church, preventing Henry from seducing anyone else; but what about those thousand years? Alexander works in two explanations. First, the chain binding Satan is, by implication, identified with the bond of excommunication placed on Henry. Thus the Concordat is not the bond itself but the condition of its cancellation, for Mother Church denies no one who seeks grace and promises satisfaction permission to return to her bosom.[15]

The other explanation is one Alexander has been nurturing since Revelation 7: the real binding of Satan began ca. 325 CE. When John says in Revelation 20:3, **He threw him into the Abyss, and locked and sealed it over him, to keep him from deceiving the nations anymore until the thousand years were ended**, he is not asserting that the emperor was imprisoned for a thousand years, but merely that he was imprisoned for *the rest of that thousand years*.[16] Of course, we are still left with Revelation 20:2, **He seized the dragon, that ancient serpent, who is the devil, or Satan, and bound him for a thousand years**, but Alexander is hardly in the mood for a close reading of the chapter. He has what he wants from it.

Revelation 20:3 tells us, **After this, he must be loosed for a short time.** Alexander explains that the loosing refers to Antichrist, who will act through the instigation of Satan. Alexander quotes Augustine at length, explaining that the binding has not prevented Satan from tempting us but merely from using his full power to do so. If he were allowed to do that, he would enmesh more souls than God wishes to see damned. When he is finally released and allowed to range free, it will be for only three and a half years. If he were not loosed at all, we would never understand his full power, nor would the endurance of the faithful in the Holy City be adequately tested.[17]

Then Alexander turns to the thrones in Revelation 20:4, and we are transported back to twelfth-century Europe for a close reading of its political and ecclesiastical history. Thomas Becket, Henry the Lion, and Frederick Barbarossa pass through, along with a host of others most of us probably have never heard of; yet in the middle of a passage concerning papal succession we do run into someone we certainly have heard of. We are told, "Alexander died and Lucius succeeded him in 1182; and in the same year, in the city of Assisi, a boy named Francis was born. His father was Pietro Bernadone." Then Alexander immediately turns to Lucius's trouble with the Romans, whom Alexander describes as adoring the beast.[18]

The conversation then switches to another beast, Saladin, and his conquest of Palestine. Speaking of the critical year 1187, Alexander breaks off the narrative and announces that "in the same year Joachim, the Abbot of Fiore,

15. Alexander, *Expos.*, 414–15.
16. Alexander, *Expos.*, 412–15.
17. Augustine, *De civitate Dei* 20.7–8 (CCSL 40:2, 442–45).
18. Alexander, *Expos.*, 427.

of the Cistercian order, prophesied that 'when 1260 years have passed, Antichrist will be born.' And he prophesied many other things some of which we will get to later." Then he returns to Saladin, still labeled as the beast, seeming to suggest that the Muslim conquerors in Palestine demanded that the Christians adore the image of the beast (Rev 13:14), which Alexander identifies as the image of Muhammad.[19] Nevertheless, he sees the complexity of the situation, since he is writing after the emperor Frederick II's crusade, which Alexander recognizes as beneficial to the Christians in Palestine. Thus he finds himself saying, without further explanation, that Muhammad was the beast and yet Frederick, although he was described as "beloved son" by one pope, was also the beast inasmuch as he persecuted the church through the inspiration of the Saracens, whose customs he imitated. The comment stands as one of many moments in which Alexander shows that he is aware of current imperial history.

In fact, as Alexander travels into the thirteenth century, he paints a grim picture of it. He comments that the density of crime created such a shadow over the world that no one could predict how bad it would get; yet God had already placed there two luminaries to counter the darkness: "Dominic and Francis, one to present an example of innocence and the other to present an example of penitence." Alexander quotes the pseudo-Joachim Jeremiah commentary at length, emphasizing the image of the crow and the dove, a passage that concentrates on the crow (i.e., the Dominicans) as exegetes and preachers. Then he cites Revelation 11:4, "These are the two olive trees and candelabras standing before the Lord," and goes on to identify Dominic with innocence and Francis with conversion.

Note that, in spite of the reference to Revelation 11:4, Alexander is still expositing Revelation 20 and is building to an interpretation of 20:6. Francis is "**blessed** because he was converted from the vanities of the world, **and holy** because he was practiced in all the virtues of good works, and on this account **he has a place in the first resurrection. . . . And the second death has no power** over Dominic, Francis, or their followers. Instead **they will be priests of God and Christ and will reign with him a thousand years,** that is, throughout eternity."[20]

At this point Alexander drops the two mendicant orders and turns back to the crusades, now relating them to the subject of those over whom the second death has no power. (He affirms his belief that the Jews will be

19. Alexander, *Expos.*, 429.
20. Alexander, *Expos.*, 436–38.

included in the first resurrection.) In the course of his comments he arrives at a thought that, given his methodology, has received less attention in this chapter than it deserves. We have seen that Alexander likes to develop parallels (sometimes specifically labeled as *concordiae*) between the Old and New Testaments, often involving numerical similarities. Here he says,

> Note that just as John presents this city as the new Jerusalem, so David ruled over a terrestrial Jerusalem. And just as John presented four animals designating the four men who wrote the gospels, so David had four who wrote the psalms. . . . John also speaks of twenty-four elders, just as David had leaders of the sanctuary. Here note the key to David's wisdom (Rev 3:7), that is, the wisdom by which he ordered his kingdom, and know that through it is opened the kingdom of Jesus Christ his son. David is estimated to have had 288 providing the religious service for himself and Solomon (1 Chron 25:7). Thus John posits twice 144,000, which corresponds to the same number. From David to Christ there were one thousand years if you subtract seventy for the captivity of the Jews. And we believe a thousand years will also be fulfilled with Christ reigning on earth, starting with the time of Saint Sylvester when the bishops began to reign. Of these, more than seventy years still remain. If God should wish to add to this number, just as in other cases during the time of David he added time so that people would have time to be converted from their sins, he has the power to do so here, for he is omnipotent.

The parallels suggested here are not rigorously developed. The whole passage seems little more than a somewhat long-winded way of asserting that the thousand years from Sylvester to Antichrist could be extended; but that in itself is worth remembering. In fact, Alexander suggests that if the reader wants to explore an entirely different interpretation, he is welcome to try the one offered by Gregory the Great, who suggests that the thousand years are meant not as a specific measure of time but as a symbol of perfection. Thus the millennium simply denotes the time of the church, no matter how long that might be.[21]

But of course, Alexander's own choice is a real millennium, and at Revelation 20:1 we arrive at its close, although Alexander seems to tell us that what needs to happen before it arrives has not yet fully occurred, and thus he still

---

21. Alexander, *Expos.*, 444. See Joachim, *Expositio in Apocalypsim*, 211, quoted in the readings for the chapter entitled "Joachim of Fiore" above.

sees it as future. **And when the thousand years are over, Satan,** that is, the devil acting through Antichrist, **will be loosed from his imprisonment to seduce the nations at the four corners of the earth, Gog and Magog** (20:7–8). Alexander recommends that we follow Augustine's interpretation: Gog and Magog are not to be understood as specific barbarous nations in some part of the world. John says they are spread over the whole earth. As for the meaning of the names, Gog means "a roof" and Magog "from a roof," in other words, "a house" and "he who comes out of the house." They are therefore the nations in which the devil was shut up as in an abyss, and the devil is coming out of them and going forth, so that they are "the roof" while he is "from the roof."[22] Alexander then quotes speculation from Isidore of Seville's *Etymologies*,[23] which he combines with Ezekiel 38 to argue that the church will be afflicted, not by one people as Augustine suggests, but by many peoples.

Alexander will in fact get back to the beloved city, but in the meantime he must interpret John's announcement that **fire descended from heaven and devoured them**.[24] We are already familiar enough with Alexander to know that "heaven" means the church, and we are prepared to find that we are again witnessing a concordance with Ezekiel 38. Alexander again reminds us that the sort of resistance against Antichrist's supporters described in Revelation 20 and Ezekiel 38 assumes a substantial number of elect. Nevertheless, he is also interested in emphasizing the substantial seductive power exerted by Antichrist in this great final confrontation and Antichrist's success in building up a following. (Here again he supports his exegesis with reference to Hildegard of Bingen, summoned to support Alexander's emphasis on the role of heresy in Antichrist's attack.)[25]

The rest of Revelation 20 is dedicated to judgment, first of Satan and then of humanity. The decks are now cleared for the descent of the heavenly city. Alexander has a surprise in store for us, more than one in fact. He begins by establishing that the heavenly city, like ourselves, will be renewed. He quotes Augustine:

> And by this universal conflagration the qualities of the corruptible elements which suited our corruptible bodies shall utterly perish, and

22. Alexander, *Expos.*, 450–51. See Augustine, *De civitate Dei* 20.11.
23. Isidore, *Etymologies* 9.26–30; 14.3.
24. Here, as elsewhere, we are contending with Alexander's often confusing revisions. I have done some adjusting for the sake of order.
25. Alexander, *Expos.*, 456, quoting *Scivias*.

our substance shall receive such qualities as shall, by a wonderful trans-
mutation, harmonize with our immortal bodies, so that, as the world itself
is renewed to some better thing, it is fitly accommodated to men, themselves renewed in their flesh to some better thing.[26]

However much the elect might rejoice in receiving a new heaven and
earth, Alexander says, they will rejoice even more in the vision of God.

For the Lord God [speaking through Jeremiah 23:24] says, "I fill the heaven
and earth." Even now there are men in God, although they may not realize it.
Thus Augustine says, "The apostle, speaking to the Athenians, said remarkable things about God that can be understood by only a few, such as that
we live, move and have our being in Him, as some of your own have said."[27]

This much can safely be said. Beyond that point Alexander's remarks
demonstrate that he sees the challenge to exegesis posed by the new Jerusalem. He pauses only for a moment on the idea that the sea is no more,
simply observing that what John means is that it isn't as it used to be. As for
the idea that time is no more, he offers several examples that imply that the
angels in heaven and the beast in the abyss seem to be existing just as before.
Alexander now turns to the vision of the holy city, the new Jerusalem,
descending from heaven. He describes the holy city as the unity of the faithful who have cast off the old man and put on the new. Once the elect have put
on their bodies and been judged, they will ascend into heaven and possess
eternal life. By this logic the new Jerusalem, too, has ascended in the persons
of the elect. Alexander also speaks of the old Jerusalem as ascending, but in a
different sense. He speaks of the terrestrial Jerusalem that ascends from the
earth, but he is actually quoting Revelation 13:11, in which the beast comes
out of the earth. That Jerusalem was marked for destruction by the prophets
and portrayed as the widow in Lamentations 1.
What, then, does John mean when he says, **Behold, the tabernacle of
God is with men** (21:3)? Alexander explains:

The tabernacle is Christ's humanity, which will be with holy men. If
through the tabernacle a body could not be designated, the apostle would
never have said, "While we are in this tabernacle we groan and are bur-

26. Augustine, *De civitate Dei* 20.16.
27. Alexander, *Expos.*, 461.

162

dened" (2 Cor 5:4). On the contrary, the voice of the terrestrial Jerusalem is heard saying, "The Lord is like the enemy of Jerusalem and has destroyed her tabernacle" (Lam 2:5). The tabernacle was changed into the temple of Christ, who is here called the tabernacle of God. It is written in another place where there is mention of Jerusalem, "God and the Lamb are its temple" (Rev 21:22).

Alexander's interpretation of the next few lines follows much the same pattern, contrasting the old, evil, earthly Jerusalem as depicted in Lamentations with what is to be in heaven. Thus it is a bit surprising when, in Revelation 21:9, **one of the angels with bowls filled with the final plagues** approaches John, and Alexander remarks,

> This is said after the last day of the city of Jerusalem, which, however, is to be built up with good works before the last day, because after the day of judgment night will come, in which no one will be able to act. And John speaks here in this final book of the city of Jerusalem, just as Ezekiel does of the city at the end of his book. And around the beginning of their works, where they see the heavens open, they are concordant in their visions of the animals. It should be known that the elect, whom we understand to be designated by the city of Jerusalem, will build it before the day of judgment, as we have said, which John clearly shows after the narrative concerning the city, saying among other things, **Let the one who does wrong continue to do wrong; let the vile person continue to be vile; let the one who does right continue to do right; and let the holy person continue to be holy** (Rev 22:11)[28]—which, without all ambiguity, must be accomplished before the final day. And also the Lord says, "Behold, I am coming soon. My reward is with me, and I will give to each person according to what they have done." Thus he clearly shows that he will come in judgment after the building of the city. This angel [i.e., with the bowl] was Innocent III.

So begins what might justly be described as a stunning example of smug mendicant self-importance. In what follows, Francis and Dominic are praised as the lynchpins of a new, final world order, but in such a way that their brethren manage to gain, if not equal status, at least unrealistically high praise, an unseemly, rollicking shout-out for their role in building the new

28. Alexander, *Expos.*, 467–68.

Jerusalem. The holy city is portrayed as very much a mendicant accomplishment, although with substantial papal aid. Nor is Alexander hesitant to name names. The entire passage is given in the readings at the end of this chapter. We pick up the end of it here.

And the kings of the earth will bring their splendor into it (21:24). Those are said to be kings who rule their territory (or that of others) well. Also, to the letter, they are the kings of the earth who now rule with Christ a thousand years, because of the devotion they bring and the glory and honor they show [the city]. Not three kings, who in spirit see over [the city] our lord Jesus Christ, the star, who says, "I am the brightly shining morning star" (Rev 22:16); but according to Isaiah (62) all the kings of the faithful who truly love God our savior and the illustrious among them who, like lamps, are illumined within it, bringing glory and honor to it. And they will do good to the poor serving the Lord within it, and that will be credited as done for God himself, for the Lord says, "Whatever you have done for one of the least of my people, you have done for me" (Matt 25:40). And this city will be called by a different name than before. It will be called "the new Jerusalem," and it will not be left derelict like the one that was destroyed after the Lord rose, when not one stone was left on another (Luke 21:6). Now kings will minister to it. **And its gates will not be closed by day** (21:25). Let the Jews consider whether this was the case in the old Jerusalem according to the vaticinium of Isaiah. **And there will be no night there**, that is, no night of ignorance and infidelity. Of this night and day the Apostle says (Rom 13:12–13), "The night is nearly over; the day is almost here." So let us put aside the deeds of darkness and put on the armor of light. Let us behave decently, as in the daytime. Although the unjust, who are the gates of Hell, rise up against the gates of justice of this city, they will not prevail against it, and the faithful will receive refuge and aid from it. If Nehemiah had possessed sufficient soldiers and arms, it would not have been necessary to close the gates of the earthly Jerusalem until the heat of the day had arrived (Neh 7:3). Thus the history says of Saint Francis, "It seemed to him that his whole house was filled with soldiers' arms, saddles, shields, spears, and other equipment. . . . And since he was bewildered by this sudden turn of events, his response was that all these arms were to be for him and his soldiers. Thus, like another David, he could liberate Jerusalem from the long-standing abuse of its enemies."[29]

29. Here Alexander utilizes Francis's vision of military weapons in the *Legend of the Three*

But the history says that he was destined to defend the celestial Jerusalem with spiritual, celestial arms, just as David once defended the old Jerusalem with material arms. "Night will come" (John 9:4) to the reprobate, "when no one can work" according to the gospel; but the Lord, who is day, having twelve hours, will illumine this city from now to eternity. Below that light, the world and the church will stand. The gates of this city will not be closed; but later, when the Lamb introduces this city, his spouse, into the kingdom of heaven, the gate will be shut. Then the unjust will come saying, "Lord, open it for us," and he will reply, "Truly, I say to you, I do not know you" (Matt 25:11–12). For whoever ignores him now in the area of good works will then be ignored.

And they will bring into it the glory and the honor of the nations (21:26). They will bring into it those who are honored and glorified among the nations of this world in order that it should be understood that they labor for nothing unless they abandon the world entirely for God and are a great example to others, who should learn from them to condemn vain glory and false honor. It should also be noted that the Abbot Joachim, almost all of whose books were received by apostolic men like Pope Lucius and Pope Urban, predicted these orders.

What follows is a long series of passages from the pseudo-Joachim Jeremiah commentary, then a quotation from Hildegard. These are introduced to demonstrate that the mendicants had already been prophesied by both Joachim and Hildegard.

Then Alexander returns to the text in order to come to terms with a line that might be expected to raise some problems: **Nothing impure will ever enter it, nor will anyone who does what is shameful or deceitful, but only those whose names are written in the Lamb's book of life** (21:27). To the extent that the new Jerusalem is used as a way of referring to heaven, that line should cause no difficulty. To the extent that it is used to refer to a new creation coming down to earth at the end of history, here too it causes no problems. The real problem is that Alexander has been using it in yet a third way. It has become his way of talking about the mendicant orders. Will that, too, remain part of his exegesis at this point? In fact it will.

Companions, ch. 2 (in *Francis of Assisi: Early Documents* [hereafter FAED], ed. Regis J. Armstrong, J. A. Wayne Hellmann, and William J. Short, 4 vols. [New York: New City Press, 1999–2002], 2:70) and *Remembrance of the Desire of a Soul*, ch. 2 (FAED, 2:245), which Francis himself originally misinterpreted, to delineate what Francis later determined to be his true mission.

Nothing impure will ever enter it, nor will anyone who does what is shameful or deceitful, but only those whose names are written in the Lamb's book of life. That is, all who consent to the devil's seductions and, in order to gain the favor of men, deck themselves out in clothes and manners that make them seem holy while they actually lack pure hearts, such people will never be assimilated to pure, pellucid gold. Those who in their pride persecute and oppress the church of God and those who pollute themselves with the abomination of fornication can in no way be called the spouse of the Lamb. The Lord, when he spoke of the just in the gospel, added, addressing the iniquitous like Judas, "I am not speaking about all of you. I know whom I have chosen." Thus these words of God are not spoken of all, but of the good alone. **The deceitful** will not enter [the holy city], that is, those who invent lies and delight in them. The Lord will condemn all those who practice deceit. Only those will be saved **whose names are written in the Lamb's book of life**, in the foreknowledge of our Lord Jesus Christ. This is he who fears Christ with a chaste fear, lest he carry out evils, and thinks upon his name with a pure love, that he should do good. Thus he says through the prophet (Mal 3:16), "a book of remembrance was written before him of those who feared the LORD and thought on his name." Saint John, who discerned these things in the spirit, said nothing of the evil people in this place, who in the sight of men are mixed with the just but whose fate is to be with the devil. John never views them as designated through this city, although many of the reprobate emerge from among the elect. Thus the blessed John, writing about the reprobate that emerged from the elect in his time, said (1 John 2:18–19), "Even now many antichrists have come. They went out from us, but they did not really belong to us. For if they had belonged to us, they would have remained with us; but their going showed that none of them belonged to us." Saint Francis, speaking of the evil mixed in with the good, said, "I do not consider those brothers who do not wish to observe my words to be my brothers until they have done penance."[30] Ezekiel saw water flowing from the temple, and later it was said to him, "This water flows toward the eastern region and goes down into the Arabah; and when it enters the sea, the sea of stagnant waters, the water will become fresh" (Ezek 47:8). And again, "On the banks, on both sides of the river, there will grow all kinds of trees for food. Their leaves will not wither nor their fruit fail, but they

---

30. Taken in slightly modified form from Francis's *Letter to the Entire Order* (FAED, 1:120).

will bear fresh fruit every month, because the water for them flows from the sanctuary" (Ezek 47:12), which is, according to the word of the Lord (Ezek 43:7), the place of his throne. "Their fruit will be for food, and their leaves for healing" (Ezek 47:12).

Having presented Ezekiel's beguiling vision, Alexander reminds us yet again that it was promised to the Jews, who didn't receive it because they didn't deserve it. That ends chapter 21.

Chapter 22 offers less contemporary relevance until the end of it is almost upon us. Then at Revelation 22:18–19, with only two verses to go thereafter, he arrives at the words **I warn everyone who hears the words of the prophecy of this book: if anyone adds to them, God will add to that person the plagues described in this book; if anyone takes away from the words of the book of this prophecy, God will take away that person's share in the tree of life and in the holy city, which are described in this book.** It seems too inviting to pass up. Alexander adds, almost *sotto voce*, "I excommunicate him, and Christ excommunicates him with me."

Who, then, is the "I" in this case? Alexander no longer feels the need to remind us, but an angel is speaking, and for Alexander angels normally stand for people, often popes. Sure enough, Alexander has papal excommunication on his mind, namely, the excommunication of Frederick II. He leaps back to chapters 13 and 20, reviewing Frederick's credentials as the beast. The inquiry seems so inevitable that we temporarily forget how exceptional it is. Up to this point Alexander has been largely consistent in keeping his exegesis tethered to a successive reading of history, but here he feels justified in making an exception.

He also feels that a final clarification is due. Alexander closes with one last series of reflections on the arrival of Antichrist, an optimistic report from the Spanish front, and a final pat on the back for the mendicants. All of this will be found in the readings.

READINGS

This is the passage in which Alexander describes the building of the city in mendicant terms. It is, as we will see, a passage that Pierre Auriol would decide needed judicious trimming and, as we will also see, one to which Nicholas of Lyra would react very negatively, seeing it as a remarkable bit of Franciscan self-advertisement. At Revelation 21:9, **one of the angels with bowls filled with the final plagues** *approaches John, and Alexander says the following.*

This is said after the last day of the city of Jerusalem, which, however, is to be built up with good works before the last day, because after the day of judgment night will come, in which no one will be able to act. And John speaks here in this final book of the city of Jerusalem, just as Ezekiel does of the city at the end of his book. And around the beginning of their works, where they see the heavens open, they are concordant in their visions of the animals. It should be known that the elect, whom we understand to be designated by the city of Jerusalem, will build it before the day of judgment, as we have said, which John clearly shows after the narrative concerning the city, saying among other things, "Let the one who does wrong continue to do wrong; let the vile person continue to be vile; let the one who does right continue to do right; and let the holy person continue to be holy" (Rev 22:11).[31] Which, without all ambiguity, must be accomplished before the final day. And also the Lord says, "Behold, I am coming soon. My reward is with me, and I will give to each person according to what they have done." Thus he clearly shows that he will come in judgment after the building of the city. This angel was Innocent III, the angel of the Lord of Hosts according to the prophet Malachi (Mal 2:7), who came through vocation and election to the sacerdotal ministry of the highest pontificate. This angel came from the seventh number of the faithful, for the seventh number stands for universality, for this present world unfolds in seven days. And in a certain canticle it is said, among other things, "since the sterile woman bore seven," which is also translated "since the sterile woman bore several" (1 Sam 2:5). This apostolic man is accustomed to use the number seven to designate universality.[32] It [the canticle] says "having vials." Vials are clean and transparent containers, through which is designated the clean heart and transparent divine wisdom of the aforesaid angels. How this pope had the vial, that is, a heart opposed to the infidels and reprobate, is fully discovered in his writings. **And he spoke to me, saying, "Come"**—in spirit, not in body—**"I will show you the bride, the wife of the Lamb"** (21:9). The angel in the person of an apostolic man called to John, who was a type of the faithful, showing him the elect, who

31. Alexander, *Expos.*, 467–68.
32. E.g., see Augustine, *De civitate Dei* 17.4.

were called the bride and wife of the Lamb and in the time of the aforesaid apostolic man to be made manifest to the faithful. **And he bore me away in the spirit** (21:10). In this it is made manifest that John saw these things in the spirit. Hence all those who wish to examine this city must necessarily be borne up in the spirit to see it (and not with carnal eyes) **on a great and high mountain. And he showed me the holy city,** the new **Jerusalem**. Thus Ezekiel on a mountain was also shown the city (Ezek 40:2). Through the mountain is designated Christ, who fills the whole world in magnitude and is highest among all. On him all the faithful are built. Daniel says of this mountain, "A rock was cut out but not by hands. . . . It grew into a huge mountain and filled the whole world" (Dan 2:34–35). By "city" is meant, as it were, the united body of citizens. Through this city is designated the Brothers Minor, who according to their history imitate the life of the apostles, and the preachers who follow the apostle Paul in their preaching. All these are called Jerusalem because they now press on toward a vision of eternal peace. He calls them "new" because they have cast off the old man and put on the new, created according to the divine pattern. Hence it is said of Saint Dominic that, like a city set on a hill, he offered a delectable display of sanctity, and of Francis the history narrates that heavenly arms were provided to him so that he, like another David, could liberate Jerusalem from its enemies. And he often repeated in his preaching the greeting that God had revealed to him, "May God give peace to us." And he often brought peace to men and women who had fallen into discord, so that Jerusalem, meaning "vision of peace," should manifestly appear. Of his brother Anthony the history says, among other things, that "the devotion of the faithful was excited by the radiant light of miracles, and, God building Jerusalem, a new dispersion of Israel was represented through the congregation. Note that in the entire book rarely do the words of the text agree so manifestly with the history as in the new Jerusalem. That the aforesaid brothers of the two orders can be designated by a single city is shown by King Solomon, who reigned in the terrestrial Jerusalem, when he says, "A brother who helps another brother is like a strong city" (Prov 18:19). And the Lord speaking to the apostles, the predecessors of this group, says, "A city set on a hill cannot be hidden" (Matt 5:14). That this order is designated as a spouse is shown when in the history it is said, "The blessed Francis, asked if he wished to take a spouse, replied figuratively, 'I will take one nobler and more beautiful than any you have ever seen, who will excel all in beauty and wisdom.'"[33] This immaculate

---

33. Celano, *Life of Saint Francis* 1.3 (FAED 1:188).

spouse of God is the true religious order he entered. The religious order of these aforementioned brothers is well described in calling it the spouse of the Lamb, and accordingly the Lord says, "I marry you to me in faith, and I marry you to me in compassion and pity." And it is also called the wife of the Lamb because, through the blessed Francis and Saint Dominic, the Lord amplifies his church with offspring of a new breed.

Descending from heaven, from God (21:2). They are said to descend from heaven, that is, from the church, because they descend in humility to the lowest grade beyond the rest of the faithful, with the aid of God. Hence the history also says of the brothers of Saint Francis, "This is the religious order of the poor crucified and the order of preachers which we call the lesser brothers. They are truly lesser and, of all the rules of this time, more humble in habit, in nudity, and in contempt of the world."[34] Often it is meant in a superior way that someone descended from heaven, and John himself, humbled and ejected from the church, heard a voice as if from heaven: "Come up here, I will show you what has to be done after this" (Rev 4:1). And in fact the Lord said to a certain city, "You, Capernaum, will you be lifted up to the heavens? No, you will go down to Hell" (Matt 11:23). On the other hand, those who humble themselves and make themselves lesser in relation to others will be eternally exalted and treated as greater in heaven. Thus the Lord says through Luke, "Whoever wishes to be greater among you, let him be least" (Luke 22:26). The name of that city, which God foreknew would in the final time descend from heaven, he will write above all those who in former times succeeded in the world. Thus he says, he who is successful I shall write on him the name of the city of the new Jerusalem that will descend from heaven. And thus the universal church will be called by the one name, Jerusalem, of which we spoke above.

It shone with the glory of God (21:11). Thus our Lord Jesus Christ says, "My Father is glorified in this: that you bear much fruit and show yourselves to be my disciples." No one would imagine himself to be illuminated by the glory of this city if he is hostile toward his brother, showing hatred toward them. Thus he says, "He who says he is in the light and yet hates his brother is still in darkness and walks in darkness and does not know where he is going because the shadows blind him" (1 John 2:9–11).

Its radiance was like that of a most rare jewel, like a jasper, clear as crystal. This jewel is firm, glowing, and transparent in its purity, just as these are according to their profession firm in the faith with which the

---

34. Jacques de Vitry, *Historia Orientalis* 2.32.

church glows. And in them is found a faithful and pure confession of that faith, hiding nothing, just as one finds in crystal. Ezekiel in describing his city mentions the wall, just as John does in describing his, saying, **having a great and high wall** (21:12). Concerning the structure of this wall the history says, "It rises on a foundation of perseverance, and in it living stones gathered from every part of the world have been built into a dwelling place of the Holy Spirit."[35] The brothers are accurately described as defenders of others through the wall, for they are great in defeating others and high lest they be defeated. Thus it is said to certain others in rebuttal, "You have not gone up to face the enemy, nor have you set up a wall for the house of Israel, to stand in battle in the day of the Lord" (Ezek 13:5). In his building Ezekiel posits twelve gates. Thus John says, **Having twelve gates**. The gates designate twelve gates of justice of the twelve apostles, and those who enter into them imitate, insofar as they are able, the twelve apostles doing justice. Of this kind of gate it is said, "Open to me the gates of justice" (Ps 117:10). Nehemiah, when the walls of the old Jerusalem were built, said, among other things, "After the wall was built, I set up the gatekeepers" (2 Esd 7:1). Thus here we have mention of the custodians of the gates.

And at the gates twelve angels. By angels are meant ministers and priors, by whom, beyond others, permission is given to receive brothers and introduce them to the imitation of the twelve apostles. For just as a wall sends to the gate those wishing to enter, so it is necessary to send brothers wishing to enter this city to the gates and to their custodians, so that through them they can be let in. In confirming the literal rule of the twelve brothers Saint Francis entered these twelve gates of justice. These brothers are called angels, as is seen above when it is said to the angel, "Do penance" (Rev 2:5), which would by no means be said concerning a spiritual angel. **On the gates the names of the twelve tribes of the sons of Israel were inscribed. On the east three gates, on the north three gates, on the south three gates, and on the west three gates** (21:12–13). Ezekiel says this about the gates of his city: On the north side, one gate for Reuben, one gate for Judah, and one for Levi. On the east side, three gates: one gate for Joseph, one gate for Benjamin, one gate for Dan. On the south side, one gate for Simeon, one gate for Isachar, one gate for Zebulun. On the west side, three gates: one gate for Dan, one gate for Asser, one gate for Nephtalim. Through the twelve tribes of Israel are designated the Jews converted to the faith, who are dispersed to the east, west, south, and north, and to whom James the apostle wrote saying, "James,

---

35. Celano, *Life of Saint Francis* 1.15.

a servant of God and of the Lord Jesus Christ, To the twelve tribes in the Dispersion: Greeting. Count it all joy, my brethren, when you meet various trials, for you know that the testing of your faith produces steadfastness. And let steadfastness have its full effect, that you may be perfect and complete, lacking in nothing" (James 1:1–4). The names of these sons of Israel are written "in the spirit, not otherwise" (2 Cor 3:3), on the gates of the city, the new Jerusalem, which is under the kingship of Jesus Christ, the son of David, just as the Jews gloried in their names being written on the gates of the old Jerusalem, to the conversion of which these brothers will contribute greatly. Also, the name of this city will be written on all Jews and gentiles who will "conquer the world by faith" (1 John 5:4) in the aforesaid way. The twelvefold number of the gates throughout the four parts of the world comprehends under the threefold number the preachers who proceed from them, who are imitators of the twelve apostles, through whom the faith and will of the holy Trinity is spread through a quadripartite world.

Here again there is a satisfactory concordance with the history, for according to the word of the Lord "many will come from the east and the west," the north and south, "and sit at table with Abraham, Isaac, and Jacob in the kingdom of heaven" (Matt 8:11). And in another place the Lord says, "It is necessary that this gospel be preached throughout the whole world, and then the consummation will come" (Matt 24:14). And that is what this bride and wife of the Lamb speaks and shouts out in the world, as is later commanded where it is said, "And the spouse calls out, 'come'" (Rev 22:17). What is mystically designated by the names of the twelve tribes of Israel is said above.

And the walls of the city having twelve foundations (21:14). Later these foundations are explained individually through the different kinds of precious stones, that is, through the virtues designated by the stones.

And in these foundations the names of the twelve apostles and of the Lamb. That is, the memory and preaching of the apostles are contained in them, which prove to be the foundations of the city. Thus Pope Gregory IX wrote to all the prelates of the church, "Since he who receives a prophet in the name of the prophet deserves to receive the reward of a prophet: Beloved sons and friars minor, who in the manner of the apostles travel about various regions of the world sowing the seed of God's word, we commend your faithful devotion all the more boldly in the measure that we ardently desire the salvation of the faithful, and in that measure wish your merit to be increased," etc.[36] And as it is said in the history of Saint Dominic, who

36. *Bullarium Franciscanum* (1759), 1:175.

began the order of preachers, "Nor should he who is found worthy to suffer contumely for the name of Jesus be robbed of the glory of the apostles."[37] And the preachers are called "apostles," that is, "sent," because according to the apostle, "how will they preach unless they are sent?" (Rom 10:15). They had the name of the Lamb, that is, of Christ, who is necessarily the foundation of all good works, written in the spirit, which they taught was to be imitated and how to imitate it. The name of the Lamb and his passion was written on Saint Francis. Thus the history says, "There appeared in him the form of the cross and passion of the spotless Lamb who washed away the crimes of the world."[38]

It should be noted that, just as the apostles preceded the apostle Paul by some time, thus Saint Francis, imitator of the apostles, preceded by some space of time Saint Dominic, who, with his group, followed the apostle Paul, who said, "I have done nothing less than those who are above the level of an apostle," etc. (2 Cor 12:11). And, "I have labored more abundantly in all these endeavors" (1 Cor 12:11). Given that the Lord encouraged so many imitators of the apostles, it would seem irrational for him not to have encouraged as well imitators of the apostle Paul, whose behavior during the time of the primitive church was also pleasing to him. Just as the apostle Paul is said to have possessed the twelfth place among the apostles, so here imitators of that apostle are understood to hold a place among the portals and foundations as well as among the names of the apostles and within the order previously approved.

And who spoke to me (21:14). It was Pope Honorius [who was] the successor of the aforesaid apostolic man. For John is apt to combine several people under a single name, as he does with Jezebel. In that case, long after the original Jezebel, he calls by the same name other women who imitate her behavior. Ezekiel (40:3) says the man who measured his city had a measuring rod. But this apostolic man **had a measuring rod of gold to measure the city** in length and width **and the gates**, that is, the defenders of others. The measuring rod means divine Scripture, by which this city is measured according to the measure of the rule that God shows to it. Because is written according to rule, holy Scripture is rightly represented by a measuring rod. The measuring rod is described as golden because of the clarity of divine wisdom, which in many places is symbolized as gold. Whence is said, "accept wisdom as if it were gold." In Ezekiel's city certain things are placed in

---

37. Petrus Ferrandi, *Vita* 20 (Analecta Bollandiana 30, 63).
38. Celano, *Life of Saint Francis* 2.9.

a square. **And the city was laid out in a square** (21:16) by the apostolic man, so that by holy works it should be spread out in orderly fashion throughout the four parts of the world. Whence the history says that some were sent to the east, some to the west, some to the north, and some to the south, so that they should equally announce the virtues to humankind.[39] **And its length was the same as its width.** By width is meant love, by length the perseverance of love. With these words the apostolic man suggests that the latitude of love should be extended to include enemies: "Love your enemies, do good to those who hate you, and pray for those who persecute and speak ill of you" (Matt 5:44). Concerning perseverance he adds, "Those who persevere until the end will be saved" (Matt 24:13).

He measured the city with the rod and found it to be 12,000 stadia in length. A *stadium* suggests a race track. One thousand is a perfect number. Thus by twelve thousand *stadia* is designated the perfection of the apostles' itinerary. The route of the preachers, who imitated the apostles with their feet, is expressed well by this number. And the history says that Saint Francis followed not only the life but the footsteps of the apostles.[40] Isaiah, who is in many ways concordant with this city, says, "The least of you will become a thousand" (Isa 60:22), that is, the friar minor, by way of his humiliation, acquires perfection. "And the smallest [is] a mighty nation" (Isa 60:22), that is, capable of weakening armed powers.

And as wide and high as it is long. It is just that the builders of this city, in the measure that they persevere in constructing the latitudinal dimension of love, should in equal measure strive to raise their thoughts to God in hope of eternal retribution.

And he measured the walls of the city, and they were 144 cubits thick (21:17). The seventy-two disciples, whom the Lord sent "without purse, bag, or sandals" (Luke 22:35), that they should work in his harvest, had 144 cubits to which their arms were attached. That is, each of them had two arms through which their work was accomplished. As an example of this they were sent in twos so that they could work on the Lord's harvest with the authority of the aforesaid apostolic men. Also the number twelve multiplied by twelve equals 144, in which the multiplex operation of the twelve apostles is expressed. **The measure of a man, that is, of an angel.** Here the ratio is in cubits, not brachia. For the measure of man, used by Ezekiel in the measuring of his city, is in done in cubits. And this was the unit of measurement

39. Celano, *Life of Saint Francis* 1.12.
40. Celano, *Life of Saint Francis* 2.166.

used by the apostolic man, who proved to be an angel of the Lord of hosts (Mal 2:7), just as earlier the priests of the churches of Asia were called angels. On that account he speaks of cubits in order to speak in a prophetic manner. What it means to say is that there are many gates of justice, more than twelve, and many ministers and custodians of them in this city beyond what are described here, and the cubits and hands laboring in the Lord's harvest now greatly exceed that number, since the Jews are seeing less of the many cubits and other things promised them for the rebuilding of Jerusalem than what is described by Ezekiel. But note that because of the devout obedience of the Christians the promise to them grows, and because of the sins of the Jews the size of what is promised to them shrinks. Thus Jerome says,

> The Lord promised a great deal of land to the sons of Israel during their exodus from Egypt, land they never possessed because they made themselves unworthy of it. Nonetheless he promised it and had the promise written down so that ever after the Jews should be confounded because they did not deserve to have it and grieved to have been denied it. In the same way, upon their return from Babylon they were promised a great deal of peace and abundance they never had. And I say the same about the temple, which is described as so lovely that the Jews, seeing and hearing of such pulchritude in a temple, mourned all the more and were all the more confounded that they did not merit it because of their iniquities. Thus it is said later, "Son of man, show the house of Israel the temple so that they may be confounded by their iniquities." It can therefore safely be said that, through this temple described here, the prophet wishes to say that the temple and its cultus will be restored. But greater glory is ascribed to the temple than it actually had, for the aforesaid reason. And I say the same of all the other excellent promises made to them, things they never received, like the altar and the cultus and the division of land and many other things memorialized in this book. Thus as was said, because of their iniquities the promise regarding a building was taken away from them, while in the case of the Christians, because of their good works, the promise of a building for them was increased.

And the wall was constructed (21:18)—that is, strong, for the protection of others. **From the precious stone jasper**—that is, from living stones glowing with the vigor of the catholic faith, called jasper because of their vigor. **While the city was pure gold, clear as glass.** Through gold is symbolized the purity of the holy works it displays to the world, and through glass the purity and cleanliness of the intentions behind these works. For the Lord says in the gospel, "Your eye," that is, the intention of your mind, "is the lamp of the body," that is, of all your action (Luke 11:34). "If your eye is simple," that is, if your intention is pure and simple, "your whole body will be bright," even though you may seem to men to possess some imperfection. If it is wicked, however, your whole body will be shadowy, that is, if a perverse intention precedes, a depraved work follows, even if something about it seems or even is just. "Therefore be careful lest the light in you be darkness," that is, lest the intention, which is the lamp of the soul, be darkened by the shadow of vice.

> *Having introduced the metaphor, Alexander seems incapable of leaving it and continues to repeat his basic interpretation of it. This is partly due to the composite nature of Alexander's commentary, but it is also a problem he has elsewhere. Eventually, however, he returns to interpreting the text.*

The foundations of the city wall were ornamented with all sorts of precious stones (21:19). The foundations of the city were the blessed Francis, Saint Dominic, and others with them, on the doctrine and example of whom the wall of the city is constructed. These foundations were ornamented with every precious stone, that is, with all the virtues. Concerning Saint Dominic the history says that he was like a vase decorated with all types of precious stone.[41] It further says what the history of Saint Francis narrates: the pontiffs of the Jews had on their garments twelve orders of precious stones. These pontiffs were betrothed to the Lord according to Hosea, "I shall betroth you to me in faith" (2:20). Thus this betrothed of the Lamb is ornamented with twelve kinds of precious stones on the foundations, and also ornamented with precious gems on the portals and on the wall. The stones of the old Jerusalem were dispersed at the head of every street (Lam 4:1), but here the stones are laid out in orderly fashion from the first foundation to the twelfth.

The first foundation was jasper. Through jasper, which is green, Christ is designated, for in the gospel he calls himself a green tree (Luke 23:31). Saint Francis built on this foundation; whence it is said in the history among other things, "always reserving to Christ his prerogative, for no one can lay another foundation but that which has been laid, which is Jesus Christ."[42]

---

41. Petrus Ferrandi, *Vita* 8.
42. Celano, *Life of Saint Francis* 1.8, describing Francis's repair of San Damiano.

*Here and in what immediately follows, Alexander is alluding to
Thomas of Celano's description of how Francis rebuilt San Damiano.
He attempts to correlate the list of gems in Revelation 21 with the
series of virtues attributed to Clare and her associates by Celano. It
proves difficult going. What Alexander gives us here is no more or
less arbitrary than what he has been wresting from the text throughout the commentary, but somehow, for one familiar with Celano
and able to recognize the role of the San Damiano story in Celano's
total argument, the way Alexander uses the text raises the question
of what he thinks he is doing in a particularly poignant way. What
follows makes sense as a tribute to the Franciscans, as a response
to their critics, and occasionally even as praise of the Dominicans
as well; yet it makes no serious effort to link all of this with the text
of Revelation.*

*Then Alexander arrives at something he can actually feel com-
fortable applying to the mendicants.*

**I did not see a temple in the city because the Lord God Almighty
and the Lamb are its temple** (21:22). In the respect that this city is built from
living stones, he did not see a temple in it, although there were churches dedicated to celebrating the divine mysteries. There were, however, no temples
endowed with prebends or other stipends from which persons who are stably
located there seek an income; yet the Lord continually contributes support
through the contributions of the faithful.

*At this point Alexander is serious about reading the text in the light
of mendicant reality. He invites us to compare Revelation 21:22–23
with Revelation 22:5.*

It must be noted that here there is mention of sun, moon, and night.
For the history says that in the beginning the friars minor had no churches.
Then John literally did not see a temple. But later they would have churches.
Thus in the later passage, where there is again mention of night, the lamp,
and the sun, he does not say that he saw no temple, because, as we have said,
they later had churches; but not so ornate that they could be called temples
by the people.

Alexander now turns to a consideration of the light question in itself.

John did not need the light of the sun or moon because he was led by the spirit onto the mountain, and in that same spirit he saw the foundations compared to precious stones, and the gates, and the wall of jasper, and the city of gold. It follows: **And the city did not need the sun or the moon to illuminate it, for the light of God will illuminate it and the Lamb will be its light.** Of the greater elect it is written, "Like the full moon at the festal season; like the sun shining on the temple of God" (Ecclus 50:6–7). These are people who exist for other people as sun and moon, examples of good works. They need no example of such things because they have people of the highest perfection, people who above others take the Lamb, the Son of God, as their example. "The glory that you have given me I have given them" (John 17:22). And again, "I am the light of the world. Whoever follows me will never walk in darkness but will have the light of life" (John 8:12). John the Baptist was "a burning and shining lamp" (John 5:35), but the Lord, who said, "I have testimony greater than John's" (John 5:36), will illumine them in this world and with all the saints in the future. Of the old Jerusalem it is said, "Nations will walk in your light, and kings in the brightness of your dawn" (Isa 60:3). Thus it is rightly said here, **The nations will walk in its light** (Rev 21:24). This is meant literally enough concerning the aforesaid elect, whose "good works shine before others" (Matt 5:16), because the nations of the faithful now existing accept from them an example of good works, so that they can "go from strength to strength" (Ps 84:7). Those who have bad eyes, that is, the envious, cannot stand the rays of this light, just as those with bad eyes cannot bear the splendor of the sun, but instead waste away and are repelled by its brilliance. Concerning eyes of this sort the Lord says in Mark, "It is from within, out of a person's heart, that evil thoughts come: sexual immorality, theft, murder, adultery, greed, malice, deceit, lewdness, envy, slander, arrogance, and folly. All these evils come from inside and defile a person" (7:21–23).

> *As he closes his commentary, Alexander offers some final observations concerning Islam and Antichrist, as well as a final shout-out to the mendicants.*

The devil is bound so that before the thousand years are completed he cannot exert his full powers on the faithful, as he will in the time of Antichrist. Thus this book does not intend to assert that Antichrist has now been born, unless they imagine it should be interpreted of the king of the Germans; nor that he will come in the year of our Lord 1260; nor that the

Saracens and pseudo-prophets are overly afflicting the church; nor that the cultus of Christianity will be blown away, unless perhaps this is particularly imagined to occur somewhere in the future. Some prophecies predict that the pope will be captured and France defeated by the king of the Germans, but the church prays that what is threatened in retribution will turn out to be salvific. Other prophecy, concordant with our views, says the pagans will be defeated by the catholic king of the Franks and placed under servitude to the Franks. The pope is clearly reigning with the priests and will continue to do so until the thousand years after Constantine are over, and during that time the church will not be subjected to any of the nations but will instead be greatly expanded among the nations. Thus Jerome says concerning Mark, "The preaching of the gospel will continue to the ends of the earth so that before the judgment the church will cry, 'I have cried out to you, Lord, to the ends of the earth.'"[43]

Although many tribulations oppress the church, which is daily assaulted by them, this book nevertheless shows that it has already weathered a great deal in the past, although the expositions of others interpret many of these things as still to come. So many things have occurred that what saints in the past anticipated as future has now largely taken place. As for many, however, whatever good things are reported seem not to please them much. The human mind is such that it praises the past and despises the present. The number 666, the years of Muhammad mentioned earlier in this book, has proved to be completed. His pestiferous doctrine extended to Spain, but that land, it is written, has now been reconquered by Christians, in which there will be 334 mothers of the church. Thus the faithful rejoice, because the angels rejoice when one sinner repents. And Daniel the prophet consoles us, saying, "The kingship and dominion and greatness of the kingdoms under the whole heaven shall be given to the people of the holy ones of the Most High" (Dan 7:27). Many sinners will rise from the death of the soul in this time. This is the first resurrection, and it is coming about through the two orders, who are now building one holy city, even though many speak ill of them. Nevertheless, on behalf of my brothers the friars minor and my neighbors the preachers, I have spoken peace of you, O Jerusalem, and on behalf of the house of our Lord, which is, according to the apostle, the church of the living God, and which will have great success in the future, I wish you peace.

---

43. Pseudo-Jerome, *Commentariorum in Marcum* 13 (PL 30:628).

THE PARIS MENDICANT MODEL

In Alexander Minorita we have seen the Revelation commentary assume a specific shape that would eventually find admirers—but not for the moment, or at least as far as we can see. That shape involved three elements, two of which were less problematic than the third.

First, the book was seen as historical. Alexander poured into his commentary all the historical sources at his disposal. The book of Revelation was *about* history. Second, that history was presented as a continuous story told sequentially as the twenty-two chapters of Revelation unfolded.

The third element, the problematic one, was hardly so to Alexander. His sequential reading of the Apocalypse allowed him a big finish. One might call it a Franciscan finish, but it would be more accurate to describe it as a mendicant finish with strong Franciscan overtones, all of which made sense in Alexander's historical context. We will see that the reading of a characteristically Franciscan apocalyptic program into Revelation would present challenges during the second half of the century and beyond, but more on that later.

For the moment, our task is to delineate a different kind of reading that became popular in the schools in the early thirteenth century. It was hardly new. There had been those in the twelfth century and even before who showed signs of interest in it, though not consistently. We find it anticipated in Richard of Saint Victor. In what follows here it will be presented in general outline, without looking too closely at what constitutes in fact a surprisingly large number of mendicant authors, works, and manuscripts to choose from.

For a thirteenth-century exegete who attempted to read his Bible in the light of a burgeoning scholasticism, two things stood out about the Apocalypse. First, it presented seven visions. Second, it portrayed a Christian history that was itself sevenfold. Note that we described it as sevenfold, not as containing seven periods. Augustine, we may recall, divided world history by seven, but it was the sixth period, running from Christ to the final judgment, that saw our time as we know it. The seventh age was in eternity.

We have seen how Jerome left the door open for a final, seventh period, and how subsequent exegetes began to slip through that door, depositing various possible interludes before the last judgment. How, then, did the seven visions relate to Christian history by the thirteenth century? Alexander had presented one possible answer, but it was not the one that dominated in Paris, even while Alexander was writing. What did dominate in the early thirteenth century appeared in a group of five Dominican and Franciscan commentaries that I discussed in my book *Olivi's Peaceable Kingdom*. At the time, I thought these five commentaries were probably written before the end of the 1260s.[1] One of the commentaries, which begins with the words *Ipse revelat*,[2] I attributed to the Franciscan Guilelmus de Militona (William of Middleton or, more likely, Guillaume de Melliton). The second commentary, beginning *Vox domini*, was published in two different editions of Aquinas's works, but in *Olivi's Peaceable Kingdom* I identified the author as a Franciscan simply because two references to Francis of Assisi seemed to suggest as much. Of the three commentaries normally considered Dominican, one was published under the name of Albertus Magnus but is now generally attributed to Pierre de Tarrantaise, while the other two, beginning *Vidit Iacob in somniis* and *Aser pinguis*, have been attributed to Hugh of Saint

---

1. David Burr, *Olivi's Peaceable Kingdom* (Philadelphia: University of Pennsylvania Press, 1993), 28–29. There I estimated that these commentaries were all written between the 1230s and the 1260s. The mendicants themselves arrived substantially earlier. Although the Franciscans did not settle into the quarters of the schools until ca. 1230, evidence of Dominican activity dates from 1217. See Jacques Verger, "Hugues de Saint-Cher dans le contexte universitaire Parisien," in *Hugues de Saint-Cher (†1263): Bibliste et théologien* (Turnhout: Brepols, 2004), 13–22, especially 21.

2. These opening words are normally referred to as the *incipit*. The *incipit* is normally the most stable way of referring to a work, since the authorship of the commentary is often in question. The actual words in the *incipit* are normally from some other passage of Scripture. Commentaries tend to begin by quoting some other book of the Bible, then provide an initial description of the book being exposited on the assumption of a parallel between the words quoted and the book. Thus two different commentaries can have the same *incipit* because they begin by quoting the same passage from some other book of the Bible.

Cher, although it also has been generally accepted that at this point commentaries were being produced by an *atelier* of sorts under Hugh's direction rather than by Hugh alone. Or so Robert Lerner argued in what I had always considered a remarkably convincing article.[3]

The discerning reader may have noted my careful use of tenses in the preceding paragraph. Recently *Ipse revelat, Vox domini, Vidit Iacob in somniis*, and *Aser pinquis* have all been the subject of other suggestions. Alain Boureau has argued that *Ipse revelat* and *Aser pinguis* were written later in the century by Richardus de Mediavilla,[4] while *Vidit Iacob in somniis* is actually by Albertus Magnus[5] and *Vox domini* is by Bonaventure.[6]

How one should feel about these adjustments is another matter. Somewhere around 2001 (the year of my retirement from teaching), at the annual Kalamazoo medieval conference, I remember describing my discussion of thirteenth-century Revelation commentaries in *Olivi's Peaceable Kingdom* as my parting gift to graduate students everywhere. So many of my attributions were uncertain that they would provide topics for a great number of future dissertations in which students would pick off my attributions one by one and reassign the works to other authors.

Now it seems to be happening. The problem, though, is that I would never have expected to see *Ipse revelat* migrate along with *Aser pinguis* from the first half of the thirteenth century to nearly the end of it and, in the case of *Aser pinguis*, change from Dominican to Franciscan in the process. In fact, if any of Boureau's reappraisals seem particularly questionable, these two are.[7] Lerner's argument still seems the more persuasive one.

3. The most important statement on this matter can be found in the masterly article by Robert Lerner, "Poverty, Preaching, and Eschatology in the Revelation Commentaries of 'Hugh of St. Cher,'" in *The Bible in the Medieval World: Essays in Memory of Beryl Smalley*, ed. Katherine Walsh and Diana Wood (Oxford: Basil Blackwell, 1985), 157–89. Lerner makes another important statement in "The Vocation of the Friars Preacher: Hugh of St. Cher between Peter the Chanter and Albert the Great," in *Hugues de Saint-Cher (†1263)*, 215–31, where he defends the same views concerning authorship and dating.

4. Alain Boureau, "Richard de Mediavilla fut-il aussi un exégète?," *Freiburger Zeitschrift für Philosophie und Theologie* 58 (2011), no. 1: 227–71; no. 2: 404–46.

5. Alain Boureau, "Albert le Grand, commentateur de l'Apocalypse," *Freiburger Zeitschrift für Philosophie und Theologie* 61 (2014): 20–43.

6. Alain Boureau, "Bonaventure, commentateur de l'Apocalypse: Pour une nouvelle attribution de *Vox domini*" (hereafter "Bonaventure"), *Franciscan Studies* 70 (2012): 139–81.

7. Boureau's attribution of *Vox domini* to Bonaventure also raises questions, but of a different sort, having to do more with the way Boureau argues his case than with any affection on my part for my original description of it as having been written between 1260 and 1263 by an anonymous Franciscan author; but more on that in a moment.

The Standard Parisian Approach and the Shape of History

In any case, the situation encourages us to be careful not only about naming authors and dating them but even about labeling them as Franciscan or Dominican. There are some things we can say, however. Speaking very generally, we can say that all of those who adopt what I called in *Olivi's Peaceable Kingdom* "the standard Parisian approach to the Apocalypse" divide the book into seven visions, world history into seven ages, and church history into seven periods. Terminology shifts. I will use the word "ages" when referring to the sevenfold division of world history and "periods" when referring to the sevenfold division of church history. To do so is to attribute more terminological regularity to the period than it normally enjoys, but doing so makes it easier to speak clearly. That will still leave some room for confusion with Joachim's threefold division of world history, for which I will also use the word "ages," but we will simply live with it.

Most of the thirteenth-century exegetes distinguish between the first four visions, which deal with all of ecclesiastical history (or, as they often say, the *status generalis*), and the last three visions, which deal only with the final times (the *status finalis*), the final times here being comprised of the time of Antichrist, the period immediately after his death, the final judgment, and eternal rewards or punishments. The *status generalis* portrayed in a specific vision can take different forms. It can be general in the sense that it speaks of Christianity in general, dealing with a specific subject without taking any great care to describe it in terms of historical development; or in the sense that it traces the development of something (e.g., preaching) throughout the full sweep of Christian history in sequential form. This is what scholars refer to as the recapitulative approach. It is called such because some of the early visions (particularly the seven seals and seven trumpets) are seen as recapitulating all of church history, rehearsing the same series of periods. For example, the seven seals are seen as describing a progression through seven periods; then the seven trumpets are depicted as describing a progression through the same seven periods, although perhaps with special attention to the development of a different thing.

Of course, reality is more complicated than that. Some commentators, succumbing to the lure of the fifth vision (the seven angels with vials), treat it as another tour through all of church history. Thus in these cases we will have a five/two division of the visions rather than a four/three division.

So far we have been speaking of the seven visions and suggesting that each of the first four might or might not present a recapitulation of all seven periods. Within those early visions, those that deal with all seven ages of church history in recapitulative style, there is room for varied readings of the historical process as the author moves from one early vision to the next. We will present an example of this phenomenon when we turn to the commentary that begins with the words *Vox domini* and look closely at the way the author deals first with the seven seals, then with the seven trumpets and seven vials.

The seven periods into which church history is divided tend to be predictable, at least in general: an initial period when the primitive church was persecuted by the Jews; a second when it was persecuted by the Roman Empire; a third when it was assaulted by the great heresies; and a fourth when it was attacked from within by hypocrites. The fifth period is harder to characterize, partly because tradition itself offers various ways of describing it. Many thirteenth-century exegetes endorse Richard of Saint Victor's suggestion that in the fifth period Satan, having failed in his project of afflicting the church with individual problems one at a time, threw all of them into the mix at once; but many commentators tend to agree in identifying the fifth trumpet with the precursors of Antichrist, those sent to pave the way for him. In fact, some exegetes explicitly characterize the fifth period as that of the precursors of Antichrist.

Precursors in what way, though? Pave the way *how*? What do they do? The commentators who answer that question emphasize heresy and corruption. The heresies mentioned are often the standard textbook ones such as Arianism, but contemporary heretics such as the Cathars and Waldensians are sometimes mentioned, and the connection between Christianity and pagan philosophy also excites interest as the thirteenth century progresses. As for corruption, some writers criticize both ecclesiastical and secular government, the latter for oppressing the church but also for grinding the faces of the poor. Corrupt *prelati* are sometimes prominently mentioned.[8]

The sixth period is always seen by these commentators as that of Antichrist, while the seventh is often portrayed as an interval after the death of Antichrist in which there will be peace, holy men will be permitted to preach freely, humankind will be given an opportunity to repent, and the Jews will be converted. As we saw earlier, this period has more to do with Jerome's interpretation of Daniel 12, which allows a period of forty-five days, than with the millennium of Revelation 20. In other words, we are dealing with the space we saw being created in the chapter on Joachim of Fiore. Forty-five days is hardly a nonnegotiable figure. Whatever figure is used—and we will

---

8. On criticism of the *prelati* see especially Burr, *Olivi's Peaceable Kingdom*, 46–48.

see the number forty-two used shortly—it tends to be seen as a minimum figure to which God can add additional time. Exegetes are of course aware that the opening of the seventh seal is greeted with "silence in heaven for about half an hour" (Rev 8:1), which might encourage scholars to anticipate a short seventh period; but then again we have those thousand years during which Satan is bound in Revelation 20. The latter is likely to be seen as Augustine saw it. It is the entire time from Christ to Antichrist and means "a long time," not precisely a millennium.

What has been said so far seems to support the idea that, however one might handle the numbers offered by Revelation and Daniel, this way of reading Revelation is heavily historical. It would probably be more accurate to say that it provides the opportunity for a historical reading. It was an opportunity someone like Petrus Iohannis Olivi was more than happy to accept, while someone like John of Wales was willing to acknowledge that opportunity but was much happier actually pursuing a course of largely atemporal, moral interpretation.[9]

If one can speak of a common mendicant approach to Revelation at Paris during the thirteenth century, this is it. To say it was common at Paris is not to say that it was common *only* there, of course. In fact, it was popular elsewhere as well. And to say it was popular is, as we have just seen, not equivalent to saying that it prohibited significant variation.

Scholarly Tools: The *Glossa ordinaria*

This is as good a time as any to pause for a moment and note that we are now in a period when scholars (often Parisian scholars) were in the process of developing not only new ways of interpreting the Bible but also aids to facilitate its study. One certainly rates major attention: the *Glossa ordinaria*, which we will refer to here simply as the *Glossa*.

One reason why this seems a good moment to speak of the *Glossa* is that, unlike most of the aids to study we will mention later, the *Glossa*

9. On John of Wales see Jenny Swanson, *John of Wales* (Cambridge: Cambridge University Press, 1989), a book useful in many ways but misleading in its failure to deal with the question of which manuscripts beginning *Spiritu magno* should be seen as containing the Apocalypse commentary by John and which should be seen as containing a very different Apocalypse commentary, probably by Vital du Four, with the same *incipit*. On that matter, see my later comments. On the commentary by John of Wales, see Alain Boureau, "L'Exégèse de Jean de Galles, Franciscain du XIIIe siècle," *Franciscan Studies* 72 (2014): 153–72.

had already received a century of attention by the early thirteenth century. Historians trace it back to at least the early twelfth century and regularly associate at least part of it with Anselm of Laon, but its text continued to develop.[10] Two decades into the fourteenth century, the author of the first and most extensive critique of Olivi's Apocalypse commentary, a man we will meet in a future chapter, treated the *Glossa* as an important authority and deployed it against Olivi.

To say the *Glossa ordinaria* was used against Olivi might seem out of place here, but it serves to remind us of the speed at which, in an era like the thirteenth century, cutting-edge scholarship could turn into rearguard scholarship. In its developing stage, the *Glossa* served as the medieval version of contemporary hypertext, combining the text with marginal and interlinear glosses that could suggest not only its meaning but sometimes a choice of meanings, which is equivalent to saying that the *Glossa* combined a wide variety of citations stretching over centuries and thus represented no single scholar's views. Nor did the *Glossa* feel even a minimal obligation to point out contradictions or offer tentative solutions to them, as Peter Lombard did in his *Sententiae*. Yet, having arrived and developed into something resembling its definitive form, the *Glossa* settled in comfortably and stayed a very long time. During the early years of printing, it would be published, and in that form it makes itself available to us in a facsimile edition today.

"Hugh of Saint Cher" and *Aser pinguis*

Meanwhile, scholarship moved on. The next big thing, a *Postilla* on the entire Bible identified with the first great mendicant Bible scholar, Hugh of Saint

10. Current study of the matter suggests that the Apocalypse was one of the earliest books to be glossed and that the history of the gloss on Revelation is a complex one. On the *Glossa ordinaria* in general see Lesley Smith, *The Glossa Ordinaria: The Making of a Medieval Bible Commentary* (Leiden: Brill, 2009). For the gloss on the Apocalypse in particular see Guy Lobrichon, "Une nouveauté: Les glosses de la Bible," in *Le Moyen Age et la Bible*, ed. P. Riche and G. Lobrichon (Paris: Beauchesne, 1984), 95–115; Lobrichon, "Conserver, réformer, transformer le monde? Les manipulations de l'Apocalypse au Moyen Âge Central," in *The Role of the Bible in Medieval Culture*, ed. Peter Ganz (Turnhout: Brepols, 1986), 2:75–95; and Lobrichon's unpublished dissertation, "L'Apocalypse des theologiens au XIIe siècle" (University of Paris, 1984). The *Glossa ordinaria* for various books is currently being published in English translation at reasonable prices. For Revelation see *Consolamini Commentary Series: The Glossa Ordinaria on Revelation*, trans. Sarah Van Der Pas (West Monroe, LA: Consolamini, 2015).

Cher,[11] combined what Dominican scholars found valuable in the *Glossa* with what they liked in more recent scholars. Leslie Smith comments that "Hugh intended his *Postilla* as a supplement to the Gloss—to bring it up to date for the thirteenth century."[12] For Hugh this meant treating the *Glossa* with the respect it deserved while simultaneously correcting it and casting what was valuable about it in a new form. What was valuable seems obvious. Scholars had much of what the *Glossa* offered: a text of the Bible with explanatory material; but the explanatory material was now in the form of a commentary. In the process, Hugh shows his respect for what he had replaced by occasionally treating it as if it were part of the Bible itself. For example, Hugh decides that the first of the four animals identified in the opening of the seals (Rev 6:1) stands for Mark, but the *Glossa* says it stands for John.[13] Hugh solves the problem in a way that would have made sense had the *Glossa* been a part of the biblical text. He makes a distinction that allows both identifications to make some sense, each in a particular context.[14]

In the quotation in the previous paragraph and in what I have said myself, Leslie Smith and I have both succumbed to the temptation offered by the manuscripts themselves, who refer to an author named Hugh; but is the "Hugh" mentioned there equivalent to the Hugh we encounter in history as prior and later cardinal? Robert Lerner thinks not. Hugh of Saint Cher was, at best, the overseer of an *atelier* that turned out commentaries, and Lerner offers some of the many good reasons for seeing the matter in that light. Since we're interested not in "Hugh's" *postillae* on the entire Bible but only in the Revelation commentary included there, it should be said that both—the longer commentary on Revelation and the shorter *postillae* on other books of the Bible—are considered to be products of the workshop. Thus the Revelation commentary, like the shorter commentaries, is the work of a group or at least members of that group.

11. Two, actually: *Aser pinguis* and *Vidit Iacob.* Lerner, "Poverty, Preaching, and Eschatology," 165–66, dates *Aser pinguis* ca. 1236 and *Vidit Iacob* between 1240 and 1244. Here we will deal mostly with *Aser pinguis.*

12. Smith, *The Glossa Ordinaria*, 222.

13. Here I am using *Biblia latina cum postillis Hugonis de Sancto Caro* (Basel: Johann Amerbach für Anton Koberger, 1498), nach 29.X.1498–kurz nach 7.XI.1502, with the Revelation commentary in the latter, as digitized by Heinrich Heine University, Düsseldorf. The digitized version has its own pagination, which I will use only when necessary. Otherwise, explicit reference to the passage being commented on in Revelation will suffice.

14. Gilbert Dahan, too, is struck by this aspect of the *Glossa* in Hugh's work. In "L'exégèse de Hugues: Méthode et herméneutique," in *Hugues de Saint-Cher (†1263)*, 65–99, especially 70, Dahan speaks of the *Glossa* as being treated almost as an "auctoritas."

As for the precise mechanism, the way the *atelier* did its work, we have no way of knowing.[15] We can say that the group of young Dominicans at Saint-Jacques included at least one scholar who knew some Greek and another who knew some Hebrew. Thus what we have is not simply exegesis but to some extent textual studies, an attempt to work from a more accurate Bible, what would have been thought of as a *correctorium*.

The goal was not a critical edition of the Vulgate as we might think of it today, but an improved text drawing on other sources such as the rather misleadingly labeled Septuagint (which occasionally seems to refer, not to the Septuagint as we now think of it, but to old Latin versions of the text). The aim was not to work back to an original text but to present variants, often culled from the church fathers (particularly Jerome, and also Origen by way of Rufinus) or from Andrew of Saint Victor. The result was a working text we now refer to as "the Paris text."

All of this had its predecessors. There was already interest in textual studies at Paris thanks to twelfth-century scholars such as the Victorines. Nor was the "Paris text" the answer to scholarly prayers. Gilbert Dahan calls it *banal, de qualité moyenne*.[16] Nonetheless, the scholars at Saint-Jacques succeeded in rolling the ball farther down the road, and they would eventually be aided by the Franciscans.

A Further Word on Scholarly Tools

Development of the "Paris text" brings us back to the subject of scholarly tools. Given time, we could point to a whole series of them that seem to have appeared in Hugh's time, allowing access to information like the meaning of names or the significance of things (for example, the meaning of the name Zebedee or the symbolic significance of an eagle), and concordances that allowed exegetes to move easily through the Scriptures, tracing words or ideas

---

15. My own sentimental favorite is to picture a group of young Dominicans sitting around a table. A verse of Scripture is read, and anyone who wishes is allowed to offer an interpretation. Some make it into the final product, and others do not. That explains the general lack of any sense that the process is tightly controlled by a single guiding principle, as well as the presence of alternate interpretations. The process is less chaotic than the *Glossa* but more chaotic than what we will see in later commentaries. There are both literal and moral interpretations, but mostly the former.

16. Dahan, "L'Exégèse de Hugues," 83.

(Hugh produced one of the early ones).[17] Such reference works gave scholars a common route by which they could pass more or less smoothly from the letter of the text to its spiritual sense, or, to put it another way, a common hermeneutical language, much of it carried over from the previous century.[18]

"Hugh's" commentary (I shall omit the quotation marks hereafter) travels the common route for the standard Parisian model: the first seal, seen as being about the primitive church, is followed by the second seal, dealing with martyrdom. What strikes one about the route in Hugh's case is the wealth of scriptural citations thrown in along the way. Here we find Matthew 10:21, John 16:2, Joshua 8:16, Judges 7:22, Lamentations 2:21, and Ezekiel 21:9 packed into a single commentary on the words "and that they should kill one another, a great sword was given to him" (Rev 6:4).

With the third seal, the devil, seeing that nothing is being gained by persecution and martyrdom, turns to heresy, defined here as perversely interpreting the Scriptures, especially concerning the incarnation. Then, with the opening of the fourth seal, we have the hypocrites. The first four seals represent not only four different kinds of attack on nascent Christianity but four orders of preachers directed against those attacks. These are followed by the fifth seal, involving the consolation of the souls of the martyrs under the altar.

The sixth seal offers us a preview of the future persecution in the time of Antichrist. It will be so strong that even the elect would be affected if that were possible. Pseudo-Christs and pseudo-prophets will provide great signs and prodigies. The exegesis offers two different interpretations of the major imagery in Revelation 6, but both are similar inasmuch as they see it as pointing to a fall within the church, not secular pressure on the church. Thus the stars that fall are seen first as "many who illuminated the church earlier," then, in a second run through the imagery, as members of religious orders falling from the former heights of religious life. Secular pursuits are mentioned, but largely because the commentary speaks of prelates engaging in them. Indeed, the passage about "the kings of the earth," "princes," and "tribunes" might seem to go out of its way to speak positively about secular princes, although a closer reading would lead us to ask if it is to be inter-

---

17. On this matter see Michel Albaric, "Hugues de Saint-Cher et les concordances bibliques latines (XIIIe–XVIIe siècles)," in *Hugues de Saint-Cher (†1263)*, 467–77, as well as Dahan, "L'Exégèse de Hugues."

18. See Dahan's brief but remarkably suggestive comments in "L'Exégèse de Hugues," 94–98.

preted as being about secular princes at all, or if, rather, it is about those people in any walk of life who are disciplined in their use of earthly goods, just as "the rich" referred to next are actually those who are rich, not in earthly belongings, but in good deeds and virtues. So far the notion of wealth is spiritualized to the point that it simply means virtue. Nevertheless, the passage will soon be subjected to an alternate interpretation, corresponding more fully to what we normally read the passage as saying, and as Revelation 6 comes to an end we are left confronting a tribulation so stark that the rich and powerful—the *real* rich and powerful—are left seeking a hiding place for all the reasons we would have anticipated.

With the opening of the seventh seal we find ourselves at the end of history, in the time after the death of Antichrist. The church will have peace, but not for long. The saints will be free to preach and will be given forty-two days to convince Antichrist's supporters, but few of the latter will be converted. Instead they will say, "Our leader may be dead, but we have peace and security." They will get married and celebrate, but even as they say "peace and security," destruction will descend on them. How much time they will have between the promised forty-two days and judgment no one knows except God the Father (Matt 24:36).

The next vision, the seven angels with trumpets, is about preaching in all periods of church history. The commentary begins this section with a great deal of general conversation about the seven virtues and the seven deadly vices but says less about the seven periods of church history, which will be important when we turn from the general to the particular and to the tribulations concerning which the preachers must speak.

The first order of preachers was that of the apostles, who first preached against the Jews, and the second that of the preachers who defied the pagans (i.e., the Romans). The third angel represents a third order of preachers, who preached against the heretics. The great star that fell from heaven represents the heretics who fell from the church, and the rivers into which it fell are the holy Scriptures. These have three parts. The first is the text of the New and Old Testaments; the second is the sayings and institutions of the apostles; and the third is the expositions of the saints. Thus the star fell in the third part, because the heretics did not accept the expositions of the saints. Or the first part is the doctrine of the Old Testament, the second is the doctrine of the New, and the third is the doctrine of neither. Or the first is the literal interpretation, the second the spiritual interpretation, and the third the perverse interpretation. Or the first is the doctrine of the evangelists, the second that of the apostles, and the third a perverse interpretation of both.

Here the group is of many minds and remains content simply to contribute possibilities.

The fourth seal could be read as being about heresy or about hypocrisy, but the fourth trumpet is clearly meant to be about hypocrisy. The preaching is described as aimed at "false brothers, morally corrupted." When a third part of the sun is struck down, the commentary notes that these were people who "held the faith but were ailing in their morals." The sun is interpreted here as the upper levels of church leadership, the prelates and doctors. Some heat up and cast light, some do the former but not the latter, and some do the reverse, casting light but no heat. The commentator responsible for this part clearly wants to make a point about word and example, and he rephrases it in different terms. Some illuminate and inflame by word and example; some illuminate but do not inflame; some do neither.

The moon represents the mid-level prelates. A third part of these are to be struck because they are greedy and without knowledge. The stars are those in religious orders who take vows of continence, obedience, and poverty. It is in the third area that the third part will be found, for they actually want to become rich. Here we find that this early Dominican *atelier*—or at least some members of it—are defenders of apostolic poverty. We will hear more from this subgroup.

We are down to the last three trumpets. Hugh gets a running start on the fifth by summarizing our progress through the first four: "After the devil discovered that by introducing individual temptations one at a time in the form of jealousy from the Jews, persecution from the Romans, the depravity of heretics, and simulation and hypocrisy from false brothers he could not get the desired result and stop Christian preaching, he attempted to achieve it through a combination of these evils." Thus we have Lucifer falling to earth and being given the keys of the abyss (Rev 9:1).

Chapter 8 ends with the eagle flying through and calling out its triple "woe." As we enter the next chapter we find ourselves moving within a powerful myth, and the commentary recognizes what myth it is. We are encountering Lucifer, the brightest star in the sky until he was cast down. Now he combines his own substantial power with what comes to him as keeper of the keys, not the keys of the heavenly kingdom but the keys of the abyss, and he opens it wide. The commentary has the sense to recur immediately to the Bible and rehearse what is said there on the subject in Isaiah 14:12–19, Luke 10:18, Daniel 8:23–25, Daniel 11, and elsewhere.[19]

19. Note that at 788a he agrees that Dan will be born from the tribe of Dan. The word *coluber* affords him the connection by way of Gen 49:7.

What follows is impressive in the sense that it is heavily loaded with references to biblical parallels and often to biblical passages that simply use the same word—which is to say that someone has worked very hard to integrate these chapters with the Bible as a whole, or that someone had a great deal of help in doing so, or that someone had access to a decent concordance. At this point in the thirteenth century, any of the three might be considered possible. Nevertheless, how it can be connected with concrete events is often hard to discern, and the problem is hardly mitigated by the fact that the commentary deals with the fifth, sixth, and seventh periods as a single unit. The sixth angel begins to blow his horn at Revelation 9:13, but the tune he plays is not appreciably different from the one offered earlier by the fifth angel. The next commentary we examine, *Vox domini*, will solve the problem partly by assigning the fifth period to the precursors of Antichrist, thus giving the period its own label and its own personality. Even in *Vox domini* what we find will hardly be a smooth, integrated trip through the ages, but at least we will pass more landmarks that suggest the trip is taking us somewhere.

One more seven-part sequence calls for investigation: Revelation 15:1–16:17, the seven bowls. As Lerner recognizes, *Aser pinguis* is following Richard of Saint Victor, who saw the seven as orders of preachers. The first six preach against oppression by the Jews, the gentiles, the heretics, Antichrist, the gentiles supporting Antichrist, and the apostate Christians supporting Antichrist. Then, according to Richard, the seventh appears after the death of Antichrist at the end of time and pours his bowl out in the air, warning the demons to expect Christ's second coming. *Aser pinguis* follows Richard concerning the first six and then, still following Richard, announces the end of the world; but what we find is a final period after Antichrist when persecution has ended and a final order of preachers will be free to preach, perform miracles, and convert the Jews to the Christian faith. This is, to be sure, a departure from Richard, but that departure is more significant than simply adding another period. Throughout his commentary, Richard is pursuing a set of ends that are very much his own, aims that might be described as less millenarian than contemplative.

In fact, judged by our normal sense of "millenarian," they are not such at all. We are using the term here in the limited sense understood by Lerner: a reading of the Apocalypse in terms of seven historical periods with the seventh following Antichrist. As the earlier chapter on Richard of Saint Victor suggests, Richard was hardly indifferent to the sevenfold structure, but he was always aiming at a rather different target. It is significant that ca. 1297 Olivi would write his commentary with two other commentaries open in front of him: those of Richard and Joachim. He often cited Richard approvingly, but in cases where he had to choose between the two he almost always chose Joachim. Olivi was, to be sure, *sui generis* (as was Joachim), but in this respect he and Hugh both belong within a long tradition that follows the trail marked by Lerner in his article "Refreshment of the Saints,"[20] then visits the places noted in Lerner's articles on Hugh of Saint Cher. Throughout this journey, a historicization of Revelation is of central importance, although it is never of sole importance.

It is impossible to leave *Aser pinguis* without further underlining the extent to which this Dominican commentary places what might seem a Franciscan emphasis on apostolic poverty. As Lerner observes, *Aser pinguis* identifies the flood of water spewing from the dragon's mouth in Revelation 12:15–16 with Constantine's donation of temporal wealth to the church and claims that it was accompanied by angelic voices announcing that "today poison has been poured into the church."[21] This statement might be taken as a high-water mark for Dominican apocalyptic attacks on wealth. They hardly disappeared after *Aser pinguis*, but they were tempered.

Thus *Aser pinguis* was highly (and, by later standards, at times dangerously) apocalyptic, but it was by no means Joachite. It certainly knew of Joachim. At Revelation 5:1, as the book with seven seals is introduced, *Aser pinguis* rings the changes on possible interpretations of the seven seals, then notes that the church could be described as a book with seven seals,

> as Joachim, who exposited this book, pointed out. The first is the washing clean of the primitive faithful through baptism. The second is their manifest persecution through infidels shedding their blood. The third is the hidden persecution or rather humiliation of the new church with God's protection. The fourth is the persecution by heretics which began in the time of the apostles but will continue to the time of Antichrist. The fifth is the glorification of the martyrs. . . . The sixth is the persecution by Antichrist. The seventh is the brief rest given to the church after the death of Antichrist, when the faithful will freely preach, announcing what has occurred and what is to be for both the reprobate and the elect.[22]

20. Robert Lerner, "Refreshment of the Saints: The Time after Antichrist as a Station for Earthly Progress in Medieval Thought," *Traditio* 32 (1976): 97–144.

21. Lerner, "Poverty, Preaching, and Eschatology," 173. Lerner provides the pedigree of this story at pp. 173–74 and points out that it also appears in *Vidit Iacob*.

22. Found at f. 766b in the Düsseldorf online edition.

Nevertheless, *Aser pinguis* shows little interest in what is now recognized as Joachim's characteristic reading of Revelation, either his twofold or his threefold pattern.

"Bonaventure" and *Vox domini*

We now turn to a second example of the standard Parisian model, different in some ways from *Aser pinguis*, and to yet another article by Alain Boureau, this one devoted to exploring the idea that the Revelation commentary beginning *Vox domini*, which I attributed to an anonymous Franciscan and dated between 1263 and 1266, is actually by Bonaventure and dates from around 1255.[23] Boureau acknowledges that he "cannot present any absolute proof, but rather an ensemble of probabilities or convergences." It is, nonetheless, an intriguing argument, one that should be considered possible and perhaps even likely. In the following discussion I will simply assume it to be worthy of serious consideration and examine what follows from it.

Knowing what we do about both the standard Parisian model and the controversies that roiled the order at that time, we can see that Boureau's dating would make sense. Thus it is hardly surprising to find that the author of the commentary beginning *Vox domini*, when he arrives at Revelation 14, spends a substantial amount of time discussing what is meant by Revelation 14:6: "Then I saw another angel flying in midair, and he had the eternal gospel to proclaim." The words "eternal gospel" are an unwelcome reminder of Gerard of Borgo San Donnino, and they send the author into a long discussion of what the word "gospel" can legitimately be taken to mean, followed by another discussion concerning what is meant when the word "eternal" is added. "That gospel is called eternal which has no new, worthier successor, as was the case when the new law succeeded the old law."[24] Boureau observes that the author's "anti-Joachite position is clear."[25]

---

23. Boreau, "Bonaventure, commentateur de l'Apocalypse," 139–81. The work in question here can be found in *Sancti Thomae Aquinatis doctoris angelici ordinis praedicatorum opera omnia*, tome 23, vol. 2 (Parma: Pietro Fiaccadori, 1869), 512–712, and elsewhere among *opera* attributed to Aquinas. Boureau, "Bonaventure, commentateur de l'Apocalypse," 140–45, summarizes that story. Hereafter, citations of *Vox domini* are taken from Aquinas's *Opera* (Vivés, 1871–1880), 32:104–821.

24. *Vox domini*, 322.

25. Boreau, "Bonaventure, commentateur de l'Apocalypse," 154.

Unfortunately, calling an author "anti-Joachite" on the basis of whether he rejects what Gerard of Borgo San Donnino said leaves one somewhat short of an accurate statement concerning what constitutes either Joachism or anti-Joachism. We speak of Olivi as a Joachite, but—as we shall see—his apocalyptic thought bore little resemblance to Gerard's, despite later accusations to the contrary. From what little we know, the same could be said about Alexander Minorita. And the historical Joachim himself was quite different from all of them. In fact, when we inquire as to what the historical Bonaventure believed and how it related to what Joachim believed, labels like this don't get us very far beyond establishing that, if Bonaventure was Joachite in some sense, it was not in the same sense as Gerard.

At last we can deal with *Vox domini*. Like others who follow the recapitulative method, the author divides the Apocalypse into seven major visions: first, that of "the correction of the churches"; second, "the revelation of mysteries of the one sitting on the throne, the book, the lamb, and the opening of the seven seals"; third, "the seven angels with trumpets"; fourth, "the battle of the woman with the dragon"; fifth, "the seven angels pouring out the vials of God's wrath"; sixth, "the damnation of Babylon, the beast, and the dragon"; and seventh, "the renewal of the elements and glorification of the saints." The author specifies that "the first four visions deal with the general state of the church from beginning to end and the last three with the final state of the church. Again, the first four are distinguished by the fact that the first is corrective, . . . the second consolatory through the revelation of mysteries, . . . the third terrible and threatening, . . . and the fourth exhortative to battle."

The last three are also distinguished from one another. That of the pouring out of the vials refers to the time of Antichrist, while the damnation of Babylon and the beast refers to the time of judgment, and the glorification of the saints refers to the state of eternal beatitude.[26]

Note that the word *status* has been given a heavy workout in the preceding passage. I have translated it as "state," but as used to refer to the second, third, and fourth visions, it also has a temporal connotation, referring to a period of church history. In the case of the fifth and sixth visions, the author explicitly uses the word *tempus* to describe what amounts to two limited periods, then uses *status* for the seventh and last vision, which is not about a period at all.

---

26. *Vox domini*, 113–14. The author says the same at the transition between the fourth and fifth visions, *Vox domini*, 335. As we will see, however, his view of the seven trumpets is more complicated.

The first vision, that of the letters to seven churches, is addressed to seven churches of Asia Minor, and these in turn are seen as standing for all churches throughout time. Thus, unsurprisingly, the advice tends to be seen as equally timeless. At one point the author suggests that the seven letters should be correlated with the seven cardinal virtues, but he then switches abruptly to a consideration of the qualities necessary in a prelate. The exegesis of this vision provides a good example of the "general state of the church" taken in one sense. There is little interest in placing the vision in the time or place suggested by the vision itself, i.e., Asia Minor in the late first century. Reference to something as specific as the Nicolaitans calls forth a brief historical explanation, but then the discussion returns to timeless admonition. Nicolaitans represent people in general, be they Jews or gentiles, orthodox or heretical, who live foolishly.[27]

The next two visions offer the *status generalis ecclesiae* taken in the other sense described earlier: each is a recapitulative trip through church history, offered sequentially. As has been said above, thirteenth-century exegetes tended to see the opening of the seven seals in Revelation 6–8 as one of the visions that dealt with all of church history as opposed to those that concentrated on the end time. Here the author of the commentary specifies that the seven seals are distinguished by the fact that the first five represent the present and past periods of the church while the two following ones pertain to the future. Thus the early ones are distinguished in the following way: the first pertains to the early building up[28] of the church in the time of Christ and the apostles. That is, it deals with the time of Christ's direct interaction with the world while he was in it, and it can be extended to the building up of the church through the preaching of the apostles after Christ's ascension.

The next three seals pertain to the tribulations of the faithful who have thus been built up. The first of them pertains to the state[29] of the church in the time of the martyrs; the second to that in the age of the heretics; and the third in the state of the false brothers.[30] That adds up to four seals. The fifth deals with the consolation of those suffering tribulation.

27. *Vox domini*, 124. Note the close relationship with Richard of Saint Victor on most of these matters.

28. Remember that the word *aedificatio*, translated here as "building up," could also be taken in the sense of "edification."

29. The word *status* could also refer to a period of time but is translated as "status" here because it is followed by *tempore*.

30. *Vox domini*, 172.

Note that the author is now talking about periods, not visions. He is saying that the second vision covers all of the *status generalis ecclesiae*, but as divided into periods, with these periods unrolling sequentially. The time of the early church is followed by that of the martyrs, then by the times of the heretics and hypocrites. This is the normal progression in the standard Parisian pattern. Notice, however, that there is a trace of ambiguity here that raises the question of whether the seals represent sharply delineated periods or things happening more or less simultaneously, or at least overlapping. This is often the case, perhaps because exegetes recognized that the various characteristics used to distinguish periods did in fact overlap. Martyrdom, heresy, and hypocrisy could be found anytime in the early church; yet in the final analysis this author is interested in separating them into periods, and shortly thereafter he repeats the whole thing in a way that makes it clear he is committed to using them as distinguishing characteristics in a division of church history into seven periods.

These are the basic dynamics of a thirteenth-century Revelation commentary. The author's presentation of a history in seven ages must proceed within the context of his recognition that historical periods do not actually have sharp, well-defined edges, that all the heresy, for example, does not get packed into a single span of years; and he must draw his sacred history from a text in which all is presented *sub figuris*, as the author of *Vox domini* likes to say. It is heavily metaphorical. In fact, from our perspective we can recognize yet another difficulty that the author must deal with but can never consciously face, namely, that beneath those *figurae* the author of Revelation is telling a story different from the one the author of the commentary expects to find there, although at times their stories do come within hailing distance of one another.

The fifth seal pertains to the consolation of those in tribulation. As the author says, the souls of the martyrs call out for a hastening of the general resurrection and judgment.[31] This section looks backward over the first four periods, which the author has presented as a story of tribulation. Now the martyred souls are calling out, "How long?" They are told to wait a little longer.

The martyred souls may be able to wait, but apparently the author cannot. At this point he leaps forward to the opening of the sixth and seventh seals, which pertain to "the final states of the church in the time of Antichrist. In the opening of the eighth is shown the peace that will be restored after

---

31. *Vox domini*, 181.

the time of Antichrist."[32] And having created an eighth seal, he proceeds to import the "other angel" of Revelation 7:2 into the discussion for a cameo appearance, bolstering the limited consolation of Revelation 6:11 with the more sustained consolation described in Revelation 7, the sealing of the elect.

Then he turns back to the tribulations of Revelation 6:12–17, and his description of them is striking in its prediction that those resisting Antichrist will be punished by secular princes. Ecclesiastics are also prominently mentioned, but as victims, not persecutors.[33]

Antichrist will reign for three and a half years; then he will be killed on Mount Olivet. A period of forty-two days will be granted so that the elect can do penance. Once it is over, Christ will come in judgment, but no one can say how long after the forty-two days have expired the final judgment will occur.[34] The author will return to this theme in his comments on Revelation 8:1, "There was silence in heaven for the space of about half an hour." Here he cites the *Glossa*, which says the forty-two days mirror the time after the crucifixion, when the Jews had forty-two years to do penance, and that it is aimed primarily at the evil, at Antichrist's followers, rather than at the good. The former will fail to take advantage of the opportunity. They will eat, drink, and make merry, taking wives and saying, "our leader is dead, but we ourselves are enjoying peace and security."[35]

All of this time the author has been discussing the career of Antichrist, mining Revelation 6:12–17 whenever he can and often falling back on the Antichrist legend when he cannot. Finally he reaches Revelation 7:2, this time in its proper order. He identifies the "other angel" as Christ, "an angel not in nature but in office."[36] A discussion of the sealing follows, in which it becomes clear that the sealed comprise, not only those who have been converted in all ages, but also those who are scheduled to be saved as members of the elect, a group consisting of both Jews and gentiles. Thus the "Israel" referred to in this chapter means "spiritual Israel."[37]

Revelation 7 contains the only two references to Francis in the entire commentary. We will examine them later.

In the meantime, we might deepen our sense of *Vox domini* as a tour of Christian history by looking briefly at the next vision, that of the seven

32. *Vox domini*, 184.
33. *Vox domini*, 186–87.
34. *Vox domini*, 188.
35. *Vox domini*, 211.
36. *Vox domini*, 190.
37. *Vox domini*, 199.

trumpets. Here, as is often the case in the Parisian model, the seven trumpets are presented as a look at history from the perspective of preaching. The tour begins with Christ and the apostles. Christ again appears in the story as the "other angel," but this time the "other angel" of Revelation 8:3.[38] Yet the main focus is on the apostles, whose preaching task involves indictment of the Jews. The second angel represents those preaching against the gentiles who persecute the church, the third those preaching against the heretics, and the fourth those preaching against the "false brothers," i.e., the hypocrites. Here again one could imagine all these things occurring simultaneously or in overlapping fashion rather than serially, and there is some sense of the latter; yet here again there is also a sense of the four as characterizing each of the first four periods of church history in turn. In the case of the first two periods, the author explicitly refers to the second as such *in order of narration and time but not in order of persons*, since many of the original preachers addressed first the Jews and then the gentiles.[39] Indeed, he recognizes that in the case of those combating heretics—the latter described as people who misinterpret the Bible—he is speaking of a group of preachers extending from the original disciples and apostles to the *sancti*, including Augustine, Jerome, and the rest, a wide temporal sweep.

As with the seven seals, some of the seven trumpets are projected into the future, but here it is the last *three* trumpets rather than the last two. The fifth deals with the precursors of Antichrist, the sixth with Antichrist and his followers, then the last with the final judgment and end of the world. The fifth trumpet—like the others, described as an order of preachers—clears up an ambiguity in the seven seals. Here it is clarified that the precursors of Antichrist, like Antichrist himself, are yet to come.

This arrangement gives the author an opportunity to develop his sense of the coming tribulation at some length. One would expect him to develop this vision, not only in terms of heresy, but also in terms of concrete moral turpitude, and he does so; yet he is remarkably interested in theology and closely identifies the coming tribulation with heresy. Like many others in the period, the author tends to see the heretics as a united front, diverse yet concordant in their attack on the church; yet his attention to the word *perfectus* might suggest that he is very much aware of the Cathars.[40] He portrays the precursors of Antichrist as disciples of the

---

38. *Vox domini*, 213.
39. *Vox domini*, 222.
40. See *Vox domini*, 242.

preceding heretics.[41] Thus, without stating the matter all that explicitly, he presents a scenario that stresses a great deal of continuity between present and future, with the heretics of his own time setting the stage for the precursors of Antichrist in the future, much as the precursors themselves will set the stage for Antichrist. Heresy looms large as a central theme.

The most serious attack will, of course, come in the time of Antichrist. The author is sparing in detail but lets us know that, once the chains that kept Satan from attacking have been unloosed, Satan will be able to count on help from worldly princes and the depraved rich. The attack will last three and a half years. That much seems to be taken literally, but the battle imagery is not. He suggests that the persecution by Antichrist and his associates is described *sub similitudine belli* and goes on to decode the imagery. The horsemen are demons, and the horses are human beings. The demons produce heretics who pretend to be perfect in observance of the divine precepts even while transgressing them.[42]

It was noted earlier that the neat four/three division between visions that cover the *status generalis ecclesiae* and those that deal with the *status finalis ecclesiae* is occasionally compromised by the temptation to read the vision of the seven vials as covering all of church history, in other words, to see it as like the visions of the seven seals and trumpets, one more recapitulative pattern producing a five/two division rather than four/three. The author of *Vox dominini* feels the temptation but does not yield to it. Or at least he does not *completely* yield to it. In commenting on Revelation 16,[43] he portrays the seven angels who pour out the vials as seven orders of preachers, and that is what he says about the angels in the previous two visions; but he then explicitly says that these seven angels "are to be interpreted as within the time of Antichrist," and the seven plagues "involve the destruction of evils [or perhaps we should read it as "the evil people"] to exist within the time of Antichrist." To be specific, the first angel will preach against the Jews who accept Antichrist, and the author underlines that in that time they will not only receive him but honor him greatly. The second angel "will preach against the gentiles who will afflict the worshipers of Christ." The third "will preach against the pseudo-apostles who will pervert the Scriptures." The

41. *Vox domini*, 236: "Here is shown the malice of the heretics, who will be disciples of preceding heretics. And, as has been shown, both the heretics and their predecessors will prepare the way for Antichrist."

42. *Vox domini*, 243.

43. Revelation 16 is covered in *Vox domini*, 344–70.

fourth will preach against Antichrist himself. The fifth will preach against the infidels, who will also subject themselves to Antichrist. The sixth will preach against the rich, and the seventh against the demons, at whose suggestion the preceding six groups will follow Antichrist. There is an obvious connection here with what we find in Richard of Saint Victor, then *Aser pinguis.*

Thus, despite the temptation to read this sequence of seven as addressing all of church history, there are times when all seven angels are portrayed as active only during the *status finalis*; yet one cannot miss the extent to which the commentator's portrayal of the first three angels dovetails with what has been said in describing the early periods of the *status generalis.* There too we find ourselves proceeding from persecution by the Jews to persecution by the gentiles, then an internal persecution by heretics (who are portrayed by the commentator elsewhere as perverting the Scriptures). In fact, at one moment the author explicitly suggests that the first two angels can be understood and in fact are commonly exposited as a double order of preachers, one part of which preached to the Jews in the early church and the other part of which preached to the gentiles. These were called different orders because their preaching to the two groups varied and their audiences differed, but the preachers were the same. Thus for a moment here the author has opened his commentary to the possibility that the seven vials are not simply about life in the *status finalis* but can be interpreted as applying to the *status generalis* as well. In fact, he makes the connection even more explicit by suggesting that the Jews bore the mark of the beast even back then, adoring the image of Antichrist long before his advent.

There is a similar connection to be made regarding the heretics, and as the exposition of Revelation 16 progresses it becomes obvious that "false Christians" primarily means "heretics." We have seen that even in the visions dealing explicitly with the *status generalis* the author manages to suggest a smooth transition from heretics to precursors of Antichrist to Antichrist himself.

All of this suggests that the author himself is not entirely consistent and that he sometimes thinks of himself as applying the seven bowls to all of church history, while at other moments he wants to apply them only to the *status finalis*; yet it could also be seen as suggesting that the author envisages a much more integrated (one might even say more homogenous) model of Christian history than the *status generalis/status finalis* distinction might at first lead one to suspect. One of the elements that tie it all together is certainly heresy, as we have seen; but another of these elements is Christ, as we will see. Yet another is the Jews, who play a much more central role as antagonists in the author's mind than might be expected, given their actual role in the problems of the church during the Middle Ages.[44] The author describes the damnation of the Jews as *durissima* and *irrevocabilis*. He acknowledges that they will be converted by Enoch and Elijah, but he cannot resist observing that the number saved will not include those who turn out to be incorrigible or who die in their error before Enoch and Elijah do their work.

In the final analysis, however, the vision of the seven vials is mainly about the *status finalis*, and it becomes more so as it progresses. That should give the author another chance to say something about the extra time given for penance after the death of Antichrist. He does, but in an odd context, as an objection. He stresses the severity of the tribulation inflicted by Antichrist and predicts that many will blaspheme against God. Some will do so because of physical injuries and others because God has, in effect, wounded them internally, in his omnipotence deciding to deny them the patience and stamina to endure. But then the author offers his objection:

> But it is objected that the faithful who erred during the tribulation will repent after the death of Antichrist, for they will be given time to do so, as is stated in the *Glossa* at the end of the seventh chapter. I respond: It seems to be said that many will repent, since they will see Antichrist brought down; yet by hidden divine justice many will remain in error, as is shown by the letter of the text.[45]

The vision of the seven vials leaves us with certain questions. One is whom the author is thinking of when he speaks of the infidels. The other is how the rich—or, as he later says, "the rich and powerful"—managed to gain one of the seven places among those singled out for special mention, particularly because he says that "through the preaching they will only become worse." He addresses neither question explicitly.

Most of what has been said so far comes from what is said in the visions dealing with the *status generalis*. Of those dealing with the *status*

---

44. This is hardly the occasion for a serious discussion of the matter, but we may be seeing here a reflection of the more general difference between the degree to which the Jews preoccupied Christians during the thirteenth century and the degree to which they logically should have, in fact, a difference in that respect running through history into the twenty-first century.

45. *Vox domini*, 349. Note that no specific number of days is given and that he refers to the *Glossa ordinaria* rather than to Jerome. The author's only comment in this chapter relating to how long the period after Antichrist will last is also on p. 353, when he says the time of the last judgment is hidden from us.

finalis, we have looked closely only at the vision concerning the seven vials. If our aim was to gain a clear view of how the author views the time of Antichrist, we would have to look particularly at his presentation of chapters 13 and 14, as well as from 17 on, where his approach is in some ways less interesting than what we have seen so far. That might seem odd, given that these chapters contain what strikes modern readers as perhaps one of the most interesting parts of the Apocalypse. What makes these chapters interesting here is the author's tendency to reduce the complex, wildly creative imagery of the Apocalypse to a series of simple interpretations that soon become predictable. For example, even by the time we get to Revelation 9 we are aware that, for the author, the servants of Antichrist are heretical and depraved, although neither their heresy nor their depravity is all that seriously investigated. Consider what a person of imagination might have done with what comes out of the bottomless pit in Revelation 9. What the author actually does with it is to identify the scene as one of heretics riding demons, then pretty much leave it there. Perhaps the problem is simply that scholastic philosopher-theologians were not the best group to deal adequately with apocalyptic imagery; yet some were, e.g., Petrus Iohannis Olivi, as we will see. Mystics like Hildegard of Bingen in the twelfth century and Na Prous Boneta in the fourteenth were accustomed to processing apocalyptic imagery creatively, but with a certain degree of risk, as the case of Na Prous suggests.[46]

What about the point mentioned earlier, Christ as a unifying element? Where is Christ in all this? At the beginning of chapter 10, the author says, "Having presented the persecution to come in the time of Antichrist, this work deals with the consolation the faithful will have then and in fact can have even now."[47] This is another sort of continuity the author stresses, and one easily ignored. The angels of Revelation 7:2; 8:3; 10:1; 14:1; 14:15; 17:1; and 18:1 are all identified with Christ.[48] The author begins chapter 14 with the announcement that, the tribulation of Antichrist having been dealt with in

46. Note, however, that Na Prous was burned, not primarily because she was a mystic, but because the content of her visions was heretical, containing the wrong message about John XXII and the contemporary church and encouraging resistance against both.

47. *Vox domini*, 248.

48. *Vox domini*, 190, 213, 248, 328, 332, 358, 370. This may not be an exhaustive list. I could have missed some. Revelation speaks of Christ as an angel in these cases because God the Father sends him to us. He is sometimes portrayed as an angel of great council. But sometimes the word "angel" might stand, not for Christ, but for a member of one of the orders of preachers, who also offer good council. Sometimes it actually stands for an angel.

chapter 13, chapter 14 deals with the aid to be given by Christ.[49] The Apocalypse is seen by this commentator and in fact by others as about tribulation and consolation. We are apt to overlook the importance of the latter, but it plays a substantial role in the author's reading of the text.

Another question easily ignored is, "Where is the author in all this?" Clearly the author of *Vox domini* feels he is living in a period prior to the opening of the sixth seal, in fact prior to the sounding of the fifth trumpet. Even the precursors of Antichrist have not yet arrived on the scene, although *their* precursors have. The point here is that the seals and trumpets order history into a discernible narrative, even as the author recognizes tribulation and Christ's comforting presence as constants that in some way transcend specific periods. Within that narrative, the angel of Revelation 7:2 is not scheduled to arrive for a while.

This brings us to the question of where Bonaventure's thoughts went from there, if indeed *Vox domini* is by Bonaventure. In 1260, at a general chapter meeting held in Narbonne, Bonaventure, who had been minister general since 1257, was entrusted with the task of writing a new biography of Francis. The result, Bonaventure's *Legenda maior*, was approved in 1263 at the general chapter in Pisa, and in 1266 the general chapter in Paris ordained that all other biographies should be destroyed.

Early in the *Legenda maior*, almost at the beginning, Bonaventure makes a remarkable statement about Saint Francis:

> Therefore, there is every reason to believe that it is he who is designated under the image of an angel rising from the east with the seal of the living God. "When the sixth seal was broken," John says in the Apocalypse, "I saw a second angel rising from the east with the seal of the living God."[50]

In other words, Bonaventure feels we have reason to think it is Francis to whom John is referring when he speaks of the angel of Revelation 7:2. He repeats this

---

49. *Vox domini*, 311.

50. Bonaventura, *Legenda maior*, in *Opera omnia* (Ad Claras Aquas [Quaracchi], 1882–1902), 8:504: "Prophetali quoque repletus spiritu nec non et angelico deputatus officio incendioque seraphico totus ignitus et ut vir hierarchicus *curru igneo* sursum vectus, sicut ex ipsius vitae decursu luculenter apparet, rationabiliter comprobatur venisse *in spiritu et virtute Eliae*, ideoque alterius *amici sponsi*, apostoli et evangelistae Ioannis vaticinatione veridica sub similitudine angeli ascendentis ab ortu solis signumque Dei vivi habentis astruitur non immerito designatus. Sub apertione *namque sexti sigilliu vidi*, ait Ioannes in Apocalypsi, *alterum angelum ascendentem ab ortu solis, habentem signum Dei vivi*."

identification in the final chapter of the *Legenda maior*. He will return to it in the *Legenda minor*, in sermons, and finally in the *Collationes in hexaemeron*.

The question is not so much what Bonaventure said but what he meant by it. In *Olivi's Peaceable Kingdom* I tried to answer that question, but from a certain perspective. I was concerned with Petrus Iohannis Olivi's interpretation of Bonaventure and the *Legenda maior*, but my major concern was with what Olivi thought Bonaventure was saying in his *Collationes in hexaemeron*. In the chapter on thirteenth-century mendicant exegesis, I attempted to place Olivi within the context of Franciscan commentaries as a whole, explaining how his decision to follow the lead of Bonaventure's *Collationes in hexaemeron* and to place himself within the sixth period of church history allowed him to read Bonaventure's identification differently than his contemporaries did. By putting themselves and particularly Francis in the sixth period of church history, Bonaventure and Olivi made it possible to take seriously the idea of Francis as angel of the sixth seal. (Bonaventure saw the sixth period as beginning well before Francis, while Olivi saw Francis as appearing at the beginning of the sixth period, in fact as a major milestone in the transition to the sixth period.) Other Franciscan exegetes placed themselves in the fifth period or earlier. Thus for them the idea of Francis as the angel of the sixth seal was more problematic. To take him as literally the angel of Revelation 7:2 would be akin to saying that the angel of the sixth seal came before the sixth period even began.

What, then, should be done with Bonaventure's announcement in the *Legenda maior*? Boureau, proceeding on the assumption that Bonaventure's words in the latter must be harmonized with his words in *Vox domini*, tries to find a different meaning for the word *adstruitur* in the *Legenda maior*, one that allows him to fit the idea of Francis as the angel of the sixth seal into "a network of similitudes" in which "the angel is taken as itself a similitude, and not as a real being."[51] What Boureau is trying to avoid is a reading of the *Legenda maior* that forces us to place Francis within the sixth period, as Petrus Iohannis Olivi "and many historians" (like myself) have done. Boureau is willing to go so far as to acknowledge that Francis as the angel of the sixth seal might be taken "as an exception or a spiritual anticipation," but Francis himself must remain in an earlier period. Boureau observes that in the prologue to the *Legenda maior* Bonaventure "is doing the work, not of an exegete, but of a hagiographer."[52]

---

51. Boureau, "Bonaventure, commentateur de l'Apocalypse," 148–50.
52. Boureau, "Bonaventure, commentateur de l'Apocalypse," 150.

There is a sense in which Boureau could be taken as correct, insofar as in *Vox domini* the author is reflecting, not Bonaventure's hagiographical assumptions, but the exegetical assumptions of *Vox domini* insofar as the author gives us any sense of what those assumptions are. Concerning the eagle flying through the air in Revelation 8:13, he comments that it stands for preachers flying through the middle of the sky (i.e., holy Scripture) due to elevated intellect, that is, neither to the right *per scrutinium majestatis* nor to the left through acceptance only of the literal sense, "because not all things should be taken as meant literally."[53] Indeed, he says, from the triple *vae* it is clear that the words of this book should be taken in the mystical sense, because eagles cannot talk.

We are reminded perhaps of Alexander Minorita on the impossibility of communicating with literal mountains, but the author of *Vox domini* is certainly correct in saying that Revelation delivers its message *sub figuris*. The real question concerns the truth value of those statements. John makes real statements about history, although he does so *sub figuris*. That much is clear. If there is one thing the author of *Vox domini* takes seriously, it is the division of the text into historical narrative and prophecy, statements about the past and those about the future. He is eager to let us know which parts refer to the former and which to the latter. He is careful with his tenses. The only two references to Francis occur in the exegesis of Revelation 7, but they place him in the past. Both reflect Celano. As for the angel of 7:2, he is interpreted in traditional fashion, as we have seen. He is Christ, as are the angels of 8:3 and 10:1. In the text Christ is referred to as an angel, but the reference is nonetheless specifically to Christ. The author cites the Septuagint version of Isaiah 9:6, where it is said that Christ will be called an "angel of good counsel." He is called an angel "not because of his nature but because of his office." Just as tribulation is suffered by Christians throughout history, so aid and comfort are available to them at all times through Christ.

In short, the references to Francis in *Vox domini* present him in hagiographical fashion without apocalyptic overtones. They occur in the context of Revelation 7, and Revelation 7 deals with the future sixth period; yet the references to Francis in Revelation 7 do not locate him in the sixth period but rather in the past, just as would be the case if the author referred to Saint Gregory the Great. It is, to be sure, intriguing that the only two references to Saint Francis in the commentary should occur in the context of Revelation 7. If *Vox domini* is by Bonaventure, then one might wonder what sort of

---

53. *Vox domini*, 229-30.

thought Bonaventure was entertaining yet feeling himself unready to express at this juncture; but we will never know the answer to that question.

What, then, should we make of the prologue to the *Legenda maior*? One might guess that, if *Vox domini* is actually by Bonaventure, then the image of Francis in the prologue to the *Legenda maior* represents something new, a new way of conceiving Francis on Bonaventure's part, although not an entirely new way of conceiving him within the order. As we saw earlier in this chapter, Gerard of Borgo San Donnino identified Francis as the angel of Revelation 7:2. This is not to say that Bonaventure was acceding to Gerard's interpretation. Whatever he meant by calling Francis the angel of the sixth seal, one can be sure it was the fruit of Bonaventure's long meditation on Francis's life and especially his stigmata in the process of writing the *Legenda maior*, as a result of which he found himself altering his sense of Francis's historical role, which is to say his apocalyptic role.

To say Bonaventure altered his sense of Francis is not to say that the entire order did so along with him. In *Olivi's Peaceable Kingdom* I pointed out that most Franciscan exegetes who followed the standard Parisian pattern inherited with it a sense of the sixth period as yet to come, and thus must have been left with a problem when it came to dealing with Revelation 7:2. They fell roughly into three categories in dealing with the angel. First, some did not mention Francis at all. Second, some offered a compromise, treating Bonaventure's identification of Francis as the angel of the sixth seal as a good subject for a sermon while avoiding any commitment to literal acceptance of the identification, which would logically imply agreement that the sixth seal had been opened. Finally, we have Bonaventure in his *Collationes in hexaemeron* and Olivi in his Revelation commentary, both of whom placed themselves and Francis in the sixth period, thus giving them substantially more latitude in dealing with Francis as the angel of the sixth seal.[54]

---

54. Something odd happens at this point in Boureau's critique of my position. In "Bonaventure, commentateur de l'Apocalypse," 149–51, he reads me as suggesting that there were two options, not three. On the one hand, there was the Bonaventuran sense of Francis as the angel of the sixth seal, a similitude without any particular chronological focus, an issue to which we will return in a moment. On the other hand, there was my option, in which I posited "a line of propagators of an identification"—a genuine historical identification—between Francis and the angel. In *Olivi's Peaceable Kingdom* I traced this line of propagators through Matthew of Aquasparta, Raymundus Rigaldi, Petrus Iohannis Olivi, and Vitalis de Furno. Thus says Boureau.

This is, of course, a misunderstanding of my position. As for everyone except Olivi, my point was (and is) that they did not—in fact could not—take the identification literally and were suggesting as much, although they were simultaneously affirming that the identification was true in another sense and could be put to excellent uses as a sermon or *collatio* topic. Their

More would follow. Boureau is silent on Bonaventure's next big project, the *Collationes in hexaemeron*; yet it was that next project that had the greatest impact on Olivi.

On Assisi 66 and Vital du Four

We will turn to the *Collationes in hexaemeron* and Olivi in a moment, but before going there we must make one final observation about the standard Parisian mendicant model.

We will attack the point to be made by leaping from the 1250s to perhaps the 1290s, from *Vox domini* to *Spiritu magno vidit* as found in Manuscript Assisi 66 and two other manuscripts at Assisi.[55] In *Olivi's Peaceable Kingdom*, I tentatively assigned one Apocalypse commentary beginning *Spiritu magno vidit* to Vital du Four. Vital began his teaching career in 1292, and in 1307 he was appointed provincial minister. Thus presumably *Spiritu magno vidit* was done between those two dates, if this is indeed Vital's commentary and it was written while he was teaching, rather than later while he was first provincial minister, then a cardinal; but the evidence concerning Vital's authorship is hardly overwhelming, and if that is the case with authorship, then the date becomes equally questionable. The matter is further complicated by

---

identification of the angel of Revelation 7:2 with Christ was long established in exegesis. What is interesting here is that the *Legenda maior* had created a situation in which Franciscan exegetes, once they had acknowledged the traditional interpretation as (in Matthew of Aquasparta's words) the principal meaning, also felt required to come to terms with the Francis identification as true in some other sense. Olivi had no such problem, and I offered him, not as the final link in a chain of propagators, but as a completely separate position.

55. I will refer to Assisi ms. 66 here. On the author see Dionisio Pacetti, "L'Expositio super Apocalypsim' di Mattia di Svezia," *Archivum Franciscanum Historicum* 54 (1961): 297–99, and my comments in my *Olivi's Peaceable Kingdom*, 44–45 and 59n68. More recently Boureau, "L'exégèse de Jean de Galles," has identified other manuscripts, including Assisi 50, with the same *incipit* as being by John of Wales, but has allowed that others including Assisi 66 are by Vital. He provides excerpts from the John of Wales commentary and seems to suggest the possibility that Vital utilized John's commentary as a model for his own, partly because John's history as a critic of Olivi suggested him as a model for Vital, who was also an opponent of Olivi. The problem here is that my reading of Vital, while it does suggest a connection with John's work, does not suggest any obvious opposition to Olivi's work. In fact, Vital's attitude toward the contemporary church seems at times remarkably like Olivi's, although Olivi is arguably harder on the Franciscans than Vital, who stands on the other side of the divide separating the spirituals from the rest of the order; although that too deserves closer analysis than it has received.

the fact that there is another commentary with the same *incipit*, probably by John of Wales, and the two commentaries, while they seem to have different authors, nevertheless seem oddly related; but that is a bigger problem than we need to handle here, where we are concerned only with the commentary perhaps by Vital.

In some ways the *Spiritu magno vidit* we are provisionally assigning to Vital is, like *Vox domini*, one more example of the standard Parisian mendicant model. For example, the opening of the seven seals reflects the seven periods of church history. The first is the time of the apostles; the second that of the martyrs or tyrants; and the third that of the heretics, heresy being seen by the author as false exposition of the Bible. The fourth period is that of the hypocrites, and the fifth that of divine consolation, protection, and remuneration. The sixth period is the time of Antichrist.[56] After the death of Antichrist comes a period of peace and tranquility in the church that will last a minimum of forty days according to Jerome, just as God gave the Jews forty years after the death of Christ before destruction of Jerusalem. Note that the minimum period of forty-something days is still accepted, but it is considered to be forty days and given an entirely different rationale. How much time there will be between the forty days and the end of the world, no one knows, unless it was perhaps revealed to someone, Vital says.[57]

So far we see nothing odd about *Spiritu magno vidit*'s version of the standard Parisian Revelation commentary other than its adjustment of Jerome's figure. Nor does the author's placement of himself within the seven periods suggest anything odd. He places himself in the fourth period, and writers of those thirteenth-century Revelation commentaries arranged in terms of the seven periods of church history tend to place themselves in the fourth or fifth period.[58]

Thus one would not expect him to follow Bonaventure in seeing Francis as the angel of the sixth seal; but what he does say is ambiguous. I suggested in *Olivi's Peaceable Kingdom* that *Spiritu sancto vidit* (that is, *this* commentary beginning *Spiritu sancto vidit* as opposed to the other one presumably by John of Wales) is one of three post-Bonaventuran Franciscan commentaries that give evidence of feeling required to make some reference to Francis in relation to Revelation 7:2, despite also feeling obliged to place the sixth period (and thus Rev 7:2) in the future. The commentary by Mat-

---

56. *Spiritu magno vidit*, 55v–60v.

57. *Spiritu magno vidit*, 71r.

58. *Spiritu magno vidit*, 75v. See my presentation in *Olivi's Peaceable Kingdom*.

thew of Aquasparta, the oldest of the three (perhaps from the early 1280s?), states that the angel of Revelation 7:2 refers principally to Christ but can also be understood to refer to Saint Francis and offers an excellent theme for preaching about him.

The commentary by Raymond Rigaud, written between the time he became a master (1287) and his death in 1296, applies the passage to Christ and then says it can also be applied to Francis.

> And then it can be taken in this way: blessed Francis, sent by Christ (*legatus a latere Christi*), is introduced in four ways through these words: blessed Francis was an angel *propter agilitatem expeditionis*, ascending *propter virilitatem executionis* from the place of the sun *propter serenitatem conversationis*, and having the seal of the living God *propter auctoritatem legationis*.

Vital's *Spiritu magno vidit* says almost exactly the same thing.

> Blessed Francis is described here *ut fidelis legatus, quantum ad agilitatem expeditionis* because he is described as an angel; *quantum ad virilitatem executionis* because he is described as ascending; *quantum ad serenitatem conversationis* because he is described as from the rising of the sun; and *quantum ad austeritatem legationis* because he bears the seal of the living God.[59]

Since publishing *Olivi's Peaceable Kingdom*, I have been reminded of yet another passage on Revelation 7:2, this time in John of Wales's commentary on Revelation as cited in Alain Boureau's article on John:

> **I saw another angel ascending from the place of the sun, having the sign of the living God.** Although these words are principally understood of the Son of God, who is an angel of great council (as appears in the exposition of the letter), they are fittingly said of the blessed Francis, in whom supersingularly and in privileged fashion *the sign of the living God* appeared when the sacred stigmata appeared on his sacred body.[60]

---

59. For all three passages see my *Olivi's Peaceable Kingdom*, 49.

60. Boureau, "L'exégèse de Jean de Galles," 169–71. Boureau also calls attention to Hal Friday, "The *Vidi Alterum Angelum* Topos in Two Sermons by Guibert of Tournai for the Feast of St. Francis," *Franciscan Studies* 70 (2012): 101–38, which is a valuable reminder, not only that

This material for a *collatio* about Francis was seen by me as one way a new, post-Bonaventuran generation of scholars could make their peace with Bonaventure's identification and still see themselves as living prior to the sixth period. I still think it makes sense to read such passages in that light. Matthew, Vital, Raymond, and John all find it easy to talk about Francis and Revelation 7:2 as material for a sermon because the angel of 7:2 was, after all, traditionally seen as a reference to Christ, and Francis was seen as one who mirrored Christ "super-singularly" (as John of Wales put it), not only in the stigmata but more generally.

Yet there is something else about the treatment of the sixth seal in Vital's *Spiritu magno vidit* that demands attention. The author of *Vox domini* had explicitly stated that Antichrist and his followers would be successful in gaining support—or at least more successful than they otherwise might have been—because the rich and powerful backed them. On the whole, though, when that commentator specified which rich and powerful he had in mind, he preferred to talk about the secular powers. His natural tendency was to describe Antichrist as supported by *principes*, and when he became more specific he seems to have thought of those *principes* as secular princes, not the great *prelati*.

Vital's *Spiritu magno vidit* is a different matter. When the author arrives at the sixth seal, he talks about both secular and religious leaders; and while he begins by writing in the future tense, we suddenly become aware that he has shifted into the present. The sun mentioned in Revelation 7 stands for prelates who should illuminate and warm (i.e., inspire) others but are instead dark and cold because of their solicitude for earthly things.[61]

Revelation 8:12, dealing with the trumpets, gives the author an even better text to work with. It says, "The fourth angel blew his trumpet, and a third of the sun was struck, and a third of the moon, and a third of the stars, so that a third of their light was darkened." Vital says, "The prelates of this time ought to be like the sun in splendor, illuminating others and setting them afire. . . . Instead some set others afire but offer no doctrinal illumination because of their ignorance; others illuminate but do not set anyone on fire; and still others do neither. This third group is the one struck."[62]

Revelation 7:2 played an important role in the scandal of the eternal gospel and thus needed to be handled carefully after the scandal hit, but that it was an important passage in Franciscan literature. According to Jacques-Guy Bougerol, "Initia latinorum sermonum laudem S. Francisci," *Antonianum* 57 (1982): 706–94, 31 of the 540 thirteenth-century sermons we know of began with that quotation, making it the most frequently utilized *incipit* of the century.

61. *Spiritu magno vidit*, 60v.

62. *Spiritu magno vidit*, 75va.

There are moments when the author gives the impression that striking down only a third is overly generous. He remarks that the whole church has become carnal and is no longer founded on the blood of the apostles; instead, "little nephews and other blood relatives" (*nepotulorum et sanguineorum*) proceed to office through family succession.[63] The day of the Lord is coming, and excessive wealth is a sign of impending judgment. Nor is the author solely or even primarily concerned about the secular rich. He specifies that the church is too wealthy. *Minoratio* and *humiliatio* will surely follow. Within the church, even the religious orders are headed for trouble. The falling stars mentioned in the Apocalypse presage the fall of religious.[64]

Does that include the Franciscans? Not necessarily. Note the reference to *minoratio et humiliatio*; and in expositing the seven trumpets, *Spiritu magno vidit* describes the fourth angel as an order of poor preachers in the fourth period (which, we recall, he labels as "the period in which we are").[65] Francis presumably also belongs in the fourth period. In dealing with Enoch and Elijah, the author observes that Elijah's rigorous lifestyle parallels that of "our father Francis." Similarities noted also include Francis's connection with animals and parallels with Christ.[66] Is the author then giving his own order positive apocalyptic significance? Apparently he is.

At least one could read *Spiritu magno vidit* in that way; yet one could read all this in any number of ways. One could argue that by the end of the thirteenth century Franciscan scholars were finding it easier to offer invidious comparisons between their order and the rest of the church; one could argue that they were finding it easier to criticize the church as a whole, themselves included; or one could argue that the comparison of *Vox domini* and *Spiritu magno vidit* says little, in fact that the total number of mendicant Apocalypse commentaries is so small as to make it hard to wring from them any general change in attitude toward the church as a whole.

One thing can be said, though. *Spiritu magno vidit* suggests that by the 1290s Olivi was not alone in offering a somewhat dystopian view of the contemporary church. In fact, if there were time for details, it would be possible to cite several that might encourage us to believe that the author of *Spiritu magno vidit* is writing close to Olivi's time and taking an interest in many

---

63. *Spiritu magno vidit*, 61r.

64. *Spiritu magno vidit*, 61r. Vital's treatment of the seven trumpets is doubly interesting because he approaches it by suggesting the outlines of a Joachite *concordia* with Old Testament history.

65. *Spiritu magno vidit*, 75va.

66. *Spiritu magno vidit*, 86v.

of the same themes. He too shows an awareness of the dangers of excessive devotion to Greek philosophy and is willing to portray it as an element in the temptation of Antichrist. Note, for example, his comment that at the time of Antichrist "stupid Plato and his disciples will be there, and Aristotle's arguments will do him no good."[67] The most interesting thing about this, though, is how far up the ecclesiastical ladder the author manages to get in his critique of the church without ever implicating the pope. This takes some doing, because he is intelligent enough to recognize that the target of Revelation 17:18 is Rome. That, of course, still gives him a great deal of room to maneuver, and he could always simply historicize the reference, interpreting it as an allusion to ancient Rome, the city of the Caesars and not that of the popes; yet he does not, or at least he does not do so completely. He comments that "John speaks for that time in which Roman idolatry was in force, or for a future time when perhaps heresy and all perfidy will thus reign." He cites Joachim to the effect that by the first king we should understand the sixth, of which it is said, "one is" (Rev 17:10); then he goes on to say that

> at that time, kings will be gathered to fight with it [i.e., Rome] and to strike at the sons of Babylon, who call themselves son of Christ and are not, but are rather the synagogue of Satan; and indeed their intention will be evil, but they will nonetheless ignorantly and unknowingly perform God's will, whether killing the just who will thus be crowned with martyrdom or bringing judgment upon the evil by whom the earth has been stained with blood. Thus after this blow—which has now already begun in part—there will be victory for the Christians and joy for those fearing the name of the Lord.[68]

What we have here is, in brief, tentative form, what we will find spelled out in detail by Petrus Iohannis Olivi. In Olivi's version, the carnal church,

---

67. *Spiritu magno vidit*, 6ov. Here, too, one might look back to *Aser pinguis*, but the result would be ambiguous at best. Lerner, in "Poverty, Preaching, and Eschatology," 166–69, suggests a real distinction between *Aser pinguis* and *Vidit Iacob in somniis*, the other revelation commentary he attributes to the Hugh workshop (rightly, I think). He sees the latter as correcting the "more ardently pro-philosophical" *Aser pinguis*; yet the subtlety of the distinction Lerner is making can be seen in his insistence that *Vidit Iacob* is "more formally 'scholastic'"; and the matter is complicated even more by passages from other postils. See Lerner, "The Vocation of the Friars Preacher," 224–25.

68. *Spiritu magno vidit*, 130ra–rb. He is expositing Revelation 17:18, "the woman that you see is a great city." See also his mention of Rome at f. 126rb and 135va.

that remarkably corrupt establishment that has installed itself in the place of the saints and seems invulnerable to reform, will be destroyed, not by reformers working within it, but by an outside power that intends to destroy Christianity itself but unintentionally saves it by stripping away the carnal shell in which it has become encased.[69]

Who is this author? Here, as elsewhere, we know too little to make a definitive judgment; yet we could perhaps come closer than we have. Some scholars might hesitate to assign the commentary to Vital, as I have tentatively done, if only because Vital is usually assumed to have been an opponent of Olivi;[70] yet it is conceivable that, in the process of opposing Olivi, Vital inadvertently adopted a few of his more interesting ideas.

It is conceivable that we should also take *Spiritu magno vidit* as evidence that by the 1290s the seven periods of church history as seen in *Vox domini* were less accepted as a "given" in making sense of the contemporary situation. The author of *Spiritu magno vidit* pays lip service to a periodization that places him in the fourth period, but his reading of his own time in terms of the seven seals and trumpets presents a much different picture. So does his reference to that blow "which has now already begun in part."

That is at least one possibility. Another is that one might see what is happening in *Spiritu magno vidit* as a continuation of what we already see anticipated in *Vox domini*, where the fourth, fifth, and sixth periods could be seen as a gradual slide from heresy to the precursors of Antichrist and then to Antichrist, in short, a fluid movement between periods that features not so much radically different problems as varying degrees of the same problem. *Vox domini* makes it clear that, however inventive Satan might seem, he works with a limited arsenal of temptations. That idea is hardly foreign to earlier commentaries. *Vox domini* also states plainly that the Apocalypse is essentially about tribulation and consolation. "Having presented the persecution to come in the time of Antichrist, this work deals with the consolation the faithful will have then and in fact can have even now." That consolation is and always has been provided by Christ, as we have seen. Thus, however much historical novelty seems implied by the notion of seven periods, it is balanced by an even stronger sense of historical continuity. As time goes by,

---

69. As we saw in the previous chapter, the basic expectation expressed here is already seen in the pseudo-Joachim commentary on Jeremiah.

70. And with good reason. See Vital's actions regarding Olivi as delineated in Sylvain Piron, "Les studia franciscains de Provence et d'Aquitaine (1275–1335)," in *Philosophy and Theology in the Studia of the Religious Orders and at the Papal and Royal Courts* (Leiden: Brill, 2012), 303–58.

the fundamental things do seem to apply. That, too, might be said for any number of thirteenth-century commentaries before Olivi's.

Does it apply to *Spiritu magno vidit*? There does seem to be a difference between *Vox domini* and *Spiritu magno vidit* in the latter's willingness to acknowledge increasing rot within the institutional church. To say this much is not to say that the author of *Spiritu magno vidit* is going where no commentary has gone before. The *nepotuli* are hardly an original creation of *Spiritu magno vidit*. One finds the word in Hugh of Saint Cher's postils, though not to my knowledge in the Revelation commentary.[71] One could say that the Hugh workshop differs from Vital du Four in historical situation. They are in the vanguard of something new and exciting, the mendicant orders, and can criticize nepotist secular prelates while implying that the Dominicans are free from that vice. As we have seen, it is possible to read a similar assumption into *Spiritu magno vidit*, arguing that when it criticizes the *nepotuli* it is implying that the Franciscans offer a remedy to the ailment. None of this can be deduced with any assurance from *Spiritu magno vidit*, however. It would be interesting to study this commentary more thoroughly than I have done here. Vital was an important figure and is well worth studying more deeply than has been the case so far. (So, in fact, is every Franciscan I have mentioned so far except Bonaventure and Olivi, who are receiving their fair share of attention.) Again we return to the fact that we have a substantial number of thirteenth-century mendicant Apocalypse commentaries that should be studied.

READINGS

It was normal to begin not only Revelation commentaries but other biblical commentaries as well with a preface. In the case of the Paris mendicant model, this preface involved exegesis of a short passage from some other book of the Bible, which was then manipulated in such a way as to make it apply to the book actually being studied. In the case of Aser pinguis *the passage is Genesis 49:20, "Asher's bread shall be fat, and he shall yield dainties to the king." Interesting though*

---

71. See Lerner, "The Vocation of the Friars Preacher," 219, for use of the word in the other postils.

it might seem to see how that thought might be read as a description of the Apocalypse, we will ignore the matter and refer the reader to a similar feat of legerdemain worked below on Psalm 29:9 in the preface to Vox domini.

In the case of Revelation commentaries, it was also common to combine this sort of preface with another commentary on yet another preface, an earlier one by an author described here as the "Magister Gallicus" and in other commentaries as "Gilbert," probably referring to the twelfth-century author Gilbert of Poitiers.[72] As will be obvious below, this preface is quoted and commented on in skeletal form by Vox domini, *but* Aser pinguis *presents it in its entirety and comments on it. The arrangement itself suggests its importance.* Aser pinguis *is set up rather like an early edition of the* Glossa ordinaria, *with biblical text presented separately and in its totality in its own columns, with the commentary proceeding in other columns around it. The Gilbertine preface (it probably really is by Gilbert of Poitiers) is presented in the column that will then contain the biblical text, probably a suggestion of the authority granted it. Here we will present first the Gilbertine preface in its totality and then the* Aser pinguis *commentary on it.*

The Gilbertine Preface

All who wish to live piously in Christ, as the apostle says, will suffer persecution (2 Tim 3:12). Son, when you come to the service of God, stand in justice and fear and prepare your soul for temptation (Ecclus 2:1). For the life of man on earth is temptation. But so that the faithful may not succumb in these things, the Lord comforts and encourages them, saying, "I am with you even to the end of the world" (Matt 28:20) and "Fear not, little flock" (Luke 12:32). Therefore the Father, seeing the tribulations that the church, founded by the apostles on the stone that is Christ, was about to suffer, decided, so that those tribulations might be feared less, to reveal them together with the Son and the Holy Spirit. And the whole Trinity revealed them to Christ according to his humanity, Christ revealed them to John through an angel, and John

---

72. I cover this matter and some of the material covered in that preface in "Olivi on Prophecy," *Cristianesimo nella storia* 17 (1996): 369–78, in the process providing a decent starting bibliography for much that I will say here.

revealed them to the church, this book being composed of that revelation. Thus this book is called "Apocalypse," that is, "Revelation," because within it is contained that which God revealed to John and John to the church, that is, how much the church suffered in the early time, and still suffers, and shall suffer in the final times of Antichrist, when the sufferings will be so great that even the elect will be shaken (Matt 24:24); and it contains what rewards will be received now and in the future, so that those currently terrified by the agonies announced will be gladdened by the promised rewards. Thus this book alone among the Scriptures of the New Testament is given the name of prophecy, and it is more excellent than the other prophecies. For just as the New Testament is superior to the Old and the gospel is superior to the law, so this prophecy is superior to that of the Old Testament prophets, because it announces mysteries concerning Christ and the church that are now largely fulfilled. Or it is also thus because, whereas other prophecies are onefold, these are threefold, encompassing past, present, and future. And the authority of the one who sent it, delivered it, and received it all concur in its confirmation. (The sender is the Trinity, the deliverer the angel, and the receiver John.)

Since these things were revealed to John in a vision, and since there are three kinds of visions, we must see which of the three it was. When we see something with our corporeal eyes, that is a corporeal vision. When we see while sleeping or even waking and discern images of things through which something else is signified, that is a spiritual or imaginary vision. Such was the case when the pharaoh saw ears of corn while sleeping or when Moses saw a burning bush while he was awake. A third kind of vision is intellectual, and that is when the Holy Spirit reveals it to us in such a way that we grasp the truth of the mystery by intellectual understanding. That is how John grasped the things related in this book. He did not merely see figures in spirit; he understood in his mind what they signified.

John saw and wrote down these things while he was on the island of Patmos, where he had been sent into exile by the evil ruler Domitian. What spurred him to write was that, while he was kept in exile on Patmos by Domitian, many vices and heresies sprang up and grew; for there were many heretics who said that Christ did not exist before Mary, because he was born of her temporally. John was rejecting this view when, at the beginning of his gospel, he said, "In the beginning was the word." And in this book he says, "Alpha and omega," that is, beginning and end. Some also said of the church that, due to the weight of tribulation, it would collapse before the end of the world and would receive no eternal reward for its labor. Wishing to destroy the errors of these people, John said that Christ was the beginning and the end. Thus Isaiah says, "There was no god before me and there will be none after me" (Isa 43:10). And the church would not come to an end through the exercise of tribulations, but was instead advancing and would receive an eternal reward.

John writes to the seven churches of Asia and to their bishops, instructing them on the aforesaid matters and teaching the whole general church through them. Thus the matter being dealt with here is particularly the state of the seven churches but more generally that of the entire church, what the church is undergoing in the present and will receive in the future. His intention is to urge them to be patient, because the time of our labor will be short and our reward will be great. This is his way of treating the matter: First he writes a prologue and salutation, which makes his listeners benign and attentive. Then he turns to narration; but before the narration he shows that Christ has existed from the beginning, since he is without beginning or end; and he presents Christ himself saying as much: "I am the Alpha and Omega," that is, the beginning and the end. Then he turns to the narrative, dividing it into seven visions; and when these are completed the book ends. But before that he begins with a prologue that says, "the apocalypse of Jesus Christ," and here you must mentally add the words, "This is," just as you would add "This is" to "the vision of Isaiah" and "These are" to "the parables of Solomon."

Here ends Gilbert's preface.

Aser pinguis Commentary on Gilbert's Preface

All who wish to live piously, etc. To this work Gilbert appends a prologue examining those things that are normally inquired about at the beginning of such books. Thus he says, **All who wish to live piously, etc.** The prologue is divided into eight parts. In the first, after briefly admonishing the faithful, it explains why God wished to reveal the future tribulations he foresaw for the church. In the second he explains the reason for the name he assigns to the book. That is, that this book is called "Apocalypse": **The whole Trinity revealed it, etc.** In the third he shows why among the Scriptures of the New Testament, only this one contains prophecy: **Thus this book, etc.** In the fourth he shows what the authority of this book is: **To confirm the authority of which, etc.** In the fifth, since the vision is multifold, he shows what kind of vision this one was: **Since this vision of John, etc.** In the sixth he shows where this vision appeared to him: **John saw, etc.** In the seventh he tells us why he wrote there: Compelling him to write there because, etc. In the eighth and last he briefly deals with the things normally covered at the beginning of books, such as what is its subject, how the author intends to treat it, and things of that sort: **John, however, writes.** And he says, **All who wish to live piously, etc.**, that is, maintaining the divine cultus. Piety is that which pertains to religiosity or the cultus of God, defined by Tullius as that which involves offering attention and ceremony to something of a higher nature. Tullius also says that piety is an emotional disposition toward a higher thing by which one is aided or at least consoled. **In Christ.** This is what is meant by "piously," as the apostle says when he speaks in 2 Timothy 3 about suffering persecution. And in Ecclesiasticus 2[:1] it says, "Son, when you turn to the service of God," "to serve whom is to reign," etc. Thus in Isaiah 49[:6] it is said, "It is too light a thing that you should be my servant to raise up," etc.

> *In what follows,* Aser *follows the Gilbertine preface closely, adding little to it except on what might be considered important issues, like whether the New Testament is superior to the Old. Here he ponders Ezekiel 1, the wheels within wheels, asking whether this implies that neither is superior to the other. His reply is that the Old Testament is in the New through explication and the New is in the Old through implication, while the Old is in the New materially and the New is in the Old formally; and thus the New is superior to the Old just as form is more elegant than matter.*

Then there is the matter of who should be considered the greatest prophet. The gospel is greater than the law, and therefore John was greater than the other prophets. But on the contrary, at the beginning of the Psalms, in the *Glossa*, David is said to have been the greatest prophet. Again, in Luke 1, where Zechariah prophesied, in the *Glossa* it is said that Zechariah was clearly the greatest of the prophets. Again, in Matthew 17:3, it says Moses and Elijah appeared with Christ, and there the *Glossa* says he [Christ] was the greatest of the prophets. Again, in Numbers 12:6 the Lord says, "If there is a prophet among you, I will make myself known to him in a vision, I will speak with him in a dream. Not so with my servant Moses."[73] Again, Deuteronomy

---

73. The passage continues (vv. 7–8): "he is entrusted with all my house. With him I speak mouth to mouth, clearly, and not in dark speech, and he beholds the form of the Lord."

24:10 says, "And no other prophet arose like Moses," and the *Glossa* says, "because Moses was greater than any other prophet of the Old Testament."

The solution to this problem is given in the *Glossa* to the Apocalypse: John was a prophet of the New Testament, and thus he was greater than all the aforesaid prophets through the profundity of what he said and the magnitude of his revelation and the authority of the man saying it. For he was an apostle, and all the apostles exceed the prophets in authority.

> Aser *cannot bear to leave the matter there, however. The author goes on to suggest a sense in which each of those mentioned could be considered preeminent.*

The three kinds of vision also present themselves as prime targets for serious discussion. Since all of this was revealed to John in a vision—as is said in 1 Corinthians 2:10, "God however has revealed to us through his spirit"—and there are three kinds of vision, we must see what kind of vision this one is. There is a corporeal vision, in which we see with our corporeal eyes something that cannot be seen by someone else, when, for example, Belshazzar saw the hand writing in Daniel 5:4–5, and Elisha saw the fiery chariot that carried Elijah to heaven in 2 Kings 2:11–12, and Moses saw the burning bush in Exodus 3, and Elisha's boy saw the fiery chariots and the army on the mountain of Samaria in 2 Kings 6:17. Nor is it called a vision unless it contains a mystical element revealed by God.

Another type of vision is spiritual or imaginary, when, awake or sleeping, we discern images of things by which other things are signified than what we are seeing. Thus the pharaoh saw ears of grain, that is, images of ears in Genesis 41. And we also have Moses with his burning bush.

With all due respect to Gilbert, this sort of vision seems more corporeal. Moses saw with corporeal eyes, and what was seen was corporeal, a bush; although it can be called imaginary insofar as he saw fire, which perhaps was not actually there. Peter's vision in Acts 10 was imaginary. In ecstasy he saw all sorts of quadrupeds, serpents of the land, and flying things of the air, and a voice said to him, "Consecrate them, Peter, and eat!" Whether asleep like the pharaoh or awake like Moses, it amounts to the same thing. It is intellectual in the case when it is revealed by the Holy Spirit to the intellect, the superior power of the mind. When the latter is illuminated, it knows the truth, as Augustine says concerning 1 Corinthians 14:4, "one who speaks tongues."

The truth of mysteries, that is, of secrets, **we understand just as it is.** This is when we see intellectual things without any image. Thus we have the

Glossa on 2 Corinthians 12: In this vision things are seen that are not bodies, nor do they bear anything similar to a corporeal form; and in what other way can we describe the operation of our intellect? In no way except by words like *love, joy, peace, faith,* and the like, those things which bring us closer to God, the same God who is all in all and from whom all things come? **How?** In the final analysis, by intellectual vision.

John saw the things referred to in this book. But the *Glossa* seems to contradict what is said in this prologue. It says that John saw images and in them he understood the truth. Thus it was an imaginary vision. Our solution: John's visions can be understood in diverse respects and accordingly can be described as imaginary or intellectual. They were imaginary because he saw visions, but intellectual because, his intellect having been illuminated by the Holy Spirit, he understood the truth. And by this it is clear that he really was a prophet, because, as the *Glossa* says citing Augustine concerning 1 Corinthians 14:2, he who speaks in tongues speaks not to men but to God. He who, like the pharaoh, sees only the images of things is less of a prophet than he who understands the truth of what he sees, like Joseph, who understood the truth of the images when the pharaoh narrated them to him. But whether one who both sees the images and understands what they mean, like Daniel in Daniel 2, is an even greater prophet, is another question. In this category we have not only Daniel but Isaiah, Jeremiah, Ezekiel, and others. Nevertheless, it should be noted that some prophets, like David, without any image whatsoever, saw the truth through the Holy Spirit and, having seen it, converted what they had seen into images through which they knew the truth, as when he [i.e., David] said, "Blessed is the man who walks not in the counsel of the wicked," etc. (Ps 1:1). Later he says, "And he will be like a tree planted by streams of water," etc. (Ps 1:3), speaking of the same man. Others see images under which they understand the truth; thus the images are presented first and then exposited, as with Isaiah and others. This is seen clearly in Jeremiah 1:13, where he sees a boiling pot, which he then explains by saying, "All evil will pour out from the north," etc. Again, John both saw the images and understood the truth expressed by them but did not explain what they meant, and on this account the book is more difficult to understand than other prophecies. There is some similarity here to the final vision of Ezekiel, which is more difficult to understand than the first, because those visions which follow from the second vision until the last explain the first, but the last is ambiguous and is not explained.

And so it goes for another page, a commentary on Gilbert's commentary, from here on without any great surprises. There are some

221

lessons to be learned, however. One has already been mentioned: we have entered a period when Scripture study is developing at a good pace, and the methodological advances tend to be cumulative. The Glossa can be seen as a stage in the development, but one that hangs on, gaining its own authority. In a sense this is explicable. A multivolume postil addressing the entire Bible, accompanied by a variety of other reference works, made sense in a center of learning like Paris, but smaller studia or monastic institutions might find it preferable to rely on a single tool like the Glossa. But that explanation might sell the Glossa short. In the early fourteenth century we will see the first and most extensive attack on Olivi's exegesis appeal more than once to the Glossa as an authority.

Another lesson to be learned lies in the way Aser and even its commentary on the Gilbertine preface manages to underline the necessity of reading Revelation in the context of the entire Bible. Certainly this "thick" reading both explains and is explained by the theory of authorship by a workshop. Later thirteenth-century and fourteenth-century commentaries simply lack the time for such an approach. Olivi, as we will see, does provide a similar sense of the Bible as a totality, but for a different reason. His Bible commentaries between 1279 and 1297 give one the impression that he is unpacking and assembling a series of elements that will eventually fit together into his Revelation commentary. More on that later, however.

Vox Domini

The following is the Vox domini preface (proemium) to that commentary. In this case Psalm 29:9 is twisted into an odd shape to make it fit, not merely with the book of Revelation, but with an application of the Aristotelian fourfold pattern of causation. That too can be found elsewhere.

This particular preface in Vox domini begins with the commentator's own thoughts as he applies the psalm to the four causes of Revelation, then pivots to a question on tribulation and its implications for theodicy. Like others, he sees the Apocalypse as primarily about tribulation and consolation. Thus as a theologian he takes time out from his role as commentator to explore the matter. The insertion of such questions into biblical commentaries was also common in the thirteenth century, an instance of scholastic method impinging on exegesis.

It is not difficult to see where the author changes direction yet again to consider the previous preface by the Magister Gallicus. Not only does he explicitly acknowledge his new focus, but he complicates the narrative from that point on by inserting words that serve as an outline of the preface by the Magister Gallicus, which he is now following. It is tempting to stop at that point, because up to this point the text is relatively orderly, but from here on it occasionally reads more like something jotted on the back of an envelope than like a coherent train of thought; yet we must keep going because in the section we are entering our commentator says a great deal about two other questions that regularly arise in prefaces by way of the Gilbertine preface. First, Gilbert argues that John is the greatest of the prophets, thus forcing all those who depend on his preface to argue for or against that idea, as we have seen in Aser's commentary on Gilbert. In view of the restricted notion of prophecy and the consequent disinterest in the Apocalypse inserted into the discussion in the thirteenth century by Aquinas, there was a great deal to be said on this score as the century progressed, and the author of this preface adds his opinion.

Another issue that the Gilbertine preface made unavoidable was what to make of the threefold classification of visions offered by Augustine and, having decided that much, whether to accept it. That too appears in the latter part of the author's preface.

The Gilbertine preface continued to move like a submarine just below the surface of prefaces throughout the thirteenth century. In the recent edition of Petrus Iohannis Olivi's Apocalypse commentary by Warren Lewis, Olivi addresses himself to it, although he does so in his exegesis of Revelation 1 rather than in his preface.

The voice of the Lord preparing the deer, and he will reveal the thickets [Ps. 29:9]. In these words, when they are diligently analyzed, a way is given to introduce this book called the Apocalypse. For in these same words can be seen the four causes that must be noted in connection with this book: that is, the efficient, final, formal, and material causes. The principal efficient cause is God himself. The blessed John, to whom the Lord showed the things contained here, is the ministerial efficient cause. Thus it is said, **The voice of the Lord**, that is, internal and spiritual, because it spoke in the heart of the blessed John, allowing him to effectively understand what was shown through an angel. The voice of the Lord has the power to teach us internally. As the psalm [29:4] says, **The voice of the Lord in power.** Thus, therefore, the principal efficient cause is shown and the ministerial cause is suggested, that is, the "I" to whom the voice of the Lord speaks. The final cause is that, through right faith and patience in adversity, the faithful should become more apt and agile when it comes to recognizing the rewards of life. Thus the text goes on to say that the voice of the Lord is **preparing the deer**, that is, preparing the faithful to run with agility toward the prize. For the deer is a very swift animal. The psalm [18:34] says, **He made my feet like the feet of a deer.** For here the blessed John intended, as can be gathered from the prologue, that, through right faith and patience in adversity, many faithful are prepared for the merit that is the fruit of sustaining tribulation. As Hebrews 10:36 says, "Patience is necessary for you, so that, doing the will of God, you may receive the promise." The formal cause is that this book is revealed and proceeds here by means of revelation. Thus it says, **And he will reveal.** That is what occurs in this book; hence it is called "Apocalypse," that is, revelation. Thus Daniel 2[:28] says, **There is a God in heaven who reveals mysteries.** The material cause is multiplex: the tribulation of the church with multiple consolations, whence it is said, **thickets**, meaning hidden and obscure things; for the Lord revealed to the blessed John many future tribulations that were not foreseen, and many consolations that were generally unexpected, in order that the church should be stronger in sustaining them; for the javelins that are foreseen are less likely to wound us. And again, consideration of the reward lessens the force of the lash. Nevertheless, although here the state of the church is shown generally as far as tribulations and consolations are concerned, the state of the church is especially and principally shown as far as the final tribulations and consolations are concerned.

And that is especially the matter of this book, namely, the state of the Asian and indeed of the entire church as far as final tribulations and consolations are concerned. And that is what distinguishes this book from other books of the New Testament. For the Sacred Page is divided into the Old and New Testaments; and the New is divided into evangelical and apostolic doctrine; and the intention of evangelical doctrine is to contemplate the head, that is, Christ, while the intention of apostolic doctrine is to contemplate the body, that is, the church; and this according to the triple state of the church militant. For in Acts the primitive state of the church is shown; in the letters of the blessed Paul and in the canonical letters the middle state of the church, that is, the present state, is described; and in this book the final state is revealed.

Here two questions can be raised briefly. The first regards the matter of this book, that is, the tribulations. Is it fitting for God to permit that his worshipers should sustain such tribulations? The second concerns the fruit of these tribulations. Should sustaining such passions or tribulations merit eternal life?

The answer to the first: God does not delight in our suffering. That would be cruel. Thus, since he loves his elect, it is not fitting that he should permit them to be so afflicted. Again, God's liberality is of the highest order; but it is manifested more by his crowning his people through good works, without afflictions. Therefore, etc.

On the contrary, it is fitting that God use whatever means might lead his faithful to life, and bearing tribulations does so. **Having been proved, etc.** [James 1:12]. Again, the law of love calls us to share in the adversity of a friend, and therefore the law of love bids us join with our truest friend, the Lord Jesus, in adversity. It is thus most fitting for God to permit his followers to be afflicted with tribulations, both as a sign of love because Christ the Lord suffered the greatest tribulations for us and thus the law of love demands that we sustain many great tribulations through our love for him (thus the apostle says in Galatians [6:14], **far be it from me to glory in anything except the cross of our Lord Jesus Christ**; and [in Gal 6:17] **I bear the stigmata of Jesus in my body**); and also as punishment for past sin, for the wiping away of guilt demands the bitterness of punishment (as the *Glossa* says, "The furnace proves the figural vase, so that whatever there is in it of impure material will be burned away"); and also for governing in the future (for as Isidore says in book 3 of *De Summo Bono*, God is harder on his elect in this life, so that, feeling the sting of the whip more strongly in this life, they will delight less in present pleasures and incessantly desire the certain peace of their celestial home); and God gives them tribulation in order that we might merit the crown (as is clear from Isidore in the same place, concerning Job 4: "God's elect are ground down by the woes of this life so that they should merit the perfection of the future life").

To the first argument it should be said that we might speak of tribulation or punishment insofar as it is merely afflictive, or insofar as it shows or promotes love, or insofar as it restricts future guilt, or insofar as it helps us to accumulate future merit. The first, whether experienced by the just or others, is not pleasing to God, nor does God permit it for that reason, but rather for one of the four subsequent reasons. Thus he does not take delight in our punishments, but rather in the benefit to us following from them. To the other argument it must be said that liberality is not commendable unless it is accompanied by wisdom, and it is different from justice. Justice demands that we sustain damage for the sake of Christ and that guilt should be punished.

After further consideration of tribulation and the conditions under which it is meritorious, the author begins to report on a completely different preface by the Magister Gallicus, which turns out to be the Gilbertine preface.

The Magister Gallicus proceeds first by presenting the foundation of what is to be said. Second follows the beginning, *Propterea videns.* The material of the following book consists of two things, tribulation and consolation. Thus in the preface he lays the foundation of what is to be said, first concerning the tribulation of the elect, and on this matter he introduces a triple authority. Second, concerning divine consolation, *Me autem*; and on this he presents a double authority. He says therefore, *Omnes.* No one who desires to worship God should be surprised if he suffers persecution. *Qui pie,* that is, worshiping God, *Volunt vivere,* for the worship of God is piety, as Titus 2[:12] says, "Soberly and justly and piously we live in this present world." *Vel pie* toward our neighbor. *In Christo* because he is our exemplary way and rule, who comes to suffer for all. *Persecutionem patientur,* and this patiently. And thus it is necessary for the servants of God to suffer many things. Thus Acts 14[:22], "We must enter into the kingdom of heaven through many tribulations." But it is objected that there are many just people who suffer no tribulation or persecution. Yet the *Glossa* replies that tribulation can refer to the mind or body. *On the contrary,* there are some who suffer bodily persecution, and yet their minds remain at peace. I respond that, according to the *Glossa,* this is understood of either the mind or body, for not only is persecution suffered at the hands of men, but persecution is suffered in the mind through demons. Nor do they constantly suffer in mind or body, but those who have suffered or will suffer can at some time experience great spiritual peace. That answers the objection.

A series of biblical citations on the matter then lead the author into the second part of the preface.

Propterea videns [**on that account seeing**]. Here follows the principal argument. Its intention is to show the multiplex cause of this book. First it deals with the cause of this book in general and diffusely; second, in particular and in a limited sense. It is accordingly large. In the first, it first demonstrates the efficient cause; second, the material cause, revelation. Third, the formal cause, thus this book. Fourth, the final cause, *Vidit autem Joannes* [**John saw**]. The efficient cause, however, is shown in a double sense, disposing and agent, concerning which we see: *Revelavit* [**he revealed**]. It says there *propterea*, because God wishes to console and confirm the faithful. Thus he has made disposition from eternity.

The agent cause is shown to be fourfold: principal (the Trinity), secondary (Christ insofar as he is man), mediated (an angel), and immediate or proximate (John).

Revelation of what, though? That is, what things are revealed? So great a question! See Matthew 24.

And now the rewards, that is, the gifts of grace and the consolations. *Ideo liber iste* [**thus this book**]. Here is shown the formal cause of this book, for it proceeds by way of prophecy and revelation.

He distributes and extols the revelations of this book in three ways: first, according to their excellence. Thus he compares these revelations with those of the Old Testament on the matter of their excellence. He posits a double explanation of its excellence: in the first place, because it is revelation of the New Testament that is now displayed. In the second, because it is a broad revelation, that is, not only of the future. In the second place he extols it because of its authority. Third, he extols it for the mode or quality of the revelation, *Cum autem Joanni* [**since however to John**], for this revelation is not so constructed as to be understood obscurely, or so that it sees figures in the spirit, but in such a way that it fully understands the things shown.

And thus it distinguishes three kinds of vision, in order to specify by what type of vision the blessed John sees these things. *Cum autem Joanni.* It says, therefore, *Ideo liber iste* [**thus this book**], because in it is revealed information concerning those things that pertain to the law of grace. *Prophetiae novae* [**new prophecies**], that is, revelations. *Censetur* [**is considered to be**], that is, it is named "Apocalypse." For just as the New Testament excels, that is, is superior to the Old, and this can be understood of all things contained in the New and Old Testaments; that is, evangelical doctrine is superior to the Mosaic doctrine in the Pentateuch; and sacraments, that is, sacred secrets predicted by the prophets, such as the passion of Christ and repair of the church, are shown as fulfilled, as we see in the book considered here. This has been fulfilled now in great part, because certain prophecies have been fulfilled, as for example concerning the final state of the church. The prophecy is unifarious, that is, to be spoken of according to one single mode of speaking, that is, all that has happened, is happening, and will happen to the church, which John has learned through the spirit of prophecy.

As for visions, one kind of vision is seen with physical eyes, just as by divine gift Elisha saw the fiery horses (2 Kgs 6:17) and Belshazzar the hand writing (Dan 5). Another is spiritual, which refers here not to the superior part of reason but to the imaginative power. Proof: Genesis 41, Moses in Exodus 3. But it might be objected to the latter example that Moses saw with corporeal eyes, and therefore his vision was corporeal rather than imaginative. Again, the *Glossa* on 2 Corinthians 12 says that a vision is spiritual or imaginative when someone in ecstasy or sleep sees not bodies but images of things.

I respond: referring that vision to what was corporeal and corporeally seen, it was a corporeal vision. Nevertheless, referring it to the thing signified by it that was thus seen, it can be called imaginative. Augustine says that Belshazzar saw the hand by corporeal vision, but Daniel saw it and opened up the vision; and thus it should be said that he and not Belshazzar was the prophet. So it is clear that what Daniel experienced was spiritual vision and what Belshazzar experienced was corporeal. He was moved corporeally and did not understand the things signified. Daniel, however, did understand. Or perhaps, as some say, the fire was seen but was not actually fire. Peter's vision, when in ecstasy he saw the quadrupeds and serpents in Acts 10, was an imaginative vision. To the other point, it should be said that the *Glossa* does not say these are the only conditions under which one can have an imaginary vision; because, as has been said, given that there is a corporeal vision, it can be considered an imaginative or spiritual vision if the spirit understands what is signified by that vision. **Like ears of grain to the philosopher**, that is, images of ears of grain, ***in the intellect***, which is the superior part, **of mysteries**, that is, of secret things, **but in what way**? That is, by intellectual vision. But against this, because the person sees visions of candelabras and many other things, as is said below in the book, therefore he sees images. I respond, he sees in an imaginative and intellectual vision in diverse respects: imaginative insofar as he sees an image; intellectual insofar as, his intellect being illumined, he understands what he saw.

Beyond this point the author of Vox domini *continues to comment on the preface of the* Magister Gallicus, *but by quoting a series of key words and phrases from that preface and only occasionally turning them into comprehensible thought. In the process there is a transition to the opening lines of the Apocalypse, and he is soon in a line-by-line commentary on chapter 1.*

The popularity of that preface by the Magister Gallicus is seen in the fact that several other late thirteenth-century commentators felt required to come to terms with it. These include the two who are granted chapters in this volume, Olivi and the author of Assisi 66 (presumably Vital du Four), although each begins by moving in a different direction, since each begins by molding a different Old Testament commentary to make it seem relevant to the Apocalypse. Instead of Psalm 8:9, the Vox domini *quotation, Olivi begins with Isaiah 30:26,* Erit lux lunae sicut lux solis *("There will be a light of the moon like the light of the sun"), and Vital with Ecclesiasticus 48:27,* Spiritu magno vidit ultima *("With a great spirit he saw final things"). Eventually, however, like the author of* Vox domini, *they pivot to the prologue of the Magister Gallicus, although Vital works it into his own* proemium *and Olivi addresses it only in the context of his commentary on chapter 1.*

BONAVENTURE'S
COLLATIONES IN HEXAEMERON

Bonaventure's roughly seventeen years as minister general were busy ones. He was confronted with the problem of what to do with the scandal created by Gerard of Borgo San Donnino, and he was plunged into a continuing controversy regarding the legitimacy of the mendicant orders, a battle known to us as the "secular-mendicant controversy." The two problems dovetailed impressively, since the scandal of the eternal gospel provided the secular clergy with ammunition. In fact, as Bonaventure himself acknowledged in two letters he wrote to the entire order in 1257 and 1266, the behavior of many friars also gave enemies of the order much to criticize.[1]

That brings us to a third major problem: standards within the order. The letters show that, whatever enemies of the order might think, Bonaventure himself felt there was substantial room for improvement. This fact bore some degree of existential importance. In the period before 1274 the Franciscans were not so thoroughly established that they could ignore the criticisms against them. Like all orders that had come into being during the thirteenth century, they recognized that their *modus vivendi* was still open to discussion.

Thus Bonaventure had to move on several fronts, but he did so skillfully, and in 1274, at the second council of Lyons, the Franciscans were one of the newer orders recognized as legitimate. In the process of reaching that goal, Bonaventure had gone a long way toward reshaping the order in his own image, but it was an impressive image, and, after his death in that same

---

1. Discussed by me in *Olivi and Franciscan Poverty* (Philadelphia: University of Pennsylvania Press, 1989), ch. 1.

year, much of him lived on in the order he had constructed. The Franciscans still had enemies outside the order and were headed for a major crisis within, the *usus pauper* (living poor) controversy, but it would be hard to blame Bonaventure for either.[2]

In this chapter attention will be focused on one thing: the *Collationes in hexaemeron* delivered to the Franciscans at Paris in 1273. Three things need to be said about the *Collationes* before we say much else. First, the work consists of *collationes*, not a formal commentary on Revelation. Thus we might be tempted to see it as more sermonic than scholarly, an appeal more to the emotions than to the intellect. That would be a serious mistake. Whatever else Bonaventure produced, it has to be seen as an important contribution to thirteenth-century exegesis of the Apocalypse. Nor is the work the only *collationes* by Bonaventure that contribute to our knowledge of his apocalyptic views. His *Collations on the Seven Gifts of the Holy Spirit* is also important.

Second, it has come down to us in the form of *reportationes*, attempts to record Bonaventure's words by members of his audience, not a carefully wrought production by Bonaventure revised after the fact. Everyone did not always hear the same thing. Much as we might wish Bonaventure had found the time to revise his work, he did not; yet on the whole we can take comfort in possessing a generally accurate report. Moreover, the work as we have it does a good job of emphasizing what in fact it is. Periodically the reporter steps outside the narrative and reminds us of his existence by speaking of Bonaventure in the third person. (For example, "And he said that we had slipped a great deal from what we should be.") Such moments are relatively rare, yet they create an odd intimacy. We are aware that he, like ourselves, is struck by what he has heard and is trying to get to the bottom of it.

That brings us to the third thing we need to say: even at the time, this was seen as an important event. One of the *reportationes* tells us that 160 friars attended in addition to those in the Paris Franciscan community. They would have had to receive permission to attend, or, as they would have described it, an "obedience." And they would have had to travel with a *socius*, a companion on the road. A significant amount of planning would have gone into the event. The order took it seriously, and so should we.

---

2. That might seem to be precisely what I do in *Olivi and Franciscan Poverty*, but in fact my point there is that while Bonaventure and Pecham were both more or less on Olivi's side in the *usus pauper* controversy, they wrote before the problem was formulated as precisely as it was in the 1280s and beyond. Thus they could hardly be expected to answer questions no one had asked yet.

Various scholars have treated the *Collationes in hexaemeron* at some length. A recent book on the subject by C. Colt Anderson does a good job of laying out several intertwining issues addressed in the *Collationes* and showing how they were interrelated.[3] Anderson sees the whole thing as an attempt to deal with three groups that threatened the Franciscan project.

One was the anti-mendicant faction among the clergy. Bonaventure's main task on a theoretical level was to argue for a subtler ecclesiology than the one that faction was endorsing, an ecclesiology that made room for the mendicants.

The second group was composed of those Franciscans Bonaventure already had attacked in his earlier letters, those whose sense of vocation was notably short of that demanded by the Franciscan rule. There is a connection with the secular clergy here, because this group had offended the latter by interfering with their sources of income. Bonaventure was trying to rein his subordinates in, making them less threatening to others in the church.[4]

Finally, there were the Joachites. According to Anderson, Bonaventure spent a substantial amount of time either contradicting Joachim or ministering to the spiritual brothers' lingering Joachite concerns by rephrasing them in the context of a non-Joachite intellectual framework.

My own discussion of the *Collationes* here will concentrate on Bonaventure's apocalyptic thought and particularly on his reading of Revelation, which is, after all, what this book is about. To limit the *Collationes* in this way is to distort its intent. Bonaventure actually does a great deal more. He begins in the same way thirteenth-century exegetes began their Bible commentaries: with a passage from another book of the Bible, applying that passage to the subject at hand. In this case Bonaventure chooses to begin with Ecclesiasticus 15:5: "In the midst of the church the Lord shall open his mouth, and shall fill it with the spirit of wisdom and understanding, and shall clothe it with a robe of glory." The first three collations are devoted to unpacking these words.

It is impossible to do justice to all the ways Bonaventure exposits the passage, but a few things must be said. First, given the totality of Bonaven-

---

3. C. Colt Anderson, *A Call to Piety* (Quincy, IL: Franciscan Press, 2002).

4. Anderson occasionally portrays Bonaventure as attacking the opposite end of the spectrum as well, the (rigidly?) pious brothers who acted according to rectitude but less according to love, i.e., the spiritual Franciscans at their worst. In effect, Anderson sees at least a shadow of the later *usus pauper* controversy. That raises a series of complex issues unfit for discussion in this venue; yet I would at least say that, although there might be some preview of the spiritual-conventual problem here, I find it hard to see Bonaventure as intentionally addressing it.

ture's work, it is hardly surprising that the idea of the Lord opening his mouth in the middle of the church should be seen here as a reference to Christ as medium. Again and again Bonaventure will emphasize the centrality of Christ. By this he certainly means that the entire Bible is centered on Christ and that the event of Christ thus furnishes the key to unlocking the meaning of all that is found in the Bible, that we must interpret it in a christocentric manner; but it also means that the Bible can be interpreted as referring constantly to Christ. As Bonaventure says at one point, wherever in the Bible there are mentions of the rivers of Paradise or fountains or the sun, they refer to Christ. This is worth pondering.

Another important theme introduced in the early collations is the insufficiency of early Greek and Roman philosophy taken on its own. The ancient philosophers accepted a truncated list of virtues that ignored faith, hope, and love. Ancient philosophy alone cannot save us. For the sort of wisdom that does save us we need access to the threefold Word—the uncreated Word that is the Father, the incarnate Word that is the Son, and the inspired Word that is the Holy Spirit—and for that we need access to holy Scripture. By the ninth collation, Bonaventure is well into an explanation of how the reputation of the early witnesses, built on merit, miracle, and martyrdom, is bolstered by later documents such as conciliar decrees and the writings of the doctors, producing an authoritative biblical message transcending the philosophers.

It transcends the philosophers in more ways than we can deal with here, but for the moment we can at least approach the subject from afar through Bonaventure's metaphor of passing over, which involves a transition beyond the study of pagan sciences to a study of holiness, then wisdom, in order to enter the gates of the city, the Jerusalem of the Apocalypse. To put the matter in this way is to introduce rather abruptly here a series of ideas developed over several collations by Bonaventure. The goal of the Christian theologian is not simply knowledge but wisdom leading to a higher, contemplative familiarity with the Word, which involves a vertical dimension, an ascent, but also a horizontal journey in time. Bonaventure's heavenly city is not only mystical but eschatological. In fact, the term "passing over" suggests both the vertical and the horizontal pilgrimage, as we will see in a moment.

If the process transcends ancient philosophy, it also transcends the synagogue. Like other Christian writings, Bonaventure's *Collationes* is aimed at distinguishing Christianity not only from Aristotle but also from Judaism. If in the former case Bonaventure is intent on comparing two distinct sources of knowledge, ancient philosophy and holy Scripture, in the latter case he is interested in comparing two different ways of reading holy Scripture. His argument is that Christian wisdom is based on the Bible, but the Bible is not to be read as the Jews read it. Their knowledge stays at the literal level; but for the Christian, "the whole of Scripture is like a single zither, and the lesser string does not produce harmony in itself, but only in combination with the others. Likewise, any single passage of Scripture depends on some other, or rather, any single passage is related to a thousand others."[5] It is a striking metaphor, suggesting as it does that no book in the Bible can be taken in isolation. To put it in Bonaventuran terms, the same uncreated and incarnate Word stands behind every word of the Bible, producing a complex tapestry that must be considered in its entirety if we are to understand its meaning at all.

That is a remarkable insight, and it would be interesting to see how widely it was observed. I refer here not to the invidious comparison with Jewish exegesis, which is based on a stereotype that faded only gradually as Christians began to study Jewish exegesis seriously, but to the zither image, which might have suggested an ambitious exegetical program. Significantly enough, Bonaventure's audience might have contained one young Franciscan, Petrus Iohannis Olivi, whose exegetical work would prove extensive enough to show how the Bonaventuran exegetical ideal might have worked out in reality; but concerning that we will say more later. For the moment we should note that the *Collationes* itself provides something of a model for what Bonaventure had in mind. The Apocalypse proves an important work for the argument Bonaventure is constructing, but that book itself is very sparsely used in the early collations, which cite a wide variety of books in building their case.

Bonaventure follows up with another metaphor, which is both about the nature of exegesis and itself a bit of exegesis:

Note that when Christ performed the miracle of changing water into wine he did not say from the very first: "Let there be wine." Nor did he produce it out of nothing, as Gregory comments. He asked the servants to fill the water jars. It is impossible to explain what he did in a literal sense, but a

5. *Collations on the Six Days*, vol. 5 of *The Works of Bonaventure*, trans. José de Vinck (Paterson, NJ: St. Anthony Guild Press, 1970), 19.7 (hereafter *Collationes*). Throughout these references I will use de Vinck's translation. The critical edition of the Bonaventure *Opera* is available online: *Doctoris Seraphici S. Bonaventurae Opera omnia . . .* , ed. the College of Saint Bonaventure (Ad Claras Aquas [Quaracchi], 1882–1902).

reason may be given in terms of spiritual understanding. The Holy Spirit does not give spiritual understanding unless man provides the jar, that is, his capacity, and his understanding, that is, his understanding of the literal sense. Then God changes the water of the literal understanding into the wine of the spiritual.[6]

Thus Bonaventure manages to suggest both the primacy of the literal sense and its ultimate insufficiency; and it should be noted that he, like others, assumes that there are four basic senses of Scripture, but in a very Bonaventuran argument he bases those four meanings on the triune nature of God.[7]

In the early collations, Bonaventure is intent on providing a series of tools for use in the interpretation of Scripture, and for these he borrows freely from previous scholarship, though always putting his own stamp on the discussion. Thus he adopts the threefold Augustinian classification of visionary experience, but in his presentation it becomes, first, purely intellectual (associated with angels); intellectual combined with imaginary (associated with the prophets); and intellectual combined with bodily senses (associated with the apostles).[8]

Another thing about the early collations is perhaps important. In the first collation he refers to the pillars of cloud and fire the Israelites followed across the desert.[9] From that point on, images of the exodus from Egypt, the time in the desert, and the need to pass over from Egypt into the desert and then into the promised land[10] reinforce a theme that, while it hardly dominates the work, provides us with a sense that Bonaventure sees himself and his colleagues in the light of those Israelites. Whatever else the *Collationes* represents, it seems to represent a plea to keep moving and not get lost in the desert.

One more general comment is in order: Francis is only sparsely mentioned. In the early collations he is occasionally invoked as an example or simply quoted, but he is not presented as an apocalyptic figure. The question is whether this trend continues to the end, a point to which we will return later in the chapter.

That brings us to our basic interest in this chapter, the *Collationes* as an apocalyptic work. My basic argument is that in the course of the *Collationes*

6. *Collationes* 19.8.
7. *Collationes* 13.11.
8. *Collationes* 9.10.
9. *Collationes* 1.3.
10. E.g., *Collationes* 19.1–4.

Bonaventure pushed exegesis of Revelation into a whole new phase, and he did so, not by refuting Joachim, but through a genuine appreciation of him. My guide here is a study so old that it antedates Vatican II: Joseph Ratzinger's *Theology of History in St. Bonaventure.*[11] It is one of the few books of which I can say that I've read it at least three times in two languages over the years, and, every time through, my admiration for it has increased.

Early in his study, Ratzinger describes the *Collationes* as "a penetrating exposition of those problems which had led earlier to the downfall of John of Parma, . . . namely the question of Joachism and spiritualism. For this reason, the work, by its very nature, was forced to undertake a fundamental treatment of the theology of history."[12] Thus Ratzinger makes it clear from the beginning that Bonaventure does not see himself as engaged in a tactical maneuver inspired by the need to wean Joachite friars away from an obviously discredited theology. The question he is raising about Joachim is, for Bonaventure, an open-ended one.

We are barely into Ratzinger's book, but already he has evaded the problem that stands between many historians and their ability to appreciate Bonaventure's theology of history, their image of Gerard of Borgo San Donnino as the voice of Joachite theology. In fact, what was rejected by the papal condemnation of 1255 was one form—to use Ratzinger's term, one *crass* form—of Joachite doctrine. There were others, some not so crass. Joachim—the real Joachim of his three major works, particularly the *Liber concordiae*—was consulted by many scholars, including Bonaventure. Ratzinger portrays Bonaventure as forsaking the standard divisions of history offered in the schools in favor of Joachim's double-seven schema in which we are presented with a *concordia* between seven periods of the Old Testament and seven of the New. That means seven periods of church history during which we can grow in wisdom. Scripture is, to be sure, "closed objectively" (as Ratzinger explains), but "its meaning is advancing in a steady growth throughout history, and this growth is not yet closed."

11. Joseph Ratzinger, *The Theology of History in St. Bonaventure*, trans. Zachary Hayes, OFM (Chicago: Franciscan Herald Press, 1971). I give the English translation rather than the original German because, although I originally read it in German as *Das Geschichtestheologie des heiligen Bonaventura* (Munich: Schnell and Steiner, 1959), it was only through Fr. Hayes's excellent translation that I began to appreciate Ratzinger's remarkable command of the subject. In fact, it was only in preparing to write this chapter and again reading Hayes's translation (after discussing the *Collationes* at some length nineteen years earlier in *Olivi's Peaceable Kingdom*, 33–44) that I finally saw how good Ratzinger's analysis actually is.

12. Ratzinger, *Theology of History*, 3. He makes the same point again on pp. 6–7.

And this meaning develops in a constant process of growth in time. Consequently we are able to interpret many things which the Fathers could not have known, because for them these things still lay in the dark future while for us they are accessible as past history. Still other things remain dark for us. And so, new knowledge arises constantly from Scripture. Something is taking place; and this happening, this history, continues onward as long as there is history at all. This is of fundamental importance for the theologian who explains Scripture. It makes it clear that the theologian cannot abstract from history in his explanation of Scripture; neither from the past nor from the future. In this way, the exegesis of Scripture becomes a theology of history; the clarification of the past leads to prophecy concerning the future.[13]

The basic elements combined in this thought are repeated at length in Ratzinger's presentation of Bonaventure. At one point he comments on the enthusiasm it excites in Bonaventure, and one can surely say the same about Ratzinger.

It is clear where the argument is tending. "The real point of Bonaventure's new vision of history is not the understanding of the past, but prophecy about that which is to come."[14] Ratzinger outlines the great double-seven schema presented in *Collationes* 16:11–31. Having given us something to use in tracing the argument, he notes that "the central point of interest lies in that small section of the sixth age which is yet to be realized, that is, in that mysterious border-line area which separates the perilous present time from that age of Sabbath Rest which is yet to come within the framework of this world."

Two things should be emphasized here. First, Ratzinger is correct in suggesting that Bonaventure anticipates, not simply joy in heaven after the final judgment, but a period of peace and contemplative joy within time. In the thirteenth collation he quotes Isaiah 11:9, "The earth shall be filled with the knowledge of the Lord," and "there shall be no harm or ruin in all my holy mountain." This applies, Bonaventure says, "to the time of the New Testament when Scripture was made evident, and mostly toward the end when those Scriptures were understood which had not been understood before.

---

13. Ratzinger, *Theology of History*, 9. If this chapter is consciously structured to remind the reader how important a single book by a brilliant historian can be in shaping our sense not only of the past but also of its impact on the present, it is also a tribute to the value of a good translator, in this case Fr. Zachary Hayes, OFM, who furnished not only an accurate translation but a graceful one.

14. Ratzinger, *Theology of History*, 19–20.

For there shall be a mountain, that is, the contemplative church. Then there shall be no harm when the monsters of heresy shall flee on account of the proper use of wisdom. But today Mount Sion is desolate because of jackals, that is, because of cunning and fetid interpreters."[15]

The second thing to be emphasized is that for Bonaventure, as interpreted by Ratzinger, the most interesting part of the future is not the final period predicted in the passage from Isaiah but that final part of the period immediately preceding it, the time of transition just before. In the fifteenth and sixteenth collations, Bonaventure presents a series of ways in which history might be divided up, based on a series of numerical patterns. In the sixteenth, immediately after noting the possibility of dividing history into six ages and a seventh running concurrently with the sixth, he suddenly breaks off to announce that, "after the New Testament, there will be no other, nor can any sacrament of the New Law be omitted, for this is an eternal testament." This is, as it were, the bottom line, the ultimate ground rule of the numerical game Bonaventure is playing. He has to stay away from Gerard of Borgo San Donnino. Immediately thereafter, he will invoke the accepted notion of two laws, the old and the new, linked as letter to spirit and as promise to fulfillment. Then he will go on to a threefold division of time, but there will be no talk of a third law.

What he does instead is certainly interesting. In collation 16:5 Bonaventure offers a parallel between a threefold temporal division of the synagogue (beginning, expansion, and consummation) and the same threefold distinction in the church, a very nonthreatening Joachite *concordia*. He does nothing much with it, but at least he has offered parallel threes that could be (and in fact are) developed by Bonaventure elsewhere without evoking Gerard.

The most important moment in all of this comes later, when Bonaventure explores the possibilities inherent in a system of double sevens. He offers a sevenfold division of Old Testament history, then does the same for the New Testament in the sense of church history as a whole. These differ somewhat from the periods offered by the standard Parisian model, because he takes the parallel between Old Testament and New Testament seriously enough to use the same categories in describing the seven periods in each; yet what he offers differs less from the standard Parisian model than one might at first imagine.

Bonaventure lines up many of the usual suspects, speaking of the primitive church, the martyrs, and the doctrinal disputes. His fourth period is

15. *Collationes* 13.6–7.

identified with the production of laws, including the Benedictine rule, Justinian's code, and canon law, and this seems a departure from the fourth period as usually delineated in the standard Parisian model; yet one can see how the standard theme of combating laxity might be specified in this way. The fifth period, according to the *Collationes*, includes confrontation with the eastern church on the one hand and Islam on the other, two themes that could be construed as reflecting the precursors of Antichrist in the standard Parisian model. Thus, by reading the first five periods of the *Collationes* in the light of the first five periods in the standard Parisian model, we can bring them at least within hailing distance of one another.

Then we arrive at the sixth period, and here we find genuine novelty. Bonaventure describes it as a time of clear doctrine, marked by peace and the advance of learning within the church, by gains in prophecy, and by the expansion of Christianity; yet he also sees it as marred by persecution and temptation. Bonaventure sees this period as having begun with Charlemagne. Thus it is already approximately five centuries old.

If the sixth period is both positive and negative, a time of both great good and great evil, can we see it as first one and then the other? Yes and no. Bonaventure compares it with the passion of Christ, in which there was light, then darkness, then light again. If we assume that the first light represents Charlemagne and the darkness Antichrist, then a third light will arrive, but when and in what form? Bonaventure is hardly clear on the matter. As for the darkness, some of it has already appeared—Bonaventure specifically mentions Henry IV and Frederick I, seen as persecutors of the church—but much more is on the way, especially in the shape of Antichrist.

One can see why Ratzinger feels that, of the two periods remaining in this time before the end, the real question touches the nature of the sixth period.[16] "In contrast with this problem, the real question of the seventh age is relatively simple." The prophecy of Ezekiel will be fulfilled, and the holy city will come down, not the heavenly city itself, but rather "the church militant conformed to the church triumphant insofar as this is possible in her pilgrim state." Ratzinger comments that "this period of time represents a state of salvation of a completely new sort. But this does not destroy its inner-worldly, inner-historical, and therefore pre-eschatological character. It is in this period that the great prophecies of Ezekiel and Isaiah will be fulfilled."[17]

---

16. So much so, in fact, that the Readings section for this chapter contains some of what Bonaventure has to say on the matter.

17. Ratzinger, *Theology of History*, 22–23.

That is, at any rate, what Bonaventure assures us; but is he at one with Joachim on the matter? So far our emphasis has been on the level of agreement between the two. Now Ratzinger raises the question of whether the agreement is complete. He considers it a question that cannot be answered until other issues have been settled, and he temporarily drops the matter. We can safely do the same and ask what else Bonaventure has to say about the sixth period.

Even so, before we proceed we might notice one more passage that comes right at the end of the sixteenth collation. Immediately after Bonaventure speaks of the holy city coming down, he says, "Then there will be a building of the city, and a restoration of it as it was in the beginning. And then there will be peace. How long that peace will last, however, God knows." We recall Bonaventure's tripartite divisions of Old and New Testament history. We know what "fulfillment" was entailed in the case of the Old Testament; but what fulfillment is entailed in the case of New Testament history? What will follow after that peace? As we will see, Olivi yields to the temptation thus presented and has more to say on the matter. Bonaventure does not.

Yet Bonaventure is not quite through with the sixteenth collation. He has one more mathematical rabbit to pull from his hat. "Since there are seven times both in the Old Testament and in the New, and each one of them is threefold in the sense that it contains three events, the sevenfold series multiplied twice by three gives forty-two, corresponding to the forty-two stages through which the promised land is reached."[18] Again we find a reference to the exodus and passage through the wilderness to the promised land. And in the nineteenth collation he comments that "if we want to come over, we must be the sons of Israel who passed over from Egypt. But the Egyptians did not pass over; they were drowned. Those alone come over who focus their whole attention on how to pass from vanity to the country of truth."[19]

If we were to look more intently at the collations, comparing them even more closely with the standard Parisian model, a great deal more could be said. For example, in the *Collationes* Bonaventure, too, sees seven periods and portrays those seven periods in connection with the seven visions of Revelation; but he seems willing to imagine that all seven periods are reflected in each of the seven visions. That makes him similar to Olivi, who also breaks with the Parisian four/three or five/two model in that way; but the *Collationes* simply does not give us enough to go on here, and in Olivi

18. *Collationes* 16.31.
19. *Collationes* 19.1.

there seems to be some difference between what he does in theory and how he behaves in practice on this matter.

There is one other way, however, in which the *Collationes* and Olivi agree on a major issue, and that issue places them strikingly at variance with the standard Parisian model: both place themselves and Francis in the sixth period. In fact, in a significant break with the standard Parisian model, Bonaventure places Francis around four centuries into it. (As we will see, Olivi places him more at its edge, but that will have to wait for the moment.) Thus what they can do with the sixth period goes well beyond what other Franciscans could do with it. First, they can see it as much more than the time of Antichrist. It can also be a time of enlightenment. Second, and following from that difference, they can both see Francis as a genuinely apocalyptic figure.[20]

How Olivi goes about doing so will be seen later. For the moment we must look at what Bonaventure claims (or seems to claim) about Francis. It is time to look at a series of passages in which Francis is barely mentioned. First, Bonaventure tells us that some of the evil princes who succeeded Charlemagne "wished to destroy the church, but the angel ascending from the place of the sun cried to the four angels, 'Do not harm the earth and the sea until we seal the servants of our God on their foreheads.'" The reference to Revelation 7:2 is clear enough, but the implied historical development is less so, because, as Bonaventure writes, the Antichrist is still to come. We have seen that the light-darkness-light parallel allows for some complexity, and we have seen that Bonaventure particularly mentions Henry IV and Frederick I, both of whom antedate Francis. How should we imagine all this as fitting together in Bonaventure's mind?[21] It is, after all, Bonaventure speaking, and, thanks to the *Legenda maior*, we like to believe that we know whom he identifies with the angel of Revelation 7:2. Is this, however, too simplistic?

---

20. This chapter hardly seems to call for a lengthy discussion of Olivi's relation to Bonaventure. Nor is one necessary, given the recent article by Sylvain Piron, "Olivi and Bonaventure: Paradoxes and Faithfulness," *Franciscan Studies* 74 (2016): 1–14. There Piron presents a brief but, I think, remarkably suggestive picture of Olivi's adherence to the Bonaventuran apocalyptic interpretation of Francis, his order, and the role of both in what was still in some important ways a Joachite reading of history. Piron also points to the way Olivi turned the Bonaventuran indictment of Aristotelian philosophy into an indictment of Averroism. Finally, he summons the evidence to show that Olivi knew Bonaventure well through personal experience, and he raises an interesting possibility that manages to bring all these things together.

21. Remember the curious anticipatory reference to the angel of 7:2 in *Vox domini*. There, of course, the periodization is different, but Bonaventure may be working through a parallel set of considerations here. As we will see, the angel of 7:2 may become Francis in the *Collationes*, but he is always also Christ, whose centrality remains unchallenged.

In fact, if Bonaventure is identifying Francis with an angel at all, then he seems to identify Francis with more angels than one. In order to gain any sense of what Bonaventure is doing we must look at a whole series of passages. In one he observes,

> The contemplative soul is sealed by God. Hence, in reference to the sixth angel, it is said that there appeared an angel having the seal of the living God. This was in the sealing of Jerusalem standing in heaven. To this angel there appeared an expressive seal regarding the mode of life consonant with this seal. . . . From the tribe of Judah, twelve thousand sealed, etc.[22]

Obviously we are still dealing with Revelation 7:2, but with additional reference to Revelation 21. Slightly earlier he ponders Revelation 21:10, "He took me up in the spirit to a great, high mountain and showed me the holy city, Jerusalem." Bonaventure says,

> How can this be? See what is said at the end of the Apocalypse. Around the middle, however, it is said, "I saw the lamb standing on Mount Zion, and with him 144,000 having his name and the name of his father written on their foreheads." But in the opening of the sixth seal it is said in the Apocalypse, "I saw another angel standing from the rising of the sun, having the seal of the living God, and he cried to the four angels authorized to harm the earth and sea, saying, 'Do not harm the earth and sea until we seal the servants of our God on their foreheads.'" This passage establishes, first, that it was those who were on Mount Sion who were sealed and, later, that one of the angels pouring out the vials—it must be the sixth— showed him the city the size of which was one hundred forty-four cubits. Around the beginning of the Apocalypse it is said to the sixth angel, that of Philadelphia, "I shall make him who overcomes a pillar in the temple of my God and write on him my name and the name of the city, the new Jerusalem," which was mentioned only at the end. There are six periods with rest. And just as Christ came in the sixth period, thus it is necessary that the contemplative church be born at the end.[23]

Here the seal and 144,000 are connected not only with Revelation 7 but with Revelation 14 (which places the 144,000 on Mount Zion with the names

22. *Collationes* 23.14.
23. *Collationes* 23.3–4.

of Lamb and Father written on their foreheads), then Revelation 16 is connected with 21:9 (since the vial-pouring angel who shows John the holy city is assumed to be the sixth). Then Bonaventure turns to yet another sixth angel, that of Philadelphia (Rev 3:7), with an implied correlation between Christ coming in the sixth period of world history (the long-accepted Augustinian pattern) and the emergence of the contemplative church "at the end." Thus what we have is not simply the angel of the sixth seal in Revelation 7:2 but an extremely complex image of "the sixth angel" useful in pulling together a good deal of what Bonaventure thinks should be said about the sixth and seventh periods.

That much is evident from another passage already mentioned, one also dealing with the angel of 7:2. Bonaventure recalls the persecutions under Frederick I and Henry IV in the sixth period and notes that there were two popes in the time of each.

> And it is certain that one of them wanted to exterminate the church, but the angel ascending from the rising of the sun cried to the four angels, "Do not harm the earth and sea until we seal the servants of our God on their foreheads." Thus the church's tribulation continues up to this time. And it was said to the angel of Philadelphia, who is the sixth one, "Thus says the holy and true one who has the key of David, he who opens and no one shuts, he who shuts and no one opens: I know your works. Behold, I have set an open door before you." And he said that now understanding of Scripture or revelation or the key of David would be given to a person or to a multitude; and I believe more to a multitude.[24]

Here again we have the angel of Revelation 7:2, now clearly associated with the persecutions and spiritual achievements of the sixth period. The angel of 3:7 turns up as well, this time in connection with the key of David and the open door, images that refer to the understanding of Scripture in the sixth period. And we encounter a hitherto undiscovered angel. Bonaventure identifies the sealing of the twelve tribes in Revelation 7:5–9 with twelve mysteries to be unlocked. Then he says,

> Note that the twelve sealings, the measuring of the city, the showing of the city and the opening of the book are under the sixth seal and under the sixth angel. And the key of David is spoken about to the sixth angel, the one of

---

24. *Collationes* 16–29.

Philadelphia (which is interpreted "preserving the inheritance"), of whom it is said, "Upon him who overcomes I will write my name and that of the city, the new Jerusalem." . . . This means I will give knowledge of Scripture to this sixth angel, but it will be bitter to his stomach, and in his mouth it will be sweet as honey. And this order is understood through John, to whom it was said, "Thus I wish him to remain until I come."[25]

Here the "sixth angel" is partly that of Revelation 3:7–13, the angel of Philadelphia, connected with the key of David (an improved knowledge of Scripture) and the new Jerusalem (another complex symbol tying together the ordered human mind, the summit of contemplation, and the community of the final age). By quoting 3:12 at length Bonaventure relates all these things to the sealing of the elect. The sixth angel of this passage is also that of Revelation 7:2, as Bonaventure's reference to the opening of the sixth seal suggests; yet the sixth angel mentioned immediately thereafter is that of neither 7:2 nor 3:7. He is at least partly that of 21:9, who guides John on his tour of the new Jerusalem and whom, as we have seen, Bonaventure chooses to see as identical with the sixth angel of 16:12.

Beyond that point we move into new territory. The "sixth angel" described here is also that of Revelation 10, who comes from heaven bearing an open book, which John proceeds to eat. Thus John becomes a symbol of the new order to whom knowledge of Scripture is given in the final age. The reference to John 21:22, "I wish him to remain until I come," suggests that this order will be the final one, apparently emerging in the sixth period and lasting until the eschaton. If the sixth angel is Francis, it is understandable why Bonaventure twists the text a bit and portrays the angel himself as eating the book.

There are other relevant passages. At one point, Bonaventure describes the sixth period as "a time of clear doctrine" when there should appear "a single order . . . similar to the order of Jesus Christ," the head of which would be "an angel ascending from the rising of the sun, having the seal of the living God and conforming to Christ. And he said that he had already come."[26] At another point he speaks in the future tense of a new understanding of Scripture, predicting a time when "our lion from the tribe of Judah will arise and open the book, when there will be a consummation of the passions of Christ which the body of Christ now suffers."[27] Here the allusion is to Revelation 5:5.

25.*Collationes* 20.29.
26.*Collationes* 16.16.
27.*Collationes* 40.15.

Thus—and the point is worth making again—in the *Collationes*, Bonaventure is not simply interested in the angel of the sixth seal but rather in the "sixth angel," and his references to that figure move well beyond the themes derived from Revelation 7:2, combining a number of passages into a rich, kaleidoscopic image that unites various elements important for Bonaventure's evaluation of Francis, the order, and their roles in the sixth and seventh periods. The image includes two different types of wisdom, namely, increased understanding of Scripture and an ecstatic knowledge that transcends the intellect. It also allows for historical development, particularly through the last two ages of church history, a development involving not only the light-filled elements of the sixth period but also the dark ones. And it ties all this together with what Bonaventure sees as the historical, indeed the salvific, significance of the Poverello.

Or does it? *Does* Bonaventure identify Francis with the sixth angel? He seems to avoid explicitly using Francis's name, although in speaking of the new order of the final times he says, "Francis seems to have been a member of this order."[28] Stanislao da Campagnola concludes from Bonaventure's reticence in naming Francis that by 1273 he was retreating from his earlier position, probably because he wanted to delimit Joachite tendencies within the order.[29] This would be odd, though. Anyone reading the *Collationes* would recognize that it is in some respects very Joachite, as Ratzinger has shown. Moreover, many things said of the "sixth angel" are also explicitly said of Francis elsewhere. Thus in the *Legenda maior* Bonaventure identifies Francis as the angel of Revelation 7:2, and in the *Collationes* he speaks of an emerging order "similar to Jesus Christ, the head of which should be an angel . . . with the seal of the living God and in conformity with Christ," then he announces that this angel has already come.[30] Whom else besides Francis could he have in mind?

Why, then, does he not explicitly make the identification? Is it because he's talking specifically to Franciscans and considers mention of Francis's name unnecessary? Would he be stunned to discover that some twenty-first-century historian feels he should have spelled it out, as if he had never written the *Legenda maior*? Or is there some reason not apparent to us why

28. *Collationes* 22.22. See also 22.23, "This order should correspond to this person" (clearly referring to Francis).

29. Stanislao da Campagnola, *L'Angelo del sesto sigillo e l'"alter Christus"* (Rome: Laurentianum, 1971), 193–97.

30. *Collationes* 16.16.

he doesn't want to do so? After all, Bonaventure's year, like ours, was composed of 365 days. In the year leading up to the *Collationes*, much happened that we haven't heard about. Is there something he should have mentioned but didn't?

In fact, though, the image Bonaventure constructs in the *Collationes* by referring to the various sixth angels and "other angels" goes beyond even the figure of Francis in two ways. First, it encompasses the order forming around him and through him. Second, Christ is placed at the center of the image. The angel of Revelation 7:2, explicitly identified with Christ in most exegesis adhering to the standard Parisian model, is not really distinguished from him in the *Collationes* either, as the citations of 7:2 make clear. In this respect at least, the *Collationes* do not depart from the standard Parisian commentary model. The book of Revelation deals with tribulation and consolation, a point made over and over in commentaries. We have seen the author of *Vox domini* identify not only the angel of 7:2 but also those of 8:3, 10:1, 14:1, 14:15, 17:1, and 18:1 with Christ. He is described there as an angel, not because he literally is one, but because God sends him to us. He is an angel not in nature but in office, as *Vox domini* says concerning 7:2. In the *Collationes* it is Christ who defends, comforts, and guides his people. Francis, head of the order, bears Christ's seal and conforms to Christ.[31]

If we plot Bonaventure's course from his Sentence commentary on, we find a man growing, not less apocalyptically oriented, but more so. As Ratzinger observes, it was the conflict with William of Saint Amour that excited an eschatological, historical awareness in him.[32] Ratzinger comments that "for the first time, in the *Quaestiones de perfectione evangelica*, a type of hierarchical thought appears which betrays the traces of the Joachite-eschatological interpretation of the Order of Francis." From that point on, his activities were such as to encourage the growth of that awareness. The scandal of the eternal gospel must have forced him to look closely at Joachim, since he was responsible for dealing with Joachites in his order. The major challenge would have been dealing with John of Parma, who had friends in high places and showed himself to be remarkably insistent on maintaining his views. We might wish for a better source concerning John's trial than the one provided

31. In the early 1990s, while writing *Olivi's Peaceable Kingdom*, I failed to appreciate the coherence of the mosaic Bonaventure constructs in his commentary on the various angels partly because I saw him as concerned with two elements: Francis and the new order. In fact, he is constantly aware of three elements: Francis, the new order, and Christ, who remains at the center of his thought.

32. Ratzinger, *Theology of History*, 109–14.

by Angelo Clareno, who displays no great love for Bonaventure, tells us little about John's position, and may be wrong in what he does tell us; but one can at least appreciate from what Angelo says how Bonaventure's attention might have been forcibly drawn beyond the problem of how to deal with John to the problem of what Joachim actually said. Add to that the task of writing the *Legenda maior* and one can appreciate how Bonaventure's thought might have been directed through channels that would have encouraged what we find in the *Collationes*.[33]

Bonaventure was never completely Joachite. According to Ratzinger, the major difference is that he adopted the scheme of double sevens but was much more cautious when it came to the three ages.[34] That is, however, remarkable in itself, because it means that for Bonaventure the dawn of a new age had broken through with Francis and his followers during the sixth period of church history, and, despite the tribulations to come (in fact, despite the projected coming of Antichrist), all the wonders of the seventh period would be attained. And those wonders would be part of what Ratzinger describes as "a thoroughly inner-worldly condition" occurring "within the church militant" prior to the end of history.[35]

Bonaventure's acceptance of a progressive element in history raises the question of how what is to come compares with what has been. As Ratzinger recognizes, the new order of the final age is prefigured by Paul, Benjamin, John, Joseph of Egypt, Moses, and Daniel, especially the first three.[36] Nevertheless, the circle of those who already have enjoyed the wisdom of the final age actually extends wider than these specific figures. The final order

---

33. Ubertino da Casale might impress us as a better source. As we saw in the chapter entitled "Early Joachism," Ubertino seems to suggest that when he visited Hugh in 1285 Hugh considered Francis to have been the angel of the sixth seal and saw him as ushering in the sixth period of church history. The question is whether he already believed that in the 1250s. Certainly Gerard of Borgo San Donnino did.

34. Ratzinger, *Theology of History*, 117–18. As I have tried to suggest, the question of whether Bonaventure was "completely Joachite" is an odd thing to ask in any case. Only Joachim was completely Joachite. Others bent him into various shapes to suit their own purposes or adopted parts of him while rejecting other parts. Bonaventure did the latter, and the part he did adopt was an important one. We have seen that at 16:2 he says, "After the New Testament there will be no other, nor can any sacrament of the New Law be subtracted, because this is an eternal testament." (Note the similarity to what is said in *Vox domini*.) Here Bonaventure is rejecting, not Joachim, but Gerard of Borgo San Donnino. As for the three ages, he stayed farther away from that side of Joachim, but even there one finds some degree of resemblance.

35. Ratzinger, *Theology of History*, 22.

36. Ratzinger, *Theology of History*, 42–44.

will enjoy what has been shared by the perfect throughout history. Ratzinger sums it up in an equation: the final age equals the first age. "At the end of time there will be a full realization of all that was present for a short time in the primitive community, and which pointed toward the future."[37] The problem faced here is predictable in any progressive historical schema. We will find Olivi, too, facing it shortly.

That still leaves us with the problem of how Bonaventure saw the connection between the Franciscan order and the new contemplative order of the seventh period. Francis founded the former and is a member of the latter, but does that make them the same? Most modern scholars have followed Ratzinger, who suggests that Bonaventure's scholarly activities and compromises as minister general can be explained by his recognition that Francis anticipated a manner of life unattainable by any thirteenth-century institution. Bonaventure, he says,

> could set aside the *sine glossa* which he knew from the Testament of Francis to be the real will of the founder . . . because the proper historical hour for such a form of life had not yet struck. . . . Bonaventure realized that Francis's own eschatological form of life could not exist as an institution in this world; it could be realized only as a break-through of grace in the individual until such a time as the God-given hour would arrive at which the world would be transformed into its final form of existence.[38]

To say this much is not to hollow the *sine glossa* out, reducing it to little more than a sentimental ideal. Bonaventure's dynamic sense of the approaching seventh period convinces him that it is really on the way and that the new order, an order already anticipated in Francis's life, will be realized. On this level, Ratzinger's suggestion makes sense. One might even ask if, during the intervening waiting period, both orders exist on parallel levels. The new order of the seventh period is not an order in the same sense that the Order of Friars Minor (OFM) is an order. Rather than being a worldly institution, it might be described as a new order of being. Francis is in it.

Are others, though? Ratzinger is aware that some evidence suggests Bonaventure may originally have identified the Franciscans with the new order.

---

37. Ratzinger, *Theology of History*, 44. As Ratzinger observes on pp. 186–87, this idea is found in Joachim's *Liber concordiae* 4.39.

38. Ratzinger, *Theology of History*, 51, and, more generally, 46–71, 155–63.

Many texts seem to indicate that Bonaventure believed that the Franciscan order was originally intended to be the final, eschatological order immediately, and was to bring about the beginning of a new era. In this case, it would have been the failure of its members that impeded the realization of this goal. Now the order would have to be purged by another final tribulation before it would be able to find its true and final form.[39]

The shift in senses of "order" occasionally impedes us from getting a clear picture of what Bonaventure is saying, but one does gain a general impression that purgation is possible and will lead to rewards. Bonaventure says,

> Consider your own call, for it is great. . . . Contemplation cannot come about except in the greatest simplicity; and the greatest simplicity cannot exist except in the greatest poverty. And this is proper to this order. The intention of the blessed Francis was to live in the greatest poverty. And he said that we had receded a lot from our state, and therefore God permitted that we be afflicted so that by those means we might be led back to our state that must possess the promised land. God promised great things to Israel, and the greatest among them were chosen as his apostles. The Jews became blind; these others were enlightened. The former gave themselves to the flesh; yet some chose to give their purses to Christ. Note also that only a few entered the promised land, and that those who discouraged the people did not go in.[40]

"This order" clearly refers to the OFM. Like the ancient Israelites, the Franciscans in his time are both recipients of a great call and notorious backsliders. They must be purified by affliction in the desert before they can enter into their inheritance. Not all will enter, but some can, and woe to him who discourages them. Bonaventure is not encouraging his brothers to wait it out patiently. He is encouraging them to strive.

Much has been made of a passage in which Bonaventure develops various ninefold orders, all correlated with the angelic hierarchy. He divides the church into laity, clerics, and contemplatives, each containing three orders. The contemplatives are divided into those who devote themselves entirely to prayer; those who strive "in a speculative way, . . . as do those who engage in the examination of Scripture"; and "those who attend to God in an elevative

---

39. Ratzinger, *Theology of History*, 53–54.
40. *Collationes* 20.30.

way, that is, an ecstatic and rapturous way."[41] The first, corresponding to the thrones, are the monastic orders such as the Cistercians. The second, corresponding to the cherubim, are the Dominicans and Franciscans. The third correspond to the seraphim. "It seems that Francis belonged to it," Bonaventure says, "but it is hard to know what it is destined to be or already is."

This passage must be balanced against another in which Bonaventure says, "This order will not flourish unless Christ appears and suffers in his mystical body. And he said that this apparition of the seraph to blessed Francis, which was both expressive and impressed, showed that this order was to correspond to that one, but was to attain to this through tribulation."[42] Through tribulation the Franciscans can attain to their status as the new order of the seventh period, the order to which Francis already belongs. In Ratzinger's words, "In his own person, Francis anticipates the eschatological form of life which will be the general form of life in the future."[43]

While none of this definitively solves the problem of whether Bonaventure intended to refer to Francis in constructing his complex image of the "sixth angel," certainly it makes us less likely to argue that he did not, and it also seems to make that problem less important. What we *can* say is that Bonaventure saw the stigmatization, not merely as a statement about Francis, but as one about the order, a statement about its ultimate destiny and the route those few Franciscans who actually achieved it would have to take in order to get there.

READINGS

Collationes in hexaemeron

Collationes 16.11–31

The original times consist of the first seven days, and the figural times run from the beginning of the world to Christ, when the New Time begins,

---

41. *Collationes* 20.22.

42. *Collationes* 21.23. "Iste ordo illi respondere debeat, sed tamen pervinire ad hoc per tribulationem."

43. Ratzinger, *Theology of History*, 50. Ratzinger's observations on the Dionysius renaissance of the thirteenth century (pp. 87–94) are important here.

although Solomon says, "There is nothing new under the sun," which is true according to nature, but this is above nature. Afterward are the times of grace. Moses began from the original times, as was necessary; for first Scripture, like a soil ready for germination, had to bring forth seed and then a tree of figures, then fruit. Seven days are posited as the original times. The first day: light formed. The second day: the waters divided. The third day: the earth made fecund. The fourth day: the sidereal light. The fifth day: the movement of life. The sixth day: the formation of the human being. The seventh day: the first quiet.

The figural times were seven: the time of created nature; of the purgation of guilt; of the election of a people; of the establishment of law; of regal glory; of the prophetic voice; and of the intermediate quiet.

In the New Testament there are similarly seven times: that of conferred grace; of baptism in blood; of the catholic norm; of the law of justice; of the sublime chair; of clear doctrine; and of final peace.

Note the correspondence. The formation of light is the seedbed of the formation of nature, and the formation of nature is the seedbed of the conferring of grace. The time of the division of waters is the seedbed of the cleansing of guilt, of the time of baptism in blood; for as the water is divided from the water, thus purgation is made in the ark, and, according to the blessed Peter, that controls the form of baptism, be it the baptism of blood, water, or fire. The day of fecundation of the earth, the time of the election of a people, and the time of the catholic norm are connected, for the earth germinated seeds, Abraham begat Isaac, Isaac begat Jacob, etc., and the church established the norm of faith, which was then passed down from generation to generation.

The day of sidereal light, the time of statute law, and the time of the norm of justice are related, for the light was divided into sun, moon, and stars; the law was divided according to method of observation, means of enforcement, and mode of living (i.e., moral, judicial, and ceremonial law), and there were canons in the church, then laws redacted into a single corpus through Justinian (what had been the property of the pagans became that of the Christians), and monastic rules like that of the blessed Benedict. The canons correspond to the ceremonial laws, the political to the judicial, and the monastic to the moral.

The day of mobile life, the time of regal glory, and the time of the sublime chair, that is, of the Roman chair. For just as one part of motive life was creeping things and another flying things, so in the church one part is composed of kings and pontiffs, another of subordinates.

The day of the human form, the time of the prophetic voice, the time of clear doctrine in which is found the prophetic life. And it was necessary that in this time there should be one order, that is, a prophetic state similar to the order of Jesus Christ, the head of which should be an angel ascending from the place of the sun, having the seal of the living God and like Christ. And he said he had already come.

The day of sabbath quiet, the time of intermediate quiet, the time of final quiet. The time of intermediate quiet was when the prophets wrote nothing. In Wisdom 18:14 it says: "For while quiet silence enveloped all things, and night in its course was now half gone, your all-powerful word leaped from heaven, from the royal throne," etc. And then there was the silence of the prophets, intermediate between the first quiet and the last. It was also quiet because then the whole world was in the greatest peace, and thus the temple of peace in Rome was closed before the coming of Christ, because in time of war it was always open and closed in time of peace. Thus at that time the doors became rusted.

Thus also at that time the emperor commanded that a census be taken. God placed this in the heart of a pagan so that the Virgin should go to Bethlehem and give birth there at an inn. And God frequently commanded that this and similar things should be included in Scripture, not by accident or chance, but for an important reason and great mystery, and those who failed to consider the matter understood nothing. Night was then in its course, for it was at the height of idolatry.

The time of created nature was from Adam to Noah; that of purging guilt from Noah to Abraham; that of election of a people from Abraham to Moses (for God elected Abraham, not Lot; Isaac, not Ishmael; Jacob, not Esau; and Judah, of whom Christ was born).

The time of established law ran from Moses to Samuel, who anointed one reprobate king and another elect one. The time of regal glory was from David to Hezekiah, in which the transmigration of ten tribes took place. The time of prophetic voice was from Hezekiah strictly speaking (but, loosely speaking, from Uzziah, who was a leper), to Zerubbabel. Under Hezekiah was that great miracle through which the day had thirty-two hours through the sun moving backwards. The time of peace and quiet was from Zerubbabel to Christ.

In the New Testament, the time of conferred grace was from Christ and the apostles, including the death of John, to Pope Clement. The time of baptism in blood was from Clement to Sylvester, because under Clement a great persecution began during which the Jews were sold and expelled from

Jerusalem, while Clement was sent with the people into exile at Chersona in Greece. During that middle time from Clement to Sylvester there were ten great persecutions.

The time of the catholic norm ran from Sylvester to Pope Leo I, under whom the Symbol [the Apostles' Creed] was given. The time of the law of justice was from Leo to Gregory the Doctor. During this period the Justinian laws, the canons, and the canonical monastic rule were established. And blessed Benedict, who prophesied concerning the blessed Gregory and blessed his pregnant mother.

The time of the sublime chair lasted from Gregory to Hadrian. During this time the empire was taken over by the Alemanni, and the empire of Constantinople was divided. Charlemagne was emperor in the western church. Pepin I of the Franks was king of Italy because, unable to bear the attacks of foreign peoples, they made him king. He fought against the king of the Lombards and prevailed.

The time of clear doctrine began in the time of Hadrian; but how long it will last, who can say or has said? It is certain that we are in it, and certain that it will last until the beast ascending from the abyss is cast down, when Babylon will be confounded and cast down, and later peace will be granted. First, however, there must come tribulations, and there no end can be predicted, for no one knows how long that time of great peace will last, for when they say "peace and security" then suddenly destruction will come upon them (1 Thess 5:3).

The seventh time, the time of quiet, begins with the cry of the angel who swore by him who lives forever that time shall be no more, but in the days of the voice of the seventh angel the mystery of God will be consummated (Rev 10:6–7).

But the apostle John comprehends the seven times of the Apocalypse in seven visions, and each of these is sevenfold, and it adds up to the number of the jubilee. These seven times are perhaps closed within the Psalter, where there are three series of fifty.

> *In the following passage, Bonaventure presents a concordance between Old Testament and New Testament history, covering the same ground already explored, but often mentioning different events. We will pick up the story at the birth of the sixth time.*

Note the correspondence between figural and salvific time. In the sixth time three things occurred: brilliance of victory, of doctrine, and of the prophetic life. Brilliance of victory was seen when Sennacherib came against Jerusalem and the angel of the Lord slew 185,000. Moreover, Hezekiah was healed in a way that defied nature, and the sun traveled backward. In similar fashion, in the time of Hadrian, victory was achieved by Charles, who miraculously achieved triumphs as if he had been an angel sent by the Lord, and the sun, that is, the tide of tribulation, retreated. Peace was achieved in the church, and later archbishops, bishops, and monasteries were created. In this time there was clarity of doctrine, because Charles called in clerics and wrote books including Bibles in Saint Denis as well as many other places. People began to read and study philosophy. [The emperor] also increased the number of people in religious communities.

In this time, it was fitting that through an order[44] there should be prophetic life. This time was twofold, however, for just as in the passion of the Lord there was light, then darkness, then light again, so it is necessary that in the first place there should be the light of doctrine, and Josiah should succeed Hezekiah, after which the Jews suffered tribulation through captivity. For it is necessary that one prince, a zealous defender of the church, should arise, one who either will be or already has been (and he added, "Would that he had not already been"), after which must come the darkness of tribulation. In this time, similarly, Charles exalted the church, then his successors opposed it. In the time of Henry IV there were two popes; and there were also two in the time of Frederick the Great. And it is certain that one of them wished to exterminate the church; but the angel ascending from the place of the sun called out to the four angels, "Do not harm the land and sea until we have sealed the servants of our God on their foreheads" (Rev 7:2). Hence the tribulation of the church continues. And it was said to the angel of Philadelphia, who is the sixth, "Thus says the holy and true one who has the key of David, who opens and no one closes, who closes and no one opens: I know your works, for behold, I have placed an open door before you" (Rev 3:7). And he said that now knowledge of Scripture or revelation or the key of David should be given to a person or to a multitude; and I believe more to a multitude.

We know these things were accomplished in the seventh time: rebuilding of the temple, restoration of the city, and peace. Similarly in the future seventh time there will be repair of the divine cultus and rebuilding of the city. Then will be fulfilled the prophecy of Ezekiel, when the city will descend from heaven, not indeed that which is above but that which is below, that

---

44. Or "through order," that is, in orderly fashion.

is, the church militant conformed to the church triumphant insofar as is possible in her pilgrim state. Then there will be a building of the city and a restoration of it as it was in the beginning. And then there will be peace. How long that peace will last, however, God knows.

Therefore, since there are seven times in both the Old Testament and the New, and each is threefold in the sense that there are three things in each, the sevenfold series multiplied twice by three gives us forty-two, corresponding to the forty-two stages through which the promised land is reached (Num 33:1). And thus it is clear how Scripture describes the succession of times. And all these things are not accidental and left to chance, but there is instead a marvelous light in them and many spiritual meanings.

EARLY OLIVI

When Bonaventure delivered his *Collationes in hexaemeron* at Paris in 1273, he spoke to a crowd of 160 friars in addition to those in the Paris Franciscan community. Here we are interested in just one, Petrus Iohannis Olivi. We know that Olivi was at Paris in the later 1260s; that he heard Bonaventure speak at the 1266 general chapter; that he also heard Bonaventure deliver the *Collationes de septem donis Spiritus sancti* in 1268; and that he was exposed sufficiently to Bonaventure to provide a striking description of the latter's physical weaknesses, a passage that contains the words "as I myself often heard him confess."[1]

There is no evidence that he was still present in Paris for the *Collationes in hexaemeron*, nor is there any that he was not. Olivi ran afoul of Bonaventure's successor as minister general, Jerome of Ascoli, at some point after the latter became minister general in 1274, and what little we know of the matter suggests that by then Olivi had returned to southern France and was teaching there. He could have been one of the 160 brothers who were given permission to go and hear the *Collationes*; but he would not have had to be there to know what Bonaventure said. If, over seven centuries later, we can account for at least three people who took notes, there were probably more who did so, and Olivi could have found his way to a copy.

Even if Olivi did not read the *Collationes*, he was very much aware of the variations they played on the Revelation commentary as seen in the stan-

---

1. See Burr, *Olivi's Peaceable Kingdom* (Philadelphia: University of Pennsylvania Press, 1993), 64.

dard Franciscan Parisian model. In their commentaries, Franciscan authors had placed themselves in the fifth period of church history at the latest. In the *Collationes*, Bonaventure places himself in the sixth. In fact, he seems to feel that the sixth period began with Charlemagne. The commentaries had identified the sixth period with the future advent of Antichrist. So does Bonaventure in the *Collationes*, but he also identifies it with a time of clear doctrine resulting from advancement of learning and peace within the church. Thus the sixth age represents both great advances and great tribulations.

If the sixth period began around the time of Charlemagne, as the *Collationes* suggests, it includes Francis. Thus the Bonaventuran pattern provides room for Francis to act as an important bulwark against temptation and as a guide into the final age. Bonaventure tells us that some of the evil princes who succeeded Charlemagne "wished to destroy the church, but the angel ascending from the place of the sun cried to the four angels, 'Do not harm the earth and sea until we seal the servants of our God on their foreheads.'" Thus we have a sixth period that actually allows Francis to act as the angel of Revelation 7:2 and to shape salvation history in the process.

It also allows Francis to act as the angel of Revelation 21:10: "He took me up in the spirit to a great high mountain and showed me the holy city, Jerusalem." Previous Franciscan Revelation commentaries provided no room for a new Jerusalem in the seventh period, a contemplative church born within the church militant. In the *Collationes* there is such a space. The sixth and seventh periods can be seen as a continuous process involving both greater understanding of the Bible and the raptures of mystical contemplation.

All this shaped Olivi's Revelation commentary, but not immediately. If Olivi had proceeded directly from a reading of the *Collationes* to his Apocalypse commentary, he might have produced a different commentary. As it happened, a young and enthusiastic Olivi, fresh from accompanying his provincial minister on a successful trip to Italy connected with the publication of the papal bull *Exit qui seminat*, began his exegetical career in Narbonne, then Montpellier, with a string of Old Testament and Gospel commentaries stretching from around 1279 until 1283, the year he was censured by a committee of Parisian scholars and deprived not only of his works but also of his teaching career. He was back teaching, this time not in southern France but in Florence, by 1288, but had to explain himself again in the early 1290s. By 1297, the year he probably finished the Revelation commentary and certainly the year before he died, he had every reason to take seriously the alternation of progress and tribulation that characterizes the sixth period as portrayed in Bonaventure's *Collationes*. He had been living it since 1279. In fact, earlier in the 1270s he had already been disciplined by Jerome of Ascoli and had been forced to burn at least one of his writings.

If we ask what Olivi's problems were about, the most obvious answer is that they were about any number of things. The trouble with Jerome of Ascoli partly concerned Olivi's view of the Virgin Mary, and the censure of 1283 was about a whole list of philosophical and theological issues. More and more, however, one could characterize Olivi's problems as centering around a split in the order over what came to be known as *usus pauper*, living poor. To what extent was it demanded by the Franciscan vow? There was not one obvious answer to this question. In fact, the number of possible answers was not even limited to two. Some friars thought the range of activities performed by the order, not to mention the range of contexts in which they were performed and the range of people performing them, demanded substantial flexibility when it came to defining the parameters of acceptable Franciscan behavior; and thus, while lack of ownership could be included in the vow, *usus pauper* could not. Others felt that those parameters had been set by primitive Franciscanism. Olivi was actually somewhere in the middle. He recognized that friars in his time had been given a wider range of responsibilities than the early Franciscans had shouldered and that they needed a wider range of educational opportunities, living conditions, etc., to fulfill them; yet he remained convinced that there were limits to the flexibility offered, and his early writings show him engaged in an attempt to contrive realistic rules of engagement.[2]

Oddly enough, one subject almost completely ignored in Olivi's early troubles was his apocalyptic thought. His early Bible commentaries were heavily apocalyptic, yet the commission that censured him shows no sign of even having read them. We will return to this matter at the end of the chapter.

This is, after all, a book about Revelation commentaries; yet it is important to say a few words about Olivi's early exegesis. Many (in fact most) of the characteristically Olivian ideas we identify with his Revelation commentary already appear in his early burst of scholarship between 1279 and 1283. If these works teach us anything, they teach us that Olivi's sense of the Bible allowed him to approach a wide variety of books and discover within them the same apocalyptic scenario he found in the Revelation commentary, although the route taken in reaching it was strikingly different.

---

2. On this problem see my *Olivi and Franciscan Poverty* (Philadelphia: University of Pennsylvania Press, 1989) and *The Spiritual Franciscans* (University Park: Pennsylvania State University Press, 2001).

This is an important point to make at least once in a book on Apocalypse commentaries. We should acknowledge at some point that an author like Olivi tended to see the entire corpus of the Bible as pointing to an apocalyptic scenario, not just the book of Revelation. Everything pointed to Christ and, to some extent, to the final times. And an author like Olivi, who saw the Bible in terms of a strong theology of history, saw its various books as related *through* that theology of history. Everything had apocalyptic significance, just as everything had christological significance. Many others undoubtedly thought the same, but we are particularly apt to notice it in Olivi because of the sheer number of commentaries by him that have survived and their strongly *heilsgeschichtliche* orientation.

Another point should be made, if only in passing. By the time Olivi arrived in Paris, Franciscan theological education was, by earlier standards, a complex affair. The students progressed through well-defined levels, and two levels of faculty, bachelors and masters, were responsible for teaching them in two different ways. By that time scholars were offering, not only two different levels of instruction (cursory commentaries on the Bible by bachelors and longer, more involved commentaries by masters) but a variety of works to aid in producing commentaries of greater precision and complexity. All of this is, of course, related to the development of the *Glossa ordinaria*, but by Olivi's time it had gone well beyond the *Glossa* and beyond the other reference works at scholars' disposal in the time of Hugh of Saint Cher. William de la Mare, a fellow Franciscan, contributed to a more accurate biblical text, while Thomas Aquinas furnished (in what would be termed the *Catena aurea*) an impressive collection of patristic and early medieval quotations that would provide others with the opportunity for one-stop shopping when it came to identifying who had said what about the text of the Bible and where.[3] These works not only aided in correcting divergent readings within the Latin text; they made some contribution to allowing a comparison with the Hebrew and Greek text and with the Septuagint translation and the Septuagint translated into Latin, which also circulated. All of this contributed to a more confident grammatical and linguistic analysis of the text; and during this period an increasing tendency to cite books of the Bible by chapter and sometimes even more precisely than that made it easier to hunt down references.

3. On Olivi and the *Catena aurea* see Louis-J. Bataillon, "Olivi utilisateur de la *Catena aurea de Thomas d'Aquin*," in *Pierre de Jean Olivi (1248–1298)*, Pensé scolastique, dissidence spirituelle et société (Paris: J. Vrin, 1999), 115–20.

Education in that time also contributed to a greater interest in classical rhetorical techniques. Olivi manages to spot synecdoche in Hosea 9:7 and uses other terms confidently elsewhere. (Notice, in what follows, his strategic uses of the word "antonomastically," especially in the later reading from the Isaiah commentary.)

Thirteenth-century exegetes also profited from historical and archeological studies. Olivi's gospel commentaries display a lively interest in the concrete geographical, political, and social stage on which the gospel events were played out. Gilbert Dahan admiringly notes that "his commentaries have a very 'modern' allure and could provide a good historical introduction to a study of the prophets."[4]

Christ's Three Advents

The first two Olivian commentaries we know of are those on Isaiah and Matthew. Olivi apparently delivered them simultaneously, probably around 1279–1281. As far as he is concerned, the Isaiah commentary is largely about what Olivi describes as Christ's three advents in the flesh, the spirit, and judgment. There the idea works as one element in a general statement concerning the nature of prophecy. Olivi already knows Joachim of Fiore by this point, and later in the Revelation commentary he will make extended use of Joachim's reading of history in terms of the three Joachite ages of Father, Son, and Holy Spirit. The three advents are both like and unlike Joachim's three ages. They divide Christian history into two parts, with Christ's first advent in the flesh roughly analogous to Joachim's age of the Son and Christ's second advent in the spirit concomitant with the age of the Holy Spirit.

This is the first commentary in which we hear of the three advents; yet at that time Olivi was hardly presenting a new idea. He had alluded to it earlier in the eighth of his *Questions on Evangelical Perfection*.

> Just as during Christ's first advent John was elected not only a prophet but more than a prophet, and none before him among the saints more fully heralded the person of Christ in the world, so before Christ's second

4. Gilbert Dahan, "L'Exégèse des livres prophétiques chez Pierre de Jean Olieu," in *Pierre de Jean Olivi (1248–1298)*, 99. Much of the preceding paragraph follows Dahan's excellent article. For fuller treatment, see his *L'Exégèse chrétienne de la Bible en Occident médiéval, XIIe–XIVe siècle* (Paris: Editions du Cerf, 2008).

advent another by the same name was elected not only a saint but more than a saint, and none of the saints before him more fully introduced and renewed the life of Christ in the world.[5]

Thus we have two of the three advents Olivi would refer to throughout the rest of his life, the third being Christ's advent in the final judgment. Notice that he refers to the first and second advents here so casually as to suggest that he knows his readers will understand what he's talking about. Note too that the Olivian three advents are more unambiguously christocentric than the Joachite three ages. And note finally that he already sees Francis, here introduced under the name "John," as marking the beginning of Christ's second advent.

In question eight he also speaks in terms of the seven periods of church history used not only by Joachim but also by any number of exegetes in Olivi's time, including Olivi himself. For Olivi the sixth period of church history marks the transition to the period of Christ's advent in the spirit. Thus, seen from the Joachite perspective, the age of the Holy Spirit begins to supplant that of the Son in the sixth period, although it will not be fully realized until the seventh. The sixth and seventh periods are also more or less equivalent to Christ's advent in the spirit. In short, Olivi, like Bonaventure and unlike most other thirteenth-century exegetes, places both Francis and himself in the sixth period, as we have seen.

In his commentary on Isaiah, Olivi explains that Isaiah deals with "the ultimate or last things to be fulfilled in humanity and especially in God's people during the final times."[6] Shortly thereafter, he tells us that Isaiah saw "the ultimate or final things to be done around the time of the captivity imposed by the Assyrians and Chaldeans; around the time of the captivity imposed by the Romans; around the time of the captivity or tribulation imposed through Antichrist; and around the time of the examination carried out through God's final and universal judgment." These, he says, "are the four ultimate or final things with which the prophets before the Babylonian captivity principally concerned themselves. And this is why they say in many places that their prophecies will be fulfilled in the final days."[7]

5. Published as *Das Heil der Armen und das Verderben der Reichen*, ed. Johannes Schlageter (Werl/Westfalen: Dietrich Coelde-Verlag, 1989), 148. (Question eight is hereafter cited as Q. 8.) This "another by the same name" is obviously Francis.

6. *Super Isaiam* (hereafter *SI*), in *Peter of John Olivi on the Bible*, ed. David Flood (St. Bonaventure, NY: Franciscan Institute, 1997), 162.

7. *SI*, 165–66.

So we have a portrayal of the prophets as predicting what would happen in their own time plus what would happen in each of the three times associated with Christ's three advents. Here we see the negative aspect of each advent, the tribulation associated with it, but Olivi is equally capable of highlighting the positive aspect. One might wonder what is "final" about these periods. One answer is that with each advent a stage of Judeo-Christian history dies away and is replaced by something that represents a step forward. Viewed from this perspective, Christian history is generally progressive, despite periods of backsliding.

How does Isaiah go about presenting his progressive history? Generally speaking, he talks about his own Old Testament world and in the process tells us about all three advents at the same time. In describing one, he describes all. Thus prophecy becomes a symbol of the Trinity, three in one.[8]

Like the Trinity, each of the three advents has its own particular properties but shares common features. The particular properties are important, underlining the fact that not every prophetic passage in Isaiah applies equally to each of the three major historical moments. The word "equally" is important here. Every word is to some extent applicable to all three advents; yet Olivi sees some passages as aimed particularly at one and some at another. Thus when Isaiah says, "Behold, a virgin will conceive" (Isa 9:6), Olivi decides he is speaking particularly of Christ's first advent; but when he says, "Behold, I will create new heavens and a new earth" (Isa 65:17), he is referring primarily to the time of the final judgment.[9]

Olivi locates himself in the period of transition between the Joachite second and third ages of world history, the ages of Son and Holy Spirit or, as Olivi prefers to state it in the Isaiah commentary, Christ's advents in the flesh and in the spirit. Thus he sees his time as one of remarkable spiritual gifts, but he also expects that in the near future Christendom will experience an intense period of tribulation. He sees Francis and his order as harbingers of the second advent, but he places Antichrist in the future.

Why does Olivi tend at this point to state his apocalyptic expectations in the form of three advents rather than the Joachite three ages? There is no satisfactory answer to this question; yet one might wonder if it is related to his reading (and perhaps even his hearing) of Bonaventure's *Collationes in hexaemeron*. In either case he would have been astute enough to notice that Bonaventure was open to the Joachite system of double sevens but was less

8. *SI*, 168.
9. *SI*, 170.

comfortable with the three ages. Olivi continued to use the Joachite threefold structure throughout his life, but he may have seen himself as "laundering" it by combining it with the idea of Christ's three advents. Or perhaps that explanation leans too heavily on its defensive function. It is hard to read the Isaiah commentary without recognizing how well the three advents work for Olivi in that context.

Olivi also felt he discovered the three advents in the Matthew commentary. If Christ was really king of the prophets, then it seemed logical that Christ would want to employ the text of Matthew to predict these advents in much the same way Isaiah had. Of course, the word "predict" would have a slightly different valence than in the case of the first advent, since Christ had already arrived; but the other two advents still lay in the future. Even the first would profit from interpretation and, being still in process, was open to prediction in its latter stages.

Of all the passages that could be used to illustrate the parallel between the Isaiah and Matthew commentaries, none is more interesting than Olivi's handling of Matthew 24, the "little apocalypse," a moment when Christ unambiguously plays the role of prophet. Jesus's disciples invite him to look at the temple, and Jesus observes that it is due to be destroyed. Later some of the disciples ask him to say more, and in his reply "Christ touches on several different periods in mixed fashion, especially three: the time of the Jewish captivity at the hands of the Romans or the demons, when they killed Christ and were ejected from the true cultus; the time of Antichrist; and the time of final judgment." In each of these periods we see four things occurring: falsehood and seduction; strife and temporal upset; persecution and martyrdom of Christ's disciples; and diffusion of the gospel throughout the world.[10] Christ's reference to the abomination of desolation (Matt 24:15) shows the magnitude of this tribulation, and Matthew 24:23–27 warns the disciples not to be fooled by those who preach false Christs and prophets. When the true Christ returns, his legitimacy will be clear to all and especially to the elect.[11] Thus,

> Just as what the prophets said about the Babylonian captivity referred as well to three other captivities pertaining to the time of Christ, and what they said about the liberation of God's people from the Babylonian captiv-

---

10. *Super Matthaeum* (*SM*), ch. 24, as found in Paris, BNF cod. lat. 15588, 113rb-va, transcribed by my former student Sarah Pucciarelli. Pucciarelli's text, while described as a transcription of the Paris manuscript, is based upon several manuscripts.

11. *SM*, ch. 24, 113va.

ity referred to the three liberations to be completed in the times of grace and then eternal glory, so Christ, in speaking of the captivity under the Romans that would occur around his own time, also included two other captivities in prophetic manner.[12]

Here again Olivi emphasizes that, although everything said can be applied to all periods, specific elements can be expected to pertain to one period more than another. For example, what is said about the multitude of pseudo-Christians and pseudo-prophets, the danger of even the elect falling into error, and the cooling of love applies more particularly to the time of Antichrist.[13]

The Mystical Antichrist

Matthew 24 proves important, not only for Olivi's view of the three advents, but also as the moment when he meets the mystical Antichrist, although

12. *SM*, ch. 24, 113va: "Ad intellegentiam autem huius partis sciendum quod sicut prophetae sub captivitate Babylonica tres alias captivitates includunt ad tempus Christi spectantes—et consimiliter sub liberatione populi Dei de captivitate Babylonica tres liberationes electorum includunt complendas in tempore gratiae et tandem gloriae aeternae—sic Christus in captivitate Romanorum circa suum tempus fienda duas alias sequentes more prophetico comprehendit. Quod quidem sicut in prophetis monstratum est fieri potuit quia sic Deus providit eas impleri debere conformiter, quod una potuit per alteram et sub altera designari."

13. *SM*, ch. 24, 113va–vb: "Ut autem omnes quodammodo innotescerent et quodammodo se invicem occultarent, sic in ceteris locis ponuntur aliqua magis proprie spectantia ad unam et alibi magis specantia ad aliam quod, cum sermo contexitur, continuatur ac si de una sola ageretur. Cuius exemplum aliquando datum est in pictura regiae imaginis aut intrica vel textura cordulae filorum diversi coloris in quo modo apparet filum album, modo viride, modo rubeum, modo hyacinthinum. Ita quod secundum diversos situs sub una textura mutuo se revelant et mutuo se occultant, sic ergo in prophetis totus textus verborum potest duci ad quamlibet partium praedictarum, quamvis quaedam ad certa tempora magis proprie dirigantur et ad quaedam minus proprie, sic et in proposito fieri potest, ut verbi gratia. Illa quae hic dicuntur de multitudine pseudochristianorum et pseudoprophetarum et de prodigiis eorum et de periculo erroris in electos et de refrigescentia caritatis magis proprie respiciunt tempora Antichristi. Quae vero de obscuratione solis et lunae et de adventu Christi in maiestate et de congregatione electorum ad eum per angelos fienda tanguntur, magis proprie respiciunt tempus extremi iudicii. Quae vero de destructione Ierusalem et de persecutione Apostolorum et de praedicatione Evangelii per orbem universum dicuntur, magis proprie respiciunt primum tempus. Quaedam vero sunt ibi quae satis communiter praedictis temporibus aptari possunt, utpote quod praeeunt proelia et pestilentiae et fames et quod abominatio desolationis ponitur in loco sancto."

without yet realizing it.[14] Some background is necessary. If we look at what Olivi has to say in the eighth of the *Quaestiones de perfectione evangelica* (Questions on Evangelical Perfection), we will find something similar in most respects to what others said in the thirteenth century. When we ask where thirteenth-century exegetes normally thought they stood within the seven periods of church history, we discover (as we have seen) that they normally placed themselves in the fifth, which they identified with those who prepared the way for Antichrist.[15] They could look outside the church for those precursors, noting Jews, Muslims, and Mongols; but they could also look within, mentioning heretics and *prelati*. Antichrist would come in the sixth period.

We have seen that Olivi differs from this standard exegetical model in placing himself within the transition to the sixth period and in seeing the near future as characterized not only by the arrival of Antichrist but also by what Olivi describes in Joachite terms as the dawning age of the Holy Spirit or, in his own terms, Christ's second advent in the spirit. Thus from Olivi's perspective the greatest temptation of history, the battle between Christ and Antichrist, is about to occur and will heavily involve "the life of Christ" recently revived by Francis, which Olivi identifies with evangelical poverty. In question eight, Olivi emphasizes that placing an excessive value on wealth is "the door to the sect of Antichrist as well as the entire Jewish and Muslim error." If we deny that the poverty chosen by the Franciscan order is better than having possessions either individually or in common, "then it follows that Christ was not the Christ promised by the Law and the prophets," and we are left waiting with the Jews for a messiah still to come.[16] Thus an error concerning the *life* of Christ implies an error concerning the *person* of Christ. There is more to the temptation of Antichrist than error about wealth and poverty, of course. Olivi has heard Bonaventure's *Collationes de septem donis Spiritus Sancti* and thus is also concerned about the dangers of an Islamicized Aristotelian philosophy; but he conceives it in such a way that he can work it, too, into the temptation of Antichrist as another overvaluation of worldly achievement.

Yet in question eight, when Olivi feels called upon to explain the route by which the church will arrive at Antichrist's door, he tells us that "divine providence permitted the church of the gentiles to be led into decline toward

---

14. I address this question in greater detail in "Olivi, Christ's Three Advents, and the Double Antichrist," *Franciscan Studies* 74 (2016): 15–40.

15. See Burr, *Olivi's Peaceable Kingdom*, 44–54; Burr, "The Antichrist and the Jews in Four Thirteenth-Century Apocalypse Commentaries," in *Friars and Jews in the Middle Ages and Renaissance* (Leiden: Brill, 2004), 23–38.

16. Q. 8, 105.

the end of the fifth period so that all but a few would err against Christ in the time of Antichrist."[17] This seems not all that different from what one finds in other thirteenth-century exegetes who speak of "the precursors of Antichrist," those who paved the way for him. It is essentially what we find in the Revelation commentary Alain Boureau assigns to Bonaventure.

In both the Isaiah and Matthew commentaries we see Olivi moving slowly toward a new way of formulating the matter. The Isaiah commentary is only marginally relevant. At one point Olivi asks himself how we should interpret the word "idol" in Isaiah. He remarks that "the word 'idol' can mystically [*mistice*] be taken, first, for heresy . . . ; second, for avarice . . . ; third, for anything loved more than God . . . ; fourth, for a fraudulent pastor or priest who has merely the appearance of a pastor and yet is honored by the people as if he were God, and in this way it is taken antonomastically for Antichrist . . . ; and fifth, for any concept or emotion that is false and perverse." Olivi then advises us that we should take the word "idol" literally when applying it to the first time; take it to mean "heresy" for the second time; and, for the third time, take it for "temporals, the cult of temporals, and Antichrist along with the fictitious pastors *with him and before him*."[18] It is a puzzling passage if we assume that by the three times he means the three advents, but not if we take "the first time" as the period Isaiah is living in and directly speaking about (i.e., his specific historical context) and assume that the second and third times actually refer to Christ's first and second advents conceived as periods. We are left wondering why he pays no attention to the third advent, but he occasionally does not.

After all, the third advent in judgment will occur at the fringe of historical time. What really matters to a denizen of the thirteenth century is the transition from Christ's first advent to his second, which is already occurring in the thirteenth century and will continue to occur in the fourteenth, as well as the Old and New Testament symbolism foreshadowing those two advents. But notice the way Olivi completes this thought. He is suggesting that the passage refers mystically (*mistice*) to Antichrist, and we should also note that it refers not only to Antichrist but to "fictitious pastors with him *and before him*." Olivi has edged beyond the standard "precursors of Antichrist" and is heading in the direction of the mystical Antichrist, though only tentatively. All of this is still vaguely stated. In fact, if we were to investigate this passage further, we would

17. Q. 8, 160.

18. *SI*, 212. The page number is misleading. The volume begins with an edition of five *principia*. The text of the Isaiah commentary begins on p. 162 and continues to p. 345.

find that Olivi is using the words "literal" and "mystical" here in a different way than will be the case later, but fortunately we need not go there at the moment.

The real leap forward comes in chapter 24 of the Matthew commentary. Olivi commented on Isaiah and Matthew simultaneously but commented briefly on Isaiah and at length on Matthew; so his exegesis of Matthew 24 may have been composed well after he wrote the passage just cited from the Isaiah commentary. Perhaps in the meantime he had been thinking more about those precursors of Antichrist.

In any case, here, as in the Isaiah commentary, he proceeds on the assumption that just as the Old Testament prophets, in describing the Babylonian captivity and its end, also predicted three other captivities and liberations, which we can summarize as three tribulations eventuating in three liberations (i.e., the three advents of Christ), so Christ, the head of all prophets, in describing the captivity under the Romans also describes two others to follow.

Here again Olivi warns us not to expect that we will be able to apply everything Christ says equally to all of the three periods.[19] Nor does Christ emphasize the same moments in all the Gospels. In Luke he more directly refers to the temporal captivity of the Jews by the Romans, whereas in Mark and Matthew he speaks more directly to later events; yet, whatever his emphasis might be in different gospels, all of his prophecy is true of all three major advents.[20] In the case of Matthew 24, Christ's words are

more properly true of the second time—that is, the time of Antichrist—except for what is said there about the destruction of Jerusalem and the day of judgment; although, I think, those words too will then be fulfilled doubly and in a double sense: that is, first mystically [*mistice*] and, as it were, through a certain conformity with the time of Christ's death when he is condemned by the pseudo-scribes and pseudo-pontiffs; then in the second place literally and openly as it were, according to the typology seen in Simon Magus, who claimed to be the son of God, and in Nero, who first persecuted the martyrs, as the apostle implies in hidden fashion in 2 Thessalonians 2[:3–12]. The rest will be easier to apply, for after the tribulation in those days the gospel will be preached throughout the world and then the end of the world will come.[21]

19. *SM*, ch. 24, 113va.
20. *SM*, ch. 24, 114va.
21. *SM*, ch. 24, 113vb. Note the absolute centrality of the life-person distinction in Olivi's thought.

Thus we have to contend with both Isaiah and Matthew, each of which will address all three advents even while emphasizing some parts of the story at the expense of others; yet we also have to contend with the existence of three Synoptic Gospels, which do the same.

Nor is that all the reader has to think about. Shortly thereafter, Olivi further complicates the problem by asking what Christ has *not* told us that we might have wished to hear. The answer is that we would have profited from hearing about

> the final temptation of the church preceding the temptation of Antichrist and disposing to it (for he could not make himself adored by the church if the church was not already seduced and blinded). It must be said that the first temptation will be aimed at blinding carnal Christians under the disguise of truth and true Christian faith rather than illuminating them. That [temptation] which is properly of Antichrist will be to punish those who are blinded and to illuminate those who will convert after his death, as well as to effect the perfect coronation of all who are martyred under him. This one [i.e., that temptation properly belonging to Antichrist] is to be preached openly, while that one [i.e., the first one] will be preached only mystically and in a hidden manner [*mistice et occulte*]. Whoever does not want to err in the second should watch out for the first, understanding, that is, the nature of that "abomination sitting in God's temple" in order to condemn the life of Christ just as Caiaphas condemned the person of Christ.[22]

Thus the Antichrist's role is less to seduce carnal Christians than to punish them for already having yielded to seduction. Olivi says the same thing in his Job commentary, which was probably first written during the same period, his next Old Testament commentary after he finished the Isaiah commentary.[23] Notice, however, that the resulting tribulation can have positive functions, leading to conversion and, in those who have resisted temptation, to the crown of martyrdom.

Some scholars have wondered whether, in using terms like *misticus* and *mistice*, Olivi is speaking as an exegete, referring to the mystical sense of Scripture. To confirm that much we should be able to look at the way he uses

22. *SM*, ch. 24, 115ra.

23. *Postilla super Iob* (Turnhout: Brepols, 2015), 526. We will return to the dating problem later.

the words *literalis* and *misticus* in his other commentaries. Unfortunately, it is not that simple. At this stage in the evolution of his terminology there may be some degree of slippage. The broad lines of his development were beautifully summarized by Gilbert Dahan in 1998.[24] Dahan notes Olivi's tendency to streamline exegesis, paying less attention to hermeneutical patterns like the four senses of Scripture while concentrating instead on the role of metaphor on the one hand and historical narrative on the other. He is obviously correct. The readings for this chapter make that much very clear; yet it remains true that Olivi inherited a rich, complex exegetical terminology and hated to throw it away completely. A term like "analogical" remained useful to him, and even at the end of his life in the Revelation commentary he was still inclined to use it in describing an image that could refer to Christ or the church.

And the reverse is true. In the early commentaries, as Olivi developed an exegetical vocabulary he found comfortable, he occasionally found himself using the same terms in what seem to be contradictory ways. We have already noted that in the passage cited earlier, where he explains what the word "idol" can mean when taken mystically as opposed to what it means when taken literally, the literal/mystical poles seem to be reversed from what we find in other passages, where he sees Christ's three advents as the literal meaning of Isaiah's words, or perhaps even in the case of the double sense of Antichrist in which what is first revealed mystically is then revealed openly. We are left wondering whether all these passages really fit together. In fact, they can be made to do so, but it would require more careful attention to the meaning of terms like *mistice* than Olivi feels required to grant them at this stage.[25]

Nevertheless, on the whole Olivi makes sense. When he applies terms like "mystically" and "openly" to the Antichrist, he certainly goes a long way

---

24. Dahan, "L'Exégèse des livres prophétiques chez Pierre de Jean Olieu," 91–114. Olivi's exegetical terminology and Dahan's comments on it are examined in my article "Young Olivi as Exegete," awaiting publication in *Percorsi di esegesi antica e medievale*.

25. I have lavished a great deal of attention on the word "mystical." In a remarkably perceptive article, Sylvain Piron pays equal attention to the word "literal," noting in particular Olivi's tendency to use the comparative, *literalior*. "Literalior: L'Englobement de Spirituel dans le litéral selon Pierre de Jean Olivi," *Annali du scienze religiose* 7 (2014): 179–95. I have found the same tendency in the early commentaries. It seems a natural choice for a man who sees prophecy as having three literal meanings, often weighted particularly toward one of the three. Piron emphasizes the rarity of the word in commentaries by other authors.

toward doing so, invoking the notion of the Antichrist as working first se-cretly and then openly.[26] Thus we have a *mysticus/literalis* contrast and a hid-den/open contrast; but the two stages described also imply an inside/outside contrast. Caiaphas and his henchmen, who called for Christ's death in his first advent, were like Antichrist working *mystice et occulte* in the time of the second advent inasmuch as they were all working inside the Jewish religion, claiming to defend it while actually corrupting it; while Simon Magus and Nero were like Antichrist working openly outside and against Christianity. One group is pseudo-Christian, the other anti-Christian.

One more contrast should be mentioned: crime/punishment, an idea that grows directly out of the destruction of Jerusalem, which serves as a visual symbol underlining God's exclusion of the Jews after their rejection of Christ. That is the area Olivi is exploring when he suggests that the An-tichrist's role is less to seduce carnal Christians than to punish them for already having yielded to seduction. The whole pattern fits together neatly like a complex puzzle. A powerful temptation works in a hidden manner (*mistice et occulte*) *within the faith* to corrupt it, then those who succumb are punished by the Antichrist working *outside the faith* in an attack openly aimed at the religion itself. Of course, this contrast is complicated by the fact that during the first advent the faith in question is first Judaism and then Christianity, and further complicated by the fact that Olivi assigns to the resultant tribulation a variety of functions, some of them salvific; yet that, too, can be incorporated into the puzzle.

Thus, in expositing Matthew 24, Olivi finally sees how the events of Christ's first advent, particularly his crucifixion and the Roman destruction of Jerusalem, can be projected upon Christ's second advent. Terminologi-cally, he still has not progressed all that far beyond those in the thirteenth century who spoke of the "predecessors of Antichrist"; yet the model of Christ's first advent is pushing him toward a more distinctive formulation for the second.

He arrives there in his commentary on John, the next gospel he lec-tures on. There he announces that "according to some people, just as the

---

26. In "Antichrists and Antichrist in Joachim of Fiore," *Speculum* 60 (1985): 564, speak-ing of Joachim's Revelation commentary, Robert Lerner says, "Just as Christ first came 'hid-denly' but will come to Judgment openly, so Satan will first send the great Antichrist to delude the faithful by trickery and then send Gog with his terrible legions to persecute them openly." The dynamics in Olivi's case are different, of course. In the Matthew commentary, Olivi is developing a contrast between the great Antichrist and what he will eventually label as the mystical Antichrist; yet he will eventually get around to Gog.

synagogue was built over forty-two generations, that is, from Abraham to Christ, thus some believe that the church progressing from Christ to the mystical Antichrist will last for forty-two generations of thirty years with a turbulent tail of three and a half years added."[27] Presumably the "turbulent tail" (and in the Revelation commentary it will be apparent that Olivi has a real tail in mind, that of the dragon) represents the tribulation under the Antichrist taken in the normal sense. Elsewhere in the commentary he notes that Christ's words "If someone else comes in his name you will accept him" refer especially to "the principal Antichrist."[28] So here, presumably in his 1281–1282 teaching, he has arrived at the point where he can distinguish between "spiritual Antichrist" and "principal Antichrist," but that still does not guarantee that he sees the former as an individual. If we see the distinction between spiritual and principal Antichrist as developing out of the thirteenth-century tendency (seen in *Vox domini* and elsewhere) to portray the fifth period as that of the "precursors of Antichrist" preparing the way for the sixth period, that of Antichrist, then one could imagine him thinking of the mystical Antichrist either as an individual or as a group; or, given what we have said so far, it might even seem possible to describe the mystical Antichrist as a process.

One other gospel commentary, that on Luke, bears mention, because even in the Matthew commentary Olivi is ready to see Christ as coordinating his messages in such a way as to speak to slightly different issues in different gospels. Thus in interpreting the tribulations predicted in Matthew 24 he observes that "the words of Luke deal more directly with the temporal captivity of the Jews carried out by the Romans, while the words of Matthew and Mark bear more directly upon the evils to occur at the end of time. And I think, just as Christ tempered his words to fit each time, so the Spirit caused one evangelist to aim his words more directly at one time and another to another, yet all spoke to all times."[29] This is a remarkable suggestion. It bypasses all the theories since proposed by modern textual scholarship and explains variants in the Gospels as the result of the Holy Spirit adjusting individual gospels to address all three advents.

Fortunato Iozelli, the editor of Olivi's Luke commentary, rightly notes that the present state of scholarship makes it impossible to say more about the date of Olivi's Luke commentary than that it was written sometime be-

27. MS Florence Bibl. Laur. Plut. 10 Dext 8 (hereafter Comm. John) 24ra.
28. Comm. John, 40vb.
29. *SM*, ch. 24, 114va.

tween 1279 and 1295.[30] Nevertheless, it is worth remembering that, when Olivi was delivering the Matthew commentary, he could hardly have expected to be censured in 1283 and barred from teaching for the next five years. Thus one can imagine him thinking seriously about Luke even as he lectured on Matthew, asking himself where the Holy Spirit actually aimed Christ's words in each; but did he hold on to those thoughts? When he returned to teaching after his rehabilitation, did he return to the interpretive scheme he had tentatively planned for Luke and Mark before 1283?

When we look for an extended statement on the three advents in the Luke commentary, something that matches the material in the Matthew commentary, we might particularly look at his exegesis of Luke 17 and 21. Luke 17 might initially seem promising because it, too, contains Jesus's comment beginning, "In the days of Noah" (Luke 17:36), which appears in the Matthew commentary and to which we will turn in a moment. Olivi begins his exegesis of the passage in Luke by noting that, since Christ already has said a great deal about his first advent, he will now turn to his second advent, and will begin by telling them not to expect it anytime soon. In fact, none of the disciples will still be alive when it occurs.

What follows is brief but centered on the second advent. In the days of Antichrist, many will claim to see Christ's advent or even to be Christ, but the elect will need to flee to supercelestial things and not descend or regress to inferior things. Olivi speaks here of fleeing Jerusalem, by which he refers to fleeing the carnal church, which will be besieged and captured, as will be explained in chapter 21; then he closes chapter 17 with the assurance that all this has been explained more fully and satisfactorily in the commentary on Matthew 24.[31]

Olivi's comments on Luke 21 are more helpful. Early in the game he reflects what he has already said in the Matthew commentary: Christ is speaking of three final judgments and, *more prophetico*, he speaks of all three together, although different parts of his literal meaning refer more to one than to the others. He notes that the entire period from Christ on might be considered that of final judgment, but, as John 12 observes, there are three

---

30. *Petri Iohannis Olivi super Lucam, et Lectura super Marcum* (hereafter Comm. Luke), 41–42. Pietro Delcorno, "Following Francis at the Time of Antichrist," *Franciscan Studies* 74 (2016): 149n10, surveys the various recent efforts to determine when the Luke commentary was written. I approach the same problem from a slightly different angle, asking not when it was written but how early Olivi might have decided how the Matthew and Luke commentaries fit together.

31. Comm. Luke, 547–50.

moments during that period that can be given special emphasis because in each we witness the end of some important preceding state. The three endings are marked by (1) the destruction of Jerusalem and the synagogue under the Romans; (2) the destruction of the carnal church around the time of Antichrist, in which the spiritual church will be purged and reborn; and (3) the final judgment at the end of time. Here in Luke 21, Olivi says, the judgment of the carnal church is distinguished less clearly from the others, and especially from the final judgment, than in Matthew 24 or in the prophets; though Luke does predict three things that pertain more literally to the time of Antichrist than to the other two times. The first is the coming of many antichrists. These can be thought of as initially all heresiarchs, pontiffs, and kings who, in the name of Christ and of pontifical or magisterial authority, impugn Christ's faith, life, and elect; but scholars tell us that the prediction refers particularly to two figures, "one of whom will say he is the messiah of the Jews promised in the Law and the other of whom will proclaim himself to be Christ or God. Whether this last, whom Ezekiel 38–39 refers to as Gog, will claim to be God is unclear to me." Before him, however, will come the mystical Antichrist with his pseudo-antichrists—that is, his accomplices— who will attack Christ's life and spirit just as Caiaphas did Christ's person and doctrine.[32]

 Much of what Olivi has said in the Matthew commentary applies here as well, although we are now clearly dealing with "antichrist" in three senses: (1) all those who impugn Christ, his person, his teachings, and the elect, and in this sense we can speak of many antichrists; (2) the mystical Antichrist (here clearly designated as such), who works within the faith (as Caiaphas did in the first century) to subvert Christ's life and spirit (read "evangelical perfection" or "the dawning third age"); and (3) the great Antichrist, who will work from outside the faith and attack Christianity itself.

 By this point Olivi has no trouble using the term "mystical Antichrist." He is seen as an individual with an entourage. Their role in relation to the great Antichrist is neatly stated.

> The mystical Antichrist, assimilated with Ananias and Caiaphas, attacks the spirit of Christ and his elect, and that being done—or rather before it is totally completed—a great battle will begin introducing the great Antichrist (as if introducing Nero and Simon Magus) and finally subverting the carnal church of the elect, subverting it like another synagogue and

---

32. Comm. Luke, 584.

fully cleansing the elect. Once that occurs, the destruction of Antichrist and his followers will follow, consummating the destruction of the entire second time.[33]

By this point Olivi has arrived at the pattern we will find in the Revelation commentary, in which a power outside the Christian church, in a blow aimed at Christianity itself, merely succeeds in destroying the carnal church. It would be interesting to know whether, had he said more about Antichrist in the John commentary, Olivi would have demonstrated that he already saw the work of the two Antichrists in that way by ca. 1281–1282; but we cannot say. What we can say is that, here in the Luke commentary, the dating of which is wide open, he is still developing the same parallels between Christ's first and second advents already explored in the Matthew commentary. The destruction of the Jewish temple by the Romans, a non-Jewish power, following Christ's crucifixion at the hands of the Jewish leaders, who represent a corrupted force within Judaism, anticipates the coming destruction of the carnal church at the hands of the non-Christian power steered by Antichrist. As far as Olivi is concerned, it is all anticipated in the Gospel of Matthew.

The question posed a few paragraphs back was this: When Olivi returned to teaching after his rehabilitation, did he return to the interpretive scheme he had tentatively planned for Matthew, Luke, and Mark before 1283? Thus narrowly posed, the question is hard to answer. To some extent he seems to have felt he had to return to the starting line, and to some extent he is asking new questions, or at least asking them differently; yet he can still cite the Matthew commentary as a reliable source concerning Christ's warnings on the destruction of Jerusalem. When one reads the Luke commentary after the Isaiah and Matthew commentaries, the sense of Olivi working through a continuous, coherent process is remarkable.

Gog and Millenarianism

We have seen that Olivi's notion of the mystical Antichrist emerges from his applying the pattern he discerns in Christ's first advent to Christ's second advent. We must now take a close look at the third advent. Late in the exegesis of Matthew 24 Olivi turns to that matter.

---

33. Comm. Luke, 586.

But it is asked how this refers to the time of final judgment. It can be proved that at that time pseudo-Christs will rise up and then some tribulation especially aimed at the saints will immediately precede the time of judgment. Concerning this it is said by certain wise people—and what they say is not unlearned—that the Antichrist who precedes the general conversion of the Jews (and who also claims to be the messiah promised in the law) is different from a certain tyrant who, after the general conversion of the Jews, will come around the time of judgment. This is what Ezekiel 38 seems to imply when, after the universal conversion and repatriation of the twelve tribes is announced in the preceding chapter, it is said in this one that Gog will come upon the people of Israel with a great army of gentiles. Hence it is said there, "After many days you will be mustered; in the latter years you will go against the land that is restored from war, the land where people were gathered from many nations upon the mountains of Israel, which had been a continual waste," etc. And farther on in the same chapter it says, "On that day, when my people Israel are dwelling securely, you will bestir yourself and come from your place out of the uttermost parts of the north"; and later, "In the latter days I will bring you against my land," etc. (38:16). But in Revelation 20, after speaking of the destruction of Babylon or the woman who is, according to him, "a great city having rule over all the kings of the earth" (Rev 17:18) and later, speaking of the damnation of the beast and the pseudo-prophet "who produced signs in his presence" (Rev 19:20) and of the incarceration of the dragon for a time, he adds that the dragon will then leave its imprisonment and seduce the nations, that is, Gog and Magog, and they will "surround the fortresses of the saints and the beloved city" (Rev 20:8), and immediately afterward the final judgment and resurrection of the dead will occur.

And the aforesaid say that the relationship of the physical death of the saints to the affectual death through which one dies to worldly affections and occupations, entering into an excess of contemplation, is equivalent to that of the tyrant designated by Gog to him who calls himself king of the Jews. For in the time of the first the first death will be introduced, and in the time of the second the death of all bodies will be consummated and then resurrection will follow.[34] This is consonant with the words of

---

34. The sentence makes sense if we assume Olivi means the first and second in historical order rather than the first and second mentioned here. Thus "in the time of the first" means "in the time of him who calls himself king of the Jews."

Christ in Luke 22(:8), "When the Son of Man comes, do you think he will find faith on the earth?" And clearly he is suggesting that the answer is, "Hardly!" Both here and in Luke 17(:26) Christ is saying openly that, just as in the days of Noah and in the days of Lot the Sodomite people devoted themselves to carnal pursuits, thus will it be at the time when the Son of Man is revealed. It is clear, however, that after Antichrist all Israel will be converted, and therefore Christ will come in judgment after their conversion. The world will again be reduced to the worst sort of cupidity and lasciviousness, to great blindness and lack of care for divine matters, and this could hardly occur in a brief time according to the common course of things.[35]

That leaves us with some serious questions. It seems hardly surprising that even Olivi should have them at this point. He is, after all, talking about an event in the distant future. In order to talk about it at all, he has to imagine a world stunningly different from the one in which he lives. Compared with imagining life in the world of Gog and final judgment, speaking of the first and second advents seems almost easy. Olivi has a whole library of sources available to aid his comments on the first advent, and, while the second advent lies in the future, it is, comparatively speaking, not that far in the future. The third advent not only lies a substantial distance ahead but, given Olivi's sense of what can be expected, will be reached only after unimaginable alterations in human society and even in the human psyche.

And what does he expect to find in that distant future? If the three-advent pattern is to be maintained, Olivi must find in the third advent not merely a judgment but a full-scale tribulation, which implies that the era of evangelical perfection Olivi expects after the death of Antichrist must eventually transmogrify into something substantially less tolerable. That "something" is cupidity, lasciviousness, and eventually Gog, who is (barely) mentioned in Ezekiel and Revelation. Note that Olivi does not refer to Gog as Antichrist, but merely as a tyrant who sees his opportunity to attack. Nevertheless, he plays a role parallel to the one occupied by Antichrist during the second advent.

The important point for Olivi's apocalyptic timetable is that, although the death of Antichrist will be followed by the conversion of the Jews and an era of peace, love, and contemplation, it too will eventually be corrupted. That will take a great deal of time, though, so we can expect a substantial

---

35. *SM*, ch. 24, 116ra–rb.

period to pass between Antichrist and Gog. Olivi is a millenarian, not in the sense that he expects the third age to last a thousand years, but in the sense that he expects it to last a very long time and then gradually turn bad.

All this will end with the final judgment. Olivi emphasizes the suddenness and unpredictability of its arrival. He continually reverts to the words "just as in the days of Noah." Noah and his family represent the elect of the final time, and the rest stand for the reprobate. "Note also that although the reprobate did not know the time of the flood, Noah knew it in advance," as Genesis 7:1–5 indicates.[36]

The Outline of a Progressive Christian History?

The commentary on John, following the Matthew commentary, adds other characteristically Olivian elements that complicate the notion of Christ's three advents. In that commentary, Antichrist becomes one of several markers along the route from incarnation to final judgment, creating a succession of people and events Olivi will still be citing years later in the Revelation commentary. In dealing with John the Baptist, he says that allegorically John the Baptist represents the Old Law, but also

> the New Testament, the end of which is perfect participation in Christ's life, just as the person of Christ according to the flesh was the end of the law. Through John is figured allegorically the monastic or ecclesiastical law mixed with temporal concerns and solicitous in the proper administration of temporal concerns, like Martha disposing to evangelical poverty and the contemplative life. Through John is figured a more external and material exposition of the faith, disposing to the fullness of spiritual understanding through an inflowing of the spirit in the elect around the time of Antichrist, leading to a more triumphal defeat of him and his sect and, that being accomplished, to a more splendid renovation of the church. This law and doctrine began from the time of Constantine, by whom temporals were given to the church and general councils celebrated. Through the multitude of schisms and heresies, especially the Arian heresy, the church demonstrated that it lacked that fullness of unction introductory to the peace of Christ described by Isaiah when he speaks of one people not raising the sword against another (Isa 2:4) and says "of the increase of

36. *SM*, ch. 24, 116rb.

this empire and of peace there will be no end" (9:7). But when the regular and clerical status around the time of Charlemagne inclined too much to the flesh and to temporal good fortune, then he loudly announced that he was not Elijah (John 1:21); and when the teachers of and commentators on Aristotle based their thought and their teaching too much on human opinion, then he protested loudly that he was not the prophet, or at least not the greatest one. The materiality of his doctrine testified to his being water in respect to the spiritual wisdom designated by fire and by the wine made by Christ at the wedding.[37]

This is Olivian biblical exegesis at its most complex. Here Constantine's importance is simultaneously recognized and relativized. He placed the church on a new legal footing, and he protected it from heresy as well as persecution. He also allowed it temporal possessions. In the Revelation commentary Olivi will make it clear that his doing so was acceptable as a temporary expedient, and he does much the same thing here by identifying the Constantinian situation with John the Baptist. The general impression given is that the period represented a salutary but lesser state disposing to the higher one that will be established after Antichrist. Here the point is quietly emphasized by noting that the church, once established and protected, is eventually swayed by material and intellectual (Aristotelian) temptations. Here as elsewhere Olivi's inclination is to make sense of the biblical text in terms of historical narrative, presenting church history as a comprehensible pattern in the past and present, but also projecting it into the future. It is comprehensible from a human perspective in the sense that we can analyze a train of events that drove and continues to drive history in a certain direction, and from a divine perspective in the sense that those events show God's purpose working itself out within history. Whatever else his accomplishments, Olivi, like Joachim before him, is a masterly arranger of symbols.

Olivi's reading is progressive in two senses. It reveals to us that the church is capable of progressing in holiness and that the revelation of that progress is itself progressive. Olivi's later analogy of the three mountains in his Revelation commentary (to be seen in the next chapter) will make both points in the process of explaining why Christ's three advents were gradually revealed with the passage of time.[38] As we journey through history, we gain

37. Comm. John, 15rb.

38. *Lectura super apocalypsim*, ed. Warren Lewis (St. Bonaventure, NY: Franciscan Institute Publications, 2015), 73–74.

better perspective concerning the course of history, and we learn that we can anticipate increased *intellectus spiritualis*. If this point is made explicitly in the Revelation commentary, it is already made implicitly yet insistently in the Isaiah commentary, where Olivi places himself in the post-Joachim, post-Francis world of Christ's second advent, though only barely in it. Antichrist is still on the way.

The prospect of Antichrist reminds us that long-term progress does not rule out periods of retrogression and tribulation. In fact, not only the period of Antichrist but that of Gog will be times of major tribulation, and other, lesser ones can be expected as well.

So far we have examined only the Isaiah and the gospel commentaries. Among the pre-1283 commentaries we have two more on the Old Testament: one on Genesis (probably being delivered while he was dealing with John) and the other on Job (begun while he was still expositing Matthew). At one point in the Genesis commentary, Olivi provides an extensive allegorical tour of Judeo-Christian history, in which Revelation 13 plays an important role, helping him to portray an age of pseudo-prophets and Antichrist occupying space in both the sixth and early seventh periods.[39] Olivi makes good use of the seven heads in Revelation 13, suggesting at another point that Antichrist is the sixth head in one way and the seventh in another, although here the distinction is a complex one, becoming first one between Jews and gentiles, then the depraved faithful and the unfaithful, then evil leaders inside and outside the church.[40]

Perhaps even more interesting, in commenting on Genesis 5 Olivi asks why Enoch and Elijah were chosen to be translated into heaven and then return to preach at the time of Antichrist. Why not use Saint Francis? Among the answers Olivi provides, he observes that, before the great flood, a sign of God's judgment to come was provided to all and in a particular way to those especially blessed by God's providence. "And thus in our time we see that, before the destruction of the carnal church symbolized in the damnation of the fornicating woman, a sign has been given to the entire church—and especially to the children of Saint Francis—in the signs of Christ's passion inflicted on our father Francis." Thus was confirmed Enoch's testimony of a double universal judgment, the first in water (as occurred in Enoch's time) and the

---

39. *Peter of John Olivi on Genesis* (hereafter Comm. Gen.) (St. Bonaventure, NY: Franciscan Institute Publications, 2007), 170–71. The first two elements in the series take place in Old Testament times.

40. Comm. Gen., 200–201. Thus we have a reflection of the inside/outside distinction mentioned earlier.

other in fire (concerning which Enoch prophesied, as Jude 14 testifies). Shortly thereafter, Olivi connects all this with Christ's three advents, remarking that at the time of the second, "which involves the battle with the great Antichrist and the conversion of the remaining Jews and Gentiles," it is deemed necessary to repeat God's promise to the faithful, and this task is entrusted to two figures from varying periods. Beyond being from different eras, one of these figures (Enoch) was married and rich, while the other (Elijah) was a virgin and is believed to have been the initiator of evangelical poverty. One lived under the law of nature, the other under the written Jewish law. Both point toward the future when all will be one, Jews and gentiles a single flock under Christ.[41]

The passage just cited actually asks and answers more questions than have been covered here, and the resultant interpretation of the passage provides a complex concordance of Old and New Testament passages. Olivi reminds us yet again that Antichrist will try to seduce the world with misleading concordances.[42] This is, in fact, important for Olivi and should be important for us. It tells us that the Olivian apocalyptic scenario is based on his sense of a concordant pattern emerging from both the Old and New Testaments. Thus, even as he delivers the Genesis commentary, Olivi is anticipating the special mission on which Enoch and Elijah will be sent according to the Revelation commentary.

The Leah-Rachel story and then the continuing tale of Joseph and Benjamin provide Olivi with a rich vein of material suitable for conversion into a series of observations on contemplation, which in turn inevitably involves him in consideration of the transition from the Joachite second age to the third. Olivi's serious thought on the matter begins early, with Genesis 29:1–3: "Then Jacob continued on his journey and came to the land of the eastern peoples. There he saw a well in the field, with three flocks of sheep lying near it because the flocks were watered from that well. The stone over the mouth of the well was large. When all the flocks were gathered there, the shepherds would roll the stone away from the well's mouth and water the sheep."[43] Olivi first notes that, "as for the mysteries" of this passage, one who flees the desert of this world and comes to the east of the eternal sun will find, in the field of virtuous activity, the well of grace and of the wisdom of God, and three flocks, that is, three groups of the faithful (the beginners, those progressing, and the perfect). After these comes Rachel, that is, the culmination of the

41. Comm. Gen., 199–203.
42. Comm. Gen., 202.
43. Comm. Gen., 463–64.

contemplative life, with her flock of contemplatives. The rock can be moved away and the well fully opened only with her arrival, or in resurrection, when all the sheep will be assembled. Shortly after, Olivi notes that there is still a great deal of time left in the day for illumination, and he associates that illumination with the third age of history, when the rock will be moved from the well through love of Rachel.

Later, dealing with chapter 35, Olivi ties Benjamin's birth into this scenario. "Rachel, that is, the contemplative church, will bear a final son, that is, a superexcess of contemplation or an ecstatic state." He goes on to say that, morally, Rachel's death signifies that the mind cannot enter the realms of superworldly excess unless it dies to this world and to itself, being crucified and buried with Christ. There is also an allegorical meaning here. Rachel's death shows that in the mother—and here Olivi sees the mother as the church itself—there is some carnal element that has to die with the birth of that full flowering of contemplation symbolized by Benjamin, just as the synagogue had to die with the birth of Christ and the Christian people. It also refers to the fact that, at the time of the final birth of the contemplative church, some of its firstborn go astray, seeking temporal rewards under the disguise of evangelical perfection, a reference to Olivi's sense that the Franciscan order is currently veering off course, departing from the path set by Francis and his rule.[44]

Who, then, is Benjamin? Allegorically he stands for Christ, without whom we cannot see the Father's wisdom; but he is also Francis, sent in the final time, in whom Christ's life is most fully revealed. Thus Benjamin points to the time in which not only the fullness of Christ's life but the heights of contemplation are finally to be revealed.[45] Olivi takes the notion of Francis as *alter Christus* seriously enough to anticipate a resurrection for him, and he does so not only in the Revelation commentary but already in the Matthew commentary.[46]

Note, however, that Benjamin is actually Rachel's second child. First she had Joseph, the prudent ruler of Egypt and eventually of his own brothers. The point here is that ecstatic *gustus* and rapturous contemplation are built upon a solid foundation of discretion and prudence. One is anterior to the other.[47]

---

44. Comm. Gen., 518–19.
45. Comm. Gen., 569–70.
46. *SM*, ch. 27, ms. Oxford New College 49 155rb–va (ms. Vat. Lat. 10900, 195ra).
47. Comm. Gen., 480. *Gustus* essentially means "taste." In Olivi's historical theology it

The Problem of the Job Commentary

The Job commentary presents a different sort of problem. In 1976, when I wrote an article arguing that Olivi's Isaiah and Matthew commentaries referred to one another in such a way as to suggest that they overlapped chronologically,[48] I observed that the same was true of the Job and Matthew commentaries. I suggested then that the Isaiah commentary is relatively short and one can imagine Olivi finishing it, then going on to the remarkably longer Job commentary while he continued to work on the Matthew commentary. One could even imagine him continuing both the Job and Matthew commentaries during the next year.

Unfortunately, Alain Boureau's recent edition of the Job commentary challenges this neat chronology, since he dates the commentary ca. 1293–1294. He reaches that conclusion on completely different grounds than those I used, never mentioning my argument, which is a shame, because the evidence for my dating is limited but striking. In the process of dealing with Job 36:6, Olivi quotes Gregory the Great to the effect that there will be two orders of the elect and two of the reprobate at the end: those saved with and without judgment and those damned with and without it. Those who supererogated and gave up all for Christ will be saved without judgment and will judge with him. That is, at any rate, how Gregory interprets Christ's comments about the twelve thrones and other passages as well; "but how this is true must more properly be touched upon in commenting on the gospels," for there are huge difficulties involved.[49] We might then expect Olivi to address the matter in his exegesis of Matthew 19:28, the only gospel passage that records Christ's remark about the twelve thrones (although Luke 22:30 mentions judging the twelve tribes). Olivi does in fact deal with the matter in exposing Matthew 19:28, citing Gregory's interpretation of Job 36:6.

Again, in commenting on Matthew 26:24, Olivi says that "wherever the punishment in Hell is referred to as death it refers to that of both soul and body. And this is how I interpreted Job's words when, in my commentary on

---

is connected with his sense that with Christ's second advent purely intellectual knowledge will be supported by other sorts of knowledge dependent on other ways of knowing.

48. David Burr, "The Date of Petrus Iohannis Olivi's Commentary on Matthew," *Collectanea Franciscana* 46 (1976): 131–38.

49. *Postilla super Iob* (hereafter Comm. Job), ed. Alan Boureau (Turnhout: Brepols, 2015), 505: "Quomodo hec sint vera, in expositione evangeliorum magis proprie tangam." Olivi goes on to explain the general problem involved, and closes by observing that it "alibi habet tradi et ideo ad presens hic omitto." In a note, Boureau explains that Olivi is referring to an "opus adhuc perditum vel non scriptum."

Job 3, I dealt with his cursing the day of his birth." What we actually find in Olivi's exegesis of Job 3 is not explicitly aimed at defending this notion but can at least be considered consistent with it.

Finally, when he deals with Job 41:34 (Vulgate 41:25), Olivi notes that Gregory says a great deal on pride and humility that "I leave aside because I have touched upon them in my own small way in commenting on Matthew."[50] He is probably referring to the little essay on humility inserted into his exegesis of Matthew 18.

I have just presented these three passages in what I take to be the order of their strength in proving my point. The first one is so impressive that one can neutralize it only by assuming that Olivi is referring to some other, later, undiscovered commentary on the Gospels. The fact that Olivi refers to the Gospels rather than Matthew in particular might seem to support such a claim, but it is equally likely that Olivi expected his audience to know where in the Gospels the twelve thrones could be found and that at the moment he and they were already headed there. The second passage can be countered only by assuming that Olivi either commented on Job twice or later revised his Matthew commentary, adding the reference.

To say this much is hardly to have settled the matter. Olivi may well have delivered the Job and Matthew commentaries, then revised them (and others as well) later. Thus Boureau's argument for a later date may also be justified in that sense. For the moment, we can only deal with the Job commentary as it sits before us.

Boureau sees the various sevenfold patterns in the Job commentary as similar to those in the Revelation commentary, and so they are. It is also perhaps worth noting that in the Job commentary he says little about the three advents of Christ, which play such an important role in the earliest commentaries, although he does mention them. That might encourage us to see the commentary as belonging to the early 1290s rather than the early 1280s; yet it is also true that he never explicitly mentions the mystical Antichrist, who plays a prominent role in the Revelation commentary after slowly emerging in the early commentaries. (He is not mentioned in the Isaiah commentary, is mentioned only by implication in the Matthew commentary, and is mentioned only once in the John commentary.) Olivi gives the word

---

50. Comm. Job, 609: "Super hoc autem loco dicit Gregorius multa notabilia de vitio superbie, de virtute humilitatis que pretermitto, quia super Mattheum illa tetigi pro modulo meo." Here in his note Boureau acknowledges that Olivi is referring to the same Matthew commentary we have today.

"mystery" an extensive workout in the Job commentary and speaks once of Antichrist "literally and mystically" attempting to assemble a *concordia* of times, but neither of these things has any bearing on the mystical Antichrist as encountered in the Revelation commentary.

What does separate the Job commentary from the other, earlier commentaries is the way, in a series of passages more or less separable from the rest of the work, Olivi presents a variety of historical patterns as possible mystical interpretations of specific elements in the text. (Olivi himself prefers to call them "mysteries.") These passages offer a variety of historical patterns based on what often seem wildly opportunistic readings of a book clearly intended for other purposes. Thus, commenting on Job 10:9-13, Olivi sees in it a series of historical moments beginning with (1) the milk of biblical doctrine being administered to the pagans, then (2) coagulated by the pressure exerted on the martyrs; then (3) the faithful being dressed in the soft furs of temporal possessions by Constantine; then (4) the church being bound together by the anchorites as if by its bones and (5) by the doctors as if by its nerves. Then, (6) the life of Christ is bestowed on it through a pouring out of grace so that (7) God's visitation should protect us from the face of the serpent. Olivi caps this section by developing a *concordia* that applies all this to the Old Testament.[51]

He next ponders Job 12:14-25, which he turns into a list of ten judgments, beginning with the fall of the angels and ending with the blinding of the Pharisees and pontiffs, "so that they continue to go astray down to the present, as if they were drunk."[52]

Next to be explained is Job 24:2-18, which deals with the three temptations of the church: (1) by the heretics; (2) by Christians, who, whether they enjoy ecclesiastical or secular power, corrupt the church through their greed; and (3) by Antichrist, "who will rise up in the early morning of evangelical life and the spiritual church to attack the poor evangelical men and Christ himself."[53]

We could look at other examples, but the point is clear enough just from looking at these three. To say he is reaching is to understate the matter. One consideration does emerge from these and other passages, however. One could argue that the Job commentary comes closer to the Revelation commentary than other texts considered here in presenting a church dom-

51. Comm. Job, 441-42.
52. Comm. Job, 442.
53. Comm. Job, 442-44.

inated by corrupt leaders who, among their many offenses, are guilty of persecuting champions of evangelical poverty. Here again we might wonder if a later revision of the Job commentary was more drastic, perhaps, in this respect, and the result was a more dystopian view of the contemporary church, more in line with what we find in the Revelation commentary; yet such an argument would have to be a more painstaking one than can be offered here, where our aim is to offer a brief description of Olivi's life as an exegete before 1283.

Conclusion

In Olivi's early Bible commentaries we find a man who believes that the prophetic words of Isaiah and Christ deal primarily with Christ's three advents in flesh, spirit, and judgment. The result is a story told in advance of its completion, a prophetic history that includes not only heroes but villains, not only Christ and Francis but Caiaphas, Simon Magus, Antichrist, and Gog. If asked where he stands in the story, Olivi places himself at the transition between the fifth and sixth periods of church history, which is equivalent to standing at the transition between Christ's first and second advents or, in Joachite terms, between the second age of the Son and the third age of the Holy Spirit. The transition is far enough along for Olivi to see Joachim as a sign of the new age and Francis as a key agent in its inception. Greater things are in store, and, although Olivi recognizes that he is too early in the process to speak with any precision about them, he is already describing the future seventh period as an age of contemplation to be understood in terms not only of propositional knowledge but of *gustus*. We have just seen this expectation revealed in the Genesis commentary, one of the last two delivered before the 1283 censure; but the language of mystical experience and ecstatic *gustus* is already being used in a major way in the Isaiah commentary, which, as I have commented elsewhere, presents a theory of prophecy that seems to blend Isaiah, Daniel, Joachim, and contemporary mysticism into a unified field theory of contemplative experience.[54]

54. David Burr, "Olivi on Prophecy," *Cristianesimo nella storia* 17 (1996): 388. In the Isaiah commentary, Francis functions more as a ghostly presence, the unmentioned elephant in the room, than as a major topic of conversation; but if we view the Isaiah and Matthew commentaries as a single conversation being carried on in two simultaneous commentaries, he becomes very important indeed.

This connection between Christ's second advent and new contemplative riches to be expected in Olivi's own time allows us to appreciate why, as early as the Isaiah commentary, Olivi assumes that reporting the experiences of a mystic he himself knows personally will aid us in understanding Old Testament prophetic inspiration. This is not the only time he cites a contemporary mystic in discussing the Bible. In the John commentary he entertains the possibility that a passage in the Gospel of John should be interpreted in a way that differs from its obvious, generally accepted sense because a mystic of his acquaintance has actually seen it in that other way.[55] The important thing here is that from Olivi's perspective Joachim, contemporary contemplatives, and Old Testament prophets are of course different, but not so different as to preclude our using one to illuminate the other. One might picture them as different points on a continuum. If, as Olivi imagines, we are in the process of entering the age of Christ's advent in the spirit, phenomena all along that continuum may increasingly become mutually explanatory.

Olivi is intensely aware of church history as *Heilsgeschichte*. Its movement is in a generally positive direction, but not completely. Satan has an important role in the story. After traveling along its own three-century trail of tears, the church is rescued by Constantine, but what he does with it is far short of perfection, and even by Charlemagne's time the church is clearly not handling its earthly power and riches entirely well. Thus it is not surprising that when evangelical perfection is ushered in by Francis it faces stiff opposition from the forerunners of Antichrist. Only after Antichrist's death will the church enter a new, extended age of peace, love, and contemplation, accompanied by the conversion of all Israel; yet even this age will eventually go bad, and Christ will have to appear again, defeat Gog, then conduct final judgment. Olivi expects the third age to be long, but not because he is applying the biblical thousand years to it. Instead, he deduces the length of the third age from the time needed to build it, enjoy it, and then corrupt it again before Gog appears.

If Gog represents Satan's final attempt to seize power, his previous one was Antichrist or, more precisely, the mystical and genuine Antichrists. The first, like Caiaphas, works within the religious establishment, while the second, like Simon Magus, works outside it. One is pseudo-Christian and the other unabashedly anti-Christian.

---

55. See David Burr, *The Persecution of Peter Olivi* (Philadelphia: American Philosophical Society, 1976), 76. Olivi seems to have known and conversed with several mystics. See David Burr, "Olivi, Apocalyptic Expectation and Visionary Experience," *Traditio* 41 (1985): 273-88.

What Olivi gives us is an *histoire de la longue durée* punctuated by vivid characters and events, because Olivi himself has a vivid imagination. To appreciate that much, we need only read his thoughts on the destruction of Jerusalem. But, equally important, Olivi sees historical narrative as the way we make sense of those characters and events. As he tells us in the Job commentary, we must counter Antichrist's bogus concordance of times with a valid one.

Olivi's suggestion that the struggle between the elect and Antichrist can be described as a battle of concordances says a great deal about his view of the scholar's task. He takes history seriously. His theology of choice is *Geschichtestheologie*; yet the other side of the matter is that, in learning to make sense of history, we learn that it is entering the age of Christ's second advent, his coming in the spirit, a new age characterized by unprecedented contemplative experience, which, among other things, produces new insight into the Bible. The Spirit that guided the prophets in composing the Bible now allows Joachim, Francis, and others to find new wisdom in it. Thus, from Olivi's perspective, Joachim is not only a major exegetical authority whose reading of the Bible alerted him to the wonders of the third age; he is also evidence that the third age is dawning.

In 1993 I published *Olivi's Peaceable Kingdom*, a study of Olivi's Revelation commentary produced shortly before his death in 1298. What I have said so far in this conclusion could be seen as a summary of that commentary, although with certain things omitted;[56] yet what I have said actually summarizes Olivi's thoughts on Isaiah, Matthew, John, Genesis, and Job in commentaries produced before 1283.[57] In other words, long before he commented on Revelation, he had already developed most of the basic interpretive structure he would rely on for the rest of his life in his biblical exegesis, including the exegesis of Revelation.

How do we explain this fact? Certainly not by asserting that Olivi saw in these books what in fact the original authors meant to say. Nor does it do much good to suggest that by the early 1280s Olivi had already produced a first redaction of his Revelation commentary and was somehow reading Isaiah, Matthew, John, Genesis, and Job in the light of Revelation. To be sure, he had read Revelation and cited it in these early works; and, to be sure, he was clearly drawn to the book. Revelation was in some ways more amenable to his view of history than was, let us say, John or Job; yet anyone who sees

---

56. One obvious omission is that, whereas in the early works he never explicitly treats the papacy as leader of the carnal church, he does so in the Revelation commentary.

57. Again, there is room for argument about the Job commentary, as I have stated above.

Olivi's exegesis of Revelation as true to the text of Revelation should try reading a few other commentaries on that book. Olivi is, as I said earlier, projecting an interpretation on Revelation, so it is of only limited value to note that he was thinking of it as he wrote those earlier commentaries.

What, then, *was* he thinking of? To some extent he was reflecting Bible scholarship in his day. Any number of Revelation commentaries in the thirteenth century offered a view of Christian history that centered persecution by the Jews in the first period of church history, by the Romans in the second, by the heretics in the third, and by the hypocrites in the fourth, followed by the forerunners of Antichrist in the fifth period and Antichrist himself in the sixth. In fact, Richard of Saint Victor offered an analogous pattern in the twelfth century when dealing with the seven angelic trumpeters.

Olivi was also definitely thinking about Bonaventure. Most commentators put themselves in the fifth period, and many of them explicitly described that period as featuring the precursors of Antichrist; but Bonaventure anticipated Olivi in placing himself in the sixth period, giving Francis a major role in that period, and seeing the period as one of major conflict between Christ and Antichrist, something that combined great tribulation and a great spiritual leap forward. Bonaventure wrote his *Collationes* toward the end of his career, but Olivi encountered it at the beginning of his, and it seems to have made a powerful impression.

Olivi was also thinking about Joachim. He entered the period of his early commentaries already a Joachite, not only in the sense that he had read Joachim, but in the sense that he admired Joachim even as he placed his own particular interpretation on what he found there. In his Isaiah commentary, he breaks off an explanation of Daniel's prophetic gift to insert a passionate defense of Joachim.

> And in this same way Joachim, in his *Liber de Concordia* and *Expositio Apocalypsis*, says he suddenly received the entire concordance of the Old and New Testaments in the form of some general rules from which, by deduction, he later deduced certain things, some of which (it seemed to him) he considered himself to know as certain conclusions, while he saw others only as probable conjectures that might be erroneous. It is just the same with the natural light of intellect joined to us from the beginning of our condition. Through it, without any argumentation, we know first principles, and from these we infer some conclusions necessarily, others only probably. In the latter case we are capable of error, yet it does not thereby follow that the light itself is false. I say this because there are those who

wish to conclude that Joachim's whole understanding was from the devil or by conjecture of the human imagination because in certain particulars what he said was merely opinion and occasionally perhaps even false.[58]

The passage makes it clear that Olivi was not only an enthusiastic Joachite but a judicious one. He balanced Joachim's three ages against his own three advents. He had read Joachim on Gog but came to a slightly different conclusion on the question of whether Gog should be described as Antichrist.[59] His view of history as *Heilsgeschichte* is like Joachim's in some ways. Olivi is almost instinctively more linear in reading history, but he is conversant with Joachite concordances and uses them often. In fact, his use of the three advents as an exegetical tool could be seen as an echo of Joachim's concordances. One gets the impression that Olivi had not read all of Joachim's works but had read some carefully enough to absorb the Joachite methodology and employ it in creative ways.[60] His treatment of John the Baptist as representing the old law in the John commentary has a remarkably Joachite feel.

Throughout this chapter we have noted Olivi's periodical references to the temptation of Antichrist as, in effect, a battle of concordances. We should take him seriously on this point. It should remind us that, in turning the Bible—the *entire* Bible, not simply Revelation—into a *liber concordiae* he is doing just what Joachim already did and what he thinks has to be done to keep Antichrist from turning it into his own story. Olivi sees his task as fitting all the pieces of the puzzle together in godly fashion.

Once Olivi's early career as an exegete was under way, the cluster of ideas we have identified here grew organically to some extent. The process becomes apparent in the Isaiah commentary, where Olivi introduces us to Isaiah as prophet of Christ's threefold advent; and the three advents become a key structural element from the Matthew commentary on, encouraging the development of the other ideas discussed here. Most of Olivi's big ideas are organically related to the three advents. His sense of them changed very little, but he spent the rest of his life exploring them. Even in the early commentaries, however, the three advents moved in tandem with the Joachite three ages.

58. *SI*, 197–98.

59. On Joachim's varying views of Gog see Robert Lerner, "Antichrists and Antichrist in Joachim of Fiore," *Speculum* 60 (1985): 553–70.

60. Kevin Madigan, *Olivi and the Interpretation of Matthew in the High Middle Ages* (Notre Dame: University of Notre Dame Press, 2003), does a good job of documenting this point. He sees no proof that Olivi had read Joachim's treatise on the Gospels, but rightly observes that doing so would not have contributed that much anyway.

Other ideas needed more time to develop. Even in the Revelation commentary, Olivi was still evolving; yet the basic building blocks of his apocalyptic thought were already available by 1283.

If they were available by 1283, then why did they play so small a role in the censure? After all, these were ideas the church saw fit to attack in 1318 and beyond. In his reply to a letter from a group of friends who had written before the censure, asking him to comment on the charges against him, Olivi notes that "some people accuse me of following dreams and fantastic visions like a soothsayer, and of busying myself with the prediction of future events." He briefly explains himself, laying down some ground rules for such prediction and insisting that he himself has avoided specificity, never asserting "that this or that would happen during that day or year, or this or that person would do this or that thing"; yet he is certain that "through a Franciscan order purged by suffering and temptation, Christianity will be renewed and the Jews and pagans converted." He is mentioning this issue, he says, even though his friends have not asked him about it.[61]

By addressing the matter of his apocalyptic preoccupations in this backhanded way, Olivi became the only person to mention it in any document involved with his 1283 censure, or at least any document that has survived. The closest the commission came to dealing with Olivi's apocalyptic thought was in looking at the eighth of his *Quaestiones de perfectione evangelica*, which did suggest a recognizable theology of history; but the commission concentrated on the debate concerning poverty and the vow, ignoring the extent to which Olivi's thought on Franciscan poverty was enmeshed in his apocalyptic historical expectations.

If question eight was the closest the commission came to confronting Olivi's apocalyptic scenario, then it seems likely that no one asked them to read the exegetical writings, for it is hard to imagine that a commission so willing to attack Olivi's idea of *usus pauper* as entailed in the vow would remain indifferent to his thoughts on Christ's second coming in the spirit in the thirteenth century, or Francis's bodily resurrection in the near future, or the possibility that Christ was still alive when stabbed by the lance simply because a mystic Olivi knew said so.[62] And if they had not read the early exegetical works, then we can appreciate that they still had a great deal to learn about Olivi.

61. Epistola ad R., in Olivi's *Quodlibeta* (Venice, 1509), ff. 51v–53r.
62. Can we also assume that *De perfectione evangelica*, q. 16, another heavily apocalyptic work, either had been overlooked or had not yet been written? That is a harder question to answer.

READINGS

Commentary on Isaiah

*Olivi, like other commentators, begins his introduction to the com-
mentary on Isaiah with a passage from some other book of the Bible,
in this case Ecclesiasticus 48:27: "With a great spirit he saw final
[ultima] things and comforted forever those mourning in Zion."
Coming to Isaiah by way of Ecclesiasticus might suggest that he implicitly accepts the accuracy of Isaiah's historical role as portrayed in
the latter, the scenario probably better known through Lord Byron's
"Destruction of Sennacherib" than through Ecclesiasticus (if it is
known at all); but Olivi actually does accept the idea that both the
Assyrians and the Babylonians (he calls them "the Chaldaeans")
led the Israelites into captivity, and in any case his concern in the
introduction is to present Isaiah's message in terms of the Aristotelian
four causes, a normal task for exegetes in that era.*

*In fact, though, he is also interested in suggesting the skeletal
structure of Isaiah's true message as he sees it, and here we finally
encounter what is remarkable about Olivi's commentary. In turning
to the second, material cause, he says, "In the spirit [Isaiah] saw the
ultimate or final things that would occur in the final days." This is, in
fact, the major theme in his introduction to Isaiah and to the prophets in general. The way he unpacks it here suggests that even at this
point in his career he has been thinking about it for quite a while.*[63]

In saying that "in the spirit he saw last things" or things to occur in the
final days, he [Isaiah] is referring to what will occur around the time of the
captivity carried out by the Assyrians and Chaldaeans; around the time of
the captivity carried out by the Romans; around the time of the captivity or
tribulation to be carried out by Antichrist; and around the time of the examination to be carried out through the last, universal judgment. These are
the four last or final things of which the prophets principally speak before
the Babylonian captivity. And thus in many places they say that in the final
days their prophecies will be fulfilled. Hence at Isaiah 2:2 Isaiah says, "In the
final days the mountain of the Lord's house shall be prepared," and Daniel

---

63. The following passage begins at *Peter of John Olivi on the Bible*, 165.

2:28, in interpreting the kings designated by the statue, says, "It is God in heaven, revealing mysteries, who showed you, King Nebuchadnezzar, what is to come in the final times." And in 10:14 the angel says, "I have come to teach you what will happen to your people in the final times."

In order to see why these are referred to as the final four things and how they are simultaneously considered by Isaiah and other prophets, we should recognize that the principal end of God's people is triple, or one end tripled. That is, [first] we have Christ's advent in the flesh and the redemption following from it, and thus the apostle says (Rom 10:4), "Christ is the end of the law, that all who have faith may be justified." Second, we have full participation in Christ's life through the inflowing of his grace, and thus 1 Timothy 1:5 says, "The end of the precept is pure-hearted love, a good conscience, and unfeigned faith." Third, we have full attainment of Christ's glory, concerning which in 1 Corinthians 15:22–23 it is said, "In Christ all will be made alive, but each in their order; first Christ, then those who are of Christ and, at his coming, believe;[64] then comes the end, when he delivers the kingdom to God the Father."

According to this, there are three solemn advents of Christ: the first in flesh, the second in spirit, and the third in judgment.[65] Concerning the first, Zechariah 9:9 says, "Behold, your king comes to you, just and a savior, poor and riding on an ass, and on a colt, the foal of an ass." And Malachi 3:1 says, "Your holy Lord whom you seek will immediately come to his holy temple." And, after it says in Isaiah 40:3, "A voice of one calling in the desert, 'prepare the way of the lord,'" it says in Isaiah 40:9, "Go up on a high mountain," etc., "and say to the cities of Judah, 'Behold, your lord will come in power.'"

Concerning the second, the apostle says in 2 Thessalonians 2:8, "Then will be revealed that iniquity whom the Lord Jesus will kill with the spirit of his mouth and will destroy by the appearance of his coming." Since it is clear that the "now" in which Antichrist is to be killed is not the "now" of the final judgment but rather of an intermediate time, it is clear that the full conversion of the Jews to Christ of which the apostle speaks when he says in Romans 11:25, "Then the fullness of the gentiles will enter and thus all of the Jews will be saved," can be understood only of a time after the death of Antichrist, because in John 5:43 Christ says the Jews will receive Antichrist,

64. "Qui in adventu eius crediderunt," which could also be translated "believe in his coming."
65. *SI*, 166.

for he says, "If another comes in his own name you will receive him." Thus it is clear enough that the advent in which Antichrist is killed differs from that in which the whole earth will be judged at the end. And as is shown from a subtle conflation of many Scriptures, it is the advent through a consummation of graces that John describes in Revelation 21:2 when he says, "I saw the holy city descending from heaven." For then all things will be restored and reformed into a perfect cultus of Christ. As Christ says in Matthew 17:11, "Elijah will come and restore all things."

Of the third advent it is said in Matthew 24:30, "Then they will see the Son of Man coming on the clouds of heaven with great power and majesty"; and in Matthew 25:31 it is said, "When the Son of Man comes in his majesty and all his angels with him."

Therefore, since first are introduced those things which pertain to some end, then finally the end of all things is introduced, and thus it is commonly said that the end is prior in intention but ultimate in execution; thus this sort of triple end is introduced in Scripture and called "the final hour." Thus of the first Matthew 20:12 says, "These last worked only one hour." There those are called "last" who were called to work in the vineyard around the eleventh hour, and concerning these it is said, "The last will be first and the first last." Of the second John says in his first canonical letter, 1 John 2:18, "My sons, it is the last hour." Wishing to prove as much, he immediately adds, "And, as you have heard, Antichrist comes, but now there are many Antichrists, so now we know it is the final hour." From this it is obvious that he properly and antonomastically calls the time of Antichrist "the final hour." Otherwise his reasoning would not be sound, because if something participates in the similitude of the time of Antichrist, therefore much more he participates in the actual time of Antichrist; which in my opinion the apostle, in Romans 11:25, calls the time of the fullness of the gentiles and of the universal conversion of the Jews.

In introducing any hour there is a certain plenitude and a certain final consummation of prior times. Thus concerning the first advent the apostle says in Galatians 4:4, "But when the plenitude of time arrived, God sent his Son," etc.; and concerning the third advent it is said in John 6:44, "And I will raise him up on the last day." And in 1 Corinthians 15:51-52 it is said, "We shall all indeed rise in a moment, in the blink of an eye, at the final trumpet, for the trumpet will indeed sound." And on the same subject it says in 15:26, "The last enemy, Death, will be destroyed." Concerning this final trumpet, Revelation 10:6-7 says, "And he swore by him who lives forever, 'There will be no more delay, but in the days when the seventh angel begins to blow his horn, the mystery of God will be accomplished just as he announced through his servants the prophets.'"

In order, however, that we might briefly comprehend and describe the principal and final boundaries containing the whole measure of things, the prophets have described them to us in terms of the four hierarchies or four animals or four wheels of the divine chariot [Ezek 1]. The first is the hierarchy of the Old Testament, lasting until Christ's advent, in which, through antonomasia and a certain propriety of the time, the veils of figures are celebrated and temporal things are in many ways promised, sought and given, procured and defended. The second is that of the calling of the gentiles to the faith, lasting from the beginning of the church to Antichrist, in which, through a certain antonomasia, spiritual battles involving martyrdom, heresy, and diverse temptations shone forth, a period that has featured an active life of obedience to Christ through many acts. The third is that of the restoration of the Israelite tribes, lasting in a certain way from the death of Antichrist to the final judgment, in which through antonomasia the quietude, tranquility, serene sweetness, and jocundity of contemplation will be given to God's people as if through a certain Sabbath. The fourth is that of the rising again of the blessed in glory, lasting from judgment into eternity, and this is the last "last thing" of all, the principal end of all.

In order that you should see how [these various endings] could be comprehended in the same prophetic letter, you should know that they were formed by God in such a way that, despite their diversity and diverse properties, they conform so fully (especially at their beginnings, ends, and middle parts) that, in a certain sense, in describing one we describe them all. And thus God contrived for these three aforesaid ends (which are simply the ends of humankind) a certain preambulatory end, which is not an end simply but only *secundum quid*, a figurative end rather than a real one, in which these three ends can be enclosed and figuratively described; and in this same is offered a symbol of Trinity in unity. For in one letter[66] the threefold truth of Christ and his church is comprehended like a tricolored light shining through a dense, dark cloud.

Now we arrive at one of the most complex passages in the Isaiah commentary. Notice, first, Olivi's way of alternating between a threefold and fourfold division, depending on whether he is talking about Christ's three advents or those advents plus the Old Testament

66. That is, one passage taken literally.

*prophecy that announces them. Notice, too, the term "hierarchy,"
which is closely related to the three advents, with each hierarchy
standing for the period introduced by an advent. Note, finally, the
way Olivi uses the terms "express figure" and "express exemplar" in
such a way that the prophets, Christ, the evangelical people at the
time of Antichrist, and the elect at the time of judgment all seem to
be connected in a progressive development.*

For God, in order to deal with the sins of the Israelite people, settled on
the well-known temporal punishment and subsequent reformation, which
included a threefold hierarchy to be fittingly introduced under Christ. And
this is one of the major reasons why the prophets were sent during the time
of the Jewish captivity begun under the Assyrians and completed under the
Chaldaeans, prophets who, in authentic prophecies concerning future times,
spoke of the future kingdom of Christ and his people. For at that time the
prophets were sent for the correction of a perverse and idolatrous people and
for their reformation, as an express figure of Christ and his apostles, who in
turn were to be sent at the beginning of the first hierarchy of Christ. And
both, that is, the prophets as well as Christ and his apostles, were an express
exemplar of the evangelical people who were to come during the battle with
Antichrist in order to introduce the second hierarchy of Christ. And all
these were an exemplar of the elect, who, around the time of judgment, will
be snatched up into the clouds to Christ. And in a similar way the fall and
perversity of the prior people is a figure of the final fall and ruin of those
following them. And similarly the first captivity is a figure of the following
captivities and punishments. And the first capturers are in the same way a
figure of the adversaries through whom the evils later inflicted were carried
out. And similarly the first healing of God's people was an express figure of
the repairs that followed, and those who administered them were an express
figure of those who administered the later repairs. And you can say the same
about all other notable circumstances of later times, always remembering,
however, that each of the circumstances has its own particular characteristics, just as the divine persons share common essence yet retain their own
personal characteristics.

In any case, that Isaiah and other prophets speak of these four will
be made more clearly evident by their exposition of particular passages.
In the meantime, it is clear from this prophet, because he repeats in many
places the things that were to be done by Sennacherib, king of the Assyrians, against the people of God and how magnificently he was later to be

destroyed by God, and how in that time the divine cult was to be raised up among the people of God. And he says a great deal about how wonderful that time would be. And in the same way he also says a great deal about what would be done by Nebuchadnezzar, king of Babylon.

And the very way Isaiah tells of these things makes it clear that they pertain to the three hierarchies of Christ, as the prudent reader will be able to see in the example I provided in the second general principle concerning Scripture in general.[67] Nonetheless, when he says, "Behold, a virgin shall conceive" [Isa 7:14] and "a baby is born to us who will be called the mighty God" [9:6], and "there will come forth a shoot from the root of Jesse" [11:1], and "surely he has borne our griefs and carried our sorrows" [53:4], and "like a lamb led to slaughter" [53:7], clearly these things are properly said of Christ as far as his first advent is concerned. And he says, "Behold, I will create new heavens and a new earth, and the former things will not be remembered" [65:17], and "no more shall the sound of weeping be heard in it, or the cry of distress" [65:19-20], and "all flesh will come to worship before me, and they will go out and see the bodies of dying men who rebelled against me, and their worms shall not die, their fires shall not be quenched" [65:23-24]. Clearly this refers to the time of the final judgment and resurrection. Where, through a certain excess, he speaks of the final restoration of his people, a thing he vehemently insists on (especially from the middle of the book on), it is clear to any of the faithful that he is speaking of the heralded conversion of the Jews to Christ, which we are still awaiting. Thus the apostle, in his letter to the Romans [9:27], refers to this matter by citing Isaiah 10:22, "For even if your people should be like the sand of the sea, only a remnant of them will be saved."

To show how this is true of the prophets as a whole, it will suffice at present to cite 1 Peter 1:10-12: "The prophets, who prophesied concerning the grace that was to be yours, searched and inquired about this salvation. They inquired as to what person or time was indicated by the spirit of Christ in them when predicting the sufferings of Christ and the subsequent glory. It was revealed to them that they were serving not themselves but you, in the things that have now been announced to you," etc.

---

67. David Flood, in *Peter of John Olivi on the Bible*, cites his edition of *De doctrina Scripturae*, pp. 73-123 of the same volume, as the *principium* Olivi has in mind. Perhaps so, yet Flood's edition of *De causis Scripturae*, on pp. 39-72 of the same volume, is in some ways closer to what Olivi has in mind. In any case, we are being introduced at this point to another form biblical scholarship took during Olivi's time.

Olivi's Matthew Commentary

While Olivi was commenting on Isaiah, he was also commenting on Matthew. The Isaiah commentary is much shorter, so it is possible that once he finished it he began his exegesis of Job, while continuing with Matthew. The major significance here is that, by the time Olivi arrived at Matthew 24, his apocalyptic thought might have progressed well beyond what we find in the Isaiah commentary.

In Matthew 24 we find Christ apparently predicting the destruction of the temple, and with some precision. Olivi says Christ replied to the questioning of his disciples that it would be destroyed "just as, to the letter, it occurred under Vespasian and Titus in the forty-second year after Christ's passion." The disciples ask Christ to elaborate on his remark, and he does so in a way that reminds us of the basic pattern we saw laid out in the Isaiah commentary.[68]

And responding Jesus said to them. In this response Christ touches in mixed fashion several times, and especially three: the time of the Jewish captivity carried out by the Romans (or by the demons) when, by killing Christ, they were rejected by the true cult of God; the time of Antichrist; and the time of the final judgment. For whatever time his words are exposited, however, they involve four things. In the first place they show that Christ's advent involves four things. First, many fallacies, seducers, battles, and commotions, many martyrdoms and persecutions of Christ's disciples, along with the diffusion of evangelical preaching among all peoples. Second, in saying, "When you see the abomination," etc. [Matt 24:15], Christ gives a solemn sign of future tribulations, explaining their magnitude. Third, where he says, "If therefore they say to you," etc. [24:26], he shows that Christ's advent will be sudden, clear, and evident, especially to the elect, and thus will hardly be in doubt as far as places or signs are concerned, nor will its particulars need to be investigated. Fourth, when he says, "Immediately after the tribulation," etc. [24:29], he shows the major signs that follow the aforesaid tribulation, preceding or accompanying Christ's advent, touching in the process on the magnificence and evident nature of that advent both for the reprobate and for the elect, although in different ways. Fifth, when he says, "From the fig tree," etc. [24:32], he confirms what he has said by a similitude. Sixth, when he says, "Truly, I say to you," etc. [24:34], he strengthens it with

---

68. *SM*, ch. 24, as found in Paris, BNF cod. lat. 15588.

an oath supporting the infallible truth of his words. Seventh, when he says, "Concerning that day, however," etc. [24:36], he shows that the hour of his advent is entirely unknown and unknowable to human beings.

To understand this part of the work, however, we must recognize that, just as the prophets, in speaking of the Babylonian captivity, were also speaking of three other captivities pertaining to the time of Christ—and similarly in speaking of the liberation of God's people from the Babylonian captivity he was addressing three liberations of the elect to be carried out in the time of grace and eternal glory—thus Christ, in speaking of the captivity to be carried out by the Romans in his time, included in prophetic manner two others that would follow. For, just as was shown in the prophets, God arranged that they should be carried out with such conformity that one could be made known by another. In order that all should be revealed in one another and yet in a way be hidden in one another, they were described in such a way that some passages concern one more properly and other passages another, yet all are woven together in such a way that each seems to refer to all three. Take the example of an image portraying a certain king, an image composed of threads of different colors woven together in such a way that we now see the white thread, now the green, now the red, and now the hyacinth.[69] Thus in one fabric they mutually reveal and hide one another. Thus in the prophets the entire fabric of words can lead us to one of the aforesaid parts, directing us more properly to one time and less properly to another. Thus, for example, those things said of the multitude of pseudo-Christians and pseudo-prophets and the prodigies performed by them and the danger of error in the elect and the cooling of love among them might more properly refer to the time of Antichrist, while what is said of the concealing of the sun and moon and of Christ's coming in majesty and of the joining together of the elect to be carried out by angels apply more properly to the final judgment. What is said of the destruction of Jerusalem, persecution of the apostles, and preaching of the gospel throughout the entire world applies more properly to the first time. There are indeed certain things said there that can be applied commonly to various aspects of the aforesaid time, such as that battles and pestilences and famines will precede them and the abomination of desolation will be installed in a holy place.

In order, however, that we should make clear how all can in some way be applied to all of the aforesaid times, we will first apply them to the

---

69. Notice that Olivi reflexively mentions four colors, not three. He is automatically including not only the three advents but the Old Testament prophecy that predicts them.

first time. Clearly in the imminent attack on Jerusalem under Titus and Vespasian there was no danger of error among the elect as posited here, nor were there many pseudo-Christs performing signs to seduce the elect. Yet there was such a danger at the time of Christ's death, as is seen in Christ's words to the apostles: "All of you will suffer scandal tonight because of me" [Matt 26:31]. At that time the Jewish pontiffs were acting as pseudo-Christs and pseudo-prophets. They were saying that Christ had yet to come, and in the process they were employing Scripture, all their authority, and all their apparent zeal, even performing signs to seduce the elect. And at that time there was, properly speaking, great tribulation in the head of the church, that is, in Christ and his mother, to whom there was no one similar nor will there ever be. And if God had not shortened those days of his death to three, the elect would have died in desperation. Moreover, when the pontiff Caiaphas and his ilk sat passing a sentence of death on the son of God, the abomination of desolation stood in the holy place. In that time, much more than at the time when Pilate placed the image of Caesar in the temple or when the equestrian statue was placed there by Hadrian, the temple and the whole synagogue was, properly speaking, entirely desolate and destitute of God's grace, spiritual union, and solace. Immediately after this tribulation the sun was hidden in Christ's death, and the stars, that is, the doctors of the synagogue, fell from the heavens, that is, from the celestial state of the divine cultus, and the angelic powers were stirred up against them. After this the apostles, filled with the Holy Spirit, were given over to various tribulations and deaths and dispersed throughout the world in a short time, and they so preached the gospel that "their sound went out through all the world" [Ps 18:5], as Paul says [Rom 10] was actually fulfilled in his time. And on this account "wars and rumors of war" followed, and the end of the synagogue came through Titus at a day unforeseen by the carnal Jews. From the time of Christ's resurrection he began to come in great power and majesty, and in the Roman emperors he came so powerfully over the Jews that all the tribes of the earth mourned. But the apostles were sent like angels to gather the elect from among the gentiles of the whole earth.

Nevertheless, these words apply more properly to the second time, that of Antichrist, except for the part about the destruction of Jerusalem and day of judgment, although I think that, too, is to be fulfilled doubly and in a double sense: first, mystically and through a certain conformity with the time of Christ's death, when he was condemned by the pseudo-scribes and pseudo-pontiffs; second, literally and openly according to the type of Simon Magus, who said he was the Son of God, and the type of Nero, in the first persecution of the martyrs, as the apostle suggests in hidden fashion in 2 Thessalonians 2. The rest is easily applied, for after the tribulation of those days the gospel will be preached throughout the world, and then the end of the world will come.

Principium de doctrina Scripturae

The various principia *edited by David Flood in* Peter of John Olivi on the Bible, *short works that comprise the first 151 pages of that book and represent the earliest stages of Olivi's thought on the Bible, are valuable in corroborating that even at that stage he had a strong interest in the Apocalypse.*[70] *The* Principium de causis *is a good example.*[71] *Like a Bible commentary, it begins with a quotation from a book of the Bible, which, as we have seen, would be from some other book and would be used to offer an entrée into the book actually being studied. In this case the subject is sacred Scripture in general, and Olivi quotes Revelation 5:1, the seven seals, a subject the early part of the* principium *will address at length once Olivi has dispensed with the task of explaining the four causes of Scripture, also a common requirement at the time.*

The seven seals are relevant because Olivi goes from quoting Revelation 5:1 to describing his topic as "the infinite sea and impermeable abyss of holy Scripture."[72] *When he describes the seven seals, they turn out to involve a series of paradoxes. They combine unity with plurality, conformity with contrariety or deformity, actuality with potentiality, generality with specificity, substantiality with accidentality, the relative with the absolute, and being as it appears with being in itself. Thus the seven seals are presented as seven ways in which the Bible is sealed to us and becomes a* hortus conclusus.[73] *Olivi's way of dealing with the resultant hermeneutical dilemma involves some remarkably suggestive comments concerning mirrors.*

---

70. Flood, *Peter of John Olivi on the Bible,* edits five but regards only three as full-fledged *principia* on the study of holy Scripture. Of these, he sees their order of composition as *De causis Scripturae, De doctrina Scripturae,* and *De Christo, medio Scripturae.* He sees all three as written prior to the Isaiah and Matthew commentaries.

71. Edited by Flood in *Peter of John Olivi on the Bible,* 43–72. (Hereafter *De causis.*)

72. *De causis,* 43: "Scripturam sanctarum pelagus infinitum et impermeabilem abyssum."

73. *De causis,* 55, cites Canticles 4:12: "hortus conclusus, fons signatus."

It also involves an ingenious commentary on John 11, in which the rock that blocked the entrance to the tomb symbolizes the weight and impermeability of the letter blocking spiritual understanding, then Lazarus coming forth from the tomb represents spiritual interpretation, and all this is combined with a remarkable double interpretation of Christ's entry into Jerusalem and, more amazing still, with 2 Kings 18:31–32, interpreted as Elijah building two concentric circles, a wheel within a wheel (as in Ezek 1), which in turn is seen as the letter of the two testaments. Elijah has four vessels of water poured into the trench, producing four literal senses of Scripture; then his prayers turn the whole thing into fire, i.e., the spiritual sense. Elijah is significant in being the father of those who live in the desert as well as the future father of the concord between Jews and gentiles; and all of this looks both forward and backward to Christ at Cana calling for those six vessels of water.[74] Olivi is able to summon these complex combinations almost at will and make them sound not only plausible but nearly inevitable.

The Principium de studio *adds another important ingredient. In it he announces that, according to Paul and Pseudo-Dionysius, "Christian wisdom consists more of spiritual* gustus *than reason."[75] In the Isaiah commentary he presents* gustus *as a central element in prophetic assurance that an experience is from God.[76] Gustus is an ingredient in the sort of religious experience enjoyed by mystics in any age, but it will be enjoyed more deeply and more regularly as history progresses through the sixth and seventh periods.*

In the Principium de doctrina Scripturae, *Olivi offers us another meditation on an imaginary work of art, again depicting a king. He has been talking about parables, and this passage can be taken as*

---

74. *De causis*, 52: "Sicut autem in eadem materia ibi fuit forma aquae et vini, aquae naturaliter, vini vero supernaturaliter, ita in eadem materia litterae est literalis sensus et spiritualis: primus tamen secundum naturam et cursum rationis communem, secundus vero secundum solam legem divini spiritus supernaturalem. . . . Sex igitur hydriae est multitudo litterae, litteraliter sex aetates mundi describentes. In sexta enim aetate est littera Scripturae sacrae consummata."

75. *Principium de studio*, 28: "Item, sapientia christiana, secundum Dionysium libro De mystica theologia et secundum Apostolum 1 Ad Corinthios 2:6–9, potius consistit in spirituali gustu quam in rationali aspectu seu actu. Et ideo potius est rimanda et addiscenda per gustum devotionis quam per industriam humanae rationis."

76. *SI*, 195.

a parable of sorts. The artist must paint a picture of the king that
represents his glory and virtues, both intrinsic and extrinsic. The
way Olivi develops the story says a great deal about the importance
of metaphor in his exegesis.

Using only visual materials, he must represent the king's interior nature, his
soul and inner powers, vastly dissimilar things. One can understand that
in depicting the royal cloak and throne he might use colors similar to their
actual colors yet not show them in precisely the same shade throughout,
because the anterior and posterior parts and the interior and exterior parts
need to be distinguished. Later you might notice that not all of the outer
tunic is visible, and even less of the inner tunic. And you would see even
less that represents the color of skin and nothing at all that matches the
colors of the muscles, bones, interior veins, and humors. And nonetheless,
by proceeding in this manner, he can produce what those who know painting would recognize as a fine work, and they would recognize from it what
such and such a color represents, and what conveys the bones, the muscles,
and indeed the king's inner soul with all its virtues. And for similar reasons
that observer would understand why just that amount of any color would
be applied in the way it was applied in that particular place, something that
would be unknowable simply by studying the natures of the colors themselves. Instead, the observer would have to understand the reasoning behind
the image and the nature of the thing being represented by it. And knowing
that much, simply by inspecting the picture the observer would understand
the entire form of both the tunic and inner tunic, and he would say that one
was under the other according to its proper proportion, and the same would
be true of the muscles, bones, and all else that is interior.

He who knows nothing about the nature of images will be able to deduce none of these things. He will simply assume that the colors are placed
in no rational order and with no truth or utility intended. If, therefore, writings were added to the images in some places—for example, if in a painting
depicting the king's humility the words "Oh, how great the humility!" were
added—these words would help to open up the meaning of the painting to
one who already understood the intention behind the image and the nature
of the thing being represented; but someone else would not understand why
these words were placed there without others that would explain what was
intended, and if he came to any conclusion on the matter it would be more
likely wrong than right. Thus the words would further cloud the meaning
rather than reveal it.

Thus the prophets, sacred writers proceeding by the order and inspiration of God, wishing to describe to us the glory of God along with his power and works, expressed in their own words and similitudes things that were, in the works of God, more distant from God, more sensible and lowly, thus more of what applied to the Old Testament than to the New, and more of what applied to temporal matters than to spiritual and eternal. And always, the more they spoke of the spiritual and divine, the more they spoke in words that were dissimilar to what they were describing. Thus under the pallium there will be a tunic, and under the tunic flesh, and under the flesh muscles, blood, and bones. Thus under the sense of the letter pertaining to the Old Testament there will be a sense pertaining to the New; and under the sense pertaining to the time of the fullness of the gentiles there will be a sense pertaining to the time of the Jews and gentiles remaining [at the end]; and under all these there will be a sense pertaining to the state of glory of angels and human beings; and under these a sense pertaining to the state of glory of the soul of Christ; and under these that which pertains to the glory of God that he possesses in himself. And always, for the most part, the more spiritual will be under the more sensible, the contemplative under the active, and the more hidden aspects under the more manifest. Thus according to Ezekiel the wheel was within the wheel. [77]

77. *De doctrina Scripturae*, 106–7.

OLIVI'S COMMENTARY ON REVELATION

After his 1283 censure, Olivi was removed from his teaching responsibilities; but he must have felt he was on track again when he was rehabilitated and by 1288 found himself teaching in Florence, then by 1290 was back teaching in southern France. Nevertheless, the Franciscan order was increasingly divided over questions such as whether *usus pauper* was included in the vow and what levels of *usus pauper* should be expected. These were debates in which Olivi had already spoken at length, and his views, while measured and practical, placed him within the group that would come to be known as the "spirituals." In 1290, Nicholas IV, the first Franciscan pope, instructed the minister general, Raymond Geoffroi, to look into "certain brothers who seemed to introduce schism into the province of Provence, condemning the state of other brethren and considering themselves to be more spiritual than others."[1] An inquisitor, Bertrand de Sigotier, OFM, took charge of the investigation. The results were submitted to the general chapter of the order in 1292, and several brothers (one source says twenty-four) were disciplined. Olivi was spared but was forced to explain his view of *usus pauper* before the chapter. He asserted that it was indeed included in the vow, but only as defined by Nicholas III in *Exiit qui seminat*. That threw the dispute into a peculiar no-man's-land, since both sides had been claiming the support of *Exiit*.

The real significance of the 1290 investigation is that it marked the moment when a hitherto Franciscan debate became a papal concern. That

---

1. On the material in the next few paragraphs see my book *The Spiritual Franciscans* (University Park: Pennsylvania State University Press, 2001), ch. 4.

is, to be sure, partly concealed by the fact that all the participants were Franciscans; yet Nicholas and Bertrand were both acting in their higher roles.

It might also be significant that, while some of the more radical brothers were punished, Olivi was not. He and Nicholas had a history. When Nicholas was Jerome of Ascoli, minister general of the Franciscan order in the 1270s, he had taken action against some of Olivi's theological views.

One can easily overstate the importance of Olivi and the controversy in southern France. By 1292 the Franciscan province of Ancona had been arguing for over a decade. The controversy had begun around 1274, and it eventuated in several brothers (including Angelo Clareno) being imprisoned. They were discovered still in prison when, presumably in 1290, the new minister, Raymond Geoffroi, discovered them during a tour of the order. Recognizing that he was powerless to protect them from their superiors in Ancona, Raymond had sent them on a mission to Armenia; then, when that did not work out for them, he had referred them to the new pope, Celestine V, who made them a separate order, an arrangement that lasted only as long as Celestine's papacy, although Angelo and many of his brethren tried to act as if it could go on forever.

We cannot say much about what was happening in southern France during the years immediately following Olivi's 1292 experience at the general chapter, but we have every reason to guess that the situation was deteriorating. Certainly that was the case in Italy, and it is partly through Olivi that we are aware of that. In 1295 he wrote Conrad of Offida, an acquaintance of his in Italy and a major figure among the more zealous Italian brethren, a letter condemning the rebellious views and behavior of brothers who questioned not only the legitimacy of Celestine V's resignation but the lawfulness of previous papal declarations like Nicholas III's *Exiit qui seminat*, which they saw as violating Francis's rule and testament. In the process of criticizing these brothers, Olivi denied that the testament was binding and warned the rebellious brothers that their assertions would play into the hands of those who had said all along that the rule was impossible to observe and thus dangerous. As a result, it would discredit the voices of serious, responsible reformers, who would be dismissed as heretical extremists.

We can compare Olivi's letter with those written by the new pope, Boniface VIII, during the same period. Boniface describes a wide spectrum of behavior on the part of people cut loose from established ecclesiastical authority and thus left free to develop their own eccentricities. How much confidence we should feel in Boniface is, of course, a problem in itself; but his words as well as his actions suggest that Olivi's letter can be taken as more than hyperbole.

More bad news of a slightly different sort was on the way. In October 1295 Boniface removed Raymond Geoffroi from the office of minister general of the Franciscan order and, in his place, appointed John of Murrovalle. Raymond was probably Olivi's friend and may well have helped him to stay out of trouble in 1292. John, on the other hand, had been a member of the seven-man commission that censured Olivi in 1283. How much we can read into the change of leaders is hard to decide, but we can certainly imagine that it ushered in a new phase in the poverty controversy.

We do not know in any detail how Olivi spent his final years, although we do know that he was at Narbonne and that, among other academic projects, he wrote the Revelation commentary. We have evidence that he was still working on it in 1297. He died in March 1298.

The General Shape of Church History

Early in his commentary on Revelation, Olivi asks and answers a series of questions he obviously considers central. The first concerns the seven periods of church history. What are they? In listing the first four, Olivi follows the well-worn thirteenth-century path, speaking of (1) the origin of the church and its break with Judaism, (2) the martyrdom inflicted on it by the pagan world, (3) the refutation of heresy, and (4) the rise of the anchorites.

From the fifth period on, something different happens. Olivi sees the fifth period as a time "of common life, partly severe and partly condescensive, among monks and clerics having temporal possessions,"[2] followed by a sixth period featuring "renewal of the evangelical life, defeat of the anti-Christian sect, final conversion of Jews and gentiles alike, and rebuilding of a church similar to the first." The seventh period, "insofar as it applies to this life, is a certain quiet and wondrous participation in the future glory, as if the heavenly Jerusalem had descended to earth. Insofar as it refers to the other life it is the general resurrection, glorification of the saints, and consummation of all things."[3]

---

2. *Lectura Super Apocalypsim* (hereafter *LSA*), ed. Warren Lewis (St. Bonaventure, NY: Franciscan Institute Publications, 2015), 20–21, offers a remarkable explanation of the *condescensio* in terms of an inevitable human weakness, the human tendency to collapse following genuine high performance (as in the remarkable achievement of the third and fourth periods), leading to a drop in quality, which in turn brought on the Muslim conquests.

3. *LSA*, 7–8.

Olivi feels some clarifications are in order on the last matter and provides them, but his general point is clear enough. The fifth period is characterized by some slippage in certain quarters, leading to a sixth period that combines tribulation and renewal, with renewal and universal conversion being given the last word. The final period will begin in the church militant and will be one of peace and contemplation. The celebration will continue in heaven.

It would be hard to miss the similarity to Bonaventure's historical pattern. Olivi begins the fifth period where Bonaventure begins the sixth, that is, with Charlemagne; then he begins his sixth period with Francis. More precisely (and here we encounter an important element in Olivi's theology of history), he says, "it begins from Francis's time, but will begin more fully with the damnation of Babylon the great whore, when the aforesaid angel signed with the seal of Christ will seal through his people Christ's future militia." The seventh period "will begin in one sense with the death of that Antichrist who calls himself God and the messiah of the Jews, and in another sense with the extreme and final judgment."[4]

Such a formulation introduces substantial ambiguity into the apocalyptic timetable. In fact, it's even more complicated than that. In commenting on Revelation 6:12–7:13, Olivi asks himself when the sixth period begins and replies that some people date it from "the revelation made to the Abbot Joachim and perhaps to some of his contemporaries concerning the third general age," which contains the sixth and seventh periods of the church. Others favor the birth of the Franciscan order, or the attack on the Franciscan rule by the carnal church, or the destruction of the carnal church. Sensibly considered, Olivi says, all of these can be taken as true, just as each of the four evangelists portrays the gospel of Christ as beginning with a different event and the beginning of the Babylonian captivity varies according to which prophet one reads.[5] What we are presented with in the latter remark is a double *concordia* in which the events of the early sixth period in church history parallel those of the sixth period in Old Testament history but also parallel the life of Christ, who ushered in the sixth period of world history. That in turn offers us a timely reminder that the same passage of Scripture can refer to several events. This multiple reference can be based on a distinction between the general and the particular, as when the beast from the sea in Revelation 13:1 is interpreted as referring to the whole beastly

4. *LSA*, 9–10.
5. *LSA*, 309–10.

crowd of reprobates opposing the elect throughout history but can also be applied in particular to the Muslims; or it can be applied to several particular phenomena other than the Muslims. As we will see, Olivi takes the same passages as referring to both the mystical and great Antichrists.

Once we begin hunting for these multiple references it becomes hard to stop, but we will move on after allowing ourselves one more example, the earthquake in Revelation 6:12. Olivi sees it as referring to the spiritual earthquake caused by conversions to the Franciscan life in Francis's time, as well as opposition to these conversions by the carnal church; yet he also sees it as referring to the Albigensian crusade; to "commotions and subversions" in Italy that he leaves unexplained; and to the Mongol invasions, especially the devastation of Hungary. Having listed all these as evidence of the second beginning of the sixth age, Olivi goes on to describe the attack on the Franciscan rule in the time of the mystical Antichrist and resultant upsets in the church as belonging to the third beginning, and events surrounding the great Antichrist's death as belonging to the fourth.[6] Olivi grants that what is said concerning the opening of the sixth seal will not be completely fulfilled until the death of the great Antichrist and the destruction of the carnal church, and thus the passage refers "more literally" to that fourth beginning, although it can be applied "in various respects and senses" to all the others.[7]

So, then, what period does Olivi actually think he's in? He's in both the fifth and the sixth, because, as he explains elsewhere, the new period grows within the old one like a baby in the womb or a chicken in the egg.[8] It can be a long gestation period, nearly a century already in this case; yet the change will be dramatic. What is being born here is not simply the time of the two Antichrists but also the time of Christ's second advent in the spirit. In the Revelation commentary, Olivi does accept not only the Joachite system of sevens with *concordiae* but also the triune ages of Father, Son, and Holy Spirit; but he also continues to employ the system of three advents featured in his early exegesis, according to which Christ came in the flesh in the first century, is in the process of coming in the spirit in Olivi's time, and will come in judgment at the end of time.[9]

6. *LSA*, 312–13.

7. *LSA*, 319–20.

8. *LSA*, 2, 34.

9. See not only the preceding chapter but also my article, "Olivi, Christ's Three Advents, and the Double Antichrist," *Franciscan Studies* 74 (2016): 15–40.

This combination intensifies the progressive note already seen in the Isaiah and Matthew commentaries. Like other commentators on Revelation, Olivi begins the prologue to the Revelation commentary with a quotation from another Old Testament book, in this case Isaiah 30:26: "There will be a light of the moon like that of the sun, and the light of the sun will be seven-fold like the light of seven days on the day that God binds up the wounds of his people and heals their injury." He goes on to say that on the day Christ came the sun of the new law was able to radiate sevenfold and the old law, which had been like the moon, was able to glow like the sun; for the veil cast over it was taken away through the light of Christ, according to Paul (2 Cor 3:13–16). Had Olivi stopped there he would have been making a point about the difference in Old Testament interpretation before and after Christ; yet even Paul goes further than that. He speaks of being "transformed into the image of Christ with ever-increasing glory" (2 Cor 3:18). Olivi speaks of being "transformed into the light and glory of Christ according to the progress and situation of the church."

It is pointless to be too literal about the image of sevenfold advancement, but it makes an important point in any case. The illumination that accompanies the transition from Old Testament to Christ will be further increased by that accompanying the arrival of the sixth period of church history and the later contemplative experiences made available by the transition to the seventh. Thus the advancement is progressive, involving not only the first century but all that occurs thereafter; and it involves knowledge in the sense that most of us would think of it, but it also involves contemplative experience beyond our present imagination.

The result of all this is not only new knowledge but new Christians through universal conversion.

Again, under the sixth angel blowing the trumpet it is written that the angel with a face like the sun descends with an open book in his hand (Rev 10:1–2). When that book was first seen it was closed (Rev 5:1). And he shouted that, in the time of the seventh angel blowing the trumpet, the mystery of God spread through his prophets would be consummated. The book was given to John, that is, to the contemplative and evangelical state designated by John, and it was said to him, you must preach to many peoples and races and tongues and kings (Rev 10:11).

That is, the advancement will constitute part of the springboard that will propel persecuted spiritual men of the new age into the preaching that will result in universal conversion of both the Jews and gentiles; but we must avoid getting ahead of ourselves. For the moment it is sufficient to notice that the way Olivi packs various angels into a single passage is reminiscent of Bonaventure's *Collationes in hexaemeron*, although Olivi is making a very different point (if indeed we can be sure what point Bonaventure is making).

We should pause for a moment to underline a statement already made earlier. There is a sense in which specific things occur in a given time (e.g., persecution in the second period or a wealth of contemplative experience in the seventh); yet everything also happens in other times. Olivi knows there were Old Testament prophets who had mystical experiences. He has also been told about Pentecost. He has learned of the desert fathers. The interesting thing about his exegetical structure—seven visions, the first five of which cover all seven periods of church history[10]—is that he can manipulate it to emphasize both the differences and the commonalities of various historical moments. Not only does the overlapping nature of periods mean that single events happen in multiple periods (just as Olivi himself was born in both the fifth and sixth periods), but the repetitive nature of much human experience means that the same things constantly happen in multiple periods (e.g., the Jews remain blind throughout the first five periods). Nevertheless, in certain periods particular things are so noteworthy that they become characteristic of that particular period. Thus we have a period dedicated to martyrdom; yet martyrdom occurs in other periods, too.

The Importance of the Sixth Period

Is there, however, one of the seven periods that deserves special attention? As far as Olivi is concerned, it is the sixth.

> The sixth member of each vision and the sixth vision of this book declare that in the sixth period of the church the singular perfection of Christ's life and wisdom will be revealed and the oldness of the prior time so universally repelled that, the old things thus rejected, it will seem that a certain new world or new church will then be formed, just as in Christ's first advent a new church was formed, the old synagogue being rejected.

---

10. There is a sense in which all seven visions do so, although Olivi acknowledges that the final two concentrate on the end time in a way the others do not. For moments when he acknowledges the difference, see *LSA*, 7, 12, 16, 32.

And that is why, . . . although in these visions a triple advent of Christ is presented [and] . . . although the second advent is in the entire development of the church and glorification of the saints, nonetheless, rightly and congruently, by a certain antonomasia it is appropriated to the sixth period.[11]

Or again,

Just as, in the sixth age, carnal Judaism and the oldness of the prior world having been rejected, the new man Christ came with his new law, life, and cross, thus in the sixth period, the carnal church and the oldness of the prior world having been rejected, the law, life, and cross of Christ will be renewed, for in the first beginning of it Francis appeared marked with the wounds of Christ and entirely crucified with and configured to Christ.[12]

It would be hard to imagine language that comes closer to declaring the sixth period to be the birth of something radically new. Or at least it would be hard to imagine the point being made without actually making a leap into heresy. Olivi has no intention of making that leap. In reality, what we have is another *concordia*, one that places Francis and his order *within* the history of Christianity, not beyond it. The sevenfold history of Christianity as accepted by thirteenth-century exegesis of Revelation is placed within the sixth and final period of world history, the period of Christianity as portrayed by Augustine. The passage allows us to see, not only that Francis should be considered *alter Christus*, but *how* he should be considered such. This passage and others like it should be considered later in this chapter when we look at the first of those fourteenth-century scholars commissioned by John XXII to evaluate Olivi's Revelation commentary. John was particularly interested in hearing what those scholars had to say about Olivi's notion that the sixth period was somehow preeminent over the first five; although neither he nor the scholar we will examine had any great interest in attempting to see what Olivi was actually *trying* to do.

We do have such an interest, however, and thus we should recognize that Olivi takes one more step in proclaiming the centrality of the sixth period. It is the key to understanding the previous periods. In other words, knowledge of those early periods depends on our understanding of the sixth

11. *LSA*, 42–43.
12. *LSA*, 70.

period and its significance. This, too, could be seen as a *concordia*. Just as our interpretation of the entire Old Testament depends on our interpretation of Christ's life, death, and resurrection, so our interpretation of church history as a whole depends on our interpretation of the sixth period.[13]

There is a sense in which Olivi is simply making a point about the value of historical perspective. His analogy of the three mountains is significant in this regard.[14] When we see three mountains from a great distance, we see them as one. Then we arrive at the first mountain and see another behind it, but we still think there are only two. Then we climb the second and see the truth for the first time. In describing this process, we could be talking about Christ's three advents as presented by Olivi or about Joachim's three ages. Certainly Olivi's generally progressive reading of history makes it easier for him to challenge Augustine than was the case with any number of previous thirteenth-century theologians. After all, Augustine witnessed only four centuries of Christian history, while Olivi has access to almost fourteen.

Francis and the New Age

Yet there is more to the centrality of the sixth period than accumulating centuries of historical perspective beyond what Augustine enjoyed. We are back to Isaiah and the sevenfold increases in light. Something new is happening, and it is telegraphed by reference to "the new man Christ." Consider another passage in which Olivi says,

> I have heard from a certain spiritual man very worthy of trust, a man on familiar terms with Brother Leo, blessed Francis's confessor and companion, something . . . I myself neither assert nor know for sure, nor do I even think it should be asserted. This person received, both through the words of Brother Leo and through a revelation made to him personally, the news that during that Babylonian temptation when Francis's state and rule is being crucified as Christ was crucified, Francis will gloriously rise again so that, just as he was singularly assimilated to Christ in receiving the stigmata, so he will be assimilated to Christ in a resurrection necessary for the confirmation and instruction of his disciples, just as Christ's resurrection was necessary for the confirmation of the apostles and in order to instruct

13. See *LSA*, 45–46, where Olivi seems to say precisely that.
14. *LSA*, 73–74.

them concerning the establishment and government of the future church. Nevertheless, in order that Francis the servant's resurrection should be clearly inferior in dignity to those of Christ and his mother, Christ rose again immediately after three days and certain people not entirely to be rejected say that his mother rose again after forty days, whereas Francis will do so only when the history of his order has progressed to the time when the order is assimilated to Christ's cross in being crucified, a crucifixion already prefigured in Francis's stigmata.[15]

What we are given here is certainly yet another example of a *concordia*, in which the larger story involving Christ in the sixth age of world history is reflected by the smaller one of Francis in the sixth period of church history; but it is much more that that. Olivi is carrying the theme of Francis as *alter Christus* to its logical conclusion. Nor is he the first to do so. There are two passages in Bonaventure that point roughly in that direction. The difference is that Bonaventure was obviously speaking metaphorically. Olivi is not. Certainly he says explicitly that he is not asserting it, and elsewhere he anticipates Francis's help coming in a way that does not tie him to a physical resurrection. For example, he says in another passage (regarding Rev 10:5–7) that "from the time of the solemn opposition and condemnation of the evangelical life and rule to be effected under the mystical Antichrist and to be more fully consummated under the great Antichrist, Christ and his servant Francis and the angelical band of his disciples will descend against the errors and evil deeds of the world."[16] In what follows, Olivi makes it clear that what he says of Francis's descent applies to the behavior of his faithful disciples within the order. In other words, Francis's descent becomes a metaphor for what his living followers will do in the face of tribulation.

Nevertheless, that doesn't allow us to explain away the other reference to Francis's resurrection as metaphorical. There Olivi is talking about a physical resurrection. Nor does he say it only in the Revelation commentary. In his Matthew commentary, written almost two decades earlier, he says this:

It has been revealed, as I have heard from a very spiritual man, that this will be fulfilled by the angel of the sixth seal with certain of his confreres in order that he should conform to Christ in his resurrection as well as in his passion, and in order that his disciples at that time, nearly enticed

15. *LSA*, 336.
16. *LSA*, 455.

into error, should have an instructor and comforter as the apostles had the risen Christ.[17]

And he's not the only Franciscan to raise this possibility. Ubertino da Casale, in his *Arbor vitae* (written in 1305), says,

> While Francis was engaged in contemplation on Mount Alverna, it was promised to him that his order would last until the end of the world, and that his rule would die then rise again. And I have heard a stupendous thing, which I do not assert with temerity but rather recite devoutly to the devout. I heard from the holy Brother Conrad and from many others worthy of faith that blessed Francis, after his glorification in heaven, revealed to the holy Brother Leo—and is said to have revealed to some others— that in this appearance Christ predicted to Francis the tribulations that would be visited upon his order and upon the church, the condemnation and corruption his rule would suffer, the great confusion that would take root in the minds of spiritual men, his sons, due to the universal attack on this rule; and Christ in his mercy promised that for their comfort and illumination he would resuscitate Francis in his glorious body, making him appear visibly to his children. That this will actually take place can be devoutly awaited but not temerariously asserted. Nevertheless, there is some reason to expect it, for just as Francis was singularly like Christ in his passion, so he may be conformed with him beyond all others in anticipating the resurrection, particularly since its purpose will be to strengthen faith and confirm the truth of the evangelical life.[18]

Like Olivi, Ubertino offers the same thought elsewhere in somewhat vaguer form. He says, "The origin, development, horrendous ruin, and glorious resurrection of the order in conformity with Christ's life was revealed, not only to blessed Francis but to several of his companions, not by one revelation but by many incapable of being doubted."[19] So both Olivi and Ubertino offer passages that give the charitable reader room to believe they're not really predicting a bodily resurrection for Saint Francis; yet each also has at least one passage in which he seems to state rather clearly that a physical resurrection is exactly what he has in mind.

17. MS New College 49, 155rb–va.
18. *Arbor vitae* 5:4, ff. 220vb–221ra.
19. *Arbor vitae* 5:3, ff. 219va.

Nor does the source they're quoting leave much room for maneuver. Obviously their source is Brother Conrad of Offida, a man both of them knew personally, and this view is enshrined in the *Sayings of Brother Conrad*. There Conrad predicts the standard decay and renewal of the Franciscan life, but then he adds, "Some say that Francis should appear in the world corporeally because of the terrible questions and tribulations that will arise."[20]

Thus, of the major spiritual Franciscan spokesmen in the final decade of the thirteenth century and first decade of the fourteenth, three out of four speculate that Francis might be resurrected so that he can help his loyal followers deal with the tribulation that will engulf the order. The fourth major spiritual, Angelo Clareno, does not predict any such thing, which is in itself interesting when we consider that parts of Angelo's commentary on the Franciscan rule reflect parts of the *Verba Conradi*, in fact sometimes word for word. That is another matter, however, leading us into the question of whether we can justifiably treat the *Verba Conradi* as an authentic source dedicated to the words of Conrad of Offida. The important thing for our purposes is that Olivi predicts Francis's resurrection.[21]

Imminent Tribulation and the Carnal Church

For the moment, the important thing about Francis's projected resurrection is its rationale. Why will he need to come back? The answer is clear: the Franciscan life is heading for its own crucifixion and will need help. We finally arrive at the dark side of living within the transition between the fifth and sixth periods. The church has been suffering through a "horrendous laxity and blindness" in the late fifth period, which will carry it into the temptation of Antichrist in the sixth.[22] It is a message Olivi delivers again and again. He portrays himself as living in an era marred

---

20. *Verba Fratris Conradi*, ch. 2, ed. P. Sabatier, in *Opuscules de critique historique*, 1 (Paris, 1903), 374.

21. The idea of Francis as *alter Christus* rising from the dead found an odd parallel at Milan in 1300 when an inquisitor had to deal with a group that saw Guiglielma as the incarnation of the Holy Spirit, currently in the process of rising from the dead, with a very public ascension to take place in the future. See my "Olivi, Maifreda, Na Prous, and the Shape of Joachism, ca. 1300," *Franciscan Studies* 73 (2015): 274–94.

22. *LSA*, 395.

not only by the great imperfection in possession and disposition of temporals witnessed in the church, but also by great pride, luxury, simony, litigation, fraud, and rapine, through which around the end of the fifth period practically the whole church from bottom to top is infected, disordered, and turned, as it were, into a new Babylon.[23]

In the complaint just quoted about "horrendous laxity and blindness," he goes on to say that the church "seems to be Babylon rather than Jerusalem, and more a synagogue of the reprobate persecuting Christ and his spirit than the church of Christ." Again, in yet another passage, he notes that "the seat of the beast (that is, of the beastly crowd) is raised up so that it prevails in numbers and power and nearly absorbs the seat of Christ, with which it is mixed in place and name." This beastly crowd, he says, is also called Babylon the whore.[24]

In these passages Olivi uses words like "as it were" (*quasi*), "seems" (*videatur*), and "nearly" (*fere*) to keep from explicitly identifying the institutional church with Babylon, but he is not consistently that careful. Certainly he makes it clear that part of the institutional church is still Christian and not allied with the beast, but the fact remains that the part of it that he calls "the carnal church," the part that will soon be destroyed by a pagan army, is already making strides in seizing control of ecclesiastical leadership. He speaks of "the carnal clergy reigning and presiding over the entire church in this fifth period" as "the seat of the beast," and he feels they are much more securely established there than among the laity.[25]

What are the issues at stake here? So far we have seen a number of ways in which Olivi sees the church as corrupt. If we had time we could add several more. He shows some interest in heresy and particularly identifies Catharism with the fifth period. He is also exercised about the influence of pagan philosophy on Christian thought. But if there is one issue that stands out, one area in which he shows particular concern, it is Franciscan poverty.

Here we have a matter that has been central in his thinking from the beginning of his scholarly career. It surfaces in a particularly significant way around 1279 in the eighth of his *Quaestiones de perfectione evangelica*, where he ties it to Christianity in a way that makes the two seem inseparable. We have seen that according to Olivi the greatest temptation of history, the battle

23. *LSA*, 38–39.
24. *LSA*, 682.
25. *LSA*, 683.

between Christ and Antichrist, is about to occur and will heavily involve "the life of Christ" recently revived by Francis, which Olivi identifies with evangelical poverty. He emphasizes that placing an excessive value on wealth is "the door to the sect of Antichrist as well as the entire Jewish and Muslim error." If we deny that the poverty chosen by the Franciscan order is better than having possessions either individually or in common, "then it follows that Christ was not the Christ promised by the Law and the prophets," and we are left waiting with the Jews for a messiah still to come.[26] Thus an error concerning the *life* of Christ implies an error concerning the *person* of Christ. We have already seen this passage, but it's worth repeating because it's breathtaking in the way it combines poverty, Judaism, Islam, and an Islamicized Aristotelianism into a neat package. The element of Islamicized Aristotelianism is, to be sure, unmentioned in the passage quoted here, but elsewhere Olivi conceives it in such a way that he can work it, too, into the temptation of Antichrist as another overvaluation of worldly achievement. He is a remarkably coherent thinker. Carnality is a basic category tying together Judaism, Islam, Aristotelianism, and the corrupt contemporary church. It might seem that Catharism is the only phenomenon that refuses to fit into the pattern, but Olivi has his suspicions about the Cathar *perfecti*, too. He tells us that they follow a literal and carnal interpretation of Scripture while placing a high value on sense experience.[27]

Olivi is convinced that in his own time things have become notably worse. Not only do most of the clergy and monks think poorly of the mendicants, but "many of those who renounce common goods say that *usus pauper* is not included in the vow."[28] The remark neatly locates Olivi within the welter of ecclesiastical battles howling around him. Within his own order, his own brethren have taken sides for or against the idea of *usus pauper* as included in the Franciscan vow. Olivi has chosen for it and finds himself in a decided minority.

Things will soon get even worse than that. Olivi fears that the pope, who has hitherto protected observers of evangelical poverty from their enemies, will turn against them.[29] He will form an alliance with an evil secu-

---

26. Q. 8, 105.

27. *LSA*, 170–71, 417. In fact, though, he thinks Catharism is a poor candidate for inclusion in the temptation of Antichrist since it "contains so many stupid and patently absurd errors that the wise can in no way be seduced by it." See the long critique in *LSA*, 411–13, arguing that Aristotle and Averroes are the more dangerous enemies.

28. *LSA*, 413.

29. *LSA*, 429.

lar ruler, and together they will attack the faithful observers of evangelical poverty. This will be the temptation of the mystical Antichrist. Which of the two, the pope or the ruler, will be the mystical Antichrist remains unclear, although if Olivi had money he would certainly put it on the pope, who will actually be a pseudo-pope, because by attacking evangelical perfection he will mark himself as a heretic.[30] The resultant temptation will be so intense that even the faithful will almost be led into error. All the standard authority figures will be united against them: ecclesiastical leaders, university professors, superiors of religious orders, secular leaders, everyone with education and position.

Conversion and the Millennium

Faced with such opposition, the small group that remains faithful will go to ground. They will find the laity more hospitable to them than the clergy, and they will discover more receptive listeners among the Greeks, Muslims, Mongols, and Jews than among the carnal Latin Christians. In these worst of all conditions, universal conversion will take place.

The conditions will continue to worsen. A non-Christian army will attack with the aim of destroying Christendom. In fact, they will succeed in destroying the carnal church, but the evangelical church will continue. It will, of course, have been handed from one set of oppressors to another, but a very different set with different aims. Pseudo-Christian leaders will have been replaced by anti-Christian leaders. The persecution of the great Antichrist will have begun. It, too, will be led by a pseudo-pope and secular ruler, and here, too, Olivi tends to favor the pseudo-pope for the title of Antichrist.

This is a story most of us might feel we have heard before, and in a sense we did hear it much earlier in Olivi's Matthew commentary, where an insider/outsider or pseudo-Christian/non-Christian contrast is portrayed by presenting us with the Jews and then the Romans; yet this is ultimately different. Olivi knows who the Jews were and are as well as who the Romans were and are. Here the challenge is to look beyond Jews and Romans, in fact beyond anything he has read about or experienced, and imagine a western Europe in which the church has been obliterated and a presumably Muslim power (or something even more foreign) is ruling with the aid of an only vaguely defined religious leader. Somehow this world has emerged after the

---

30. Olivi is also open to the possibility that he will not be canonically elected, either.

temptation of the spiritual Antichrist, whom Olivi can at least imagine because he feels it is pretty much the present situation intensified; but after that he is in unexplored territory. Thus he is remarkably shy when it comes to explaining what the temptation of the great Antichrist will look like, how it will end, or how the church in the seventh period will comport itself.

Here the problem is compounded by the fact that, whereas *Vox domini* and other similar Franciscan commentaries have only a brief post-Antichrist repentance period to consider, Olivi projects a third age of close to one thousand years. Among Olivi's contributions, one should certainly include his sense of a third age that will be substantially more than a half-hour of silence (as Rev 8:1 would put it). I have examined Olivi's apocalyptic timetable at some length elsewhere,[31] concluding that he manipulated a great variety of numbers culled from various passages of Revelation and followed where they led, which is to say in various directions, though Olivi proves skillful at making them lead toward the early fourteenth century as he seeks a date for the dawn of the third age. One of the most important passages, though, involves the thousand years in Revelation 20:2, which provides him with a near-millennium from Constantine to around the end of the thirteenth century. Given a bit of latitude, that could be seen as leading to the two Antichrists.

That gives him a virtual millennium of the second age, the age of the Son. What about the age of the Holy Spirit, then? Olivi cites an ancient Hebraic belief that there will be two thousand years before the law, two thousand more under it, and two thousand under the messiah. That might suggest a third age only around half as long as the second. Olivi observes that some people draw that same conclusion from Revelation 8:1. The significant thing here is that years earlier, in the Matthew commentary and elsewhere, Olivi had already decided that the important thing is not to argue for a specific number of years for the third age but simply to establish that it will last a long time, long enough for it to be established and enjoyed, then fade into disorder, until things are so bad that Christ will feel required to come again, this time for final judgment.

This sense of three ages becoming established, blooming, and then fading out has its effects, not only on Christ, but on Gog. Once more Olivi reviews the interstice between the first and second advents, then that between the second and third. The first involves Antichrist and the second Gog; but for Olivi the names become to some degree interchangeable. In

---

31. Burr, *Olivi's Peaceable Kingdom*, ch. 7.

his exegesis of the dragon in Revelation 12 and then in Revelation 17, he offers alternate expositions. In the first, the mystical Antichrist will be part of the fifth head of the beast, the great Antichrist will be the sixth head, and Gog will be the seventh. In the other interpretation, the sixth head will be the mystical Antichrist, the seventh will be the great Antichrist, and *Gog novissimus* will be the tail. In dealing with Revelation 20, after noting that the period from Pope Sylvester's death to the imminent end of the thirteenth century is approximately one thousand years, Olivi remarks that, if you take this period as running not to the future Gog around the time of the last judgment at the end of the seventh period, but rather to Gog insofar as the name refers to both the mystical and the open Antichrist in the sixth period, then it is unknown whether the seventh period, from the death of Antichrist to *Gog novissimus*, will literally be another thousand years. If we look at the double sense of "Gog" already noted by Olivi in the Matthew commentary, we recognize that Olivi had been concerned about the problem since the early 1280s, even as, in the meantime, his sense of the double Antichrist had developed notably.

Life in the Third Age

In asking himself what the church might look like during an extended seventh period or third age, Olivi does have two things to rely on: Joachism and Franciscanism. The two in combination allow him to explore life in the seventh age from the perspective of central issues such as knowledge and leadership. In *Olivi's Peaceable Kingdom*, I suggested that both were important, but the Franciscan model was the more important of the two.[32] Here Bonaventure's *Collationes in hexaemeron*—with its seventh period of peace and enlightenment mirroring the original state of the church to some extent, yet also modeled on Francis to some extent, a period in which the church militant "will be conformed with the church triumphant so far as is possible on the pilgrim way"—offered Olivi an important direction in which to look in his effort to describe the seventh period.

For Olivi, that meant a return of the church to apostolic poverty. It also meant peace conceived as an end not only of warfare but of heresy and schism. Seen from another perspective, it promised universal conversion, a conversion aided by the fact that, in order to escape persecution by the

---

32. Burr, *Olivi's Peaceable Kingdom*, 186–95.

carnal church, spiritual children of Saint Francis would live among Mongols, Muslims, Greeks, and Jews, who would gradually be converted. It meant inner peace, leaving us free to explore new spiritual possibilities. Thus the Franciscan invocation, "Peace to this house," pointed toward a whole new state to be realized by the world in the seventh period.

Peace and conversion would be closely related to increased spiritual knowledge. Here again we are dealing with a phenomenon Olivi saw as already evident in Francis but also (as we have seen) increasingly discernible in other mystics, including some he personally knew. What is at stake here is fuller understanding of the Bible and of church history, but also mystical experience unmediated through writings or spoken words. This expectation "is already being fulfilled, will be fulfilled *secundum quid* in the church militant, and will be fulfilled *simpliciter* in the church triumphant."[33]

Church government will also change. Olivi shows little interest in ecclesiastical structure but great concern with the quality of leadership. Leaders will be not only poor but humble. They will see themselves not as lords but as servants, and they will forbid their subordinates to honor them. That will inspire the subordinates to honor them all the more. Thus the basis of leadership will be charismatic rather than juridical. Such a refurbished church deserves a new capital. Olivi suggests that it will be centered in Jerusalem.

This portrait of a renewed Christianity, lovely as it seems, must be balanced against Olivi's conviction that eventually decay will set in and Christ will be forced to return in judgment. In this respect he is faithful to Joachim, and he is faithful to the thoughts on an extended seventh period laid out earlier in his gospel commentaries.

In fact, there is little in the Revelation commentary that is not anticipated in his early biblical scholarship. In most respects, Olivi arrived at his views early and stuck to them. Moreover, in most respects these views reflected the standard Parisian model; yet in certain cases (like the extended seventh period and his placement of both Francis and himself in the sixth period) he broke from that model in ways that significantly changed his historical perspective. In the latter case he was following Bonaventure, and doing so allowed him to see the sixth period in both a negative and a positive light. It was the period of Antichrist, but also the period of Christ's advent in the Spirit. In his reading of the sixth period, the highs were higher and the lows lower. Like *Spiritu magno vidit* (presumably, as we have seen, by Vital du Four) in some ways, Olivi offered a dystopian view of the church in the

---

33. *LSA*, 845–46.

sixth period, but an even more dystopian one than *Spiritu magno vidit*, one in which a pope not only would serve both the mystical and real Antichrist but would probably *be* both the mystical and real Antichrist. Yet, unlike *Spiritu magno vidit*, Olivi pictured the persecution of the real Antichrist as giving way to an era of peace and spiritual perfection lasting close to a millennium.

That much might seem enough to say about Olivi's millenarian visions, yet much more might be offered. Certainly, more could be said comparing him with Joachim, but it would then be necessary to say more about the connection with Francis's leadership as seen in early Franciscan sources and, perhaps more surprisingly, John of Parma as portrayed by Salimbene, Angelo Clareno, and others. There is a sense in which Olivi is tapping into a vision of Franciscan leadership that, somewhat like the Camelot legend, remains aspirational, yet trembles on the brink of realization in the minds of many friars, the dream of a once and future minister general.

The Condemnation of Olivi's Revelation Commentary

Examination of the Revelation commentary began almost immediately after Olivi's death, continuing at a leisurely rate for the first two decades.[34] On his deathbed he had submitted his work to the pope for correction, so the commentary was sent to Boniface VIII along with other works by him. Boniface apparently gave it to Gilles of Rome for examination, but little or nothing came of that for some time. During the first two decades after Olivi's death, his apocalyptic thought hardly went unnoticed, but the spiritual-conventual controversy was in full swing, and the argument was mainly about the nature of true Franciscan poverty. The Franciscans found themselves at odds over whether the order needed serious reform, a question that Pope Clement V tried unsuccessfully to settle at the council of Vienne in 1312.[35] Apocalyptic thought was an ingredient in the discussion, but the focus was on what sort

---

34. A good summary of the process is found at Sylvain Piron, "La consultation demandée à François de Meyronnes sur la *Lectura super Apocalipsim*," *Oliviana* 3 (2009), http://oliviana.revues.org/330, posted online April 3, 2009, accessed December 21, 2016; and by me in *Olivi's Peaceable Kingdom*, chs. 9–10; but Piron's article includes sources not yet discovered when I wrote the book and identifies other sources I did not identify. Thus it represents the current state of scholarship on the basis of which my book should be corrected.

35. It is this problem that I principally address in *The Spiritual Franciscans*, especially chs. 5–9. Some of the apocalyptic elements in this period are discussed in *Olivi's Peaceable Kingdom*, 198–203.

of life was demanded by the Franciscan rule and vow, then on the question of obedience.

The discussion during these years was, to be sure, among prelates and Franciscans, with some of both on each side of the debate; yet a third group had begun to notice what was going on. One of the most interesting things about Olivi is that he seems to have been carrying through a definable project among the laity during the latter part of his life. It goes back at least to his time in Florence but can be said to have taken off after his return to Languedoc, his home territory. At that point we can define it with some confidence as an effort to educate the laity by translating works originally written in Latin and by writing a number of short works in the vernacular. Olivi was certainly a major force, but he must have enjoyed the aid of other spiritual Franciscans. At any rate, an increasingly literate laity was being armed, not only with devotional and moral works written specifically for them, but with some or all of the Revelation commentary in translation.[36]

Clement V had at least tried to see both sides and to forge a settlement that would hold the order together. His successor, John XXII (1316–1334), decided to settle the matter by forcing the spiritual Franciscans to obey, and he stayed alive long enough to make life miserable for them; yet inquisitorial documents from the period suggest that what he achieved was not so much victory as serious resistance, not only among the spirituals but among their lay supporters. By the end of May 1318, four spiritual Franciscans had been burned at the stake, and others were under investigation by inquisitors. Many became fugitives and were in hiding, protected by supporters who eventually managed to produce an underground railroad of sorts that smuggled spirituals out of France and all the way to Sicily.

The time seemed ripe for a serious investigation not only of the spirituals but of the Revelation commentary that seemed to inspire them; and the inquisitor Michel Le Moine, OFM, in sentencing the first four to be burned in 1318, had already encouraged attention to it by announcing that the heresy of the Franciscan spirituals stemmed from Olivi and especially from his Revelation commentary. He observed that Olivi's works had already

---

36. Antonio Montefusco and Sylvain Piron, "In vulgari nostro," *Oliviana* 5 (2016), http://journals.openedition.org/oliviana/904, posted online June 5, 2017, accessed March 24, 2018; Antonio Montefusco, "Il progetto bilingue di Olivi e la memoria dissidente," in *Pietro di Giovanni Olivi Frate Minore* (Spoleto: Centro Italiano di Studi sull'Alto Medioevo, 2016), 185–209. Both articles are valuable not only in themselves but also for the bibliography they contain. Although still young, Montefusco has been engaged in this work for some time now and has built up an impressive bibliography on the subject.

been condemned and burned by his own order but had now again been submitted to certain cardinals and masters for judgment by Pope John XXII. In the meantime, they were not to be read, nor should Olivi be revered as a saint. The latter reminds us that after Olivi died in 1298 and was buried at Narbonne, his tomb had become a popular pilgrimage site, and he himself was credited with miracles. All of that was still going on in 1318, even though it was forced into secrecy.

In 1318, Guido Terrini, a Carmelite, and Pierre de la Palud, a Dominican, read and judged an abridged version of Olivi's Revelation commentary in the vernacular.[37] The investigation picked up momentum when John XXII entrusted a single cardinal, Niccolo da Prato, with the task of overseeing the Olivi process, and then Niccolo in turn extracted several passages and gave them to a single theologian identified by Joseph Koch as probably the Dominican Guillaume de Laudun,[38] but more recently identified by Patrick Nold as the Augustinian hermit Gregory of Lucca.[39] Nold's identification is far from definite, yet it has so much to recommend it that we will call the author "Gregory" here. Gregory reported his findings before the end of 1318. Selected passages were then submitted to an eight-man commission that included two Franciscans. We have Gregory's entire work in a single manuscript,[40] although we might wish we did not. It is repetitious, devoid of folio numbers, and large parts of the manuscript are either illegible or nearly so.

Nevertheless, Nold provides an excellent reading of Gregory's critique. Just as important, he is the first person to identify the plentiful annotations in the manuscript as by John XXII and include them in the discussion. He sees that the date they were added must be considered a separate issue. He recognizes that John could have written them as early as 1319, but he prefers to see them as roughly concurrent with the period 1324–1326 when John prepared a list of issues on which he asked a group of consultants to give their opinions, then issued his final opinion. More on that in a moment,

37. We know from inquisitorial sources as well that Olivi's commentary was translated at least in abridged form and thus made available to the laity. Was this the same translation?

38. Joseph Koch, "Der Prozess gegen die Postille Olivis zur Apokalypse," *Recherches de Théologie Ancienne et Mediévale* 5 (1933): 304, so identifies him, though without explaining the choice.

39. Patrick Nold, "New Annotations of Pope John XXII and the Process against Peter of John Olivi's *Lectura super Apocalipsim*," *Oliviana* 4 (2012), http://oliviana.revues.org/521, posted online March 14, 2013, accessed December 26, 2016.

40. Ms. Paris, bibl. lat.3381A (hereafter 3381A).

however. In the spring of 1319, at the Franciscan general chapter meeting in Marseilles, Olivi's commentary was condemned by a commission of twelve masters and in fact by the order. The pope took a great deal longer. In 1322, he reserved the final decision for himself. Then he extracted what he saw as significant passages from the commentary and sent them out to individuals for comment. Much had changed by February 1326, when John XXII finally issued the condemnation. In the meantime, he had issued significant bulls that changed the official interpretation of Franciscan poverty and had found himself increasingly at odds, not only with the emperor Ludwig the Bavarian, but also with a notable segment of the Franciscan order, including the minister general, Michael of Cesena. Among the Franciscans, John faced not only a truculent minister general but groups of fugitive first-order Franciscans in Italy and France, as well as resistance among third-order Franciscans in southern France. Inquisitors were busy weeding out the dissenters, burning some and imprisoning others. That, however, is a longer story than we need to tell here. The important point for us is that by 1326 John was speaking to a very different situation, one that had changed significantly since Olivi's death and even since 1318. It had not changed so significantly since 1318 that it is impossible to imagine John producing the annotations in 1319 rather than later. John and the contents of Olivi's Revelation commentary were always on a collision course. Nevertheless, on balance Nold's later date has much to recommend it.

In fact, this different situation in the mid-1320s complicates the matter less than one might at first imagine. Certainly Gregory, writing in 1318, occasionally acts as if the spiritual Franciscans being condemned in 1318 are saying the same thing Olivi said in 1297. His assumption is seen in comments such as his assertion that spirituals in 1318 are heretical in agreeing with Olivi that the pope cannot dispense from the contents of the Franciscan rule, "just as he could not dispense from the contents of the Gospel, and that the evangelical perfection which Christ and his apostles observed is nothing other than the way of living according to that rule."[41] When spiritual Franciscans from 1318 on made such a statement, they did so in the face of a pope who saw such utterances not only as defiance of papal authority but, partly for that very reason, as heresy.

---

41. 3381A, 17v: "quod papa non potest immutare aliquid circa illam sicut nec circa evangelium, nec dispensare circa contenta in regula sicut nec circa contenta in evangelio, et quod perfectio evangelica quam Christus servavit et eius apostoli non est nisi in modo vivendi secundum illam regulam."

It is hard even for modern historians to remember how open to debate the Franciscan poverty question was before John's accession in 1316. Clement V intended to settle it in 1312, but after his death in 1314 two radically different positions within the Franciscan order managed to stake out territory, both claiming obedience to Clement's decision. Olivi, writing in 1297, had even less to come to terms with in the way of papal authority. He simply attempted to claim compatibility with *Exiit qui seminat*, Nicholas III's 1279 bull, and *Exiit* had predated the *usus pauper* controversy. Had Gregory been prone to thinking historically, he might have asked himself how Olivi got away with teaching Franciscans his interpretation of *usus pauper* as late as 1297.

Of course, Gregory was not given to thinking in that manner. This was hardly a major problem for him, though. On the whole he stays with what he reads in Olivi's Revelation commentary, and on the whole he reads it correctly. Moreover, his evaluation of what he reads is correct when seen from John XXII's perspective. In a curious way, Olivi's commentary anticipated not only Christ's second advent but John XXII's advent as well. Placed within the Olivian apocalyptic scenario, John made an excellent mystical Antichrist. He did more or less what Olivi expected the mystical Antichrist to do, a point not lost on those laity who remained faithful to Olivi's position concerning Franciscan poverty.

Gregory presents his critique in eighty-four articles. John annotates the first eighteen, then jumps to the eighty-second and eighty-third. Perhaps after the first eighteen, which are very repetitive, he felt safe in leaping to the end.

The first article offered and challenged by Gregory is that in Olivi's commentary "the sixth period is always described as notably preeminent over the first five and as the end of the earlier ones, and as the beginning of a new age purging the old age, just as the time of Christ purged the Old Testament and the oldness of humankind. Thus, as it were in circular fashion, it is joined to the first time of Christ as if the entire church were a sphere and as if in the sixth period a second period of Christ begins, one having its seven periods just as the whole history of the church has."[42] Gregory observes that

42. 3381A, 1r: "Septimum est quare sextus status semper describitur ut notabiliter preeminens quinque primis et sicut finis priorum, et tanquam initium novi seculi evacuans quoddam vetus seculum, sicut status Christi evacuavit vetus testamentum et vetustatem humani generis, unde et quasi circulariter sic iungitur primo tempori Christi ac si tota ecclesia sit una sphera et ac si in sexto eius statu secundo [*recte* secundus] incipiat status Christi habens sua septem tempora sicut habet totus decursus ecclesie, sic tamen quod septimus status sexti sit idem cum septimo statu totius ecclesie."

if the sixth period is preeminent as Olivi claims, it is superior to the period of the apostles, the primitive church, and the apostolic, evangelical life.

Gregory, a careful man, is willing to acknowledge that Olivi may not have meant to say that. Nevertheless, he feels that, whether he meant to say it or not, that is what his words suggest, and words used incautiously can lead to heresy. In fact, these particular words seem to imply two errors of the eternal gospel, in which it is claimed that those in a later age will be more perfect and that preachers in that age will speak with more authority than preachers in the primitive church. To make such claims, Gregory says, seems erroneous or at least temerarious and presumptuous.

Three elements in this evaluation are worth noting. First, Gregory has read Olivi's commentary carefully, so carefully that he fixes on the circle metaphor and tries to take it seriously in the context of the entire passage, as we will see in a moment. Second, he makes some effort to recognize that Olivi might not have intended to say what his words suggest. Third, his comparison with the eternal gospel would have been inaccurate if it had not been limited to two aspects of Gerard's thought, but he has the sense to limit it in that way.

Gregory sees in this first article another error touching directly on the connection between the sixth period and the Franciscan order. Olivi, he says, sees the first five periods as those of the apostles, martyrs, hermits, doctors, clerics, and religious having income in common. The sixth period is from the time of Saint Francis and involves those living according to his rule as Olivi understands it. That it is wrong to say, as Olivi does, that the mode of life embodied in that rule is the end of all preceding is clear, because the end (in the sense of final end or goal) is better and more perfect than that of which it is the end, and that would mean it is better and more perfect than the way of life of the apostles and the primitive church. Gregory takes a great deal of space explaining why such a view is incorrect, but one can sum it up in a single line: "The way of living of the sixth period either is not perfect or it is the same as that of the first period and thus is in no sense its end." Gregory sees the apostles as the *non plus ultra* when it comes to perfect observance of the gospel, and that is the end of it. He also invites Olivi to consider the implications of comparing the transition from the fifth to the sixth period with the transition from synagogue to church. After Christ one could not be saved without rejecting the synagogue and transferring to the way of life represented by the church. Does that mean that after the advent of Francis in the sixth period there can be no salvation in the state of riches? Gregory observes that such an assertion is similar to what the Waldensians have been saying.

The third error in this first article involves Olivi's statement that the sixth period is like the beginning of a new age. Gregory marshals his New Testament sources to argue that there will be no new age. This one will end with final judgment. Thus what Olivi sees as Christ's three advents should be shrunk to Christ's two advents, omitting what Olivi sees as Christ's advent in the spirit.

The fourth error has to do with the same passage. Gregory says the parallel between the Old Testament and the fifth period would imply that no one who died in the fifth period while having wealth either individually or in common would be saved, and that in the sixth period surrendering such wealth would be required for salvation. If it is objected that wealth held in the fifth period would entail corruption, but not so much as to make salvation impossible—in other words, it would prevent evangelical perfection but not salvation—Christ has promised that the church will never be so corrupted that there will not be some who practice Christ's perfection living within it. Gregory calls our attention to the fact that Olivi has not singled out the fifth period as opposed to the entire first five, but has said the sixth has primacy over all five. Even if he limited it to the fifth period there would be a problem, however. Gregory quotes Augustine and Acts to show that having possessions in common is a form of evangelical perfection, and such perfection continued in the fifth period.

The fifth error is seen by Gregory as entailed in Olivi's evocation of the sixth period as joined in a circular motion to the first. A circular path would entail moving through a point totally opposite, like the light of day slowly giving way to the darkness of the carnal church, then the light returning to perfect day and the conversion of the whole world. The problem for Gregory is that such a view is necessarily erroneous, because "never, either now or in the future, will the church be so darkened that it will be the opposite of the life of Christ and will fall from evangelical perfection, for just as, as long as the sun stands above the earth it cannot be night on earth (although the sun might be darkened by clouds), so the Sun of Justice has promised to stand with the church to the end of the world." In this case Gregory could be accused of overinterpreting the metaphor. Olivi assumes that even in the fifth period, indeed even in the temptation of Antichrist, there will be some elect to persecute. Thus he anticipates, not total eclipse, but the same scenario Gregory accepts.

The sixth and last error is entailed in these words: "In the sixth state, the state of Christ begins a second time, having its seven time periods just like the entire course of the church." Gregory considers this erroneous because Olivi is suggesting that the state of Christ will have collapsed completely in the church except in those in whom there is abdication of all things individually and in common, just as the Rule of Saint Francis has it, and that in the whole church before blessed Francis there was neither the life of Christ nor evangelical life.

The second article extends a theme that Gregory has touched on in the first article: Olivi's negative attitude toward the contemporary church. He quotes Olivi's statement that "The sixth [vision], which is about the damnation of the whore and of the seven-headed beast as well as the new nuptials of the Lamb and his spouse after the damnation of the whore, deals more directly with the rejection of Babylonian oldness and renovation of the form of Christ, as well as the septiform nature of the aforementioned rejection and renovation, for in the killing of the first head of the beast was the first renovation, and in the killing of the second was the second, and so on concerning the others." Gregory protests that "even though there are some within the church who morally fornicate, separating themselves from God, nevertheless the church in itself should not on this account be called a whore. On the contrary, it is perennially a virgin because in it there are always some good people in whom it principally consists. . . . All who share the faith and unity of the church and are not divided from it by heresy or schism are said to be of the church, and in reference to these the church might be called a whore *secundum quid*, but not *simpliciter*." Olivi, however, "understands by this whore and by Babylon the universal and catholic church of which the Roman church is the head, mother, and mistress" and "says that this church is to be destroyed in this age except for the elect on which the spiritual church will be founded."[43]

Another error has to do with the marriage of the lamb after the whore is dealt with. Gregory observes that, if the old church is destroyed and Christ is married to a new one, then he would have to be incarnated again. But of course Olivi's fantasy of a second marriage is incorrect from Gregory's perspective. Gregory asserts that, if the whore is understood according to the true sense of Scripture, it is the congregation of adherents to the Antichrist, whose damnation will occur with the final judgment, not the modern church, as Olivi seems to imagine. In fact, the damnation of the whore and the marriage cannot occur before judgment day, "for if the whore is taken according to the true sense of Scripture, that is, the community of the evil or the congregation of Antichrist, the universal damnation of this group

43. 3381A, 4r.

will not occur until the day of judgment, for the damnation of the whore as all Scripture portrays it is eternal damnation, not temporal, and the whore is permitted to flourish in the world so that it can be damned eternally in hell." He cites Revelation 18:21 and 19:3, then adds, "If indeed the whore is taken according to his false interpretation, namely as the modern church that in his opinion has gone whoring and abandoned God, especially the Roman church with its pomp, its gold, silver, and precious stones, all of which abound in the Roman church, then in calling the bride of Christ adulterous he is speaking blasphemy."[44]

In addressing what he sees as the third error in this second article, Gregory continues his attack on the identification of the church with the whore. He again calls it blasphemous but adds that it is heretical as well. John XXII, in the margin, agrees.

In presenting a fourth error, Gregory contends, it is "[Olivi's] intention that the church that now exists, the Roman church, which rules over the universal church, is the whore riding on the beast." By interpreting Revelation 13 in this way he is perverting Scripture, taking it other than as the Holy Spirit intended, and thus doing violence to the letter, which is a mark of heretics, as Gregory the Great tells us in his commentary on Job. Nor is Olivi correct in going on to suggest in his exegesis of what follows that it refers to the church being renewed seven times or its oldness rejected seven times. The church has the use of evangelical doctrine, through which it will be renewed until the end. The old man was crucified once with Christ, and Christ does not need to suffer many times again before the end of the world. To say otherwise is to suggest that Christ's passion was not efficacious.

As we said above, Gregory presents his critique in eighty-four articles. John annotates the first eighteen, then leaps to the eighty-second. We have examined two articles in cursory fashion. Obviously we cannot afford to continue reading the entire text, nor do we have to do so. We can see where Gregory and John stand on the sixth period as the hinge of history. For both Gregory and John, all roads really do lead to Rome, so the idea of the pope as head of the carnal church could hardly be expected to gain much credence. And that *is* what Olivi is saying. Not necessarily *this particular pope*, John XXII, who arrived on the scene well after Olivi's death; yet when we look at the bulls concerning Franciscan poverty (and Christ's poverty) promulgated by John in the early 1320s, it is not difficult to image what Olivi would have thought of them.

44. 3381A, 5r.

Nor should we be surprised that Gregory and the pope find Olivi's apocalyptic interpretation of Saint Francis hard to accept. As they see it and as Gregory actually says in the sixth article, Olivi is claiming that

> the church in the fifth period, which he calls "that of having something of one's own or in common," will fall so far from the life of Christ and evangelical perfection in life, knowledge, and doctrine that it will be totally cast aside and renewed in the form of a newly founded spiritual church in which the life and image of Christ will be reformed through those who live according to the rule of Saint Francis.[45]

Is this an accurate portrayal of the relationship between Franciscanism and the new age as seen through Olivi's eyes? Yes and no. Olivi sees Francis as an apocalyptic figure, as does Bonaventure before him. Both grant him an important role in the sixth period. Both feel that they themselves are already in the sixth period, although neither claims to have seen the Antichrist yet. Both anticipate that, once the Antichrist does come and has been destroyed, the church will experience spiritual joys beyond anything hitherto encountered, at least on such a large scale.

The latter qualification reminds us that both Olivi and Bonaventure anticipate a seventh period, but both see the seventh period as bringing the elect back to the spiritual level already attained by the apostles. Olivi could be read as less certain about how this should be handled, and at times he seems to jettison the idea in favor of a more consistently progressive historical pattern; but he does try to present Christ's second advent in a way that does not leave the apostles consigned to the dustbin of history. All of this tends to decrease the perceived distance between Olivi and Gregory, despite Gregory's effort to expose the inconsistencies in Olivi's exegesis; yet there is clearly a major difference of opinion between them.

There is also the question of whether Olivi's picture of universal conversion in the period from Antichrist on really entails everyone adopting the Franciscan rule. Certainly he thinks leaders of the church after Antichrist will behave as if they were Franciscans, but that is not equivalent to saying that everyone will do so or what would be entailed in their doing so. Olivi seems to realize how far beyond any chance of accuracy he is getting when he speaks of the world after Antichrist, and his predictions are not all that clear.

45. 3381A, 9r.

What *is* clear is that Olivi not only fails to insist that everyone before the sixth period should have been without goods individually or in common; he explicitly says the opposite early in the commentary.

> Christ's pontificate as originally bestowed upon Peter and the apostles in the first period of evangelical and apostolic life was later commuted to a state allowing temporal possessions. This was usefully and rationally done, and it lasted at least from Constantine's time to the end of the fifth period. Nevertheless, insofar as many priests were monks and, in both their writings and their hearts, they preferred the poverty of Christ and the apostles over all the temporal possessions given to the church, the first order of apostolic priesthood remained preeminent. It is fitting, therefore, that at the end the priesthood should rise and return to its first form, as befits the law of primogeniture, greater perfection, and greater conformity with Christ.

We are left with a general impression that Gregory saw his task as that of finding holes in Olivi's argument, even if it meant continually giving Olivi's exegesis a worst-case interpretation. Had he not proceeded on that basis, he would have encountered a commentary that followed the pattern of the standard Parisian model up to a point but broke with it by self-locating in the sixth period and seeing that period as the time, not only of Antichrist, but of huge spiritual progress modeled on Saint Francis. It saw that progress as mostly in the future but already occurring to some extent. It also broke with the Parisian model in treating the seventh period as a lengthy era of peace, contemplation, and *intellectus spiritualis*. In short, Gregory would have encountered a theology of history in some ways like Bonaventure's in the *Collationes in hexaemeron*. Gregory, whose exegetical theory is closer to the Parisian model as more generally encountered in the early and mid-thirteenth century (e.g., in *Vox domini*) than to the *Collationes in hexaemeron*, would still have found Olivi's apocalyptic scenario hard to agree with. That is, looking at what was said by Olivi in the passage quoted above about the priesthood returning to its original form, he might well have found something to complain about; but he might also have recognized that what he disagreed with had more coherence and more to recommend it than is actually suggested in his critique.

Instead, much of Gregory's time is spent tracing what he sees as the heterodox implications of Olivi's exegesis. This is not a matter of ignorance concerning the standard exegetical theory of his day. He is good at quoting the Bible, the fathers, the *Glossa*, and Richard of Saint Victor. Olivi, who constantly seems to work with the Revelation commentaries of Richard of Saint Victor and Joachim of Fiore open before him, would have appreciated that attention to Richard, although, as we have seen, in cases where he cites the interpretations of both Richard and Joachim he normally chooses to go with Joachim. Gregory feels that Joachim is a heretic. A serious conversation between Olivi and Gregory concerning exegetical theory would have been illuminating.

What happens instead is less so. Gregory does occasionally contradict Olivi on specific matters of exegesis such as when the Jews are to be converted, and these are moments when we recognize him as a man whose theological formation has prepared him for serious biblical scholarship; yet his sense of his perceived duty to showcase Olivi's heresy from as many angles as possible regularly leads him in a very different direction. For example, he quotes Olivi's comment that "Some, drawing on the many things that Joachim writes concerning Frederick II and his offspring, and based on those things that blessed Francis revealed secretly to Brother Leo and to certain others of his companions," believe that in the time of the mystical Antichrist Frederick will be revived in some of his offspring, acquiring both the empire and the kingdom of France. He will also install "a certain false religious as the pseudo-pope, who will plot against the evangelical rule, devising deceitful dispensations from it and promoting to bishoprics professors of the aforementioned rule who consent to his actions. Moreover, he will expel the clerics and prior bishops opposed to Frederick's offspring, and especially to that emperor and the beast and its statue. And so the outcome will be that he will expel all those who shall desire fully to observe the aforementioned rule in a plain and simple way and defend it."[46]

One might imagine that such a scenario would provide Gregory with a great deal to work with; yet what he does with it seems a waste of good material. He rightly assumes that the rule in question is the Franciscan rule, then observes that according to Olivi this rule is the very one Christ observed and had written into the Gospels. Olivi considers any pope who dispenses from that rule a pseudo-pope; yet all the popes from the beginning have changed the rule in some way or another by their bulls concerning it. Gregory then decides that the whole intellectual structure thus created would blasphemously label Nicholas III a pseudo-pope since he issued *Exiit qui seminat*, a declaration on the rule, and he promoted many members of the order who

---

46. 3381A citing *Lectura*, 615–16.

observed the rule according to that declaration, "anathematizing that sect who believed and did the opposite. And the same can be said of Nicholas IV, a religious."

Nicholas manages to get through this without asking himself what Olivi actually *said* about either Nicholas, or what sect Nicholas III might have been anathematizing. In fact, Olivi relied heavily on *Exiit qui seminat* when arguing the case for his notion of *usus pauper* as part of the vow. His relationship with Nicholas IV may have been more fraught, but in that period he seems to have escaped the storm of disciplinary action that struck other friars in southern France, and it is hard to find any later comments by Olivi specifically aimed at Nicholas IV. Nor, while we're considering individual popes, is there any reason to think that Olivi saw Boniface VIII as anything other than a legitimate pope, and here there is good evidence to work with, since we have Olivi's letter to Conrad of Offida saying as much. In other words, Gregory's attempt to drag every heretical implication possible out of Olivi's commentary and hold it up to inspection encourages him to construct a straw man and attack it instead of the historical Olivi.

There is, in fact, a sense that Gregory is loading the exegetical dice against Olivi even when he purports to be doing straightforward exegesis. This much is clear, for example, within Gregory's fifty-seventh article, in which he attacks Olivi's exegesis of Revelation 16:11. Olivi says, "Certain people say that through intestine battles of kings and kingdoms the strength of the Roman church will be dried up or will decline and the multitude of its armies will be decreased, and this will be preparation for the following destruction of the carnal church."[47] Gregory calls this a bit of "temerarious divination" if Olivi is referring to corporeal strength, "unless perhaps he is speaking of the time of Antichrist, when it is certain that the strength of the armies of the church will be entirely lost, just as in other times of persecution; and in these cases the church triumphed through endurance alone. But if it is meant concerning spiritual strength and the armies of angels, the idea that the church lacks such spiritual strength is erroneous because celestial support is always sent to the sons of Israel and to the city of Jerusalem." Gregory cites the *Glossa* on Judges 3:9, "they cried to the Lord, who provided them with a savior," which takes as the mystical significance of the passage the idea that God provides help to those who sincerely call out for it.

Gregory goes on to say that the passage is erroneous because it predicts the destruction of the carnal church, by which Olivi means the Roman

---

47. *Lectura,* 686.

church. Gregory cites the gloss on 2 Chronicles 23:17 in support of the idea that the Roman church will remain and indeed grow until the end of the world. He then corrects Olivi's thoughts on the conversion of the Jews in a brief passage tying together John 19:15, Daniel 9:26, Judges 11:7, and Augustine's thoughts on Joseph and his brothers.

There is more—quite a bit more—said on this particular article, but this much is sufficient to make an important point. Gregory goes into battle against the Olivian interpretation of Revelation armed with the ecclesiology presented to him by the church as defined by John XXII and himself, and on that basis alone he feels justified in saying Olivi was dangerous, possibly heretical (although that is a word Gregory uses sparingly); yet in arguing his case he is armed with an exegetical overview of the Bible that depends, not simply on his interpretation of Revelation, but on his interpretation of other books as well. That is one reason why it was worthwhile to devote an entire chapter to Olivi's early exegesis. In the 1279–1283 period, in the process of commenting on other books than Revelation, Olivi was building a *Gestalt*, a total view of Scripture based on slow, line-by-line interpretation of the books on which he specifically lectured, but also on an impressive acquaintance with other books such as Mark, Luke, Daniel, and (of course) Revelation, all of which played an important part in his early exegesis. Thus Olivi's view of Revelation was based on a comprehensive reading of Scripture as a whole and a complex sense of how it all fit together. That was the work of a lifetime.

The same is true of Gregory. He, too, continually goes back to books such as Matthew, Job, and Genesis, the same books Olivi commented on before 1283; but Gregory approaches them differently and fits them together in a different *Gestalt*. We lack that *Gestalt*. That is why we find it so easy to describe Gregory's quarrel with Olivi on the basis of his ecclesiology but so difficult to describe the complex net of exegetical assumptions and scriptural interpretation that Gregory would have seen as supporting the ecclesiological quarrel. It would be fascinating to place him in his natural habitat.

One thing *is* clear, though. In his commentary, Olivi suggests that a corrupt church, including the pope, will be instrumental in seducing Christians, tempting them to fall from grace, and eventually the pope will orchestrate a persecution leading in that direction. There is no way of ignoring that much. And that much was enough for Gregory, as it was for John XXII. Here, despite Gregory's complicated attack on Olivi's commentary, the issue becomes very simple. When the angel says that Babylon has fallen, what is Babylon? And when the two beasts appear, who are they? For Gregory, "Babylon signifies the same as the two beasts, but through them, as has been said, it is not the church that is signified but the congregation of the evil persecuting it." (At that point he quotes Richard of Saint Victor.) On occasion he manages to suggest that, when the *Glossa* speaks of many prelates dominating and oppressing their subordinates, it is referring to members of Olivi's sect being oppressed by good prelates seeking justice, for it is Olivi's sect and other heretics who are rightly called Babylon. That, of course, is nonsensical as a reading of the gloss in question; yet it hardly prohibits us from noting that Gregory is correct in seeing a huge gap between Olivi's notion of the beast and his own.

For Olivi, the ecclesiastical poles are reversed. In the sixth period, in the temptation of the spiritual Antichrist, the church as an institution will fall into carnal hands and will become the carnal church, while the persecuted elect, the true church, will find themselves outside the institution until the institution is destroyed by an outside force. They will thus go into hiding and work on projects such as universal conversion. Gregory, like John XXII, finds it impossible even to imagine the institutional church in which he lives, moves, and has his being ever falling into such disarray. Olivi has no trouble whatsoever imagining it.

READINGS

Prologue

Olivi's commentary on the Apocalypse begins with a lengthy prologue, an effort to state in general what he thinks the Apocalypse is about. In the course of that prologue, Olivi asks and answers thirteen basic questions about the work. Only at the beginning of chapter 1 does he finally turn to the questions addressed in the earlier prologue utilized in Vox domini *and elsewhere. The following passages are from the seventh and eighth of these questions[48] and demonstrate the central role played by the sixth period in Olivi's interpretation*

---

48. *LSA*, 36–47. I am grateful to Warren Lewis for allowing me access to his forthcoming translation of Olivi's commentary. It has been helpful to follow Lewis through the text not only in Latin but in English. Over the years he has shown himself to be both perceptive and collegial. I have learned a great deal from him.

of the Apocalypse. Notice that in the first of the following arguments he is thinking in terms of the three advents, but also in terms of the Joachite three ages.

As for the seventh matter, that is, why the sixth period is always described as notably preeminent over the five previous ones, as their completion, and as the beginning of a new age supplanting the old one, I have offered some arguments on this score in the fifth part of the response section in the first of my *Questions on Evangelical Poverty* [identified with *Questions on Evangelical Perfection*, q. 8], in my *Commentary on Isaiah*, and in many other places. Here it will suffice to touch briefly on three arguments.

The first involves the celebration [*solemnizatio*] of God's three persons and Christ's three final perfections or properties, the first of which is that a single person consists of both divine and human nature, from which he derives the property of redeemer. Through this he was the end of the old [law] according to the apostle in Romans 10.

The second property is his singular and exemplary life, which he imposed on the apostles, exemplified in himself, and caused to be solemnly written down in the gospels [*in libris evangelicis*]. The perfect imitation of and participation in this life is and ought to be the end of all our activity and life.

The third involves the eternal glory of Christ according to his deity and humanity. And in this lies the end and final object of our beatitude. Therefore, just as it was fitting that, through the celebration [*solemnizatio*] of the person of Christ the redeemer, the old should be driven out and the whole world of the gentiles should be renewed according to his faith and grace, and this at some solemn time and through some solemn works, thus it was fitting that, for the even wider celebration of his life, some following time should be established in which, the old being changed, the world should again be renewed through the light and grace of his life, and thus in a third time the world should be renewed and consummated through Christ's glory and in Christ's glory.

Whence, in the words of Isaiah quoted earlier, it is said, "The sun's light shall increase sevenfold in the day when he will bind up and heal the wound of his people" [Isa 30:26]. For on the third day of the aforesaid third end, the wound of sin and death will be bound up. Thus will be begun in the first day what proceeds on in the second and is consummated in the third. And thus, just as in Christ's first advent the sun shone seven times more brightly than before, so it will be in the sixth period of the church and even more fully so in the seventh.

And from this flows a most solemn and glorious representation of God's Trinity and unity. For according to this, the time of Christ's forefathers expressly represents God the Father, fecund and totally oriented to generation of the Son. Thus all of the law and prophets and the whole prior people of God were made fecund by God and totally oriented to prefiguring, promising, and giving birth to Christ.

Christ, indeed, as the Son of God and man redeeming and renewing the world, is himself properly Son of God; and that people propagated from him and incorporated into him was expressly the image of himself.

The holy and singular participation in and celebration of his holy life and love is appropriated throughout the Scriptures to the Holy Spirit, proceeding from the Father and Son and illuminating each. Thus it is fittingly represented by a following time when the world is renewed through Christ's life, in which the former people of the Jews, who were the image of the Father, and the people of the gentiles, who, after they received Christ, now almost all defect from the pure faith of Christ and will do so even more under Antichrist, will be restored and revived under the living and life-giving heat and life of Christ's life through his and his Father's one unifying Spirit. The state of eternal glory that follows the aforesaid three ages is assimilated to the unity of essence of the three persons, because there "God will be all in all," and all things will be one in him.

The second argument proceeds from the diverse perfections or the diverse levels of perfection to be introduced, in a distinct and ordered manner, into the church of Christ. For just as there are many levels of perfection between the lowest and highest, just so it was fitting that the church should ascend from the lowest to the highest through intermediate levels disposing it to the highest form. Thus, in order that there should be a concordance between the end of the church and the end of the synagogue or of the prior time [seculi], in the sixth age [etate] of which Christ came as end of the prior time [seculi], God chose the sixth period [tempus] of the church to express more perfectly his form and life in Christ.[49]

49. This passage is hard to translate and even harder to understand because in it a *concordia* of three different moments in history seems to be suggested. First, there are the seven periods of world history, with Christ initiating the sixth. All the rest of world history unfolds within that sixth period, because the seventh period corresponds to life in heaven. Second, there are the seven periods of Old Testament history from Adam to Christ's advent in the flesh, leading to the end of the synagogue as God's chosen religious institution. Third, there are the seven periods of church history ending (in the sense of "being fulfilled") with the sixth period, which marks Christ's advent in the spirit. Thus what we have here is a *con-*

Olivi then faces the objection that the fifth period of church history is not superior to the first four periods. In fact, on the basis of what has been, it would seem to be inferior to them, since it involves a broader, more inclusive church gained through condescension to the weak. Olivi replies in three ways. First, although it is true that the condescension of the fifth period to take in the weak involves something less perfect, it is nevertheless also true that in the saints—who cleave to the arduous perfections of earlier times in their mental habits and condescend only through love, for the good of the weak— this condescension actually increases perfection, just as was the case with Christ when he condescended to the weak. Second, even when the fifth period begins, the first four periods remain, at least in reputation and in heavenly reward; and thus, when the fifth period is added, the totality of all five periods represents greater perfection than the first four alone. Third, even a fall from perfection contributes in some way, albeit in a tangential way, to the final perfection, since it is punished by divine judgment. Moreover, opposites placed in juxtaposition serve to clarify the nature of the conflict and challenge the elect. Thus what is new about succeeding periods often is not fully understood, nor is the new period fully implemented, until the old period has undergone decay.

Olivi then provides a striking example of how what seems a step backward actually fits into God's greater plan.

In the same way, Christ's pontificate as originally bestowed upon Peter and the apostles in the first period of evangelical and apostolic life was later commuted to a state allowing temporal possessions. This was usefully and rationally done, and it lasted at least from Constantine's time to the end of the

---

cordia of world history, Old Testament history, and New Testament history, but organized around another *concordia* of Christ's two advents in the flesh and spirit. Thus the sixth period of church history witnesses a new sort of advent on Christ's part, his advent in the spirit that begins a transition to the Joachite third age of world history, which will be perfectly realized within the seventh period of church history. Notice that in the middle of all this Olivi refers to "a concordance between the end of the church and the end of the synagogue," which *seems* to suggest that the third age will see the end of the church as God's chosen organization just as the second marked the end of the synagogue; yet it cannot mean that, because the seventh period of church history is still to come. As the last two chapters have suggested, one has to take Olivi's sense of "end" as meaning something more like "fulfillment" than "extinction" or "rejection." Nevertheless, one can see why all this set off alarm bells in Gregory of Lucca's mind.

fifth period. Nevertheless, insofar as many priests were monks and, in both their writings and their hearts, they preferred the poverty of Christ and the apostles over all the temporal possessions given to the church, the first order of apostolic priesthood remained preeminent. It is fitting, therefore, that at the end the priesthood should rise and return to its first form, as befits the law of primogeniture, greater perfection, and greater conformity with Christ.

And this return will be aided, albeit tangentially, not only by the many imperfections seen in the way the church possesses and dispenses its temporal goods, but also by the many excesses in pride, extravagance, simony, conflict, litigation, fraud, and robbery suffered at that time [*occasionaliter*], as a result of which the church around the end of the fifth period is, from the soles of its feet to the top of its head, almost completely infected, disordered, and turned, as it were, into a new Babylon.

The third argument proceeds from the fact that two peoples, the gentiles and Jews, are to be converted through Christ. Although the Jewish people would have been the first to be solemnly led to Christ and exalted [*magnificandus*] through him had they not rebelled outrageously against him and his grace, and had their previous sins not rendered them unworthy, and had the incomprehensible, most just order of divine predestination not ordained otherwise, nevertheless that people was not to be entirely excluded. On the contrary, around the end of the world some solemn time of universal conversion and exaltation [*magnification*] would be reserved for them.

From this observation proceeds a twofold argument leading to our conclusion. The first is that if, through the conversion of the gentile people, there occurred a solemn renovation of the whole world, having in itself its own times and activities, it is no less fitting that in the universal conversion of Israel the whole world should be solemnly renewed yet again. In fact, insofar as Christ and his mother were closer to this people according to the flesh, and the salvation of this people was more expressly prophesied through the prophets to the fathers by God with the strongest possible guarantees, it is all the more necessary that this people should be more solemnly exalted by Christ and in Christ. Thus it is not without merit that this event should have been scheduled for the end of history and of the church, so that the beginning and end of Christ's church should lie in this people and the gentile people should be given the role of middle link in the process.

The second argument is that the gentile people were so blinded by idolatry and disordered by rude customs that, when they first entered into the faith of Christ, they were not sufficiently disposed to understand the faith perfectly and perfectly imitate Christ's life. Thus it was necessary that, over a period of time, they should gradually come to understand the faith and, through the example of various periods and holy leaders, should progressively be raised up to the perfection of Christ's life.

Furthermore, just as every day has its morning, noon, and evening, so does every time of God's people. In eternity it will always be noon, with no night. Thus the time of the fullness of the gentiles under Christ also had to have its morning, noon, and evening before the conversion of another people (that is, the Jews). And thus even now we see the process completed and described by John in this book. For the morning of the gentile people, mixed with the shadows of idolatry, lasted from the beginning of the gentiles' conversion up to the time of Constantine. Its noon came in the distinguished teaching and contemplation of the doctors and anchorites, and its evening is only too apparent around the end of the fifth period. And when Babylon the whore and the beast carrying her are at their height, there will be the darkest night, of which the psalmist says, "I have spread out the shadows and it has become night" (Ps 103:20). These are the beasts formed in the sixth day, after which man was formed in God's image (Gen 1:27), because after these things occur Israel will be converted along with the rest of the gentiles, and the Christiform life and image of Christ will appear.

From the aforesaid it should be apparent why the sixth and seventh visions principally describe only the final age of the church. This is to show more fully that the sixth and seventh periods contain a solemn end of the prior times and a certain new and solemn world.

*Later Olivi makes an even stronger statement concerning the pivotal
role of the sixth period.*

The sixth member of these [first five] visions and the sixth vision of this book declare that in the sixth period of the church the singular perfection of Christ's life and wisdom will be revealed and the antiquity of the prior period so universally swept away that a certain new age or new church seems to be formed, old things having now been cast aside, just as in Christ's first advent a new church was formed, the old synagogue having been cast aside.

And thus it is that a threefold advent of Christ is presented in these visions: the first in human flesh, redeeming the world and founding the church; the second in the spirit of evangelical life, reforming and perfecting the church founded earlier; the third in judgment, glorifying the elect and bringing all things to their consummation. Although the second advent is present in the whole history of the church and also in the glorification of the saints, nevertheless through antonomasia it is rightly and congruously appropriated to the sixth period.

Chapter 7

As we would expect, Olivi deals with the sixth period of church history not only in the sixth vision but in the sixth part of various other visions. In fact, some of his most interesting comments are found in the latter. The following is taken from his exegesis of the second vision, that of the seven seals. Here he turns to Revelation 7:2 and the opening of the sixth seal.[50]

And I saw, when he had opened the sixth seal, etc. In this opening seven things are touched upon. The first is a certain terrible judgment upon and banishment of the previous age; the second an obstacle impeding spiritual preaching and grace after that judgment, in the passage beginning, **After these things, I saw four angels**; third, the removal of that impediment by an angel having the sign of God, in the passage beginning, **I saw another angel**; fourth, the signing of the twelve tribes of Israel under a certain and a mystical number by that same angel, in the passage beginning, **And I heard the number of them that were signed**; fifth, the conversion to Christ of a countless number from all the peoples of the earth, their glorious and triumphal placement before Christ, and the strong, joyful praise, sounded by them, in the passage beginning, **After this, I saw a great multitude**; sixth, the adoration and jocund glorification of God by all the angels, in the passage beginning, **And all the angels**; seventh, the laudatory declaration by one of the elders concerning the merit and reward of the aforesaid who were converted to Christ, in the passage beginning, **And one of the ancients answered**.

In order to understand this sixth opening we must first remember what was said above in the thirteen things to be considered, and especially how it was shown there that the life of Christ would be clarified in a special way in the sixth and seventh periods of church history, and that its greatness would be shown in the final consummation of the church and the conversion of all Israel.

50. *LSA*, 306–22.

It is clearly established, therefore, through the authentic testimony and confirmation of the Roman church, that the rule of the Brothers Minor produced by the blessed Francis is truly and precisely that gospel which Christ himself observed, imposed on the apostles, and caused to be written in his gospels. Nonetheless, this point is also clearly established through the indisputable testimony of the gospel books and other holy Scriptures, as well as through their holy interpreters, as is more than abundantly shown elsewhere. It is also clearly established by the indubitable testimony of the most holy Francis and confirmed by his ineffable sanctity and by innumerable miracles of God (especially the most glorious stigmata impressed upon him by Christ) that he is the angel of the opening of the sixth seal having the sign of the living God, the sign, that is, of the crucified Christ's wounds, and also the sign of his total transformation and conformity to Christ and in Christ. And this is established through a revelation that is clear and worthy of faith, as Brother Bonaventure, a most solemn master of sacred theology and former general minister of our order, solemnly preached at Paris in a chapter meeting of our brothers. I was there and I heard it.

Having said this much, we must still explain when this sixth opening begins. It seems to some that it starts with the beginning of the order and the holy rule. To others it seems that it starts with the solemn revelation by the Abbot Joachim (and perhaps by some others contemporary with him) of the third general age, which contains the sixth and seventh periods of church history. It seems to still others that it begins with the destruction of Babylon— that is, the carnal church—to be carried out by the ten horns of the beast, i.e., the ten kings. Yet others feel that it begins from the resuscitation of the spirit or of certain people to the spirit of Christ and Francis, at a time when his rule is evilly and sophistically attacked and condemned by the church of the carnal and proud, just as Christ was condemned by the reprobate synagogue of the Jews. For this will occur before the time of the destruction of Babylon just as the condemnation of Christ and his followers by the Jews came before the time of the synagogue's destruction.

It should be recognized, however, that the four aforesaid views, understood in the proper manner, are not contradictory but rather concordant. For just as Luke begins the gospel of Christ from the priesthood of Zechariah, to whom it was revealed that Christ would soon come, and from John [the Baptist], Christ's immediate precursor, while Matthew begins with the human birth of Christ, Mark begins with the preaching of Christ and John [the Baptist], and John [the evangelist] begins with the eternity and eternal generation of the Word, so this sixth opening had a certain prophetic beginning in the revelation of the abbot and similar writers, then found the beginning of its birth and planting in the renewal of the evangelical rule through its observer Francis. It will find the beginning of its reburgeoning and reflowering in the preaching of a spiritual people to be awakened and in a new Babylon that is to be condemned. It will find in the destruction of Babylon the beginning of its clear distinction from the fifth period and its clarification. In the same way, we say that the things of the law were slain with Christ's passion and resurrection, then buried and made truly dead with the full promulgation of the gospel and with the destruction of the temple of the law by Titus and Vespasian.

You find much the same thing in the prophets. The beginning of the seventy years of Babylonian captivity and devastation of the temple by the Chaldeans is counted in one way from the thirtieth year in the reign of Josiah (under whom Jeremiah began to prophesy) and terminated the first year of King Cyrus [Jer 1:2; Ezra 1:1–2]. It is counted in another way from the destruction of the temple itself and terminated in the second year of Darius, the son of Hystaspes, as we see in Zechariah 1[:1–2]. In fact, the things touched upon here in connection with the opening of the sixth seal are not to be completed fully before the destruction of the Babylonian temple, and for that reason they more literally and more principally refer to the fourth beginning of the sixth opening. For the seventy weeks of years in Daniel begin more literally from the rebuilding of the temple under Esdras and Nehemiah than from the one beginning under Zerubbabel and conceded by King Cyrus [Dan 9:24],[51] yet it can nonetheless be seen as beginning in a shadowy and incomplete way from what occurred under Cyrus. Thus, those things touched upon here can, in a limited and partial fashion, be applied in the prior ways, or at least in the second and third ways.

It can be applied to the second, for through Francis, from the beginning of this order to the present, there has been a great signing of individuals into a spiritual army of the evangelical rule, and beyond that a great crowd of people have been, thanks to their example, led to penance and to the grace of Christ. Nor was there lacking an earthquake of remorse and the exchange of an evil life for a good one. In many others there has been an earthquake of anger toward evangelical men and their profession, so that many who seem like the sun because they are masters and prelates are made so dark that even today they think and teach that the state of evangelical

51. Cf. also 2 Chr 36:23; Ezra 1–6; Isa 44:28; 45:1; Dan 9:2.

mendicancy is a state of damnation, or at least of less perfection, and that to have common possessions is more perfect and more evangelical than not to have them.

Just as, once David had been anointed by the Lord and the Lord's spirit had come upon him, the Lord's spirit departed from Saul and he was tormented by an evil spirit, as 1 Samuel 16[:14] says, so in the same way, when the spirit of God was manifestly placed in the evangelical poor, calling them by apostolic authority to the preaching office, many began to be stirred up against them by a diabolical spirit, and these people were cast deeply into simony, lechery, avarice, and pride. Thus **the sun** of faith and ecclesiastical regimen **was made black**, and like a sack woven from the hair of swine and wild beasts. On this account the **moon**—that is, the people subordinate to these leaders—**became as blood**, that is, foully stained with the blood of lechery and murder. Moreover, many in religious orders, who were earlier like **the stars from heaven, fell upon the earth**, that is, into earthly desires and into a life that was openly earthly or worldly.

Because of these things, however, **the heavens**—that is, the heavenly purity and sublimity of the ecclesiastical state—**departed as a book folded up**, that is, they were hidden in a few good people and, in the rest, mixed up with many evils. Furthermore, these evils became all the more obvious when evangelical men first came along and began to preach zealously against them; and as they strongly opposed them and made it known that the wrath of the judge would soon be felt, **the princes and tribunes and the rich**, as well as the poor, were very terrified. Thus they **hid themselves in the caves and in the rocks of mountains**—that is, in a secret and strong relationship with the most sublime saints—turning humbly to seek their protection. And they said **to the mountains and the rocks**—that is, to the most sublime saints, firm in the faith—"**Fall upon us**" through good will and condescension "**and hide us**" through your intercession "**from the face**" (that is, from the censure) "**of him that sitteth upon the throne**," that is, of God who reigns, "**and from the wrath of the Lamb**," that is, the man Christ. **And who shall be able to stand** before such a terrible and angry judge, as if they were to say, "If a just man is barely saved, what will occur to us sinners?" [1 Pet 4:18].

Furthermore, when Francis's order was first begun, there was an earthquake in many places, for example in the county of Toulouse, which was devastated at that time by crusaders. In fact, in the third or fourth year of this order, they demolished the city of Béziers, where I grew up. Moreover, in Italy, as well as in lands beyond the sea, there were at that time stormy times and disruptions. Indeed, the Tartars openly captured and laid waste many lands in the east and west as well. Around the thirtieth year of our order they entered and practically destroyed Hungary, a Christian land.

As far as the third beginning of the sixth opening is concerned, there will be a great earthquake shaking the faith of many in the truth of the evangelical rule and the spirit of the evangelical life. Then the sun will more fully turn black and the moon turn cruel and bloody through dissension and battle both among the elect and in themselves.[52] Thus battles in the church uprooting isles and mountains—that is, cities and kingdoms—will precede the stirring up of the spirit. It will also be preceded or accompanied by schisms among the clergy and those in religious orders, shaking certain states and groups. As a result, many stars will fall through apostasy from their heavenly or regular states, even many within the evangelical state who seemed above all others to be stars. The reason for their fall is that they were not mature figs, filled with the sweetness of devout love. Nor were they small through humility, but rather were blown up by pride and immature through lack of inner virtue. Thus they were blown by the wind of vanity and temptation and fell from the fig-tree of the holy state. Because of this, many not only among the good but also among the evil will be terrified not only by seeing and experiencing such evils but also by the expectation of experiencing even greater ones. And then many will be signed as part of a spiritual army, although they will be few in comparison with the multitude of the reprobate.

You might ask why Francis and his first colleagues in the order were not personally involved in the third and fourth beginnings. After all, Christ and his apostles were present in the time of preaching and crucifixion at the beginning of the new law (events corresponding to the third beginning of this sixth opening). Moreover, Peter and Paul, Christ's apostles, died under Nero and Simon Magus (who pretended to be Christ), at a time in which Judea began to be destroyed by Vespasian, who had been sent by Nero. Shortly thereafter it was totally destroyed. This time corresponds to the fourth beginning of this sixth opening, in which the carnal church will be struck and, shortly thereafter, the eleventh horn of the beast (a sort of Nero) will arrive along with the Great Antichrist, who is to be raised up by the horn, just as Simon Magus was by Nero. But practically the entire thirteenth century will have passed before this happens, a long wait after the time of Francis and the beginning of his order.

---

52. Presumably meaning among the hierarchy and within the church as a whole.

Again we see the importance of concordia *for Olivi. Here what is at stake is not the larger* concordia *between Old Testament and New Testament but the smaller one between Christ's first and second advents. A chain of events that unrolled between the beginning of Christ's ministry and the destruction of Jerusalem during the first advent is taking an entire century to occur during the second advent. Why the delay? Remember that even in his early years Olivi pointed to the danger of the Antichrist using phony concordances to mislead the faithful. Here we have room for diabolical legerdemain. Olivi takes the danger seriously.*

An eightfold explanation might be given. The first is general in nature. It was not expedient or fitting that these later events should correspond to the earlier ones in every particular. On the contrary, each should have its own special properties. Thus, simply because the two agree in one respect, we should not conclude that they do so in every respect.

Second, one order composed of many persons corresponds to the person of Christ in the sixth opening. It grows up just as Christ did.

Third, the Christian people were to be increased by evangelical men and called to penance with at least a threefold citation punctuated by fitting pauses to give them time for response. For just as under Noah people were given a hundred years to repent [Gen 6:3], so it is here, more or less. Moreover, under Isaiah the ten tribes were given sixty-five years from the time the prophets (for example, Hosea or Amos) first began to prophesy the captivity of the ten tribes until that event actually occurred. Thus in Isaiah 7[:8] he says, "In sixty-five years Ephraim will cease to be a people," beginning from the twenty-fourth year of King Uzziah. According to Richard,[53] from the death of Elisha, who, along with Elijah, called Israel to penance, a little over one hundred years passed. Moreover, ninety-three years passed from the destruction of the ten tribes, which occurred in the sixth year of the reign of Hezekiah, to the thirteenth year in the reign of Josiah (the year Jeremiah, the last prophet to call them to repentance, first began to prophesy the captivity of Jerusalem). In the same way, considering the call to repentance made to the Jews in Christ's advent, if you begin counting from Zechariah, John's father, or from Simeon and the prophetess Anna, who preceded Christ in the spirit and received him in the temple [Luke 2], then you have a good hundred years to Christ's death or at least to the destruction of Jerusalem.

53. I have not found this reference.

Fourth, as I showed in connection with the gospels, it was deemed fitting that Christ should have few years to live among us and even fewer to preach.[54] Nor was it deemed fitting that his disciples be given the fullness of the Spirit until after his death and resurrection, or that his church should be solemnly established by them until then. Nor did Christ himself need much time to be strengthened in order to face condemnation by the high priests of the Jews and all who consented to their verdict. On the other hand, unless the evangelical order is renewed by Francis in many ways and given two or three generations to develop, neither it nor the people it was supposed to lead could be sufficiently prepared to undergo a real persecution like the one Christ sustained.

Fifth, the temptation accompanying this condemnation should be so seductive that even the elect barely avoid falling into error. It should involve the elect being persecuted with the utmost zeal. Thus it was necessary that the aforesaid order exist long enough beforehand so that it would have time to ascend from morning to high noon, and from there begin to decline toward evening, and that in the process there should emerge from it a group extremely anxious for it to achieve carnal glory, a group that would oppose those zealous to preserve its original, pure spirit. And it was fitting that the order should deserve this temptation by virtue of its tepidity.

Sixth, just as the person and life of Christ served as exemplar for the entire future church, so it was fitting that the first part of this order's history running down to the destruction of Babylon should be the type and image of the entire following part, so that the beginning should correspond with the beginning, the middle with the middle, and the end with the end.

Seventh, the first part should conform with the beginning, middle, and end of the fifth period, with which it is concurrent, and also with that of the entire church, the beginning of which was humble and poor, the middle eminent and spread wide throughout the world, and the end darkening and tepid. Moreover, according to some it can be compared as well with the three years and three months from Christ's baptism to his death, taking each year as thirty years, Christ's age at his baptism. Some would add to this the three months of John the Baptist's preaching, which would bring the total to 105 years.

Taken together, the sixth and seventh considerations show Olivi staring his own nightmare in the face: the danger of producing, if not

54. *Lectura super Iohannem*, MS Vat. Ottob. lat. 3302, dealing with John 7:39.

the sort of phony concordiae *favored by Antichrist, at least something analogous in the form of* concordiae *within* concordiae *within* concordiae, *like a set of nesting matryoshka dolls. Here he sees the temptation and seems to counter it by issuing a warning to himself.*

It should be recognized, though, that comparisons like this have no certitude unless they can be supported by hard evidence from events or by unquestionable revelation or unless they can be unquestionably supported by the authority of holy Scripture. Such comparisons can be formed in many, in fact in innumerable ways. Thus we can say that one year should be thought of as one hundred years, or a thousand, or forty, or ten, and so on.

Eighth, spiritual errors concerning the evangelical rule first had to be sown and firmly rooted before they could produce perfect thorns and vomit out all their poison. The founding of the evangelical order and its rule gave many people an opportunity for envy and bitter opposition against it as well as an opening to work against it. Thus, just as the first Herod slaughtered the infants in order to kill Christ, so in the early infancy of this order, while the kings of the world were devoutly adoring Christ's poverty in it, the new Herods, the carnal doctors, were damning the state of evangelical mendicancy, and through this, many of the young, tender developments recently born in many were slaughtered. This error has sent out many roots and will continue to send out many more until the second Herod arises. It was also necessary that, on the other hand, the elect should be educated with equal zeal and effort concerning this error so that, in the day of temptation, they should be less wounded and shaken by the anticipated darts.

Because what is written here concerning the sixth opening refers more fully to its fourth beginning—in which the new Babylon is overthrown by the ten kings, and then many are signed to be brought to the faith and at length martyred by the great Antichrist, and then after the latter's death the whole world is more fully signed—we will exposit the literal meaning of the text as it refers to this fourth beginning. It says, "**And behold there was a great earthquake.**" Of this it is said below, at Revelation 18, "**And a mighty angel took up a stone, as it were a great millstone, and cast it into the sea, saying: With such violence as this shall Babylon, that great city, be thrown down and shall be found no more at all**" [18:21]. By the sea, as will be touched upon later, is meant the flow of infidel nations, and also the great bitterness of such a submersion or ruin.

Of this it is also said, below at Revelation 11, after the killing and resurrection of Christ's two witnesses and their ascension into heaven, that "**at that**

hour there was made a great earthquake, and the tenth part of the city fell" [11:13]. Although this passage refers more literally to the earthquake that will occur at the death of the great Antichrist, of which it is said that "the Lord shall go forth, and shall fight, and his feet shall stand in that day upon the mount of Olives, and the mount of Olives shall be divided with a very great opening, and you shall flee as you fled from the face of the earthquake in the days of Uzziah king of Judah" [Zech 14:3–5],[55] it can nevertheless be said that in various ways and senses it refers to both earthquakes, because the full signing or conversion of the twelve tribes of Israel will not occur until after Antichrist's death, even though according to Joachim it will begin before.[56] These will receive Antichrist, as Christ says in John 5[:43], but lest they be deprived of the glorious martyrdom to be carried out under Antichrist, some will first be signed into a noble militia to be martyred by Antichrist. Each of these times is touched upon without being clearly distinguished, as is the manner of prophetic Scripture.

It follows, **And the sun became black**, etc. Taken in one sense, this is what Matthew 24[:29] touches upon when Christ says, "Immediately after the tribulation of those days" (through which even the elect will barely escape being led into error), "the sun shall be darkened and the moon shall not give her light and the stars shall fall from heaven and the powers of heaven shall be moved." For at that time the entire state of the church as it is based in prelates, laity, and religious will be destroyed except for what remains hidden in a small number of elect. Then, too, in the eyes of the infidel and in those of the faithful who apostatize or die in despair, the light of solar faith will grow dark, and the church will seem like a moon that has been made bloody. Such will be the case, not only due to the slaughter of those killed, but also because then it will become more fully evident how abominably bloodied the church has become by lechery as well as by filthy impiety and cruelty. At that time many will commit apostasy, people who seemed like stars but were actually hypocrites, figs who were large on the outside but

---

55. This is a truncated quotation. The actual passage is, "the Lord shall go forth, and shall fight against those nations, as when he fought in the day of battle. And his feet shall stand in that day upon the mount of Olives, which is over against Jerusalem towards the east: and the mount of Olives shall be divided in the midst thereof to the east, and to the west with a very great opening, and half of the mountain shall be separated to the north, and half thereof to the south. And you shall flee to the valley of those mountains, for the valley of the mountains shall be joined even to the next, and you shall flee as you fled from the face of the earthquake in the days of Uzziah king of Judah."

56. Joachim, *Expositio in Apocalypsim* (Venice, 1527; reprint, Frankfurt am Main: Minerva, 1964), 121ra (hereafter *Expos.*).

empty within. Then the **mountains**, that is, the rulers of the church, **and the islands**, that is, the monasteries and great churches placed in this world as if in the earth or the sea, will be **moved out of their places**. That is, they will be devastated, and their people will be led into death or captivity. Then, due to that temporal destruction which they understand has come upon them by God's judgment whether they wish it or not, and because of that despairing fear of eternal judgment which will come upon them after death, all of them—the great, the middling, and the lowly—will be so horribly stunned and terrified that they will want the mountains and rocks to fall suddenly upon them. From fear they will flee, hiding themselves in caves and among the rocks of the mountains. The new Babylon will be judged at that time just as carnal Jerusalem was, because it did not receive Christ but instead rejected and crucified him. Thus in Luke 24 [23:28–30] Christ predicts evils like these, saying, "Daughters of Jerusalem, weep not over me; but weep for yourselves." And shortly thereafter, "Then shall they begin to say to the mountains: Fall upon us. And to the hills: Cover us."

Olivi now turns to Revelation 7:1.[57]

After these things, I saw, etc. Here is shown how, after the aforesaid judgment and destruction of the carnal church, demons and impious humans attempt to impede the preaching of the faith, the conversion of the world to faith, and the preservation of faith among the faithful already received into the faith. Thus he says, **After these things**—that is, after the aforesaid judgment—**I saw four angels standing on the four corners of the earth**. According to Richard, these four angels are all the demons, wishing at that time to possess the entire world within its four corners. They are standing because they are pausing to consider fixedly those throughout the entire world whom they might devour. And according to him, just as the whole world is designated by the four corners, so through the four angels are designated all the demons, or their princes.

According to Joachim, however, through these are designated the infidel peoples or heretics within the church who prohibit Christian doctors from preaching God's word to those subject to them. Or, according to him, taking this in good part, the four angels are four kinds of preachers to whom has been given the power to harm, ceasing from God's word because of sin, as it is said later concerning the two prophets that "they have power to close

---

57. *LSA*, 332–36.

heaven in the days of their prophecy" [Rev 11:6].[58] These can also be taken for good angels, through God's justice retaining a flood of graces, permitting them to be impeded by demons and impious humans.

Holding the four winds of the earth, that is, according to Richard, impeding the doctrine of the four gospels by which the world is inspired through preachers. Or, according to Joachim, the four winds are four spiritual meanings through the doctrine of which the earth was normally made fruitful.

Again, through these four winds are understood all the inspirations of the Holy Spirit according to Ezekiel 37[:9], "Come, spirit, from the four winds, and blow upon these slain, and let them live again." For one wind is from the east of Christ's humble incarnation and of our low origin; another is from the west of Christ's death and of our miserable death; another is from the north of Christ's temptations and ours; and the fourth is from the south of Christ's love and glory, which is promised to us.

That they should not blow upon the earth nor upon the sea, that is, according to Richard, on the evil who love earthly things and are tossed about upon the sea of this world. **Nor on any tree,** that is, on the good raised up high and fruitful. And he says that because the good already intrinsically possessed by the good is offered from on high to the evil, in the case of the evil it is said "upon the earth," etc., but for the good it is not said "upon," but rather "on any tree." Or, following the pattern seen later in this book, by the earth is meant the place of the carnal faithful and by the sea the place and people of the infidels tossed about by error. Thus vegetable gardens and fruit trees do not grow well there. At that time, though, many in each place will be converted, although at first the devil will prevent it. In the case of the first beginning of this sixth opening, however, by the earth is meant the religious orders and by the sea the secular world, which is tossed by the waves of worldly negotiations and upheavals.

The third part follows, in which we see a prohibition of the aforesaid impediment by the next angel: **And I saw another angel,** that is, another besides the four just mentioned, and another not only in person but also in his power and office. The other four are evil and impede good, but this one is the opposite in both ways.

Joachim says of this angel that it is he who will reflect Christ through concordance at the beginning of the third age. He will rise from the place of the sun because, in order that people should not fear the uncertainties of

---

58. See Joachim, *Expos.*, 120va.

present life, he will predict with clear evidence the coming of the True Sun and the approaching resurrection of all the just. Before the power of his proclamation the opposing forces will become silent and, though unwillingly, will not oppose the rejoicing that, in the sixth part of this book, is predicted for the period between the fall of Babylon and the battle of the beast and earthly kings against him who sits on the white horse, just as Peter, after catching the 153 great fish, was called to dine with Christ, but soon, the dinner over, heard Christ say, "Follow me" [John 21], that is, to the cross. For that night, when Peter had fished without success until dawn, signifies the first tribulation. The meal, eaten in the morning after fishing, signifies the joy that will follow the tribulation of this night. That having occurred, the great battle will begin, that described in the sixth part of the book, namely in the nineteenth chapter, where it says, "Then I saw the beast gathering the kings of the earth and their armies in order to fight against the one sitting on the horse and his army" [Rev 19:19]. Thus says Joachim.[59]

Therefore this angel is Francis, renewer and, after Christ and his mother, highest observer of the evangelical life and rule to be propagated and celebrated in the sixth and seventh periods. **Rising from the place of the sun**, that is, from that life which Christ, the sun of this world, brought us in his first advent. For in Francis, Christ reascended the ten shadow lines of Ahaz's sundial [2 Kgs 20:11], back to that morning of Christ's birth. He was also from the place of the sun because he derived the basis and beginning of his ascent from the Roman seat, which is, among the five patriarchal churches, principally seat and city of the sun, that is, of Christ and his faith. Isaiah refers to it in a typical sense when he says, "On that day, there will be five cities on the earth," etc., then says, "One will be called the city of the sun" [Isa 19:18].

And he ascends from the place of the sun, i.e., around the time when the sixth and seventh solar day or third general state of the world began. Again, through this is to be understood the crowd of his disciples to arise in the third and fourth beginnings of the sixth opening, who are also to appear from the place of the sun, for it will be a group in which his example, merit, and heavenly guidance are singularly apparent, so that whatever is good in them should be ascribed to him rather than to them.

Moreover, I have heard from a certain spiritual man very worthy of trust, a man on familiar terms with Brother Leo, the blessed Francis's confessor and companion, something consistent with this passage, yet something

---

59. *Expos.*, 120vb–121ra.

I myself neither assert nor know for sure, nor do I even think it should be asserted. This person received, both through the words of Brother Leo and through a revelation made to him personally, the news that, during that Babylonian temptation, when Francis's state and rule are being crucified as Christ was crucified, Francis will gloriously rise again so that, just as he was singularly assimilated to Christ in receiving the stigmata, so he will be assimilated to Christ in a resurrection necessary for the confirmation and instruction of his disciples, just as Christ's resurrection was necessary for the confirmation of the apostles and in order to instruct them concerning the establishment and government of the future church. Nevertheless, in order that Francis the servant's resurrection should be clearly inferior in dignity to those of Christ and his mother, Christ rose again immediately after the three days, and certain people not entirely to be rejected say that his mother rose again after forty days, whereas Francis will do so only when the history of his order has progressed to the time when the order is assimilated to Christ's cross in being crucified, a crucifixion already prefigured in Francis's stigmata.

Chapter 13

And I saw a beast, that is, a bestial crowd and sect, **ascending**, that is, to high dominion, public status, and power, **from the sea**, that is, from an infidel nation of paganism.

> *This is another chapter that could be included in its entirety, but we will pick it up at Revelation 13:11, at which point Olivi clarifies his expectations.*[60]

And I saw another beast, because in Antichrist's time, along with the aforesaid beastly people and their king, there will be a beastly crowd of pseudo-prophets who arise, not from the sea of infidel nations, but from the land of Christianity. They will move in concert with the first beast because they will join with it in a single erroneous sect that is a conflation of both. Here he deals with this second beast. He deals with it in the second place for three reasons: first, because, after the exaltation of the first beast, this one will follow; second, because this second beast will rise up and prevail, not

60. The passage translated here is found in *LSA*, 599–602. The entire chapter is found in *LSA*, 580–631.

by its own strength, but through that of the first beast; and third, because this second beast will produce false signs and various other evils in support of the first beast.

Joachim and other great scholars have thought that the head of this second beast will be a pseudo-pope whom the king of the first beast, the monarch of the entire world, will cause to be worshiped as God by the whole world, because that king has been deceived and driven out of his mind through false miracles, hypocritical feigning, and fallacious arguments drawn from worldly philosophy. Perhaps the king will also do so because he has been aided through the activity and instruction of this second beast and of the devil in the acquisition of his empire and monarchy, or in fuller and firmer establishment of it. For this second beast will be a familiar of the prince of demons and will be full of his crafty stratagems. The devil will assist him in revealing secret things and performing miraculous deeds. Thus he is also called a pseudo-prophet in what follows.

Some think that, just as Julian the Apostate was made emperor and was against Christ, so the apostate Antichrist will obtain the rule of his world empire through fraud, and then many pseudo-prophets will arise from among the false Christians to praise him and produce false signs that will cause him to be adored. They will preach the law he has proclaimed and make it seem to be true. Thus these are called the second beast, and the king, who is Antichrist, is called the first beast. It is he in whose service they produce the false signs, and it is he whom they cause to be adored.

I myself do not care much whether he who will be Antichrist, who will be adored as if he were God and will claim to be messiah of the Jews, will be the king, the pseudo-pope, or both together. It is sufficient for me to know that he will be a fraud and against Christ.

As for what some people have said and written, namely that he will be trained and educated from his mother's womb by the devil—in fact, that he will be more or less a devil himself, filled and inhabited by the devil from the beginning—and that God will permit all this knowing his future malice, many people do not think these things could be true. In the first place, this would provide a great excuse for and reduction of his sin, because from the womb he would be acting not so much on his own but at the devil's instigation. It would follow from this that he would not be one of the most culpable people in the story, and the saints say just the opposite. In the second place, it simply would not be fitting for God to permit that from his mother's womb he should be, as it were, necessarily seduced and driven to perform such evils. In the third place, if such were the case, his sin would not be similar to

Lucifer's, for the latter voluntarily apostatized and through apostasy fell from the highest and most righteous state in which he was created.

Thus it is not improbably concluded by the learned that he will be an apostate from Christianity and, in fact, from the highest religious order. Thus he will be especially skillful at simulating genuine religious behavior and subtly devising the cunning errors of his false doctrine and law.

> *Having generously hinted that the pseudo-prophet will be an apos-*
> *tate Franciscan (Olivi has no trouble deciding which religious order*
> *is the highest one), Olivi has gone a long way toward predicting what*
> *will occur. He seems to have concluded that an evil king will combine*
> *forces with a pseudo-pope who will bolster the king's rule with fake*
> *miracles and signs. The problem is that in other passages he has*
> *made it clear that he expects two Antichrists, the mystical one and*
> *the great one. Which has he been discussing? For the moment, he*
> *simply doesn't say. In the following exegesis, though, he applies Rev-*
> *elation 13:17-18, the mark and number of the beast, in an interesting*
> *way. First he interprets it as many other contemporary exegetes do,*
> *converting the numbers into letters to spell out the possible names*
> *of Antichrist, each of which is given a meaning. Then, however, he*
> *says something that seems more important to him.*[61]

Certain people, however, go beyond this in stating (purely as an opinion) that this signifies the number of years the Saracen sect will rule. For from the year of our Lord 635, in which according to the chronicles the Saracens conquered Persia and gained rule over it, until the year 1300 is 666 years. From the year of our Lord 648, in which the Saracens took Africa, having first taken Damascus, Phoenicia, Egypt, and Jerusalem, until 1290 years from Christ's death—that is, until 1323 years from Christ's nativity—adds up to 666 years. If, therefore, the number prefixed in Daniel 12 is seen as running from the time the yoke of sacrifice was taken away from the Jews until the time of Antichrist,[62] then from the time the kingdom of the Saracens was spread out solemnly through Asia and Africa to the time of Antichrist will be 666 years, of which we have twenty-three years left to go. And if the

---

61. *LSA*, 611-17.

62. Dan 12:11-12: "And from the time when the continual sacrifice shall be taken away, and the abomination unto desolation shall be set up, there shall be 1,290 days. Blessed is he that waits and comes unto 1,335 days."

three years of Antichrist's tribulation are included in the number just written, then we have only twenty years to go before the beginning of those three years. What will actually come to pass, however, I don't know. God knows.

It should be recognized, however, that wherever the great Antichrist is discussed in this book, the time of the mystical Antichrist preceding the great one is implied in prophetic manner. According to this reasoning, the beast ascending from the sea signifies the bestial life and people of the carnal and secular Christians; since the end of the fourth period it has had many heads in the form of carnal princes and prelates, and this has been going on for six hundred years now. In this sixth centenary, one head has been almost killed through Francis's evangelical state; for the higher, more widely, and more perfectly evangelical poverty and perfection are impressed upon and magnified within the church, the more powerfully the head of earthly cupidity and vile carnality is killed in it. But now this head, almost destroyed, is reviving so much that carnal Christians admire and follow its carnal glory.

When, however, the apostate beast from the earth of the religious ascends on high with its two horns of pseudo-religious and pseudo-prophets falsely resembling the true horns of the lamb, the most powerful temptation of the mystical Antichrist will occur. Then will arise the pseudo-Christs and pseudo-prophets who will cause cupidity and carnality or the earthly glory of the secular beast to be admired by all. And they will provide great signs on that account. The first sign will be that of ecclesiastical authority, contradiction of which will seem to be disobedience, contumacy, and schismatic rebellion. The second sign will be that of universal opinion, the agreement of all the masters and doctors of the church as well as the common agreement of the whole multitude, contradiction of which will seem foolish, insane, and even heretical. The third sign will be that of arguments and falsely twisted Scriptures, as well as of some superficial, ancient, and complex religion confirmed and solemnized through long succession from antiquity. Thus with these signs they will seem to make the fire of divine wrath descend on those who contradict them, and they will seem to make the fire of holy and apostolic zeal descend from heaven on those people's disciples. They will decree that whoever does not obey should be anathematized, ejected from the synagogue, and, if necessary, turned over to the secular arm of the first beast. They will make the image of the beast—that is, the pseudo-pope raised up by the king of the first beast—adored in such a way that he is believed in more than Christ and that his gospel is honored as if he were the god of this world.

The number of the name—that is, of the famous sect and of its glory— will be 666 both because the three states (the laity, clerics, and religious or the inferior, middling, and superior) will take pride in perfecting themselves, and perhaps because from the end of the fourth period to this time 666 years will pass. For the fifth period, starting from Pepin, already has run 560 years; and, if you begin counting from the devastation wreaked on the anchorites and other of the faithful living in Persia, Syria, and Egypt, the number is already completed. For, as I said above, the Saracens captured the kingdom of Persia and two years later captured Jerusalem.

Some people, working from many things Joachim said about Frederick II and his seed and from certain things the blessed Francis is said to have revealed secretly to Brother Leo and certain others among his companions, opine that the aforesaid Frederick and his seed will be, as it were, the slain head in regard to this time, and that in the time of the mystical Antichrist he will be so revived in one of his descendants that he will gain not only the Roman Empire but the kingdom of the Franks as well, having conquered the Franks. Five other Christian kings will adhere to him, and he will establish as pseudo-pope a certain false religious who will plot against the evangelical rule and make deceitful dispensation, promoting to bishoprics some professors of the aforesaid rule who will obey him, accordingly expelling clerics and previous bishops who were opposed to the seed of Frederick, to him in particular and to his state, and consequently all who wish to observe and defend the aforesaid rule purely and fully. They say that the fall of those clerics and of the kingdom of France, as well as some other related things, are designated through the earthquake at the beginning of the opening of the sixth seal, although the latter also designates, beyond that, the subversion and blinding of nearly the entire church that will occur at that time. How much of this will or will not occur should, I think, be left up to God.

The aforesaid people add, however, that at that time, the words of the apostle in 2 Thessalonians [2:3] will be fulfilled, namely, "Unless there come a revolt first." For they say that at that time almost everyone will fall away from obedience to the pope and follow the pseudo-pope, who will indeed be "pseudo" because he errs in a heretical way against the truth of evangelical poverty and perfection, and perhaps also because he will not be canonically elected but schismatically introduced.

PETRUS AURIOLI

The same year that Gregory was asked to write his critique of Olivi, Pierre Auriol (Petrus Aurioli) became the new Franciscan regent master of theology at Paris. In July 1318, Pope John XXII had written asking that Pierre be appointed. Pierre served in that capacity until 1320 or 1321, when John made him bishop of Aix-en-Provence. Thus we can probably assume that Pierre composed his Revelation commentary around 1319 or 1320. It was not a freestanding commentary but rather part of his *Compendium of the Literal Sense of the Entire Divine Scripture*, a bracing run through the entire Bible.[1]

The most interesting thing about Pierre's commentary is his decision to revert to the basic exegetical approach used by Alexander Minorita: he portrays Revelation as a narrative of Christian history beginning in Revelation 1 and progressing through Revelation 22. The intention of the Apocalypse is to predict "all the notable sufferings, changes, persecutions, and novelties occurring in the church, and not just the persecution under Antichrist." That represents a huge challenge, and Pierre tells us he sees little reason why God would want to waste space by repeating the same general pattern over and over. "It does not seem rational that what is said in chapter 7 should refer to the end of the world, then at the beginning of the eighth we're back to the early church."[2] Obviously Pierre has a point of sorts. There was always something odd about the notion that each sevenfold pattern in Revelation

---

1. *Compendium sensus literalis totius divinae scripturae*, ed. Philibertus Seebeek (Quaracchi: College of St. Bonaventure, 1896).
2. *Compendium*, 456.

should cover the entire historical pattern from beginning to end, although many exegetes did give it some sense by suggesting that in each sequence a different aspect of church history is being examined (for example, that the trumpets represent preaching). The question for Pierre is whether one experiences any advance in coherence by reading Revelation straight through and trying to match it with church history. Either way, it's a struggle.

Given that fact, and given the fact that, as far as we know, the Alexandrine straight-through pattern had been used only by Alexander himself during the thirteenth century, and especially given the fact that Pierre had studied at Paris and was now teaching there, one is tempted to look around for a less exegetically oriented and perhaps more existentially oriented explanation for Pierre's choice. Could he have decided that it would be a good idea to get as far away from Olivi's recapitulative exegetical strategy as possible? Of course, the recapitulative approach to Revelation had been used steadily throughout the thirteenth century. If there was some unwelcome novelty in Olivi's work, it certainly was not the recapitulative strategy. And Olivi's commentary would not be condemned by John XXII until 1326 in any case, although as John's protégé Pierre would certainly be aware of which way the wind was blowing, and the Franciscan order would have carried out its own condemnation in the spring of 1319.

And of course the Alexandrine commentary had its own problems, committed as it was to early thirteenth-century Joachism; and it is noteworthy that Pierre is cautious at precisely those points. He tries to stay away from sources such as the pseudo-Joachite *Super Ieremiam*, to which Alexander gave significant attention, and he eliminates the sustained apocalyptic celebration of the mendicants that Alexander had packed into his interpretation of Revelation 21–22. The new Jerusalem turns out to refer, not to the mendicants, but to heaven.[3] Francis and Dominic are mentioned in relation to Revelation 20:5, but in a more subdued form than Alexander would have thought appropriate. This strategy made sense when one considers that, even as Pierre wrote, John XXII was on the verge of doing battle with the Franciscans concerning what he obviously saw as their overly grandiose self-image. What Pierre says about the mendicants and Revelation 20:5 can hardly be described as self-effacing, but the praise is dialed down remarkably when compared with that of Alexander or, for that matter, Olivi.

It is important to remember, of course, that what Pierre produced was not a stand-alone commentary on Revelation but a compendium dealing

---

3. *Compendium*, 550–55.

with the literal sense of the entire Bible. The book of Revelation represents the home stretch of that compendium. That would have helped Pierre control himself concerning passages such as Revelation 20–22.

Of course, there was Revelation 7:2, a passage that had inspired serious thought in various Franciscan exegetes after Bonaventure's *Legenda maior*. Some had ignored it, while others explained it away, accepting the traditional identification of the angel as Christ while welcoming the connection with Francis as an invitation to preach a sermon about him rather than to identify him as literally the angel in question.

For Pierre the problem is softened by his reading of Revelation as a progressive historical narrative. By chapter 7 he is at the age of Constantine, whose role in the story is important enough to encourage identification of him as the angel of 7:2, with the evil emperors Maximian, Severus, Maxentius, and Licinius in the role of the preceding four angels (Rev 7:1). The rules of the game are thus changed, and Pierre may have taken the alteration as a good excuse to avoid the matter, which by this point had been the source of some irritation among non-Franciscans. By John's pontificate some prelates felt free to make it clear that Francis, while a saint, was not the only saint and should not be treated as somehow in a class by himself.

Thus one might be moved to see Pierre and Olivi as standing at opposite poles of the spectrum when it comes to Francis as an apocalyptic figure; yet that would be putting the matter too simply. Francis appears in the story alongside Dominic, but, as we have noted, that combination had appeared in the thirteenth century with apocalyptic overtones, and in a larger sense Pierre's view of history is not totally opposed to what we find in Olivi. Like Olivi, he sees the mendicants as contributing to a period of improvement within the church.

Of course, what Pierre produces is primarily not so much an ode to the Franciscans or even the mendicants as it is a triumphalist tribute to the institutional church. The enemies are all external. They are the Jews, the heretics, the Greeks, the Muslims, and those German emperors who challenged ecclesiastical authority. The Mongols rate mention, too, since Alexander identifies them with Gog and Magog; but in the final analysis Pierre feels required to agree with Augustine that Gog and Magog represent evil people throughout the world, not a specific people.

The Muslims are important to Pierre, and that importance is reflected in the amount of space he devotes to the crusades. He inherits from Alexander a solid number to apply: 666. Alexander saw it as a prediction of how long Islam would last, and the figure worked well for him insofar as it had not yet expired by the time he wrote. By Pierre's time it had. He notes that some Muslims feel they have exceeded the duration predicted for them by the prophets and are now living in a grace period of sorts, while others feel the 666 years did not begin until the reorganization of the faith and correction of the Qur'an that began after Muhammad's death, in which case the allotted years have not yet expired. Pierre confesses that he himself does not know what to think.[4]

There is also the matter of the thousand years in Revelation 20:7, after which Satan is released and, according to Alexander, Antichrist appears. Here again Alexander, who starts the clock with the election of Pope Sylvester in 316, feels there is still time. Antichrist should appear in 1316; yet for Pierre that number, too, has elapsed, and if Alexander's calculation is accepted, Antichrist should now be three years old. Here again he feels caution is the better part of prophetic valor and suggests that the matter be left up to the Holy Spirit.[5]

On the whole, Pierre is optimistic. The Christian church has struggled against powerful enemies, but it is doing well and will of course triumph. Moreover, the Christian church that will triumph is the institution headed by the pope, not a small group struggling against the carnal institution.

READINGS

The commentary begins with Pierre's revisionist sense of how many visions the Apocalypse contains and what is in each.

The General Structure of the Apocalypse and the Structure of History[6]

According to the literal sense, it can be said that these six visions contain future events covering tribulations and persecutions that the church was to suffer, especially in the time of Antichrist. The entire development of the

4. *Compendium*, 505.
5. *Compendium*, 548.
6. *Compendium*, 454–58.

church can be divided into seven smaller periods in the way that the story of the whole world is divided into seven periods. Thus the entire development of the church can be divided into seven ages. These are:

- First, the period of its foundation in the time of Christ's apostles and disciples.
- Second, the period of its persecution in the time of the emperors and martyrs.
- Third, the period of prosperity and exaltation in the time of Constantine, who bestowed on it honor and abundance of temporal goods.
- Fourth, the period of division and dismemberment in the time of the heretics.
- Fifth, the period of perfect pacification and expansion in the time of Charlemagne and succeeding emperors. This period has led to the expansion and pacification of the church as well as the foundation of many monasteries.
- Sixth, the period of new persecution in the time of Antichrist and his disciples.
- Seventh, the period of rewarding the good and punishing the evil after the day of judgment and after the destruction of Antichrist.

Each vision proceeds according to this sevenfold pattern. For in the first there are seven seals, with the first seal corresponding to the first age, the second to the second, and so on. In the second, that of the seven angels, the first angel corresponds to the first angel with a trumpet and so on. In the third vision, that of the dragon and the woman, attention is primarily devoted to the sixth period, the persecution of Antichrist. Indeed, according to this way of expositing the book, every vision is primarily devoted to that.

These ages can be described in another way, however. In this way what has been described as the third age, the time of Constantine, is omitted. For then the dissension and division of the heretics under Arius began, and according to this pattern the time of Antichrist belongs to the fifth age, and then the sixth will be computed from the death of Antichrist to the end of judgment. The seventh will then be attributed to the period from the end of judgment and so on.

But because, according to this whole way of expositing the book, the entire prophecy concentrates on persecutions inflicted by Antichrist and consequently many things are omitted—especially those things that occurred in the church during the intermediate time, such as the separation of the Greeks from the wholeness of the church, the translation of the empire from the Greeks to the Germans through the person of Charlemagne, the persecution of Christians begun by Khosrow beginning in Jerusalem and the east, that is, spreading from Persia into Syria and devastating the church, and the persecution begun by Muhammad that converted Persia, Arabia, Syria, Egypt, Africa, Spain, Gascony, and Provence from the faith of Christ to infidelity and Saracenism—it therefore seems irrational that this and much more that was noteworthy and was inflicted upon the universal church during this time should have been omitted by John in this prophecy.

Yet because he himself says in the beginning, "The Apocalypse of Jesus Christ, which God gave to him to pass on to his servants, and which is to happen soon"; and further on he says, "The time is close at hand"; and in the fourth chapter he says, "I shall show you what is to happen immediately after this"; and in the sixth chapter he says, "You must prophesy to all people and tribes and to many languages and kingdoms," through which it is to be understood that he prophesied in this book not only about the nefarious kingdom of Antichrist but about much else; and because the prophets of the Old Testament prophesied not only about the ultimate tribulation that the Israelites were to suffer under the Romans but about others they were to suffer under other monarchies—for all these reasons it has seemed to others that in this book are predicted all the notable sufferings, changes, persecutions, and novelties occurring to the universal church and not only the persecution of Antichrist. And this is the case especially because it does not seem rational that what is said in chapter 7 should be referred to the end of the world and then at the beginning of the eighth we are back to the beginning of the church, and we must do that often if the aforesaid method of exposition is to be followed.

Thus, by harmonizing with this prophecy those histories of the past in which notable events occurring to the church are written down, we can say that whatever is described in the latter historically is contained here prophetically.

According to the histories the ages of the church can be divided as follows:

- The first time was from the foundation of the church by the disciples and apostles to Julian the Apostate, in which time the church was, as it were, closed and sealed under the persecution of the pagan emperors, and all this age is dealt with in the first vision of the seven seals.

- The second time was from Julian's, Jovinian's, and Valentinian's deaths to the emperor Justinian, or to Mauritius, in whose time Pope Gregory the Great lived. During this entire time the church was, as it were, under angels sounding trumpets, because it was under the persecution of heretics, for in the entire period many emperors were Arians and infected by other heresies; and this entire time is contained in the second vision.
- The third time was from the emperor Phocas, who succeeded Mauritius, to that emperor Constantine who was blinded by his mother Irene. In this time the empire of the Greeks was transferred to Charlemagne and the Germans. And in that time the church suffered the persecution of the dragon, that is, Khosrow, and of the beast, Muhammad, and the persecution of the Saracens; and all this was prophesied in the third vision.
- The fourth time was that of Charlemagne to Henry IV, in which time the church was subjected to certain plagues and vials full of God's wrath, due to schisms and certain adversaries, as will appear later. And all this is prophetically predicted in the fourth vision, where we encounter the seven angels with seven plagues.
- The fifth time was from the time of the aforesaid Henry and lasts to the time of Antichrist, in which the church had victory over Babylon the harlot under Kings Baldwin and Godfrey, and rested for a while, and that is described in the fifth vision.
- The sixth time will be from the persecution of Antichrist to the day of judgment, after which we will have the glory of paradise and the consummation of the mysteries of God, and the sixth vision corresponds to this.

Constantine as the Angel of Revelation 7:2

In the place where it says, **After these things I saw four angels**, where the seventh chapter begins, John foretells the end of the whole persecution, the peace of the Christian religion, and the time of tranquility.

First, he introduces the shameful behavior of the four tyrants. As we have read, after Diocletian and Maximian laid aside their imperial positions in one day, Galerius and Constantius were made emperors. Galerius instituted two Caesars, one in Italy named Severus and the other in the east named Maximian; but in the city of Rome, Maxentius, the son of Maximian, was made emperor.

But Constantius and Helen bore Constantine the Great, who was made emperor after the death of his father, and he assumed the position jointly with the emperor Licinius, who was admittedly at first peaceful toward the Christians but afterward became a persecutor. Therefore the four angels of Satan, messengers and ministers of persecution, were Maximian in the east, Severus in Italy, Maxentius in Rome, and Licinius in Egypt and Alexandria. And thus they stood upon the four corners of the earth as John says, and they held the winds so that they should not blow on the earth because, after Diocletian and Maximian came to power, believing teachers could not preach on the earth, nor in the sea, nor on any tree, that is, to any believers.

Then John introduces the triumph of the liberator. For we have read of Constantine that first at Marseilles he beheaded Maximian, the colleague of Diocletian, who wished to control the empire. Then, marching on Rome against Maxentius and concerned about war, he had a vision from heaven that he should conquer in the sign of the cross. And, with the sign of the cross shown to him, it was said to him through angels, "Constantine, in this you will conquer." Therefore he made the sign of the cross on his forehead and put it on his banners. And having been strengthened for war against Maxentius, he was victorious. And when he came in triumph to Rome, the senate erected an image in his honor, and ordered that a banner with the cross of the Lord on it be put to the right of his image, and [decreed that] under it should be written, "This is the sign of the invincible living God." Therefore this Constantine is the other angel ascending from the east, because he went to Rome through revelation and divine or angelic inspiration, having the seal of the living God. And he cried out against those four angels who were ministers of evil persecution, about whom something has already been said. Indeed, he cried out, striking fear and waging war so that they would not harm the earth, or the sea, or the trees, that is, any Christian, until all were sealed on their foreheads through the free reception of baptism. For he passed an edict that every person throughout the whole Roman world was free to be baptized and signed with the cross, and churches could be built, and everywhere images of the crucifix could be depicted on them. Moreover, he, too, was baptized and sealed publicly.

Francis and Dominic (Rev 20:5)[7]

This is the first resurrection predicts the useful institution, fruitful in the world, of two religions, the order of minors through Francis, the confessor of Christ, and the order of preachers through that excellent father and doctor Dominic. For it is read that in the time of Pope Innocent III and the emperor Frederick these two saints, destined by the Lord to be two lights, instituted two religions through the doctrines, exhortations, merits, and examples of which all Christianity, as it were, seems to have risen with Christ and, in respect to the preceding time, walked in new life.

Thus, since the resurrection is twofold, one spiritual through grace and truth and consecration and holy life while the other is corporeal, with souls united to bodies at the end, in the advent of these two orders the first resurrection seems to have begun and the whole world to have been renewed. For before that time it was filled with errors and shameful acts.

The Antichrist (Rev 20:7)

And when a thousand years had passed. Here the introduction and bitter persecution of Antichrist is predicted, and it is predicted that such will occur after a thousand years, and then **he will be released for a short time** (20:3). But the question is: from what date should those thousand years be computed? Clearly they could not be counted from Christ's nativity, since it has been over a thousand years since then already and Antichrist still has not appeared. Thus others, with greater probability, compute it from Constantine in the time of Pope Sylvester, when Christ and the church began to reign and the honor of the empire was translated to the person of Sylvester. Then the Roman church, and the bishops and priests, who for three hundred years had been atrociously slaughtered by pagan emperors, were honored like kings.

Sylvester became pope in the year 316, and subtracting that from today's date we find that the Antichrist has been born and should be three years old. For that reason we should avoid speaking with any certainty on the matter, leaving it up to the Holy Spirit.

7. *Compendium*, 547–48.

NICHOLAS OF LYRA

The last Revelation commentary to be considered at length here is that of Nicholas of Lyra, who was the Franciscan regent master at Paris in 1308–1309.[1] The commentary itself is later, however. In its present form it was produced as part of his literal commentary on the entire Bible, begun in 1322 and completed in 1332 or 1333. Nevertheless, he had already commented on Daniel, the Psalms, and, for all we know, perhaps Revelation before that. Scholars tend to see the Revelation commentary now available to us as having been done ca. 1329.

Nicholas is considered an important figure for any number of reasons. First of all, he followed Alexander Minorita and Pierre Auriol in reading Revelation as a continuous historical narrative. This is hardly to say that he followed them all the way. They took the train to the end of the line, assuming that the entirety of Revelation covered the entirety of history and

---

1. He is also listed as a bachelor of theology present at a hearing concerning the Templars in 1307 and as a master of theology in a quodlibet in 1309, then as a master of theology again at a hearing concerning Marguerite Porete in 1309 or 1310. Philip Krey, in the introduction to *Nicholas of Lyra's Apocalypse Commentary*, TEAMS Commentary Series (Kalamazoo: Western Michigan University, 1997), his translation of Nicholas's Revelation commentary, provides an instructive history of Nicholas's career, as does Deeana Copeland Klepper, *The Insight of Unbelievers* (Philadelphia: University of Pennsylvania Press, 2007), in the introduction and indeed elsewhere. *Nicholas of Lyra: The Senses of Scripture*, ed. Philip D. Krey and Lesley Smith (Leiden: Brill, 2000), offers an excellent introduction to Nicholas of Lyra's life and works as well as essays by Lyra scholars on specific topics. I am particularly indebted to Krey for allowing me to employ his translation, thus saving me the effort of providing my own.

their task was to follow it there, whereas in chapter 17 Nicholas stops reading Revelation as a continuous narrative of past events and begins to treat it as the story of what will occur in the present and future. The transition at the beginning of chapter 17 is jarring, like running into a wall.

> **Then one of the seven . . .** According to those who say that the whole text from here to that place: **When the thousand years are ended** (around the middle of chapter twenty [20:7]) has been fulfilled in the past, the seventh plague is now described more specifically. First I will present their whole interpretation of [this section], and then afterward I will say what seems to me the true interpretation of it.

It will soon become clear to the reader—or at least the reader who has read this book so far—that the "they" to whom he refers here are Alexander, Pierre, and anyone else who might have followed their lead. Nicholas is informing us that he is about to present an exegesis with which he does not agree, then critique it. Obviously he cannot present an exegesis that does full justice to both men since they themselves differ, but he doesn't need to do so. All he has to do is mark out a trail from the twelfth century, where chapter 16 left the story, extending it to 20:7. Where the trail goes is less important than having a historical narrative to reject.

Much of the passage will be presented here in a moment and thus need not be summarized in detail. The important point for now is that when Nicholas reaches 20:7 he finally tosses the grenade he has been holding since 17:1, blowing the whole thing up.

> On account of this and many other things that could be said against this exposition, it seems (I submit myself to better judgment) that the whole text from the beginning of chapter seventeen to this place is not yet fulfilled. And because I am not a prophet or the son of a prophet [Amos 7:14] I will not say anything about the future except what can be taken from scripture or from the words of the saints and established teachers. Therefore I leave interpretation of this text to the wise. If the Lord were to grant me understanding of it, I would be glad to share it with others.

Then Nicholas launches his exegesis of 20:7, where he seems to feel that Scripture actually does give him something to say about Antichrist, Gog, and Magog.

To say this much about what happens in the passage just quoted is to present such a general picture of Nicholas's interpretation as to distort it noticeably. The fact is that Nicholas cannot bring himself simply to present the interpretation he is about to reject and then reject it. As a man who has absorbed a substantial number of historical sources, he feels required to critique details of the interpretation he is presenting even though he realizes that he is presenting it merely to destroy it in its totality. Where the source he is citing interprets the beginning of Revelation 20 as referring to Pope Callixtus, Nicholas says as much and then cannot stop himself from remarking that "if one were to interpret this text as if it were fulfilled in the past, it seems (I submit myself to better judgment) that it would be better to interpret this text as if it were about Pope Innocent III, who approved the orders of the friars minor and the preachers, through whom the teaching and preaching of the church were in a certain way renewed and the power of the devil was restricted." Nor is this the only moment when he feels required to correct details of the story before rejecting the story as a whole.

In fact, as Philip Krey observes, there seems to be something else involved here as well. It looks very much as if at some moments we are encountering a later revision in which Nicholas is recording his own change of mind about something he himself had said earlier. "More than likely," Krey says, "he re-edited the whole commentary in 1329, having changed his mind about a number of issues."[2] The result can be challenging. Nicholas can find himself arguing against the total interpretation he presents but will eventually reject as incorrect, against details of the totally incorrect interpretation, or against details of the interpretation he once considered correct but then changed his mind about. It is hardly surprising that scholars have occasionally misunderstood what he intended to say.

If there is perhaps unintended humor in the result, there is intended humor as well, provided we include irony within the boundaries of humor. His stated willingness to share any later enlightenment with us certainly qualifies in that category. Knowing even as little as we do about Nicholas, he doesn't strike us as a man who plans to contact us to report future mystical experiences. In fact, one could find it easy to see a degree of irony in his regular offers to submit himself to better judgment. Nicholas was a born historian. He settled comfortably into scholarly life at Paris; but he was also, one might guess, tolerably comfortable in the various leadership roles he

2. Krey, *Nicholas of Lyra's Apocalypse Commentary*, 199.

held within the order, including election as provincial minister of France in 1319, then provincial minister of Burgundy in 1325. It was a time of serious battles between elements within the Franciscan order, between at least part of the order and the pope, and between the pope and the king of France. Nicholas remained in the thick of things. His name pops up in connection with a remarkable number of crises, and yet, as Krey observes, he seems to have navigated his way through them adroitly.[3] He was a man with a strong respect for his own abilities and probably with a good deal of faith in his own stated opinions. The demands of Christian humility might have encouraged him to submit to better judgment when he encountered it, but he might not have expected to encounter it all that often.

Which brings us to another aspect of Nicholas's exegesis. If Pierre Auriol's commentary can be described as triumphalist, Nicholas's can be described as realistic. Krey uses the term "hard-nosed,"[4] and there is much to be said for that description. Krey notes that "after Lyra's revisions, church history looked different. . . . The heroes and villains of history become harder to identify." Here we are speaking not so much of Nicholas's revision of his earlier opinions as of his revision of Alexander Minorita and Pierre Auriol. Whereas in describing the investiture controversy Pierre Auriol clearly sides with Gregory VII against Henry IV, Nicholas avoids assigning blame, and Krey goes on to observe that "if [Nicholas] were forced to choose the instigator, it would not be Henry."[5]

It would be fair to say that, although Nicholas could be described as specifically Francophile and more generally as a man who appreciated the historical role of secular government in defending the church, in the final analysis he must be characterized as "imbued with a profound sense of the ambiguities of history."[6] He realized that the closest thing to the truth could only emerge from an exploration that involved finding as many as possible of the best sources available and reading them carefully, balancing them off against one another. Krey attempts to mention a few of the ones important to Nicholas, and the list is an impressive one.[7] If what emerges from Revelation at his hands is an impressive historical reading of Christianity, it is not because that is what John meant to write but because Nicholas, starting

---

3. Krey, *Nicholas of Lyra's Apocalypse Commentary*, 9.
4. Krey, *Nicholas of Lyra's Apocalypse Commentary*, 11.
5. Krey, *Nicholas of Lyra's Apocalypse Commentary*, 20.
6. I quote Krey's words, *Nicholas of Lyra's Apocalypse Commentary*, 23.
7. Krey, *Nicholas of Lyra's Apocalypse Commentary*, 19–20.

with the assumption that such a sequential historical pattern underlay the text, marshaled the sources to read such a pattern into it, accumulating so many sources and absorbing them so successfully as to produce a more complex map of Christian history than either Alexander or Pierre had managed to achieve. It was a remarkable achievement on Nicholas's part, and one can understand why in the Renaissance and early modern period his commentary took its place alongside the *Glossa ordinaria* as a standard aid in interpreting the text.

But there seems to be more involved here than a better collection of sources. When he reaches the descent of the heavenly Jerusalem at the end of Revelation, Nicholas turns to Alexander's reading of it in terms of the mendicant orders and proceeds to destroy it.

> Although this exposition is able to be preserved in some mystical sense, it is not possible in the literal sense as I believe. First, because it is said that the angel who is introduced here teaches John, saying, "Come, I will show you" (21:9). One cannot say that of Pope Innocent, since he lived more than one thousand years after John. Similarly, because it is said about this city, "I saw no temple in the city" (21:22). These orders, however, have churches. Similarly, because it is added, "And the city has no need of sun or moon" (21:23), and afterwards, "But nothing unclean will enter it, nor anyone who practices abomination or falsehood" (21:27). . . . These orders, however, need the illumination of the sun and moon, neither are all who enter them unstained, nor do all who are good when they enter persevere in the good, but many become apostate and the worst of persons.

What lies between Alexander's commentary and Nicholas's is not simply better historical scholarship but decades of experience, much of it bitter experience. Between the time Nicholas became a master of theology and the time he finished the Revelation commentary he had seen a protracted struggle between the spirituals and the rest of the order. He had seen two popes attempt to end that battle without success, then an emperor dragged into the melee. He had seen inquisitorial involvement leading to the imprisonment and even execution of some Franciscans. And the strife continued. Having witnessed all that, he understandably felt it might seem odd to identify his order with the new Jerusalem. Nicholas probably saw that lesson written clearly not only in his study of Franciscan history to date but in his own experience. Krey states the matter neatly: "Although he was a Franciscan administrator (perhaps *because* he was an administrator), he did not see the Apocalypse as a tool of propaganda for the order."[8]

But, again, it is important to emphasize that the difference extends beyond his view of the order. Nicholas is less sanguine than Alexander and Pierre about a whole series of things, including the crusades and Islam. On the former he is more realistic in estimating motives and results. On the latter he is clear-eyed enough to state bluntly that instead of fading away Islam is getting stronger.

Two other aspects of Nicholas's scholarship should be mentioned, one important to his Revelation commentary and the other less so. The latter is his degree of success in learning Hebrew and integrating what he found in Jewish biblical scholarship into his own biblical studies. This was in some sense his greatest achievement, yet it was less important for his interpretation of Revelation than his mastery of Latin historical sources.

The other aspect of Nicholas's scholarship has more direct bearing on his Revelation commentary: his acceptance of a double literal sense, allowing one meaning for the prophet's own time and another for the future. The important thing is that both meanings can be considered literal.

For example, according to Nicholas's sequential reading of Revelation, chapter 11 describes the Eutychian heresy in the sixth century. The two witnesses of 11:3 are Sylverius and Menas, who stood steadfastly against the heresy; yet, as Nicholas observes, 11:3 is normally interpreted as referring to Enoch and Elijah, who will be killed in the future for their opposition to Antichrist. Both references are to be taken as literally true. Nicholas goes on to propose a more complicated example involving Solomon.

That entire passage will be included in the readings in this chapter. For the moment we simply need to ask whether, granting Nicholas's affection for the double literal meaning and his modern connection with it, he in any sense pioneered it. The answer is that one can find other exegetes using something remarkably similar, if not identical to it. Thus, in commenting on Isaiah in the commentary mentioned earlier in this book, Olivi presents passages in Isaiah as prophesying events in the immediate future, but also Christ's three advents in flesh, spirit, and judgment. Thus the same prophetic words are directed at the prophet's own time, Christ's incarnation in the first century, his advent in the spirit in the fourteenth century (presumably), and his advent at the time of the final judgment. Oddly enough, the only one of these four predictions that is not explicitly described as literal by Olivi is

8. Krey, *Nicholas of Lyra's Apocalypse Commentary*, 23.

the first one, and even in that case he occasionally includes it as part of the literal meaning, giving him a quadruple literal sense.

One more comment is in order. Nicholas's quarrel with the sequential historical interpretation of Revelation as practiced by Alexander and Pierre is in one way oddly like Pierre's problem with the recapitulative interpretation. Pierre feels that the recapitulative approach, by constantly rehearsing history, leaves us with excessive concentration on a few things at the expense of all the other elements in church history that should be mentioned. Nicholas recognizes that the sequential interpretation leaves him with more room to work in a variety of people and events, but he feels that Pierre and particularly Alexander have limited its scope by treating it as if it covers all of history. If history is in its final days, then that makes sense; but Nicholas prefers to keep the interpretive door open by assuming that what lies beyond Revelation 17:1 has not yet occurred.

READINGS

The following readings are from Nicholas of Lyra's Apocalypse Commentary, *ed. and trans.* Philip D. Krey, *TEAMS Commentary Series (Kalamazoo: Western Michigan University, 1997). I am grateful to Philip Krey for his kindness in allowing me to use his translation.*

Revelation 11:1-12 and the Double Literal Sense

Then I was given a measuring rod like a staff. After the consolation of the Church he addresses the fruit of devotion, and, second, John returns to the burden of a certain tribulation for the church at the place, **And they will trample over the holy city** (11:2). Concerning the first, one must know that Pope Felix, who presided over the Roman Church at the time, instituted a feast of dedication of the church to be celebrated every year. For that dedication the bishop encircles the church and conducts himself as if he were measuring the eternal walls, and on the floor of the church from corner to corner he writes crosswise the Greek alphabet; thus, in a certain way, the interior is measured. According to this, John prophesies speaking in an image of the Church. **Then I was given a measuring rod.** To dedicate the temple he carries an aspersory in his hand. **Come and measure the temple.** This is the word of Pope Felix to every bishop to dedicate the church.

But do not measure the court outside the temple. This establishes that the mass is only to be celebrated in a consecrated place. **For it is given over to the nations.** Who offer their sacrifices not only in consecrated places but also in profane ones. **And they will trample.** Here Saint John returns to describing a certain tribulation of the church incited by Anthimus, patriarch of Constantinople, who, because he had been corrupted by the Eutychian heresy, was deposed by Pope Agapetus. In his place the monk and servant of God, Menas was instituted. Nevertheless Empress Theodora, infected by the same heresy, sought to restore Anthimus through Pope Sylvester, as is clear in *The Legend of Saint Sylvester*. Angered by his refusal to do this, Theodora and her husband Justinian began to persecute the ministers of the Church; thus Sylvester was deposed and sent into exile by Belisarius, the patrician, and Menas, the servant of God, was tormented in prison. And this is what John says **over the holy city,** that is, the church, which is called the holy city, for it is the unity of the citizens gathered by the Holy Spirit. **They will trample,** that is, Anthemus, Justinian, Theodora and Belisarius, by grievously oppressing the ministers of the church **for forty-two months.** For such a period or thereabouts this persecution is said to have lasted, namely for three and a half years.

3. **And I will grant my two witnesses.** Supply perseverance and wisdom. These were Sylverius and Menas, the servants of God, who stood steadfastly against the followers of the Eutychian heresy by preaching the truth. Therefore it is added **Authority to prophesy for one thousand two hundred sixty days.** These days equal the same as before, namely three and a half years or thereabouts. **Wearing sackcloth,** that is, with common vestments, because Pope Sylvester was stripped of his papal garb and was dressed in monastic garb.

4. **These are the two olive trees** because of the richness of their devotion **and the two lampstands** because of the ardor of their love **that stand before the Lord of the earth** by the steadfastness of the truth.

5. **And if anyone wants to harm them** as was done by the noted persecutors of the church. **Fire pours from their mouth** The words proceeding from the fervor of faith. **And consumes their foes** By conferring on them the sentence of execution; therefore, it is added: **Anyone who wants to harm them** With the material sword. **Must be killed in this manner** By the spiritual sword.

6. **They have authority to shut the sky** With the keys of the church. **So that no rain may fall during the days of their prophesying** For the benefits

of the church are not offered to those justly excommunicated. **And they have authority over the waters** That is, the doctrines of the heretics, concerning whom it is said in Prov. 9:17, "Stolen water is sweet." **To turn them into blood** By demonstrating their error. **And to strike the earth** The heretics fixed on earthly things, when Augustine says, "If you love the earth, you are earth." **With every kind of plague** To burden with the spiritual sentence of excommunication.

7. **When they have finished their testimony** By constantly defending the truth. **The beast that comes up from the bottomless pit** That is, Belisarius, the patrician—to the extent that he was a cruel man, he is called a lion or a rabid dog. **Will make war on them** In the manner said before. **And kill them** By civil death by sending them into exile.

8. **And their dead bodies will lie** They were considered common, just as a cadaver lying on the ground. **In the street of the great city** That is, among the congregation of the faithful, which at that point was very large. **Which is spiritually called Sodom** On account of the baseness of the vices. **An Egypt** As a result of the obscurity of their errors. **Where also their Lord** Namely, Christ. **Was crucified** Because he was preaching against the vices of the scribes and pharisees they conceived invidious and hateful things against him, by which their understanding was obscured concerning Christ, which they had through the writing of the prophets, as I have said more fully concerning Mtt. 21:38, "The servants said to themselves 'This is the heir.'" Thus blinded, they proceeded to kill him.

9. **Members of the peoples and tribes and languages will gaze** Their civil death and exile to different peoples of diverse languages was noted. **For three and a half days** Here a day is understood as a year according to Ez. 4:6, "I assign you one day for each year." Their exile lasted that long, as was said before. **And refuse to let their dead bodies be placed in a tomb** That is, the leaders of the Eutychians by not letting them experience any human kindness.

10. **And the inhabitants of the earth** That is, the Eutychian heresy, which was dominant on earth. **Will gloat over them** Concerning their exile. **And exchange presents** As a sign of joy. **Because these two prophets had been a torment** By excommunications and aggravations.

11. **But after three and a half days** That is, after three and a half years. **The breath of life from God entered them** Because they were restored to their former state and were thus revivified from civil death. Sylverius assumed the papal seat again in the year 536. **And those who saw them were terrified** That is, the Eutychians.

12. Then they heard a great voice from heaven That is, from the church militant restoring them to their former honor. Nevertheless, Saint Sylverius after being returned to exile died there, and thus went to heaven with the martyr's crown; the same should be said concerning Menas, the servant of God; thus it is possible to expound this passage otherwise. **And I heard a great voice** Namely, the voice of God calling them to glory.

While their enemies watched them Through their miracles witnessing to his glory. It is written in the *Legend of Saint Sylverius* that, after his death in the place of exile, many came who were ill and were healed.

However, the passage interpreted above is commonly interpreted to refer to Enoch and Elijah, who are said to be the future witnesses of Christ preaching against the wickedness of Antichrist for three and a half years. **Wearing sackcloth** That is, in worthless clothing, they are called **two olive trees** because of their exuberant devotion, and **the two lampstands** by the ardor of their love. **Standing** In the sight of God by their constancy against the wickedness of Antichrist. For here it is said that **Fire pours from their mouth.** That is, the word of fervent preaching by which the malice of Antichrist and of his own is disclosed, and the word of devoted prayer by which Antichrist and a great part of his army will be deservedly thunderstruck, just as it was more fully said in 2 Thess. 2. Thus they perform true wonders over against the lying signs of Antichrist, by which Antichrist and his followers will be struck down. Therefore it is added, **They have authority.**

Finally, Antichrist, who is here called the beast because of his cruelty, **Rising from the bottomless pit** Because of the power of his own demon. **Will kill them, and their dead bodies will lie in the street** To terrorize the Christians. **Of the great city** That is of the congregation adhering to Antichrist, which will be especially great. **Called Sodom and Egypt** That is, vile and shadowy. **Members of the peoples and tribes and languages and nations will gaze** Because from all the nations many will follow Antichrist. **For three and a half days** Namely, natural days and a part of a fourth. **And the inhabitants of the earth will gloat** That is the followers of Antichrist. **But after three and a half days, the breath of life . . .** Because they will be resuscitated and transferred to heaven as a testimony to the truth of their preaching.

This exposition harmonizes with the text more than the preceding one. Both, nevertheless, are able to be called literal. It should be known that a figure of another thing is necessarily something in itself, because what is nothing cannot figure or signify something. Therefore a figure can be taken in three ways. In one way only as the figure in and of itself. In another way only as the figure of another. In the third way as the thing in itself and the figure of another. This threefold manner is frequently found in the Holy Scripture by the gift of the Word.

Concerning Solomon it is frequently said in 1 Kings 11:4, "His wives turned away his heart after other gods." This is said only with reference to himself and in no way as the figure of Christ that he was, and thus the literal sense refers only to Solomon. This is what is said concerning him in Ps. 72:1: "Blessed be his name forever, enduring as long as the sun." This is not to be understood as referring to Solomon in and of himself, but only as he was a figure of Christ; on that account the literal sense refers only to Christ, just as in the same place it was proclaimed more fully. That, moreover, which the Lord said concerning him in 2 Sam. 7:14, "I will be a father to him, and he will be a son to me," is understood to refer to Solomon himself and to affirm that he was a figure of Christ, because he was the son of God through the grace of adoption, especially in the beginning of his reign, as is clear in 2 Samuel. He was a figure of Christ, who is a son of God by nature, which sonship is more perfect than the other.

Thus there is a double literal sense, one referring to Solomon by reason of his adoptive sonship, the other referring to Christ by reason of his natural sonship figured through this. In this second way the apostle intends the noted passage in Heb. 1:5 to prove the divinity of Christ, which proof is not effectively done through scripture unless it is understood in the literal sense, as Augustine says against Vincent the Donatist.

Thus the double literal sense is in the case in question. One was fulfilled in Pope Sylverius and Menas, servants of God, who were figures of Enoch and Elijah; the other will be fulfilled in Enoch and Elijah, with whom the letter agrees more, as was seen, and will be fulfilled more perfectly in them; therefore the sense principally intended refers to them.

Nicholas on the Final Chapters

At the beginning of chapter 17 Nicholas warns us that something new is about to happen.

17:1: **Then one of the seven ...** According to those who say that the whole text from here to that place **When the thousand years are ended** [i.e., 20:7] has been fulfilled in the past, the seventh plague is now described more specifically. First I will present their whole interpretation; afterwards I will say what seems true to me concerning this.

Nicholas now works systematically through what "they" say about everything from here to 20:7. He occasionally suggests an alternate reading, but only occasionally. On the whole he simply presents what "they" think. Then he tells us he believes none of it.

Therefore it is clear how it is possible to explain the text from chapter seventeen to this place as already completed. Nevertheless, this exposition seems incorrect in many things and forced; first, because it was said in chapter seventeen that the beast with seven horns is to be understood as the king of Egypt and the woman of fornication as the king of Turkey, and afterwards it was said that one of the seven heads, namely, the sixth, was the king of Turkey. This contradicts what preceded, especially since the king of Egypt and the king of Turkey were enemies with one another, as it was said in that chapter and earlier.

Similarly, in chapter eighteen, where the punishment of the Saracen sect is treated under the name "Babylon," many things are discussed such as that its total destruction would seem to be understood when it says, **Fallen, fallen is Babylon the great! It has become a dwelling place of demons** [18:2]. Similarly, on account of this it is added afterwards, **Therefore its plagues will come in single day—pestilence and mourning and famine—and she will be burned with fire** [18:8]. Similarly, on account of what happens in the same chapter: **With such great violence Babylon the great city shall be thrown down, and will be found no more** [18:21]. On account of which its total destruction seems to be understood in the previous exposition.

Nevertheless, the Saracens remained in the kingdoms of Egypt and Turkey, which at that time were not acquired by the Christians, nor afterwards, but only one part of Syria and Judaea. The Christians lost these places for the most part at the time of Saladin, although after seventy years they were occupied by the Christians; afterwards those which remained Christian, namely Acre, Tripoli and certain others, were partly destroyed by the Saracens and partly held.

Similarly, afterwards parts of the nineteenth chapter are interpreted with regard to king Baldwin. **On his head are many diadems** [19:12] On account of the regal cities he acquired. But this seems improbable because his kingdom never grew but remained rather small. Similarly, because it is added there, **He has a name inscribed that no one knows but himself.** Because the name of this king and his condition were known by others. Furthermore, the concealment of such a name seems appropriate only for a divine person. "No one knows the Son except the Father, and no one knows the Father except the Son" [Matt. 11:27].

Therefore this text seems to refer not to King Baldwin but to Christ. Thus it is added there, **And his Name is called the Word of God** [19:13]. This name is only appropriate for the Son of God, as is clear in John [1:14], "and the Word became flesh."

Similarly, because afterward it is added, **On his robe and on his thigh he has the name inscribed, "King of Kings and Lord of Lords"** [19:16]. This is explained according to the literal sense of Christ, by the saints and catholic doctors.

Similarly, that which is inserted in the same place, **And the armies of heaven . . . were following him** [19:14], is interpreted by reference to the Templars and Hospitalers, but this does not seem well said. The notable victory which is described there was in the fifth year of Baldwin's reign, as was said above. He began to rule in the year 1100. The order of the Templars, moreover, was approved in the year 1128, and through the example of the Templars the Hospitalers began to take up arms, although they had been instituted before them, as Jacques de Vitry says in chapter sixty-five. Thus it does not appear that they were in the army of King Baldwin, who only ruled for twenty-eight years, as that same bishop says in chapter ninety-three.

Moreover, according to this exposition, everything written in these three chapters of this book has been completed for two hundred years or more, as is clear from the above, and the text immediately following is interpreted by all as referring to the Antichrist. But that John wrote nothing about the state of the church with so much history left (since as yet the coming of Antichrist does not seem to be near) does not seem fitting, especially since it is commonly said by the doctors that in this book John writes the notable events that occur in the church to the end of the world.

On account of these and other things that could be said against this exposition, it seems (I submit myself to better judgment) that the whole text from the beginning of chapter seventeen to this place is not yet fulfilled. And because I am not a prophet, or the son of a prophet [Amos 7:14], I will not say anything about the future except what can be taken from scripture or the words of the saints and established teachers. Therefore I leave the interpretation of this text to the wise. If the Lord were to grant me its understanding, I would be glad to share it with others.

When the thousand years are ended [20:7] Here the persecution of Antichrist is described concerning which scripture and the saints speak in many places, as it is said: **When the thousand years are ended,** That is, the time of the church to the time of Antichrist.[9] **Satan will be released** Whose power was restrained by Christ's preaching, and his passion, and by the apostles' teaching, and by that of the saintly preachers, which will be slackened at the time of Antichrist. Therefore it is added:

8. **And he will deceive the nations at the four corners of the earth** [20:8] Having been seduced by Antichrist's preachers, some from all parts of the earth will adhere to him and the devil will cooperate with "lying wonders" [2 Thess. 2:9], just as the gospel was proclaimed through the apostles, "while the Lord worked with them and confirmed the message by the signs that accompanied it" [Mk. 16:20] **Gog and Magog** By Gog, which means "roof," is understood Antichrist, who will be the dwelling place of the devil. By Magog, which means "from the roof," those who follow Antichrist are understood, as has been said more fully in Ez. 39. **In order to gather them for battle** Against the body of the faithful.

9. **They marched over the breadth of the earth** [20:9] To force everyone to obey Antichrist. Nevertheless, here the future is spoken of in the past tense because of the certitude of the prophecy, which is frequently done in prophecies. **And surrounded the camp of the saints** That is, Jerusalem, which will be inhabited at that time by Christians, as was said in Ez. 39. **And fire came down from heaven** Because Antichrist will be struck by the Archangel Michael, directed by Christ, and a great part of his army will perish with him, as was said in 2 Thess. 2.

> *Lyra's exposition of the following verses, Revelation 20:10–15, can be skipped over, although it is worth noting that in the process he rejects the notion that the Tartars are the force besieging Jerusalem, because the Tartars did not blockade Jerusalem at any time when it was inhabited by Christians, nor, a fortiori, did fire come down and destroy their army. Moreover, Antichrist dies at 20:9, his remaining forces are destroyed as they besiege Jerusalem (20:10), and the final judgment commences (20:11). There is no room for any final period in between, no space for one final opportunity to repent.*
>
> *Revelation 21:1–8 will also be omitted. We will concentrate instead on what Nicholas has to say about his fellow mendicants from 21:9 on. Nicholas will obliquely address the matter again through his reference to 22:11.*

9. Note that Nicholas does not agonize over dates here. Presumably he sees the figure as symbolic, not a literal thousand years.

9. Then one of the seven angels . . . came and said to me Here the status of the church after the judgment is described more specifically. One should know, however, that some explain this concerning the time before the judgment, and also before the coming of Antichrist, which they strive to show on account of what is included in the following chapter: **Let the evildoer still do evil and the filthy still be filthy, and the righteous still do right** [22:11]. After the judgment there will be no time nor place for merits or demerits. They say, therefore, that this angel introduced here is understood to be Pope Innocent III, who approved the orders of the Friars Minor and Preachers, who are called here the new city, Jerusalem, according to Prov. 18:19: "A brother helped by a brother is like a strong city."

Both orders were instituted for the same work, namely, preaching the Gospel. Therefore they say that Francis and Dominic, the founders of these orders, are the foundation of this city. Moreover, there are twelve foundations, it is said [21:14], because they are imitators of the twelve apostles; the wall is the regular observance through the precepts and rules; the gates are entering from the four parts of the earth, because some are entering these orders from all parts of the earth; the angels standing at the gates are the ministers and provincial priors, who by themselves or through others receive those coming to the order. Thus, as they are able, they adapt other words here to their proposition.

Although this exposition is able to be preserved in some mystical sense, it is not possible in the literal sense as I believe. First, because it is said that the angel who is introduced here teaches John saying "Come, I will show you" (21:9). One cannot say that of Pope Innocent, since he lived more than one thousand years after John. Similarly, because it is said about this city, "I saw no temple in the city" (21:22). These orders, however, have churches. Similarly, because it is added, "And the city has no need of sun or moon" (21:23), and afterwards, "But nothing unclean will enter it, nor anyone who practices abomination or falsehood" (21:27). . . . These orders, however, need the illumination of the sun and moon, neither are all who enter unstained, nor do all who are good when they enter persevere in the good, but many become apostate and the worst of persons. As Augustine says, "Just as I have not found any better than those who live their professions well in monasteries, so also I have found none worse than those who have fallen into sin in monasteries."

On account of these things and many others which can be raised against this interpretation, insofar as they speak of the literal sense, it seems to me that the city described here is the heavenly Jerusalem.

Having clarified that chapter 21 is really about heaven, Nicholas fits it into the entire historical (and biblical) pattern.

21:9. **Come, I will show you the bride** That is, the heavenly Jerusalem, as was said in the first chapter, which is called the wife of the Lamb in a special manner because it is joined to him inseparably and eternally. Thus it is not the church militant that will cease to exist at the end of the world but the imperfect at the coming of the perfect and the figure at the arrival of the thing figured. Just as the Old Law was imperfect and was a figure of the New Law, so the church militant is a figure of the church triumphant, whose status will be perfect in every way in the general resurrection. The elect will be separated from the reprobate, and they will be perfectly blessed in body and soul. They will rise in glorious bodies because the glory of the soul will return to the body.

10. **And in the spirit** This he says to show that he does not see the glory of the elect at that time, as it will be in itself; he sees a representation of it, namely, in the city which is described below, which he saw by an imaginary vision whose significance he understood, otherwise it would not be a prophetic vision, as was presented in the first book of the Psalms and the first book of Daniel.

Final Thoughts

We have now started the book and ended it, always conscious that history itself did not begin with John of Patmos and end with Nicholas of Lyra. The decision to choose a beginning and an end is ours, based on criteria imposed by us or by our editors. While conscious that any such decision is to some extent arbitrary, we can also hope that it is based on criteria convincing to someone besides ourselves.

Beginnings and Endings

In John's case, one could object that apocalyptic literature (and its more respectable cousin, prophetic literature) was around long before the book of Revelation, and much of it is important in explaining John's text. A serious effort to lay a foundation for any decent understanding of Revelation would require examination not only of the Old Testament but of intertestamental Judaism as well as a series of other prophetic texts popular in the Greco-Roman world. But that would be another story, demanding another book. (As I hope I've indicated, that book is largely extant in the form of Richard Bauckham's *Climax of Prophecy*, a breathtaking piece of scholarship.)

On the other end of the story, we have the question of why Nicholas of Lyra should be chosen for our grand finale. Here again one could object that the last two chapters are misleading inasmuch as they leave the reader with an impression that when Pierre Auriol and Nicholas of Lyra abandoned the recapitulative approach and turned back to reading the Apocalypse as a continuous historical narrative, everyone else did as well. Certainly Auriol and Lyra did, but others continued to find the recapitulative approach more comfortable. Auriol and Lyra are important, not because everyone followed their example, but because in them we see two prestigious scholars returning to what in the thirteenth century had been very much a minority opinion, and that raises the question of why they did so.

We will turn to that question in a moment, but first we should point to another feature of Revelation commentaries that remained notable throughout the period covered in this book: they were very historically oriented. That is, they sought the meaning of the Apocalypse and with it the meaning of history in a story with a discernible shape. That was what the Apocalypse was *about*. Richard of Saint Victor, a contemplative who seems to feel the world would be better off without change and who sometimes views John's Patmos exile with something resembling envy, nonetheless feels required to present the Christian story as a series of events. For Joachim, the meaning of Christianity is discovered in a complex historical pattern. The Franciscans, to whom we have dedicated entire chapters, use the space we allotted them to provide their own theologies of history. Here at least Auriol and Lyra are very much like their predecessors.

We can now return to the question asked earlier: Why did Auriol and Lyra abandon the recapitulative approach? The answer to that question might strike the reader as disappointing—in essence, it is that we don't know the answer—but it is worth asking anyway. And if one attempts an answer, two possibilities seem inviting. First, we might suggest that the way of reading Revelation chosen by Auriol and Lyra might have seemed safer to them, less apocalyptically charged. Seen from this angle, the rejection of the recapitulative view would be closely related to the condemnation of Olivi's Apocalypse commentary. After all, the same pope who presided over the condemnation of Olivi's Revelation commentary intervened to advance Auriol's career.

That might be the case, but if it is, we might ask whether scholars were throwing the baby out with the bathwater. By that point they had been pursuing a recapitulative approach for well over a century without any perceived ill effects. It had worked well enough for a succession of Parisian scholars going all the way back to Richard of Saint Victor, whose approach was at least partly recapitulative. The commentary assigned to Bonventure by Alain Boureau depends heavily on recapitulation.

In other words, the problem with Olivi's commentary was hardly an inevitable result of the recapitulative technique. The problem was, rather, what sort of history Olivi thought was being recapitulated. It was his interpretation of history, not the form in which he interpreted it. Auriol and Lyra were intelligent enough to recognize this much. And if that is the case, then perhaps we should ask ourselves whether they chose a sequential reading of the Apocalypse for precisely the reasons given by them. They decided that John's revelation was essentially a prophecy of Christian history, all of it. For Auriol, that meant the Holy Spirit wouldn't have seen much point in repeating some things over and over at the cost of leaving other things out. For Lyra, that much was true, but there was also a second issue. The latter part of the Apocalypse should leave room for the rest of history beyond the present. There must be things prophesied in that part that are yet to occur.

Lyra offers a convenient stopping point for us because his name is intimately associated with medieval biblical scholarship, so much so that his *Postillae* were the first Bible commentary printed. They and the *Glossa ordinaria* were often combined into a single edition, offering those institutions with limited libraries a handy reference work for Bible readers. He was, in short, an important figure who carried biblical scholarship through to the end of the Middle Ages. Anyone who needs proof of Lyra's stature as a medieval Bible scholar and his lasting influence as such need only read Luther's thoughts on him.[1]

Even as Luther was praising Lyra, of course, a whole new sort of biblical scholarship was being developed, a scholarship identified with the Renaissance. Lyra is not entirely extraneous to that story either, since he was also important for his use of Hebrew, especially Rashi; but, as we observed earlier, that part of his contribution is of less importance in his commentary on Revelation. More significant in this case is his development of the double literal sense; but, again as noted earlier, here one would have to ask whether Olivi had already gone down an analogous path. Not only am I inclined to think he had done so; I would suggest that much of his apocalyptic exegesis depended on it.

What, then, was so great about Lyra's Revelation commentary? The answer is partly that when Alexander, Pierre, and Nicholas decided to abandon the recapitulative approach and treat Revelation as a continuous reading of Christian history, the Apocalypse became somewhat analogous to a *roman à clef*. We could call it an *histoire à clef*, in which the narrative of Revelation traces history in coded form. Alexander, Pierre, and Nicholas seem to have

---

1. In fact, one might also note Luther's methodology when it comes reading the Apocalypse, although Luther's interpretation differs from Lyra's, which is hardly surprising.

seen it in much that way. The basic question was always, "To what event does this sentence actually refer? What historical figure is represented by that angel?" If that was the game being played, then the exegete who came to the table armed with the fullest and most accurate historical understanding had a remarkable advantage. That historian was Nicholas. It was he who could match the biblical narrative with such a knowledge of Christian history.

That is, of course, only half the explanation. For the other half we must listen seriously to Nicholas's tone. Call it "realistic" or call it "hard-nosed" with Philip Krey; whatever you call it, it goes well with the century and with Nicholas's administrative functions within that century

Thoughts on Olivi

If we recognize that Lyra emerged in the fourteenth century as the premier voice of biblical scholarship, we might at least note in passing that during the same period another voice was posthumously silenced. Olivi's scholarship was of a different sort. Whereas Auriol and Lyra covered the entire Bible, Olivi dug deeply into individual books. More important, Olivi was a radically different sort of scholar when it came to apocalyptic speculation. Auriol and Lyra were by definition apocalyptic, since they were commenting on the book of Revelation. Olivi, however, was apocalyptic to the bone. His exegetical methodology was Joachite, not simply because he repeated Joachim (although he often did) but because he sensed how Joachim read the Bible, what he was seeking there; and Olivi was seeking much the same thing. The result in Olivi's case was a radically historical reading based on patterns like Christ's three advents, which enabled him to read a passage such as Matthew 24 not only as a reference to the destruction of Jerusalem in the first century but also as a prediction of the destruction of the carnal church in the relatively near future at the time of Christ's second advent, then the tribulation at the time of Gog in the distant future on the way to Christ's third advent. It also allowed him to see that the great Antichrist in the nearer future would be preceded by a mystical Antichrist. It was all there in the Bible. He might not be able to unpack it completely, but to the extent that he could unpack it at all, he would be better prepared to deal with the tribulations to come.

This, too, was history, but of a radically different sort. In comparison with Nicholas, Olivi referred to remarkably fewer names and events between the early church and his own time, just enough, in fact, to lay out an outline. Constantine, Charlemagne, and Francis served as place-markers, but Olivi's

forte was hardly providing a full, factual narrative. Instead, he hurried between the centuries, knitting them together into a pattern that was as diverse
yet coherent as his threefold advent of Christ. The result was, in effect, a
speculative map of the future.

It is important to realize that, however we might regard such considerations as the threefold advent today—however odd they might seem to us
and however appealing Lyra's terse, ironic refusal to indulge in them near
the end of his Revelation commentary might be to us, however sensible, in
fact, his insistence on reading events in terms that would be acceptable on
the *PBS News Hour*—the fact remains that a great deal of what went before as
examined in this book had more to do with what Olivi was attempting than
with Lyra's aspirations. The thirteenth century was a profoundly apocalyptic
age. We see as much, not only in Olivi, but in the way the pseudo-Joachite
commentary on Jeremiah echoed through Alexander Minorita's Apocalypse
commentary, Petrus Iohannis Olivi, and even Vital du Four. We see it in the
way Joachim was given sanctuary in Bonaventure's *Collationes*, not to mention Salimbene's chronicle, and in a great deal else we have left unexamined
here. Much of what was said in the way of apocalyptic thought might strike
us as opportunistic and insincere—much of the apocalyptic element in attacks on Frederick II might strike us as such, for example—but then again
much of it does not.

Nor did the educated of the world collectively and definitively lose
interest in apocalyptic speculation once people like Nicholas of Lyra talked
sense to them. In 1977 at Oxford, I found myself sharing Joachim's works
with a professor of modern history who had begun to see Joachim as a key
to modern intellectual history.

Olivi's commentary is important because it represented more than just
another reading of the apocalyptic timetable. It attempted to cast light on the
future of the Franciscan order and, in an odd way, on the future of the institutional church. At a time when the institutional church and its hierarchy
had been tightening its control over western Christendom, Olivi's commentary seriously raised the question of how far one could go in trusting that
hierarchy and what might be done if one stopped doing so. When aimed at
a lower level in the life of the church, it raised the same question concerning
the Franciscan order. The Olivian understanding of Franciscan poverty was
closely tied to his apocalyptic expectations and was contested within the
order throughout the last two decades of the thirteenth century. Remember
that, by the time he died in 1298, Olivi had begun to write not only for his
fellow Franciscans but also for the laity, and after his death a thriving Olivi

cult sprang up at his tomb in Narbonne. Among the vernacular writings he left behind was material that advised caution about apocalyptical prognostication, but someone among Olivi's followers translated a good deal of Olivi's Revelation commentary, evidence that the Olivi legacy was shared by both his Franciscan disciples and his faithful lay admirers. In fact, it was evidence that the disciples and lay admirers had made significant contact with one another, and it was precisely their close contact that produced an explosion in Languedoc.

The result was a small group of Franciscans in southern France who stood for a higher level of observance and were supported by a contingent among the laity. This situation was hardly unique in the order. In Italy there were also groups of Franciscan zealots who found themselves at odds with their fellow Franciscans yet at one with zealous laity. This should hardly be news to anyone. I have described the whole thing in *The Spiritual Franciscans*. What matters here is that, when the dynamics of this situation led to Olivi's condemnation by his order in 1318–1319 and then by Pope John XXII in 1326, the condemnation took the form of an attack on his Apocalypse commentary. Much more was entailed in the pope's judgment concerning the order, as the order itself would discover when John XXII moved from condemning Olivi and several other forms of dissent to a revision of the Franciscan self-understanding; but, as a result of the way events unfolded, the Olivian apocalyptic reading of history was placed dead center in the papal condemnation.

Something like this had occurred earlier when Gerard of Borgo San Donnino was imprisoned; yet that case was in some ways strikingly different. One has to remember that in condemning Gerard of Borgo San Donnino in 1254 the church was attacking a view that Joachim of Fiore had never actually held. Gerard saw Joachim and his eternal gospel as replacing the church, but Joachim did not. There were those who wanted to blame the whole thing on Joachim, but at the time the pope had been unwilling to participate. Gerard's view was, by the standards of the time, so obviously heretical that it practically condemned itself; but Joachim's subtler, more splendid thought was apparently deemed acceptable by the pope.

What Alexander IV saw, John XXII seems to have missed in Olivi as well as in Joachim. In the first opinion offered concerning Olivi's Apocalypse commentary, Gregory, as we have seen in chapter 12, began with an attack on Olivi's description of the sixth state of church history as "notably preeminent over the first five ones, . . . as if it were the end of previous ones, and, in the same way, the beginning of a new age emptying out the old, just as the state of Christ emptied out the Old Testament and the oldness of humankind." Gregory notes that this view "seems to involve two errors of the so-called eternal gospel for which Gerard was condemned."

What follows depends on innuendo. Gregory tends to indulge in argumentative overkill and, in the process, links Olivi's position with some odd notions. John is willing to join him at least occasionally. They find themselves arguing against theses Olivi would never have dreamed of defending, like the idea that there can be no salvation for those who possess riches individually or in common. (Gregory and John not only attribute this idea to the Waldensians but imply that it follows naturally from Olivi's argument.)

Nevertheless, the basic problem here is worth considering. Olivi had described the sixth state of church history as the end of the previous five, and by "end" he meant the goal of the first five periods, the state they were directed toward achieving. That made sense from Olivi's perspective. God is carrying out a purpose in history. The second age, the age of the Son, leads to the third age of the Holy Spirit. Christ's first advent in the flesh prepares the way for his second advent in the spirit. There is a noticeably progressive element in Olivi's view of history.

This is precisely the problem from Gregory's perspective. He feels that to speak of the sixth period as the fulfillment or goal of the first five is to see it as superior to the state of the apostles, and according to Gregory such a view "is erroneous and temerarious, or at least appears presumptuous." Later Gregory applies the lesson directly to the Franciscan rule: "Clearly it is erroneous to posit the way of living of that rule, however you understand it, to be the end of the five preceding ways of living, because the end is better." John XXII, who, we recall, is reading this part of Gregory's critique, cheers him on from the margin.

In a conceptual world that chooses to see the primitive church as its model, any progressive view of history has its difficulties. Bonaventure recognizes as much in the *Collationes* and tries to arrange his argument accordingly. Olivi also sees as much and does his best to create a safe space for the primitive church that will allow its virtue to remain unsurpassable. Whether he succeeds or not is another matter. As much as he wants to give the apostles some degree of superiority, his own enthusiasm about the future often seems to betray him.

Oddly enough, Olivi's strong suit in this debate with himself is, paradoxically, his remarkable tendency to see human virtue as prone to periodical slippage. He is more than willing to grant that, after remarkable progress from Constantine to Charlemagne, the church will descend into such disarray that the just will be reduced to hiding out not only among the Christian laity but among pagans, Muslims, and Jews. Moreover, he sees another great collapse happening again at the end of the third age, this time precipitating Christ's third advent for the final judgment. Conversely, in the middle of the most abysmal times he sees individuals or small groups rising to remarkable spiritual achievement. Witness that future courageous few who, hounded by the carnal church, will go to ground among non-Christians and succeed in converting them, then the rest of the world after them. The story as Olivi tells it is ultimately one of God working through charismatic individuals and groups. It is not primarily about how God shapes an institution to function as God's unquestionable spokesperson.

Is there cognitive dissonance in the Olivian mind? Certainly! But in such dissonance he finds an odd strength. In it he finds depth, which gives him the ability to live with uncertainty and ambiguity. In it he discovers the courage to face a future in which the institutional church will find itself under the control of Antichrist, then find itself devastated by non-Christians; yet the faith will survive. Olivi had never heard of Paul Tillich, let alone read the final pages of Tillich's *Courage to Be*; yet there are moments when he comes very close to echoing the Tillichian message. On this matter we could do no better than to consult young Olivi's paradoxical reading of the seven seals in his *Principium de causis* or his thoughts on Pseudo-Dionysius in the *Principium de doctrina Scripturae*, both mentioned in the chapter on Olivi's early work.

All of which is to say that, whatever book of the Bible Olivi is expositing, his exegesis becomes a voyage of discovery. It is impossible to miss the way he radiates the excitement produced by that discovery. It is equally impossible to miss the fact that what he does with the text is often wildly creative.

Gregory's critique, on the other hand, is in the service of a highly organized church used to imagining that it has assumed the institutional form God wishes it to enjoy. Olivi assumes instead that institutions are part of God's plan for us as God guides us through history, but they are still only as reliable as those who lead them, and he knows the moment could come when the more righteous among us might need to take cover. Thus for many of us, and perhaps for most of us in the early twenty-first century, Olivi ought to be fascinating not only because he is a brilliant, exciting exegete but because he displays an oddly contemporary sensibility in his attitude toward authority.

A Tale of Two Scholars

Olivi was condemned and his body disinterred, then quietly disposed of. The conflict within the Franciscan order was decided in favor of the Franciscan leadership, then decided again by reinterpreting the nature of Franciscan poverty to fit the new reality within the order, recasting it in a form Francis would not have recognized. In the form of life that emerged, Olivi's witness could continue only as a protest movement.

Nicholas of Lyra, on the other hand, prospered both as an administrator and as a realistic guide to what might be expected of leaders. And in the meantime, he prospered as a biblical scholar, not the same kind of scholar as Olivi, but perhaps, like Olivi, the most important Bible scholar of his time. The story might be said to have two heroes. We can choose.

Bibliography

Primary Texts

Alexander the Minorite. *Expositio in apocalypsim.* Monumenta Historiae Germanica, Quellen, 1. Weimar: Hermann Böhlaus Nachfolger, 1955.

Augustine of Hippo. *De civitate dei contra paganos.* Corpus Christianorum Series Latina, 48. Turnhout: Brepols, 1955.

Bede. *Chronica.* Monumenta Germaniae Historica Auctores antiquissimi, 13. Berlin: Weidmann, 1892.

———. *Explanatio apocalypsis.* Patrologia Latina, 93:129D–206D. Edited by J.-P. Migne. Paris, 1841–1865.

Biblia latina cum glossa ordinaria. Editio Princeps. Strassburg, Adolph Rusch, 1480–1481. Facsimile reprint, with an introduction by Karlfried Froehlich and Margaret T. Gibson, 4 vols. Turnhout: Brepols, 1992.

Bonaventura da Bagnoreggio. *Collations on the Six Days.* Translated by José de Vinck. *The Works of Bonaventure,* 5. Paterson, NJ: St. Anthony Guild Press, 1970

———. *Opera omnia.* Ad Claras Aquas (Quaracchi). College of St. Bonaventure, 1882–1902.

Bullarium franciscanum romanorum pontificum. Edited by Giovanni Giacinto Sbaraglia. Rome: Typis Sacæ Congregationis de Propaganda Fide, 1759–1804.

Conrad of Offida (?). *Verba Fratris Conradied.* Edited by P. Sabatier. Opuscules de critique historique, 1. Paris, 1903.

Francis of Assisi. *Ecrits.* Latin text, edited by Kajetan Esser. Sources Chrétiennes, 285. Paris: Éditions du Cerf, 1981. English translation: *Writings.* Edited and translated by Regis Armstrong et al. 3 vols. New York: New City Press, 1999–2001.

The Glossa Ordinaria on Revelation. Translated by Sarah Van Der Pas. West Monroe, LA: Consolamini, 2015.

Haimo of Auxerre (attributed to Haimo of Halberstadt). *Expositionis in Apocalypsim B. Joannis Libri Septem*. Patrologia Latina, 117:937C–1220D. Edited by J.-P. Migne. Paris, 1841–1865.

———. *In Epistolam I ad Thessalonicenses*. Patrologia Latina, 117:765B–778B. Edited by J.-P. Migne. Paris, 1841–1865.

———. *In Epistolam II ad Thessalonicenses*. Patrologia Latina, 117:777C–781D. Edited by J.-P. Migne. Paris, 1841–1865.

Hildegard of Bingen. *Scivias*. Patrologia Latina, 197. Edited by J.-P. Migne. Paris, 1841–1865. Corpus Christianorum Continuatio Mediaevalis, 43–43A. English translation: *Scivias*. Translated by Mother Columba Hart and Jane Bishop. New York: Paulist Press, 1990.

Hugh of Saint Cher. *Biblia latina cum postillis Hugonis de Sancto Caro*. Basel: Johann Amerbach for Anton Koberger, [1498]. Revelation commentary, as digitized by Heinrich Heine University, Düsseldorf.

Isidore of Seville. *Etymologies*. Edited by W. M. Lindsay. Oxford: Oxford University Press, 1911, available in corrected form at http://penelope.uchicago.edu/Thayer/E/Roman/Texts/Isidore/home.html. Two English translations: *Isidore of Seville's Etymologies*. Translated by Priscilla Throop. Charlotte, VT: MedievalMS, 2005; and *The Etymologies of Isidore of Seville*. Translated by Stephen Barney. Cambridge: Cambridge University Press, 2010.

Jacques de Vitry. *Historia Orientalis*. Edited by Jean Donnadieu. Turnhout: Brepols, 2008.

Jerome. *Commentariorum in Danielem libri III*. Corpus Christianorum Series Latina 75A. Turnhout: Brepols, 1964.

———. *Commentariorum in Esaiam libri XVIII*. Corpus Christianorum Series Latina 73–73A. Turnhout: Brepols, 1963.

———. *Commentariorum in Matheum libri IV*. Corpus Christianorum Series Latina, 77. Turnhout: Brepols, 1969.

Joachim of Fiore. "*De vita sancti Benedicti ed de officio divino secundum eius doctrinam*." Edited by Cipriano Baraut. *Analecta sacra Tarraconensia* 24 (1951): 33–122.

———. *Expositio in Apocalypsim*. Venice, 1527; reprint Frankfurt am Main: Minerva, 1964.

———. *Il libro delle figure dell'abate Gioacchino da Fiore (Liber figurarum)*. Edited by L. Tondelli, M. Reeves, and B. Hirsch-Reich. Turin, 1954.

———. *Liber concordiae novi ac veteris testament*. Venice, 1519; reprint Frankfurt am Main: Minerva, 1964. Modern edition of books 1–4 of Abbot Joachim of Fiore, *Liber de Concordia Novi ac Veteris Testamenti*. Edited by E. R. Daniel. Philadelphia: American Philosophical Society, 1973. Book 5 still has no modern edition.

———. *Psalterium decem chordarum*. Venice, 1527; reprint Frankfurt am Main: Minerva, 1965. Modern edition edited by Kurt-Victor Selge. Monumenta

Germaniae Historica, Quellen zur Geistesgeschichte des Mittelalters, 20. Hanover: Hahnsche, 2009.

———. *Tractatus super quatuor evangelia.* Edited by Ernesto Buonaiuti. Fonti per la Storia d'Italia, 67. Rome, 1930.

Nicholas of Lyra. *Nicholas of Lyra's Apocalypse Commentary.* Edited and translated by Philip D. Krey. TEAMS Commentary Series. Kalamazoo: Western Michigan University, 1997.

———. *Postilla super totam bibliam.* Strassburg, 1492; reprint Frankfurt am Main: Minerva, 1971.

Pierre Auriol. *Compendium sensus literalis totius divinae scripturae.* Edited by Philibertus Seebeek. Quaracchi: College of St. Bonaventure, 1896.

Petrus Iohannis Olivi. *Epistola ad R.* in Olivi's *Quodlibeta,* 51v–53r. Venice, 1509.

———. *Expositio in Canticum Canticorum.* Edited by Johannes Schlageter. Editiones Collegii S. Bonaventiurae ad Claras Aquas. Rome: Grottaferrata, 1999.

———. *La Caduta di Gerusalemme. il commento al libro delle Lamentazioni di Pietro di Giovanni Olivi.* Edited by Marco Bartoli. Rome: Istituto Storico Italiano per il Medio Evo, 1991.

———. *Peter of John Olivi on Genesis.* Edited by David Flood. St. Bonventure, NY: Franciscan Institute Publications, 2007.

———. *Peter of John Olivi on the Acts of the Apostles.* Edited by David Flood. St. Bonventure, NY: Franciscan Institute Publications, 2001.

———. *Peter of John Olivi on the Bible.* Edited by David Flood. St. Bonventure, NY: Franciscan Institute Publications, 1997. (Contains *Principia quinque in sacram scripturam, Postilla in Isaiam, Postilla in I ad Corinthios, Quaestio de oboedientia,* and *Sermones duo de S. Francisco.*)

———. *Petri Iohannis Olivi super Lucam, et Lectura super Marcum.* Edited by Fortunato Iozelli. Editiones Collegii S. Bonaventurae Ad Claras Aquas. Grottaferrata, 2010.

———. *Postilla super Iob.* Edited by Alain Boureau. Turnhout: Brepols, 2015.

———. *Postilla super Matthaeum,* chapter 24. Edited by Sarah Pucciarelli based on Paris, BNF cod. lat. 15588, and corrected from other mss. Unpublished.

———. *Quaestiones de perfectione evangelica,* question 8. Edited by Johannes Schlageter. In *Das Heil der Armen und das Verderben der Reichen.* Werl/Westfalen: Dietrich Coelde-Verlag, 1989.

———. *Quaestiones de perfectione evangelica,* question 9. In Petrus Ioannis Olivi, *De Usu Paupere: The Quaestio and the Tractatus.* Edited by David Burr. Florence: Leo S. Olschki, 1992.

Pseudo-Dionysius the Areopagite. *The Complete Works.* Translated by Colm Luibheid. Mahwah, NJ: Paulist Press, 1987.

Pseudo-Jerome. *Commentariorum in Marcum.* Patrologia Latina, 30. Edited by J.-P. Migne. Paris, 1841–1865.

Pseudo-Joachim of Fiore. *Commentarius in Ieremiam.* Venice, 1525.

Ricardus de Sancto Victore. *In Apocalypsim Joannis Libri Septem.* Patrologia Latina, 196. Edited by J.-P. Migne. Paris, 1841–1865.

Salimbene da Parma. *The Chronicle of Salimbene de Adam.* Translated by Joseph L. Baird and John Robert Kane. Binghamton, NY: University Center at Binghamton, 1986.

Secondary Texts

Albaric, Michel. "Hugues de Saint-Cher et les concordances bibliques latines (XIIIe–XVIIe siècles)." In *Hugues de Saint-Cher (†1263): Bibliste et théologien*, edited by G. Dahan et al., 467–77. Turnhout: Brepols, 2004.

Anderson, C. Colt. *A Call to Piety.* Quincy, IL: Franciscan Press, 2002.

Bataillon, Louis-J. "Olivi utilisateur de la *Catena aurea de Thomas d'Aquin.*" In *Pierre de Jean Olivi (1248–1298)*, 115–20. Pensé scolastique, dissidence spirituelle et société. Paris: J. Vrin, 1999.

Bauckham, Richard. *The Climax of Prophecy.* Edinburgh: T&T Clark, 1993.

Bougerol, Jacques-Guy. "Initia latinorum sermonum laudem S. Francisci." *Antonianum* 57 (1982): 706–94.

Boureau, Alain. "Albert le Grand, commentateur de l'Apocalypse." *Freiburger Zeitschrift für Philosophie und Theologie* 61 (2014): 20–43.

———. "Bonaventure, commentateur de l'Apocalypse: Pour une nouvelle attribution de *Vox domini.*" *Franciscan Studies* 70 (2012): 139–81.

———. "L'Exégèse de Jean de Galles, Franciscain du XIIIe siècle." *Franciscan Studies* 72 (2014): 153–72.

———. "Richard de Mediavilla fut-il aussi un exégète?" *Freiburger Zeitschrift für Philosophie und Theologie* 58 (2011): no. 1, 227–71; no. 2, 404–46.

Burr, David. "The Antichrist and the Jews in Four Thirteenth-Century Apocalypse Commentaries." In *Friars and Jews in the Middle Ages and Renaissance*, 23–38. Leiden: Brill, 2004.

———. "The Date of Petrus Iohannis Olivi's Commentary on Matthew." *Collectanea Franciscana* 46 (1976): 131–38.

———. "Ecclesiastical Condemnation and Exegetical Theory: The Case of Olivi's Apocalypse Commentary." In *Neue Richtungen in der hoch- und spätmittelalterlichen Bibelexegese*, 149–62. Munich: R. Oldenbourg Verlag, 1996.

———. *Olivi and Franciscan Poverty.* Philadelphia: University of Pennsylvania Press, 1989.

———. "Olivi, Apocalyptic Expectation and Visionary Experience." *Traditio* 41 (1985): 273–88.

———. "Olivi, Christ's Three Advents, and the Double Antichrist." *Franciscan Studies* 74 (2016): 15–40.

———. "Olivi, Maifreda, Na Prous, and the Shape of Joachism, ca. 1300." *Franciscan Studies* 73 (2015): 274–94.

———. "Olivi on Prophecy." *Cristianesimo nella storia* 17 (1996): 369–78.

———. *Olivi's Peaceable Kingdom*. Philadelphia: University of Pennsylvania Press, 1993.

———. *The Persecution of Peter Olivi*. Philadelphia: American Philosophical Society, 1976.

———. *The Spiritual Franciscans*. University Park: Pennsylvania State University Press, 2001.

———. "Young Olivi as Exegete." Awaiting publication in *Percorsi di esegesi antica e medievale*.

Caird, G. B. *The Revelation of St. John the Divine*. London: A & C Black, 1984.

Collins, Adela Yarbro. *The Combat Myth in the Book of Revelation*. Missoula: Scholars, 1976.

Coolman, Boyd Taylor, and Dale M. Coulter, eds. *Trinity and Creation*. Turnhout: Brepols, 2010.

Dahan, Gilbert. *L'exégèse chrétienne de la Bible en Occident médiéval, XIIe–XIVe siècle*. Paris: Les Editions du Cerf, 2008.

———. "L'exegèse de Hugues. Méthode et herméneutique." In *Hugues de Saint-Cher (†1263): Bibliste et théologien*, 65–99. Turnhout: Brepols, 2004.

———. "L'exégèse des livres prophétiques chez Pierre de Jean Olieu." In *Pierre de Jean Olivi (1248–1298)*, 91–114. Paris: J. Vrin, 1999.

Daniel, E. R. "A Re-examination of the Origins of Franciscan Joachism." *Speculum* 43 (1968): 671–76.

Delcorno, Pietro. "Following Francis at the Time of Antichrist." *Franciscan Studies* 74 (2016): 149.

Fekkes, Jan. *Isaiah and the Prophetic Traditions in the Book of Revelation*. Sheffield: Sheffield Academic, 1994.

———. *Revelation*. Minneapolis: Fortress, 1991.

Friday, Hal. "The *Vidi Alterum Angelum* Topos in Two Sermons by Guibert of Tournai for the Feast of St. Francis." *Franciscan Studies* 70 (2012): 101–38.

Harkins, Franklin T., and Frans van Liere, eds. *Interpretation of Scripture: Theory; A Selection of Works of Hugh, Andrew, Richard and Godfrey of St Victor, and of Robert of Melun*. Turnhout: Brepols, 2012.

Howard-Brook, Wes, and Anthony Gwyther. *Unveiling Empire: Reading Revelation Then and Now*. Maryknoll: Orbis, 2005.

Klepper, Deeana Copeland. *The Insight of Unbelievers*. Philadelphia: University of Pennsylvania Press, 2007.

Koch, Joseph. "Der Prozess gegen die Postille Olivis zur Apokalypse." *Recherches de Théologie Ancienne et Mediévale* 5 (1933): 102–15.

Konrad, Robert, ed. *De ortu et tempore Antichristi*. Kalmünz, 1964.

Lerner, Robert. "Antichrists and Antichrist in Joachim of Fiore." *Speculum* 60 (1985): 553–70.

———. "Joachim of Fiore's Breakthrough to Chiliasm." *Cristianesimo nella storia* 6 (1985).

———. "Poverty, Preaching and Eschatology in the Revelation Commentaries of 'Hugh of St. Cher.'" In *The Bible in the Medieval World: Essays in Memory of Beryl Smalley*, edited by Katherine Walsh and Diana Wood, 157–89. Oxford: Basil Blackwell, 1985.

———. "Refreshment of the Saints: The Time after Antichrist as a Station for Earthly Progress in Medieval Thought." *Traditio* 32 (1976): 97–144.

———. "The Vocation of the Friars Preacher: Hugh of St. Cher between Peter the Chanter and Albert the Great." In *Hugues de Saint-Cher (†1263): Bibliste et théologien*, 215–31. Turnhout: Brepols, 2004.

Lobrichon, Guy. "Conserver, réformer, transformer le monde? Les manipulations de l'Apocalypse au Moyen Âge Central." In *The Role of the Book in Medieval Culture*, edited by Peter Ganz, vol. 2, 75–95. Turnhout: Brepols, 1986,

———. "L'Apocalypse des théologiens au XIIe siècle." Dissertation, University of Paris, 1984.

———. "Une nouveauté: Les glosses de la Bible." In *Le Moyen Age et la Bible*, edited by P. Riché and G. Lobrichon, 95–115. Bible de tous les temps, 4. Paris: Beauchesne, 1984.

Madigan, Kevin. *Olivi and the Interpretation of Matthew in the High Middle Ages.* Notre Dame: University of Notre Dame Press, 2003.

Manselli, Raoul. *La "Lectura super Apocalpsim" di Pietro di Giovanni Olivi.* Rome: Istituto Storico Italiano per il Medio Evo, 1955.

McGinn, Bernard. *Antichrist: Two Thousand Years of the Human Fascination with Evil.* New York: Columbia University Press, 2000.

———. *The Calabrian Abbot.* New York: Macmillan, 1985.

Montefusco, Antonio. "Il progetto bilingue di Olivi e la memoria dissidente." In *Pietro di Giovanni Olivi Frate Minore*, 185–209. Spoleto: Centro Italiano di Studi sull'Alto Medioevo, 2016.

Montefusco, Antonio, and Sylvain Piron. "In vulgari nostro." *Oliviana* 5 (2016). http://journals.openedition.org/oliviana/904, posted online June 5, 2017, accessed March 24, 2018.

Moynihan, Robert. "The Development of the 'Pseudo-Joachim' Commentary 'Super Ieremiam.'" *Mélanges de l'Ecole française de Rome, Moyen Age* 98 (1986): 109–42.

———. "Joachim of Fiore and the Early Franciscans: A Study of the Commentary 'Super Hieremiam,' Volume 1." Dissertation, Yale University, 1988.

Nold, Patrick. "New Annotations of Pope John XXII and the Process against Peter of John Olivi's *Lectura super Apocalipsim*." *Oliviana* 4 (2012). http://oliviana.revues.org/521, posted online March 14, 2013, accessed December 26, 2016.

Pacetti, Dionisio. "L'Expositio super Apocalypsim' di Mattia di Svezia." *Archivum Franciscanum Historicum* 54 (1961): 297–99.

Pagels, Elaine. *Revelations: Visions, Prophecy, and Politics in the Book of Revelation.* New York: Penguin, 2012.

Parisoli, Luca. *Gioacchino da Fiore e il carattere meridionale del movimento francescano in Calabria.* Collana Pensatori Italiani. Davoli Marina: Associazione Radici del Tempo, 2016.

Piron, Sylvain. "La consultation demandée à François de Meyronnes sur la *Lectura super Apocalypsim*." *Oliviana* 3 (2009). http://oliviana.revues.org/330, posted online April 3, 2009, accessed December 21, 2016.

———. "Les studia franciscains de Provence et d'Aquitaine (1275-1335)." In *Philosophy and Theology in the Studia of the Religious Orders and at the Papal and Royal Courts,* 303–58. Leiden: Brill, 2012.

———. "Literalior: L'Englobement de Spirituel dans le litéral selon Pierre de Jean Olivi." *Annali du scienze religiose* 7 (2014): 179–95.

———. "Olivi and Bonaventure: Paradoxes and Faithfulness." *Franciscan Studies* 74 (2016):1–14.

Potestà, Gian Luca. *Il tempo dell'Apocalisse: Vita di Gioacchino da Fiore.* Rome and Bari: Laterza, 2004.

Rainini, Marco. *Disegni dei tempi: Il "Liber Figurarum" e la teologia figurativa di Gioacchino da Fiore.* Centro Internationale di Studi Gioachimiti, Opere di Gioacchino da Fiore, testi e strumenti, 18. Rome: Viella, 2006.

Ratzinger, Joseph. *Das Geschichtestheologie des heiligen Bonaventura.* Munich: Schnell und Steiner, 1959. Translated by Zachary Hayes as *The Theology of History in St. Bonaventure.* Chicago: Franciscan Herald Press, 1971

Reeves, Marjorie. *The Influence of Prophecy in the Later Middle Ages.* Oxford: Clarendon, 1969.

———. *Joachim of Fiore and the Prophetic Future.* London: SPCK, 1976.

Reeves, Marjorie, and Beatrice Hirsch-Reich. *The Figurae of Joachim of Fiore.* Oxford: Clarendon, 1972.

Ruiz, Damien. "Es tu infatuatus sicut alii qui istam doctrinam secuntur?" In *Experiences religieuses et chemins de perfection dans l'occident médiéval,* 277–92. Paris: AIBL, 2012.

Sackur, Ernst. *Sibyllinische Texte und Forschungen.* Halle, 1898; reprint, Turin, 1963.

Schmolinsky, Sabine. *Der Apokalypsenkommentar des Alexander Minorita: Zur frühen Rezeption Joachims von Fiore in Deutschland.* Monumenta Germaniae Historica. Studien und Texte, 3. Hannover, 1991.

———. "Merkmale der Exegese bei Alexander Minorita." In *Neue Richtungen in der hoch- und spätmittelalterlichen Bibelexegese,* 139–48. Munich: R. Oldenbourg Verlag, 1996.

Schüssler Fiorenza, Elisabeth. *The Book of Revelation: Justice and Judgment.* Philadelphia: Fortress, 1985.

Smalley, Beryl. *The Study of the Bible in the Middle Ages.* Notre Dame: University of Notre Dame Press, 1964.

Smith, Lesley. *The Glossa Ordinaria: The Making of a Medieval Bible Commentary.* Leiden: Brill, 2009.

Stanislao da Campagnola. *L'Angelo del sesto sigillo e l'"alter Christus."* Rome: Laurentianum, 1971.

Swanson, Jenny. *John of Wales.* Cambridge: Cambridge University Press, 1989.

Troncarelli, Fabio. "Fiorenzo d'Acri e la condanna di Gioacchino." *Frate Francesco* 68 (2002): 111–36.

———. "La chiave di David." *Frate Francesco* 69 (2003): 5–56.

———, ed. *Il ricordo del future.* Bari: Mario Addia Editore, 2006.

Ubertino da Casale. *Arbor vitae.* Turin: Bottega d'Erasmo, 1961.

Verger, Jacques. "Hugues de Saint-Cher dans le contexte universitaire Parisien." In *Hugues de Saint-Cher (†1263): Bibliste et théologien*, 13–22. Turnhout: Brepols, 2004.

Wadding, Luke. *Annales minorum.* Rome: Typis Rochi Bernabò, 1731.

Wessley, Stephen. "Bonum est Benedicto mutare locum." *Revue Bénédictine* 90 (1980): 314–28.

———. *Joachim of Fiore and Monastic Reform.* New York: Peter Lang, 1990.

Witherington, Ben, III. *Revelation.* Cambridge: Cambridge University Press, 2003.

Index of Names

Parisoli, Luca, 131n3
Pepin I, 253, 358
Peter Abelard, 39
Peter Lombard, 39, 130–31, 138–39, 186,
   253
Petrus Iohannis Olivi (Peter of John
   Olivi), ix, xii–xiv, 39, 90, 156, 185–86,
   192–93, 195, 203, 205, 207–8, 212–14,
   215, 222–23, 229, 231n2, 234, 240–41,
   248, 359, 360–61, 373, 385–86, 387–91,
   392
Philippus, emperor, 152
Phocas, emperor, 365
Pierre Auriol (Petrus Aurioli), xiv,
   167–68, 368, 371, 384–86, 387
Pierre de Tarrantaise, 181
Piron, Sylvain, 214n70, 241n20, 269n25,
   322n34, 323n36
Pliny, 24–25
Potestà, Gian Luca, xiv, 85–87, 88
Pseudo-Dionysius the Areopagite, 40,
   65, 301, 391
Pseudo-Jerome, 179n43
Pseudo-Joachim, xii, 90, 135, 360, 388

Rainini, Marco, 87, 90, 131n3
Raniero da Ponza, 131
Rashi, 386
Ratzinger, Joseph, xiii, 236–38, 239–40,
   245, 246, 247–49, 250
Raymond Geoffroi, 304, 305, 306
Raymond Rigaud, 210, 211
Reeves, Marjorie, 84n19, 85n21, 87, 132,
   134n11
Remigius, 124
Richard of Saint Victor, ix, xii–xiii, 1, 90,
   130, 148, 180, 184, 192–93, 196n27, 201,
   288, 333, 336, 347, 351–52, 385
Richardus de Mediavilla, 182
Ruiz, Damien, 131n4, 133–34, 135, 137

Sackur, Ernst, 33n47
Saladin, 89, 100, 122, 158–59, 379
Salimbene da Parma, 131–32, 133–34,
   135–42, 145, 322, 388
Schüssler Fiorenza, Elisabeth, 3, 5, 6n7,
   11n11, 14, 17n16
Selge, Kurt-Victor, 79n1
Severus, emperor, 150, 361, 365–66
Smalley, Beryl, 39n1
Smith, Lesley, 186n10, 187, 368n1
Stanislao da Campagnola, 245
Swanson, Jenny, 185n9
Sylvester, Pope, 112, 150, 160, 252–53, 320,
   362, 367, 373, 375–77, 378

Tertullian, 23
Theodora, empress, 375
Thomas of Celano, 177, 206
Tillich, Paul, 22
Titus, emperor, 297, 299, 344
Trajan, emperor, 24
Troncarelli, Fabio, 131
Tullius, 219
Tychonius, 31n39

Ubertino da Casale, 137–38, 247n33, 314
Urban, Pope, 112, 165
Urban III, Pope, 130

Verger, Jacques, 181n1
Vespasian, emperor, 297, 299, 344, 346
Vincent the Donatist, 378
Vital du Four, xiii, 185n9, 208–15, 229,
   321, 388

Wadding, Luke, 133n8
Wessley, Stephen, 80n5, 133n10
William de la Mare, 259
William of Saint Amour, 246
Witherington, Ben, III, 4n4, 5n5, 5n6,
   11n12, 26

Index of Subjects

Aaron, 94, 155

Abbey of Saint Victor, Victorine school, 39–40, 131, 188; exegesis, 39–41, 87–88, 90

abomination of desolation, 28, 263, 268

Abraham, 59, 91, 93, 101, 143, 251–52, 271

abyss, 126, 161, 191; beast from, 96, 119, 121, 253

Adam, 26, 59, 97, 101, 118, 252, 338n49

advents of Christ, three, 265–68, 269–76, 277–80, 283, 289–90, 292–96, 297–300, 308, 341–42, 373–74, 387–88; first, 260–61, 262–63, 266, 270, 272, 276, 293, 296, 310, 337, 341, 347; first and second, 266, 274, 285–86, 309, 319, 347–48, 387, 390; second, spiritual, 260–62, 265–66, 270–72, 274–76, 279–80, 286–87, 308, 311, 326, 331, 341–42, 387, 390–91; third, 266, 274–76, 293, 387, 390–91

Albigensian crusade, 308

allegory, 106, 277, 279, 281

Anagni commission, 142–44, 145

anagogy, 68–69

angels, 12, 17, 44, 69, 72, 150, 241–42; fallen, 21, 72, 126, 150, 153, 365–66; four bound, 7, 150; Jesus Christ appearing as, 43, 50, 51, 52–53, 74, 76, 106, 198–99, 203–4, 206, 210–11, 246,

352–53, 361; judgment, executing, 12–13, 14, 18, 150; messengers, 15, 16–18, 100, 119; Michael, 10, 381; preachers, 51, 57, 82, 200–201; of seven churches, 5–6, 76, 120, 150; seven with trumpets, 7–8, 32, 50–54, 55–56, 82, 154; sixth, 242, 242–46, 254; sixth seal, 137, 204–7, 209–11; as symbols for humans, 143, 150–51, 167, 168–69, 171, 174–75; vials, seven, 58–59, 104, 123, 125, 154, 200–201, 242–43

Antichrist, 29, 58, 126, 141; abomination of desolation, 28, 263, 268; apostate Christian, Franciscan, 355–56; as beast, 36–37, 56, 63, 354–56, 377; birth, 141, 159, 178, 362, 367; Christ and, 101–2, 115, 265, 272, 288, 295, 317; church and, 265–66, 391; concordances, 280, 287, 289, 347–49; deception, heresy, 32, 37, 101–2, 161, 280, 287, 355, 377; dragon and, 117–19; fall of, 124–25, 126–27; Gog and, 101, 126–27, 160–61, 289, 381; great, 101, 270n26, 273–74, 280, 308, 313, 318–20, 346, 349–50, 356–57, 387; idea, legend of, 35–38, 198; Jews, 37, 200–202, 350; martyrs, 268, 284, 294, 297, 349–50; messiah, 37, 275, 307, 355; mystical, 264–67, 269–71, 273–74,

405

history, 144–45; Jerusalem, new, 170–71, 176, 177, 372–73; Joachism, 131–34, 138, 139–40, 246; Joachites, xiv, 134, 140, 232, 236, 241n20, 245–47; laity and, 323, 326, 388–89; leadership, 321–22, 392; Order of the Friars Minor (OFM), 248–49, 367, 370, 382; Paris, 231, 256–57, 359, 368; poverty, *usus pauper*, 193, 249, 258, 265, 290, 304–6, 316–18, 320–21, 322–23, 325–26, 330, 333–34, 344–45, 349, 388, 392; as preachers, 344–45; rule, standards, 230–31, 325, 329, 331–34, 343–46, 349, 358, 390; scholarship, 259–60, 288; seventh period, 320–22, 327; spirituals, 304, 312–15, 321–22, 323–26, 353–54, 372–73, 389; tribulation, 313–14, 315

Franks, 179, 253, 358

fulfillment, 26, 227–28, 240, 261; future, 369–70, 380–81

Genesis commentary, Olivi, 279, 285

Germany, Germans, 153, 364, 365, 364; kings, emperors of, 96, 178, 179, 361

Gilbertine preface, 216–22, 223, 226

Glossa ordinaria, 34, 222, 333, 336, 372, 386; citations, 198, 202, 225, 226, 334; development, 185–88, 216, 222, 259; prophets, 219–20; visions, 220–21, 228

Gnosticism, 37

God, 66–67, 225; gifts, 43–44, 72, 227; glory, 302–3; history, 89–90, 278; sons of, 53–54; tabernacle with humans, 162–63; victory over evil, 19–20; voice of, 223–24. *See also* wrath of God

Gog, 29, 97, 103, 273, 279, 285; Antichrist, 101, 126–27, 160–61, 289, 381; devil and, 102, 126–27; Ezekiel, 161, 273, 275; Magog, 103, 161, 275, 361, 381; as nations, all, 161, 361; Satan and, 286–87; time of, 13, 275–77, 319–20

gospel, preaching, 18, 52, 64, 73–75, 98, 108–9, 382

Gospels, 107–8, 139, 307, 333, 337, 343–44; Synoptic, 2–3

Goths, 110, 112

grace, 46, 67, 76, 93, 98, 227, 251

Greek empire, 96, 110, 363–64, 365; Antiochus, 97; Macedonian, 91–92, 95–96

Greek language, 2, 4, 56, 188, 374; number of the beast, 15, 56, 154

Greek philosophy, 213, 233, 241n20, 265; Aristotelian, 213, 222, 233, 241n20, 265, 278, 291, 317

Greeks, 68, 128, 361; church, 361, 363–64; conversion, 135, 318, 321

harlot, whore, Babylon, 58–60, 123, 156, 307, 316, 341, 365, 379; church as, 329–30; Rome as, 14–17, 27

heaven, 62–63, 65, 66–67, 70, 237; church as, 161, 170; Jerusalem, new, 165–66, 360, 372, 382–83; martyrs in, 6, 7, 17, 377; temple, 9, 13, 132; winds of, four, 107–9, 351–52, 365–66

heresy, heretics, 31–32, 49–52, 58, 135, 149, 153, 189, 197, 217–18, 351; Antichrist and, 32, 37, 101–2, 161, 280, 287, 355, 377; Arian, 27, 82, 109, 110–12, 116, 120, 153, 184, 277–78, 363, 365; Cathars, 82, 135, 184, 199, 316, 317; eternal gospel, 140–41, 142–43, 194, 211n60, 230, 246, 327, 389–90; Eutychian, 373, 375–76; Gnosticism, 37; Patarene, 116; Scripture, misinterpreting, 199, 200, 209, 238, 357; star, falling, 190–91; tribulation, 193, 199–200, 275; Waldensians, 184, 327, 390

hermits, 108–9, 112, 132, 327

Herod, king, 99–100, 101, 119–20, 121, 349

Hezekiah, king, 252, 254, 347

history, world. *See* world history

Holy Roman Empire, 86, 134–35; Frederick II, emperor, 131, 134–37, 138–40, 159, 167, 333, 358, 388; Henry VI, 134

Holy Spirit, 42, 47, 57, 108, 299; age of, 83–84, 144, 260–61, 265, 285, 319; freedom, 128–29; grace, 46, 67, 76, 93, 98; illumination, revelation, 68, 152, 217, 220–22, 338; Scripture composition, 271–72, 287, 352, 386

Hospitalers, 380

Index of Scripture References